THE CHINESE TRANSFORMATION OF BUDDHISM

KENNETH K. S. CH'EN

THE CHINESE TRANSFORMATION OF
BUDDHISM

PRINCETON UNIVERSITY PRESS
PRINCETON, NEW JERSEY

TO PROFESSOR THOMAS A. BAILEY,
WHO BY HIS INSPIRED TEACHING FIRST OPENED
THE VISTAS OF SCHOLARSHIP TO THE AUTHOR

ACKNOWLEDGEMENTS

To carry out this study, I received financial assistance from the University Committee on Research in the Humanities and Social Sciences and the Coordinating Committee on Foreign and International Affairs of Princeton University. This assistance is gratefully acknowledged here. I am also grateful to the Trustees of Princeton University for an appointment as McCosh Faculty Fellow during the academic year 1969-1970, which enabled me to spend some time doing research on the Tun-huang manuscripts in the Bibliothèque Nationale in Paris and the British Museum in London. To Mr. K. P. Gardner, Keeper of Oriental Printed Books and Manuscripts of the British Museum, and Madame M. R. Guignard of the Bibliothèque Nationale, I wish to acknowledge deep felt gratitude for their assistance in placing the Tun-huang manuscripts at my disposal. Research fellowships granted by the Committee on International Exchange of Persons and by the Guggenheim Memorial Foundation enabled me to spend the academic year 1964-1965 in the library of the Research Institute for Humanistic Studies at Kyoto University. For this assistance I am most grateful. I wish also to thank the following publishers for permission to quote from their books: G. Allen Unwin of London: from Arthur Waley, *The Life and Times of Po Chü-i* (London 1949); Ronald Press Co.: from E. O. Reischauer, *Ennin's Diary, The Record of a Pilgrimage to China in Search of the Law*, translated from the Chinese (New York 1955); Princeton University Press: from Kenneth K. S. Ch'en, *Buddhism in China* (Princeton 1964); the Editors of the *Harvard Journal of Asiatic Studies*: from the *HJAS* 28 (1968), 81-97; École Pratique des Hautes Études, Service des Publications, and Mouton & Company from their forthcoming volume: F. Aubin (ed.), *Etudes Song, In Memoriam Etienne Balazs* (Série II, Civilisation). Finally, I would like to express my appreciation to the following individuals: Mr. René-Yvon Lefebvre d'Argencé, Director, and Mr. and Mrs. Clarence Shangraw, Curators of the Brundage Collection in the M. H. de Young Memorial Museum of San Francisco, for providing me with working space in the museum; to Denise Landry of the Department of Religion, Princeton University, and Eileen A. Scanlon and Mary Pottala of the Department of Oriental Languages, University of California, Los Angeles, for typing the manuscript; to Mr. James S. K. Tung, Special Assistant University Librarian and Curator of the Gest Oriental Collection at Princeton University, for his cooperation in providing library assistance; to Mrs. Polly Hanford of Princeton University Press for her editorial assistance; and to my wife Man Hing Y. Ch'en, head of the Oriental Library at UCLA, for her kindness in putting the facilities of the Oriental Library at my disposal and for her valuable assistance in the final preparation of the manuscript.

Kenneth K. S. Ch'en

CONTENTS

THE CHINESE TRANSFORMATION OF BUDDHISM

LIST OF ABBREVIATIONS

BEFEO	*Bulletin de l'École Française d'Extreme-Orient*
CCC	*Po-shih ch'ang-ch'ing-chi*
CKC	*Chi ku-chin fo-tao lun-heng*
CSM	*Chi Sha-men pu-ying pai-su teng-shih*
CSTCC	*Ch'u-san-tsang chi-chi*
CSTP	*Chin-shih ts'ui-pien*
CTS	*Chiu T'ang-shu*
CTW	*Ch'üan T'ang-wen*
Ennin	Ennin, *Nittō-guhō junrei gyōki* in *Dainihon Bukkyō zensho*, Vol. 113
FTLT	*Fo-tsu li-tai t'ung-tsai*
FTTC	*Fo-tsu t'ung-chi*
FYCL	*Fa-yüan chu-lin*
HJAS	*Harvard Journal of Asiatic Studies*
HKSC	*Hsü Kao-seng-chuan*
HMC	*Hung-ming-chi*
HTS	*Hsin T'ang-shu*
JRAS	*Journal of the Royal Asiatic Society*
KHMC	*Kuang Hung-ming-chi*
KSC	*Kao-seng-chuan*
KYL	*K'ai-yüan-lu*
SBE	*Sacred Books of the East*
SKSC	*Sung Kao-seng-chuan*
SPPY	*Ssu-pu pei-yao*
SPTK	*Ssu-pu ts'ung-k'an*
SSL	*Seng-shih-lüeh*
T	*Taishō Tripitaka*
TFYK	*Ts'e-fu-yüan-kuei*
THY	*T'ang-hui-yao*
TLSI	*T'ang-lü su-i*
TLT	*T'ang-liu-tien*
TP	*T'oung-pao*
TPKC	*T'ai-p'ing-kuang-chi*
TSCC	*Ts'ung-shu chi-ch'eng*

ONE

INTRODUCTION

At the Tercentenary Celebration of Harvard University in 1936, the late Dr. Hu Shih presented an address entitled, "The Indianization of China," in which he discussed the role played by Buddhism in Indianizing Chinese life and thought.[1] Dr. Hu contended that the plain, simple religion developed by the ancient Chinese consisted primarily of worship of ancestors, of natural forces, and of T'ien or heaven; of belief in the efficacy of divination; and of some vague notions of rewards and retributions. After Buddhism was introduced into China, the simple, practical Chinese were confronted with a hierarchy of heavens peopled by deities, some of whom have forms, desires, and passions just like ordinary human beings, others with forms only but no desires for sensual pleasures, and still others with no forms but only consciousness. Parallel to these heavens were a series of hells, hot and cold, in which the torments became progressively more tortuous and terrifying. In place of the vague notions of rewards and retributions, the Chinese learned that there was an all-pervasive force called karma, which operated inexorably to reward good deeds with meritorious rebirths, and evil deeds with rebirth in one of the evil modes of existence. The Chinese were also told that the phenomenal world is illusory, like a mirage or shadow, that life is suffering and transitory, that sensual pleasures are undesirable and therefore ought to be suppressed or eradicated, that the ideal pattern of life was withdrawal from society and family to a life of celibacy and mendicancy. The Chinese also learned that because of rebirth, their ancestors could very well be reborn as animals, and hence it would be wise to follow a vegetarian diet.

[1] See his *Independence, Convergence, and Borrowing* (Cambridge, Mass. 1937), 219-247.

3

Slowly but steadily, such Indian ideas spread among the Chinese and found acceptance as the Chinese embraced Buddhism. By the T'ang dynasty, such ideas had permeated all elements of Chinese society. India was looked upon as the fountainhead of religious truths, and generations of pious Chinese monks braved the trackless sands of the Central Asiatic deserts and the awesome peaks of the Himalayas to go to India to drink of the words of wisdom there.

With the coming of the Sung dynasty, a reaction set in. The rational philosophers who emerged then sought to revive the ancient Confucian philosophy as a counterforce against what they considered to be the antisocial, individualistic, and other-worldly philosophy of the Buddhists. To their immense satisfaction, they found that the ancient Confucian texts, with some slight reinterpretations, discussed the same problems of life and the universe that the Buddhist texts did, but with the bonus that this Confucian philosophy, unlike the Buddhist, was directed toward the ordering of the family, the state, and the world. Though professing to be anti-Buddhists, these rational philosophers, Dr. Hu contended, were in fact subtly influenced by exposure to the Buddhist tradition, and were reinterpreting their ancient systems in the light of that tradition. He concluded that what the rational philosophers did was to secularize Buddhist ideas and, by so doing, spread them beyond the Buddhist monasteries to the whole Chinese population.

As an example of such Indianization, Dr. Hu referred to the suppression of human emotions and sensual desires. In pre-Buddhist China, Dr. Hu contended that there was no prohibition against the remarriage of destitute widows. The Sung rational philosophers proclaimed, however, that death by starvation is a small matter, but violation of chastity is a very important matter. The acceptance of such an idea by the Chinese gave rise to countless stone tablets erected in honor of chaste widows. By their suppression of human emotions and desires, and the eradication of simple human joys and pleasures, the rational philosophers were considered by Hu

Shih to have been the most effective agents for the Indianization of China. Because Buddhism was the vehicle of this Indianization, Dr. Hu had on more than one occasion condemned Buddhism as one of the greatest evils to have befallen China.

While Dr. Hu has presented a strong case in favor of this thesis of Indianization, one is inclined to think that he has not presented a balanced account of the development of Buddhism in China. It is true that the process of Indianization did take place, but it is also true that another process was going on, namely, the adaptation of Buddhism to Chinese conditions. While Indian ideas were gaining ground, the Chinese were also fashioning changes in the Indian ideas and practices, so that Buddhism became more and more Chinese and more acceptable to the Chinese. I call this process the Sinicization of Buddhism in China.

When Buddhism was introduced into Ceylon, Burma, and Thailand, it found ready acceptance among the people in those countries. There Buddhism was the civilizing influence. With little or no attainments in the arts, literature, and thought, the Ceylonese, Burmese, and Thai welcomed Buddhism in the hope that their own cultural levels would be elevated by the superior civilization brought in with the religion.[2] In China, however, the situation was different. Already possessed of a high level of civilization when Buddhism was introduced about the beginning of the Christian era, the Chinese were not totally overwhelmed by the new religion. It is true that for a few centuries, the Chinese were captivated by the overpowering religious panorama brought in with Buddhism, but in time, what some scholars call the basic personality or the local genius of the Chinese began manifesting itself. By this local genius or national character is meant the sum total of the cultural traits which the vast majority of the Chinese adhered to, traits that had been developed by

[2] H. G. Quaritch Wales, *The Making of Further India* (London 1961), 246 pp.

INTRODUCTION

them during their long history.³ It was through the manifestation of this local genius that they were able to choose ideas from the Indian religion and modify them to fit the Chinese situation.

Examples of such modifications may be seen in the concept and image of the bodhisattvas Avalokiteśvara and Maitreya. In Buddhism there are two traditions concerning Avalokiteśvara. According to the first, found in Chapter Twenty-four of the *Lotus Sutra,* Avalokiteśvara is the epitome of mercy and compassion. He is ever on the lookout for people who are suffering, but he is specially concerned for those who are endangered by fire, water, demons, fetters, and sword. The second tradition is found in the *Pure Land Sutra,* which teaches that the Buddha Amitābha presides over a Western Paradise or Pure Land where all beings who have absolute faith in him will be reborn. When such beings die, they will be escorted to the Pure Land by the bodhisattva Avalokiteśvara, the chief helper of Amitābha. Amitābha does not leave his heavenly abode—he remains there forever—and so he has to rely on Avalokiteśvara to rescue beings in the human world.

In Indian Buddhism, the bodhisattva appears in iconography in the male form, and after introduction into China there was no change, as his numerous images in Yün-kang and Lung-men bear testimony. Even paintings found in Tunhuang and dated as late as the latter half of the tenth century portray Avalokiteśvara with a moustache.⁴ There is no question then that within the Buddhist tradition Avalokiteśvara was regarded as a male deity.

With popular Buddhism, however, there is a different tradition which presents the bodhisattva in the delicate, beautiful, and slender female form so universally admired not only in East Asia but also throughout the art world of the West. In this popular form the deity is commonly referred to in the

³ Quaritch Wales, *The Indianization of China* (London 1967), xxiii-xxiv.
⁴ See Matsumoto Eiichi, *Tonkōga no kenkyū* (Tokyo 1937), plate 98b, dated 943; plate 222, dated 968.

6

West as the Chinese Madonna, in the East as Sung-tzu Kuan-yin, or Kuan-yin, the Giver of children. How and when such a metamorphosis took place is still a point of controversy among scholars. Eduard Erkes studied a stele dated in the sixth century which he claims contains a female representation of the deity, but this identification is by no means certain.[5] It is more likely that the change was brought about under the influence of Tantric Buddhism, which became prominent in China during the eighth century through the translations and activities of the Tantric masters Śubhakara-siṃha, Vajrabodhi, and Amoghavajra.[6] In Tantric Buddhism, the female element assumes a prominent position, and all the Buddhas and bodhisattvas are said to have female consorts. The female consort of Avalokiteśvara is called the White Tara, or in Sanskrit, Pandaravāsinī, Clad in white. In Chinese art of the T'ang dynasty may be found paintings of a female deity called Pai-i Kuan-yin, Kuan-yin, Clad in white. As for the Sung-tzu Kuan-yin, it is possible that this was developed out of the tradition in the *Lotus Sutra* that Avalokiteśvara has the power to grant children to any woman who prays to him. It is also possible that the development grew out of the connection in Tantric Buddhism of Pandaravāsinī with the mandala Garbhakośadhātu, or Womb-Element Treasury. This connection with the womb could have led the Chinese to evolve the concept of the deity as the giver of children. A woman who was without child and desired one would have her wishes fulfilled if she went to the temple and paid her respects to the bodhisattva.

Maitreya likewise underwent a transformation in China. Very early in the Pāli tradition Maitreya appears as the future Buddha waiting to be reborn on earth to purify the religion in some distant future. In the meantime he is a bodhisattva living in Tushita Heaven. On the whole he does not

[5] Eduard Erkes, "Zum Problem der Weiblichen Kuanyin," *Artibus Asiae* 9.4 (1946), 316-321.
[6] H. Maspero, "The Mythology of Modern China," in J. Hackin (ed.) *Asiatic Mythology* (New York 1932), 352-358.

play an important role in Indian Buddhism. Only after he was introduced into China did he become an important figure. By the fourth century A.D., there was a Maitreya cult in which the devotees vowed to be reborn in Tushita Heaven in order to see Maitreya face to face. The popularity of the cult may be evidenced by the large number of Maitreya images in Yün-kang and Lung-men during the fifth and sixth centuries. In these early images there are no particular features to distinguish them from other images. After the seventh century the cult declined, to be replaced by the cult devoted to Amitābha and Avalokiteśvara. When Maitreya reappeared in the thirteenth century, he took the form of a fat, laughing image, and he was referred to as the Pot-Bellied Maitreya or the Laughing Buddha. It appears that this image of Maitreya was based on legends surrounding the life of a tenth century Chinese monk with a wrinkled forehead and a mountainous belly. Apparently this monk was very popular with the ordinary people, who regarded him as a barometer for the weather. Whenever they saw him sleeping on the market bridge, they could expect good weather, but when they saw him scurrying for cover, they could expect rain.[7]

At present this image of the pot-bellied and laughing Maitreya greets the visitor as soon as he enters a Chinese temple. Often he has a bevy of children climbing all over him. These features of Maitreya are very likely responsible for his popularity among the Chinese, who see in them representations of the life ideals of the Chinese. The fat belly denotes prosperity, for only a rich person can afford to eat sumptuously. The children denote a large family with many offspring, another ideal sought after by the Chinese.

The metamorphosis of these important Mahāyāna bodhisattvas took place in China, not in India or Central Asia, and through these changes the bodhisattvas became much more closely identified with Chinese life ideals and therefore more acceptable to the Chinese.

[7] F. D. Lessing, *Yung Ho Kung* (Stockholm 1942), 21-37.

Further examples of such Sinicization may be cited here. One is the classification of the Buddhist sutras according to chronological periods, which may be attributed to the Chinese predilection for history. During the centuries after the introduction of Buddhism into China, a tremendous body of literature, conveying the widest assortment of doctrines and ideas, was translated into Chinese. This huge body of literature must have been a constant source of amazement to the Chinese, for how could one individual preach such a variety of teachings during his brief span of life? Moreover, how could one explain the numerous doctrinal differences taught in the Hīnayāna and Mahāyāna sutras? These problems led the Chinese Buddhists to undertake the task of organizing and classifying the entire corpus of literature according to periods and doctrines. By classifying the sutras according to chronological periods, the Chinese succeeded in bringing some order out of chaos. They accepted the tradition that all the sutras were preached by one person, but they claimed that the different sutras were preached by the Buddha during different periods of his life. The differences in doctrines were explained by the theory that the Buddha was preaching to different audiences during the different periods, hence he had to adjust his teachings to the intellectual capacities and the spiritual attainments of his listeners.

The T'ien-t'ai School founded by Chih-i (538-597) was the first to perfect this theory of classification by periods. According to Chih-i, the Buddha immediately after enlightenment preached the *Avataṁsakasūtra*. However, the abstruse doctrines and ideas contained in this sutra were far too advanced for his listeners, and the Buddha felt obliged to shift his emphasis. This inaugurated the second period of his ministry, during which he preached the simple Hīnayāna sutras, stressing such easy to understand doctrines as the four noble truths, the eightfold path, and dependent origination. After twelve years of such preachings, the Master now felt that his followers were ready for something more advanced, so in the third period, which lasted eight years, he preached the elementary Mahāyāna sutras, which stressed the superiority of the bodhisattva ideal over that of the arhat. With this preparation out of the way, the Buddha next preached those advanced Mahāyāna sutras known as the Wisdom Sutras, which taught the doctrine of *śūnyatā* or emptiness, according to which all phenomenal existence is empty and illusory, and only the Absolute remains, unconditional, undefinable, and eternal. This period lasted twenty-two years. Finally in the last period, which took up the last eight years of his life, the Buddha preached the *Lotus Sutra,* which stressed the absolute identity of the contrasts, as opposed to the nonexistence of the contrasts taught in the fourth period.

Besides classifying the sutras according to periods, the T'ien-t'ai School also worked out a scheme according to the methods of teaching, and another according to the nature of the teachings.

The T'ien-t'ai School with its classification represented the Chinese attempt to establish an all-embracing school of Buddhism that could include all the manifold and diverse teachings of the master. The Chinese genius for organization and classification and the emphasis on history may be said to be the forces behind this comprehensive and encyclopedic venture.

Likewise, the Chinese genius may also be behind the establishment of the Ch'an School during the T'ang dynasty. By that time, besides the enormous body of literature translated, magnificent temples and monasteries had been constructed throughout the empire, and within them were beautifully decorated images of the Buddhas and bodhisattvas, all serving as objects of worship and fervent adoration by the faithful. The translations of sacred texts, the construction of imposing temples, and the ritualistic adoration of images were all performed for the sake of merits which the performer hoped to reap as a reward for his deeds. For example, during the first half of the sixth century, Liang Wu-ti, one of the most avid supporters of Buddhism ever to sit on the Chinese throne, was reported to have said, "Ever since the beginning of my reign, I have built so many temples, copied so many sutras, and fed so many monks. What do you think my merits should be?" Also, excessive reliance was placed on the written word. Many of the Buddhist schools in China seized upon one text and regarded that as the authoritative word of the Buddha, thus giving rise to what might be called sutra-dogmatism. The T'ien-t'ai School placed its reliance on the *Lotus Sutra*, the Hua-yen on the *Avataṁsaka*, and the Pure Land on the *Pure Land Sutra*.

During the seventh century, some Chinese monks began to protest against this excessive reliance on the external paraphernalia of the religion and argued that the true essence of the religion was an inner experience. These protesting monks condemned the sutra-dogmatism that regarded one sutra as the norm of truth, and instead sought to return to that which was prior to the sutras. Accordingly they coined the following slogans: "Not relying on words or letters"; "An independent transmission outside of the teaching"; "Directly pointing to man's mind"; "Seeing his original nature and becoming the Buddha."

Against the prevailing practice of looking to the Buddha and bodhisattvas for support in achieving spiritual progress, the Ch'an masters shouted to their followers that if they should encounter the Buddha and bodhisattvas, they should kill them, for the Buddha was said to be just a barbarian devil and the bodhisattvas just so many dung-heap coolies. Of course, these words are not to be taken literally. They are used to make the point that one should not rely on such external aids but should rely rather on meditation, which was considered the essence of Buddhism, as it was through meditation that the Buddha achieved enlightenment under the bodhi tree. Through meditation, one can awaken the original nature which is the Buddha nature or Buddha mind in all of us, and thus achieve enlightenment directly, completely, and instantly. There is no need to depend on reading and studying scriptures, worshiping images, or performing meritorious deeds. Ch'an was therefore the product of the Chinese mind and environment; it was, as Dr. Hu Shih puts it, "a revolt against Buddhist verbalism and scholasticism."[8] It was also a protest against the long period of spiritual training prescribed in the Indian system. Through Ch'an, one can put aside the butcher's knife and become the Buddha.

By investigating the role of Buddhism in the ethical, political, economic, literary, educational, and social life of the Chinese, in the ensuing chapters, I hope to demonstrate further how the Indian religion gradually became Sinicized and accepted as an integral part of the Chinese way of life. Some might question why nothing is said about Buddhist art in China. This noninclusion is the result of a deliberate decision. I feel that since this is such a specialized field, it is the better part of wisdom to leave such discussions to the trained Buddhist art historians.[9]

[8] Hu Shih, *op.cit.*, 237.

[9] Major works on Chinese Buddhist sculpture in Western languages written during the first few decades of this century were by Osvald Siren and Edouard Chavannes, with works on Tun-huang specifically by Paul Pelliot and Aurel Stein. More recently, J. Leroy Davidson's book, *The Lotus Sutra in Chinese Art* (New Haven 1954), contains an extensive bibliography of works on Buddhist art. Studies in Japanese have been contributed principally by Mizuno Seiichi and Nagahiro Toshio covering the major northern Chinese cave complexes of Yün-kang and Lung-men, and by Matsubara Saburō covering the material outside of these complexes. Alexander Soper, in *Arts of China: Buddhist Cave Temples, New Researches* (Kodansha, Tokyo 1969), adapted, with extensive commentaries, a Japanese work on recent Chinese mainland discoveries and research. He also translated an important work by Ōmura Seigai entitled *Literary Evidence for Early Buddhist Art in China*, Artibus Asiae (Ascona 1959), and has also written several important articles on Buddhist art. Many recent discoveries in mainland China of new materials and of cave complexes such as Mai-chi-shan, Ping-ling-ssu, and Wan-fo-ssu near Ch'eng-tu have been reported in monographs of the Cultural Press and archaeological journals such as *K'ao-ku, K'ao-ku hsüeh-pao,* and *Wen-wu.* Such materials have only begun to be available in English, notably in Michael Sullivan's *The Cave Temples of Mai-chi-shan* (Berkeley and Los Angeles 1969). A very useful book is Deitrich Seckel's *Art of Buddhism* (New York 1964), which puts Chinese Buddhist art in perspective.

Some explanation may be in order concerning the writing of some Indian words. The reader will find in some instances the same Sanskrit words written with the diacritical marks, and in other instances, without. The examples that come to mind are sutra (sūtra) and nirvana (nirvāṇa). These words are so commonly used that they have passed into the English vocabulary and accepted as English words, and when the words are used as such, the diacritical marks are not used. However, when these same words appear as part of the title of a text, then they are considered as Sanskrit, and hence the diacritical marks are used. For instance, when speaking of enlightenment just "nirvana" is used, but in a title, then *Nirvāṇasūtra*.

TWO

ETHICAL LIFE*

THE traditional Chinese social system was based on the family, not the individual, and to preserve the family, Confucian ideology insisted that filial piety or *hsiao* be the foundation of its ethics. To the Chinese, family existence, clan harmony, social peace, and the preservation of Chinese culture all rested on the proper observance of this virtue. In the *Hsiao-ching*, or the *Classic on filial piety*, we read, "Filial piety is the basis of virtue and the source of the teachings. We receive our body, our hair, and skin from our parents, and we dare not destroy them. This is the beginning of filial piety. To establish ourselves and to practice the way, so that we will perpetuate our name in later generations, thus glorifying our parents, this is the end of filial piety. For filial piety starts with serving our parents, continues with serving the ruling prince, and ends with establishing ourselves." In practicing piety, the same classic goes on to say, "The filial son serving his parents should be most respectful to them while living, most joyful in supporting them, greatly worried at their illness, deeply grieved at their death, and utterly solemn at the sacrifices." Furthermore, we are told that "of the 3,000 offenses included under the five punishments, none is greater than unfilial conduct."

As models of filial conduct, Chinese literature usually refers to the twenty-four examples of filial sons performing prodigious feats for the welfare of their parents. One individual, Wang Hsiang of the Chin dynasty, stripped off his clothing in deep winter and reclined on ice in the river, so that his bodily warmth melted the ice and enabled him to catch

---

* Portions of this chapter have been published in an article, "Filial Piety in Chinese Buddhism," *HJAS* 28 (1968), 81-97.

some carp for his mother. Another example had as its hero an eight-year-old boy, Wu Meng, also of the Chin dynasty, whose family was so poor that it could not afford to buy even a mosquito net. In order to protect his parents from the mosquitoes, the boy slept naked, so that the insects stung him instead of his parents. The extreme example concerned an individual of the Han dynasty, Kuo Chü, who planned to kill his own son in order to save some food for his mother.[1]

Buddhism as a religion in India aimed at individual salvation in nirvana, a goal attainable by leaving the household life, to use the familiar phrase in Buddhist literature, and entering the houseless stage, which meant the life of celibacy and mendicancy. Upon assuming the monastic robe, the Buddhist monk terminated his ties with family and society, so that his wife became a widow; his children, orphans. When this religion was introduced into China, where filial piety and family life were the dominant features of society, the conflict was joined.[2]

From the very beginning, Buddhism was attacked as un-

[1] For Wang Hsiang and Wu Meng, see *Ku hsiao-tzu chuan*, *TSCC* ed., 18, 33. For Kuo Chü, see *Hsiao-tzu-chuan* 1 ab, *Shih-chung ku-i-shu* ed., *FYCL* 49, *T* 53.658c. See also Chao Meng-chien, *Chao Tzu-ku erh-shih-ssu-hsiao shu-hua ho-pi* (Pei-p'ing 1933).

[2] Japanese scholars have published a number of studies dealing with the role of Buddhism in the ethical life of the Chinese. Among these, Michihata Ryōshū occupies the preeminent position, and this chapter is greatly indebted to him for his contributions. Of particular importance are the following: (*a*) "Bukkyō to jissen rinri," in his *Tōdai bukkyōshi no kenkyū* (Kyoto 1957), 299-380; (*b*) "Chūgoku shakai ni okeru bukkyō rinri no keitai," in Miyamoto Shōson (ed.), *Bukkyō no kompon shinri* (Tokyo 1956), 707-728; (*c*) "Chūgoku bukkyō to sosen sūhai," *Bukkyō shigaku* 9.1 (1960), 1-17. In 1968, he published his *Bukkyō to Jukyō rinri* (Kyoto), 326 pp., in which he sums up the results of a lifetime of research on this problem. This is by far the most exhaustive book on the subject of Buddhist and Confucian ethics. See also his *Chūgoku bukkyōshi no kenkyū* (Kyoto 1970), 348 pp.

Further studies, by Ogasawara Senshū, include:
(*a*) "Chūgoku rinri to Tōdai bukkyō," *Bukkyō shigaku* 3.3 (1953), 234-245; (*b*) "Chūgoku shomin seikatsu to bukkyō rinri," in Miyamoto (ed.), *op.cit.*, 729-752.

15

filial. In the *T'ai-p'ing-ching*, a work dating back to the latter part of the Han dynasty, there is already criticism of Buddhism as being unfilial.[3] Soon after that, in the treatise *Mou-tzu li-huo-lun* (*Treatise on the settling of doubts*), portions of which could be dated back to the third century A.D., there are several passages reflecting this criticism of Buddhism. In one section, the critic of Buddhism charged that the Buddhists were unfilial when they shaved off their hair, for in so doing they were violating the teaching of the *Hsiao-ching*, which stressed the necessity to return our body, hair, and skin intact to our ancestors. To answer this charge, Mou-tzu recalled an incident in the kingdom of Ch'i. A father and son were crossing a river and midstream the father fell into the water. Fortunately, the son was quick-witted enough to pull him out, and then turned him upside down to let the water run out through his mouth. Now the son's holding his father upside down was a most unfilial act, but the son thereby saved his father's life. Mou-tzu also referred to the example of T'ai-po of Chou, who cut off his hair and tattooed his body, yet he was praised by Confucius as being perfect in virtue.[4] Going further, Mou-tzu pointed out the following cases of individuals who mutilated their bodies: Yü Jang, who covered his body with lacquer;[5] Nieh Cheng, who slashed his face and

[3] T'ang Yung-t'ung, *Han Wei Liang-chin Nan-pei-ch'ao fo-chiao-shih* (Shanghai 1938), 104-105.

[4] E. Chavannes, *Mémoires historiques* (Paris 1895), 1.215-216. Comment by Confucius in *Lun-yü* 7.1, translated in J. Legge, *Chinese Classics* (China 1939), 1.207. The example of T'ai-po was also commended by Sun Ch'o in his *Yü-tao-lun, T* 52.17b.

[5] Yü lived in the 5th century B.C. See P. Pelliot, "Meou-tseu ou les doutes levées," *TP* 19 (1920), 364, n. 147; H. A. Giles, *Biographical Dictionary*, no. 2525. Yü Jang was a native of Chin. After his master was killed by the prince of Chao, he vowed revenge, disguised himself by covering his body with lacquer, and swallowed charcoal to make himself dumb. The assassination attempt was unsuccessful, and when he was brought into the presence of the prince, he said that he would die without regrets if he could pierce Chao's robes with his sword. Chao complied with his wish, and then Jang stabbed himself.

killed himself;[6] Po Chi, who trod on fire;[7] and Kao Hsing, who mutilated her face.[8] For their deeds, Mou-tzu wrote that "gentlemen considered them as brave people who died for righteousness. I have not heard anyone blaming them for their self-mutilation. Compared to the deeds of these four people, the act of monks cutting off their hair and shaving their beard is mild indeed."[9]

In another section the critic charged that monks were abandoning their wives or were not marrying, and by not having offspring, they were unfilial. In answer to this, Mou-tzu referred to the examples of Hsü Yu,[10] who perched on a tree, and Po I and Shu Ch'i, who died of famine in Shou-yang.[11] Even though they were without offspring, Confucius

[6] Pelliot, *op.cit.*, 364, n. 148; Giles, *op.cit.*, no. 1565. Nieh, 4th century B.C., native of the Han kingdom, was a famous assassin in Chinese history. After he had killed a minister in the Han kingdom, he disfigured his face, gouged out his eyes, and disemboweled himself, in order to make himself unrecognizable and thus not implicate his sister in the crime.

[7] Pelliot, *op.cit.*, 364, n. 149. Po Chi, 6th century B.C., was a daughter of Duke Hsüan of the kingdom of Lu. After ten years of marriage she became a widow. When fire swept through the palace in which she was living, people asked her to leave, but she replied that a woman should not leave her apartment without being accompanied by a directress of the inner apartments, and so she was burned to death.

[8] *Ibid.*, n. 150. Kao Hsing was a native of Liang during the period of the Warring Kingdoms. A very beautiful woman, she became a widow at an early age and was sought after by numerous men. The prince of Liang joined the ranks of her suitors but the widow cut off her nose and thus put an end to all these attempts to woo her. The prince was greatly impressed by her act, and conferred on her the title, *kao-hsing*, lofty in conduct. Po Chi and Kao Hsing were both cited by Sun Ch'o in his work *Yü-tao-lun*, T 52.17b.

[9] T 52.2c-3a.

[10] For Hsü Yu, see Pelliot, *op.cit.*, 367, n. 163.

[11] Po I and Shu Ch'i were sons of the prince of Ku-chu, located in present-day Hopei. The prince wanted to pass power to the second son Shu Ch'i, but this son refused to antagonize his older brother, and fled the kingdom after the death of his father. After the fall of the Yin dynasty, the two brothers refused to serve under the Chou dynasty, preferring to die of famine. Cf. Pelliot, *op.cit.*, 367, n. 164; Chavannes, *op.cit.*, 1.217; *Shih-chi*, ch. 67.

17

praised them for their wisdom and humanity.[12] In succeeding centuries, this charge of unfilial conduct against the Buddhists was emphasized again by Hsün Chi during the sixth century, Fu I during the seventh, and Han Yü during the ninth.[13]

The Buddhists were quick to realize that mere refutation of the Confucian charges was negative in spirit and not sufficient to gain a favorable hearing for Buddhism among the Chinese. In a society where filial piety was emphasized, the Buddhists recognized clearly that their religion must develop and stress its own ideas concerning piety if it were to flourish in China. Only through such a positive approach could the religion hope to compete with the Confucians on favorable terms. Having recognized the problem that they faced in China, how did the Buddhists proceed to adjust to this ethical milieu, so as to present a better image of their religion as far as filial piety was concerned? Briefly, they sought to make Buddhism acceptable to the Chinese by three methods: first, by pointing out the numerous sutras in the Buddhist canon which stress filial piety; second, by forging a body of apocryphal literature which emphasizes piety as its central theme; and third, by contending that the Buddhist concept of filial piety was superior to that of the Confucians in that it aimed at universal salvation (this would include all previous ancestors in different forms), while the Confucian piety was limited to just one family. The following discussion will elaborate on these points.

The Chinese Buddhists did not admit that the relationship

[12] *T* 52.3a.

[13] Hsün Chi's attack is preserved in the *KHMC*, *T* 52.128c-131b; *Ch'üan Hou-Wei wen* 51.12a-14b. See K. Chen, *HJAS* 15 (1952), 185-192. Fu I's criticisms may be found in *KHMC*, *T* 52.134a-135b; *CTS* 79.4a-5a; *HTS* 107.1b-2a. See also Ogasawara Senshū, "Tō no haibutsuronsha Fu Eki ni tsuite," *Shina bukkyō shigaku*, 1.3 (1937), 83-93; A. Wright, *Journal of the History of Ideas* 12 (1951), 33-47. Han Yü's memorial against Buddhism may be found in the collection of his works, *Ch'ang-li hsien-sheng chi* 39.3a-6a, translated in E. R. Reischauer, *Ennin's Travels in T'ang China* (New York 1955), 221-224.

between parents and children was destroyed as soon as one was converted to the religion. In fact, they argued, this relationship is stressed in a number of sutras preached by the Buddha. There are, first of all, the numerous translations in Chinese of the *Sigalovādasutta* in the *Dīghanikāya: Shih-chia-lo yüeh liu-fang li-ching*, translated by An Shih-kao, Han dynasty, *T* 1.251b; *Fo-shuo shan-sheng-tzu-ching*, translated by Chih Fa-tu of the Western Chin dynasty, *T* 1.254a; *Ch'ang-a-han-ching* by Buddhayaśas and Chu Fo-nien, fifth century, *T* 1.71c; and *Chung-a-han-ching*, by Sanghadeva, fourth century, *T* 1.641a. In this sutra a son is called upon to serve and respect his parents in five ways: (1) to serve them in such a way that they are not lacking in anything; (2) to inform the parents beforehand of all his activities; (3) to respect and not go contrary to the actions of the parents; (4) not to disobey the commandments of the parents; (5) not to terminate the traditions of the parents.[14]

The Parthian monk An Shih-kao also translated another sutra stressing the debt owed by children to their parents. This is entitled *Fu-mu-en nan-pao-ching* (*Parental love is difficult to be repaid*), and in it we find the following passage: "The Buddha proclaimed to the monks, 'Parents are most helpful and beneficial to the child. The mother breast-feeds and nurtures the child at all times to help him grow. When the child is grown up, he should not entertain any ill-feeling toward his parents, even though he should carry his father on his right shoulder and his mother on his left for a thousand

---

[14] *Ch'ang-a-han*, *T* 1.71c. There are some variations in these five duties. The translation of *An Shih-kao*, *T* 1.251b, indicates that the son should do the following: (*a*) support his parents; (*b*) rise early in the morning and order the servants to prepare breakfast for the parents; (*c*) not cause his parents to worry; (*d*) seek a doctor immediately if his parents should become sick; (*e*) reflect on the love of his parents for him. The *Chung-a-han*, *T* 1.641a, lists the following five duties: (*a*) to increase the material wealth; (*b*) to manage all the business of the parents; (*c*) to respond immediately to their wishes; (*d*) not to go contrary to their desires; (*e*) to present all their private possessions to them. For the Pāli version, see *Dīghanikāya* (London 1911), 3.189.

years, supposing this is possible to do so. Yet even this deed is not sufficient to repay for the love of parents.' "[15]

Of the examples of filial conduct mentioned in the Buddhist sutras, probably the most famous concern Shan-tzu (Śyāma in Sanskrit, Sāma in Pāli) and Mu-lien (Maudgalyāyana in Sanskrit, Moggallāna in Pāli). The story of the former is told in the *P'u-sa Shan-tzu-ching*,[16] translated probably during the Western Chin dynasty by an unknown monk. The Chinese title has *ching*, sutra, but there is no doubt that it is based on the *Śyāmajātaka* in the Pāli collection of *Jātaka* stories.[17]

In this *Jātaka*, a bodhisattva scanned the world and saw a blind couple who had no children and who wanted to retire into the forest to lead the life of a recluse. Sensing that the blind couple would be confronted with all kinds of dangers in the forest, the bodhisattva chose to be reborn as the son of the couple in order to serve them. As the son, who was named Shan-tzu, grew up, he devoted himself entirely to the service and support of his blind parents, and the latter soon forgot their vow to retreat to the forest. One day Shan-tzu reminded them of their vow and assured them that he would serve them just as before if they should retire to lead the life of a recluse. With this assurance, the blind parents sold all their earthly possessions and retired to the forest.

In the new surroundings, Shan-tzu served his parents as before; he helped them build a hut of grass and branches, and

---

[15] *T* 16.778c-779a. This idea of children carrying their parents on both shoulders as a sign of gratitude is very likely inspired by a passage in the *Lotus Sutra*, which reads: "If we were to carry [the Buddha] on the top of the head, or bear him on both shoulders, and exhaust ourselves in deference to him for *kalpas* as numerous as the sands of the Ganges, . . . still we would not be able to repay [the Buddha] for his favors." *Miao-fa-lien-hua-ching* 2, *T* 9.18c.

[16] *Śyāmajātaka*, first mentioned in the catalogue of Tao-an now preserved in *CSTCC* 3, *T* 55.17c.

[17] For the Pāli version, see Fausböll, *Jātaka* (London 1896) 6.68-95. The English translation is in E. B. Cowell and W.H.D. Rouse, *Jātaka Stories* 6.38-52 (London 1957). There is also a *Śyāmajātaka* in the *Mahāvastu* 2.209-231, translated in J. J. Jones, *The Mahāvastu* (London 1952), 2.199-218, where the account in general follows the Pāli version.

tied ropes to guide them from one place to another. As he fetched food and drew water for his parents, he became such a familiar figure in the forest that all the animals and birds accepted him as one of them, and did not harm him or his parents. In going to the spring for water, he would don a covering of deerskin so as not to disturb the deer at the watering place.

It was when he was in this disguise that he was accidentally shot by the king of the land, who was out hunting. Knowing that he was mortally wounded by the arrow, Shan-tzu cried out that by killing him, the king had killed three persons, for his blind parents were entirely dependent upon him for food. When the king heard this human voice, he hurried to where Shan-tzu was lying in pain, and asked him who he was, and why he was wearing the deerskin. Shan-tzu explained everything to the king, saying that he had lived in the forest for twenty years, serving his parents, and never once was he harmed by the wild animals. Now he was shot by a man.

Suddenly, a storm arose and the birds and animals cried out in grief. This frightened the king, who told Shan-tzu that he had shot him by mistake. Shan-tzu assured the king, however, that his own karma was responsible, but that he was worried about his blind parents. The king was so moved by this attitude of filial piety that he promised to look after the blind parents if Shan-tzu should die, and asked the latter for directions to the parents' hut. Shan-tzu gave the necessary directions, and died.

When the parents heard the sad news from the king, they were overcome with grief, and asked to be taken to the corpse. This the king did. The father embraced the legs of Shan-tzu, while the mother embraced his head. She then licked the wound, hoping to suck out the poison, so that Shan-tzu would live while she would die. In their agony, they uttered the Act of Truth[18] that if it were true that Shan-tzu was

---

[18] *Satyakriyā* in Sanskrit, *saccakiriyā* in Pāli. For discussion of this concept in Indian and Buddhist thought, see W. Norman Brown, "The Basis for the Hindu Act of Truth," *Review of Religions* (November

the paragon of sincerity and filial piety, then let this arrow be plucked out, the poison eradicated, and Shan-tzu restored to life.

When Sakka heard this Act of Truth and saw what was happening, he descended with his retinue of deities to where

---

1940), 36-45; E. W. Burlingame, "The Act of Truth," *JRAS* (July 1917), 429-467. Burlingame writes "An Act of Truth is a formal declaration of fact, accompanied by command or resolution that the purpose of the agent shall be accomplished" (429).

Numerous instances of the operation of this concept may be found in Buddhist literature. In *Jātaka*, no. 463, Fausböll 4.139-143, we read that the Buddha in one of his previous rebirths was a master mariner who became blind through the continuous spraying of salt water on his eyes. However, so skillful a mariner was he that sailors insisted on having him on board despite his blindness. On one trip the ship was rapidly drawn into a whirlpool. With disaster facing the ship and the sailors, the bodhisatta decided to resort to the Act of Truth to save the ship. He was bathed in scented water, clothed in new garments, and placed on the bow of the ship. He then said, "As long as I can remember, since I became one with knowledge, I am not conscious of having killed one living thing intentionally. With this Act of Truth, may this ship return to safety." With one leap, the ship returned to port, making a month's journey in one day.

Another instance may be found in the *Milindapañha* 121-123, translated in T. W. Rhys Davids, *The Questions of King Milinda* (New York 1890) I.184. Here we read about a certain courtesan Bindumati, who was able to turn the waters of the Ganges upstream. King Ashoka was surprised by this feat, and wondered how a woman of loose morals could possess such powers. She admitted she was a wicked person, but that she did possess the power of the Act of Truth. Asked to explain this, she replied, "Whoever, O King, gives me gold, be he a noble or a brahman or a tradesman or a servant, I regard them all alike. When I see he is a noble, I make no distinction in his favor. If I know him to be a slave, I despise him not. Free from fawning and from dislike do I do service to him who has bought me. This, Your Majesty, is the basis of the Act of Truth by the force of which I turned the Ganges back."

The basic idea seems to be that different people occupy different positions and each person must perform with sincerity and singleness of purpose the duties incumbent upon his particular station in life. When each person performs his duties according to the best traditions of his profession, then he achieves personal integrity and conforms to the cosmic purpose. When such conditions are fulfilled, then the wishes of the agent of the Act of Truth must be accomplished.

Shan-tzu was, and forced some medicine into Shan-tzu's mouth. Immediately the arrow popped out, and Shan-tzu was restored to life. The story ends with the words of the Buddha that people with parents must be filial to them.[19]

Judging from the number of times the account is mentioned in the Chinese canon, it is obvious that Shan-tzu's exemplary conduct was just the model of filial piety sought after by the Buddhists. Two other translations of the *Jātaka* were made, one by the monk Sheng-chien of the Western Chin dynasty, *T* 3.438b-440a; and the other by K'ang Seng-hui of the kingdom of Wu, and included in the *Liu-tu chi-ching, T* 3.24b-25a. A synopsis is found in the Buddhist encyclopedia *Fa-yüan chu-lin*, c. 49, *T* 53.656ff, and in the *Ching-lü-i-hsiang*, c. 10, *T* 53.51b-52c. Reference to the story was also made by Hsüan-tsang in his *Ta-T'ang Hsi-yü chi*, c. 2, *T* 51.881b.

Such an example of filial piety in Buddhist literature obviously was no different from what the Confucians advocated, and it comes as no surprise to find that by the Sung dynasty it was accepted in the popular literature as one of the twenty-four standard models of piety in China. Some changes crept into the story during the process of transition. Shan-tzu became Yen-tzu, a native of the Chou dynasty. His parents were blind, and they wanted to drink some deer's milk. So Yen-tzu donned a covering of deerskin and went into the forest to obtain the milk. There he was almost killed by a hunter.[20]

---

[19] *T* 3.436b-438b. The Pāli version contains some variations from the Chinese translation. First, when the couple retired into the forest, they were not yet blind, and became so through the poisonous gas emitted by a snake in the forest. Second, when Sāma was shot by the king's arrow, there was no storm, no howling of winds, and no crying of birds. Third, the Pāli introduced a goddess, a mother of Sāma in a previous rebirth, who joined in uttering the Act of Truth which led to Sāma's revival. Finally, when Sāma regained life, his parents also regained their sight.

[20] Chao Meng-chien (1199-1295), *Chao Tzu-ku erh-shih-ssu-hsiao shu-hua ho-pi*, n.p. The complete account is as follows: "Yen-tzu of the Chou dynasty was most filial. His parents in their old age both suffered from eye ailments, and wanted to drink deer's milk. Yen-tzu donned a deerskin and entered amidst a herd of deer in the mountains to get

Even more famous is the story of Mu-lien whose filial piety toward his mother is told in the *Yü-lan-p'en-ching*,[21] translated by Dharmaraksha during the Western Chin dynasty. According to this sutra, Mu-lien, upon attaining arhatship, wished to repay his parents for their love and kindness to him. With his divine eyes he surveyed the three worlds to see where they were, and to his disappointment, he found his mother reborn as a hungry ghost, emaciated and famished. Out of compassion for her he took a bowl of food and presented it to her, but the food turned into burning charcoal as soon as she brought it to her mouth. Mu-lien was sorely grieved by this, and returned in tears to report to the Buddha.

The Buddha told Mu-lien that his mother's offenses were indeed most serious, and could not be alleviated by his (Mu-lien's) individual efforts, even though his piety was sufficient to move heaven and earth. What was required for her release, the Buddha suggested, was the divine powers of all the monks of the ten quarters. The Blessed One then instructed Mu-lien to have prepared a sumptuous offering of the hundred delicacies, fruits, utensils, and sweet-scented oil, and on the fifteenth day of the seventh moon to present them to the monks of the ten quarters on behalf of present and deceased parents for seven generations back. On this day, all the monks of great virtue, no matter where they are, must accept the offerings and observe the commandments. The virtues of the multitudes of monks are vast indeed, and through the power of such virtues, the present parents and relatives would escape from the three evil modes of existences. If the parents

---

the milk. A hunter spied him and was about to shoot him with an arrow, but stopped when Yen-tzu informed him of the situation."

In none of the different versions of the *Ku-hsiao-tzu chuan* as preserved in the *Shih-chung ku-i-shu* is Shan-tzu or Yen-tzu mentioned. It is only when we come to the work of Chao Meng-chien of the Southern Sung dynasty that we find Yen-tzu included in the list of twenty-four examples for the first time.

[21] For a detailed study of the Mu-lien legend in China and Japan, and an analysis of the term *yü-lan-p'en*, see Iwamoto Yutaka, *Mokuren densetsu to urabon* (Kyoto 1968), 245 pp. See also Appendix at end of this chapter for further discussion of the term.

are still living, they would live up to a hundred years, and deceased ancestors for seven generations back would be reborn as deities in heaven.[22]

Mu-lien carried out these instructions, and as a result his mother was rescued from her evil existence as a hungry ghost. The monk then asked the Buddha whether or not it was permissible for pious and filial sons in the future to hold such a feast, called *yü-lan-p'en*, for the purpose of saving or rescuing parents and ancestors. The Blessed One answered in the affirmative and urged his followers to celebrate such a festival on the fifteenth day of the seventh month. He closed with these words of exhortation, "Those disciples of the Buddha who are filial and obedient to their parents should constantly remember their parents in their thoughts, and make offerings to them back to the seventh generation. Every year on the fifteenth day of the seventh month, they should remember their parents and ancestors with piety and compassion, and repay their parents for their care and love by preparing a *yü-lan-p'en* feast for offering to the Buddha and the monks."[23]

On account of the unequivocal emphasis on filial piety, this sutra was welcomed by the Chinese and became exceedingly popular not only among the Buddhists but also among the common people. Among the latter, it took the form of popular stories, recited during temple festivals by story-telling monks or traveling ballad-singers. Such popular stories have been preserved in a style of literature known as *pien-wen* (Texts of marvelous events), samples of which have been discovered among the Tun-huang manuscripts. The presence of such *pien-wen* as the *Mu-lien pien-wen*,[24] *Mu-lien yüan-ch'i*,[25] and

[22] This notion of an offering for the hungry ghosts or *peta* (Sanskrit *preta*) is already found in the Pāli canon. See the *Khuddakapāṭha*, translated by Ñāṇamoli, *The Minor Readings* (London 1960), 7-8.

[23] *T* 16.779a-779c.

[24] Three manuscripts of this are kept in Peking. See Ch'en Yüan, *Tun-huang chieh-yü-lu* (Peking 1931), 541. One of these versions is edited and published in Yang Chia-lo, *Tun-huang pien-wen* (Taipei 1964), 2.756-760.

[25] Manuscript in Paris, Pelliot 2193. Text published in Yang, *op.cit.*, 2.701-703.

the *Ta-Mu-kan-lien ming-chien chiu-mu pien-wen ping-t'u*[26] attest to the popularity of this story among the masses.

In the *Mu-lien yüan-ch'i*, Pelliot 2193, the story is told in much greater details. Mu-lien's family was very well-off. His mother, named Ch'ing-t'i, lived with her son, named Lo-pu, after her husband died. She was described as evil, greedy, and avaricious, while the son was religious and compassionate. One day the son decided to go away to distant lands to make his fortune. Before leaving, he divided his property into three portions, one for his own use, one for his mother, and one to be distributed to the poor and to Buddhist monks. The mother agreed to this arrangement. After the son left, the mother disregarded his words, and whenever monks came for alms to her house, she abused them and chased them away. When the needy came for food, she set dogs to keep them away.

Lo-pu returned one day after having amassed a fortune. His mother assured him that she had carried out his instructions concerning the distribution of the third portion. However, Lo-pu heard from others in the town that the mother never performed any charitable deeds to the monks and the needy. When he questioned his mother about this, she angrily replied, "I am your mother, you are my son. The affections between mother and son are as weighty as the mountains. Now you do not trust my words, but instead consider as truth the words of others. If what I say this morning is not the truth, then let me swear that within seven days I will descend into the deepest Avīci hell." Upon hearing this oath, Lo-pu naturally believed his mother.

[26] *The Pien-wen concerning the great Mu-lien going to the nether regions to rescue his mother, with illustrations.* Many copies of this version were found in Tun-huang. The text of the copy now kept in the British Museum (Stein 2614), is published in *T* 85.1307a-1314a; Yang, *op.cit.*, 2.714-755. There is another copy in London (Stein 3704). In the Bibliothèque Nationale are four manuscripts: Pelliot 2319, 3107, 3485, 4988, while in Peking may be found three manuscripts: *Ying* 76, *Li* 85, *Shuang* 89. There is an English résumé in A. Waley, *Ballads and Stories from Tunhuang* (London 1960), 216-235.

The mother died after seven days and was reborn in the Avīci hell, to suffer the interminable tortures there. Lo-pu observed the mourning period of three years, then joined the Buddhist saṅgha, where by his diligent cultivation of the religious discipline he achieved arhatship and took the name of Mu-lien. He now felt that he must repay his parents for the benefactions and favors they had bestowed upon him, so he scanned the three worlds to see where his parents were. He saw his father in one of the heavens, but nowhere was his mother to be found. He went up to the Buddha for help. The Buddha told Mu-lien that his mother, because of her avariciousness and deceit, was reborn in the Avīci hell. Mu-lien told the Buddha that he wanted to see his mother, so the Buddha endowed him with the necessary powers to descend to Avīci hell. (Here the narrative presents a most vivid description of the tortures suffered in Avīci; some beings climbing up mountains of sharp knives; other beings having molten bronze poured into their mouths; some swallowing red hot iron balls while others were scorched all over by fire.) When Mu-lien saw his mother enduring such torments, he wept. The mother confessed her evil deeds.

Mu-lien then returned to seek the aid of the Buddha in rescuing his mother from her pitiful state. The Buddha instructed Mu-lien to prepare a feast and offer it to the Buddhas of the past, present, and future and to the monks of the ten directions. By so doing, his mother would be rescued from Avīci hell.

Mu-lien did as instructed by the Buddha, and as a result, his mother was able to get out of Avīci hell, only to be reborn as a female dog that ate impurities all day. Mu-lien with his divine eyes saw his mother in the form of the dog, and went to her side. The dog became happy in his presence. Mu-lien beseeched the Buddha for help. This time the Buddha advised him to invite forty-nine monks and order them to chant the scriptures and pray for seven days. He should also burn incense and light lanterns, save living creatures, and recite Mahāyāna sutras. Mu-lien performed all these things, and his mother was thereby rescued from her rebirth as a dog and re-born in one of the heavens. (End of story.)

Now this account says nothing about the mother's being reborn as a hungry ghost. This, however, is contained in Pel-liot 2319, entitled *Ta-Mu-kan-lien ming-chien chiu-mu pien-wen* in one *chüan*. This is a much more detailed narrative, although the general outline is similar to the contents of the *Mu-lien yüan-ch'i*. Portions of the legend are found in several other manuscripts recovered from Tun-huang, but they do not add materially to the story.[27]

[27] In Pelliot 2319, we read that after Avīci, the mother was reborn as a hungry ghost, then as a black dog. In this form she was found. Mu-lien then led the dog to a stupa, where for seven days and nights he recited sutras. This meritorious deed enabled the mother to aban-don rebirth as a dog to become a woman again and to hang the dog's form on a tree. Then Mu-lien and his mother sat under the sal tree to worship the Buddha. After this, he asked the Buddha whether or not there was any residue of evil karma left in his mother. The Buddha surveyed the situation, concluded that the evil karma had been ex-hausted, and caused her to be reborn as a deva in Tushita Heaven.

Pelliot 3485 contains only a fragment of the story, but this fragment presents an interesting variation. In this account, Mu-lien found his father and asked him what had become of his mother. The father told him that his mother had not practiced meritorious deeds during her lifetime, hence she was reborn in hell. He instructed Mu-lien to search for a certain A-niang and that if he found her, she would be his mother. Mu-lien in his search appeared before the deity presid-ing over hell, and asked for A-niang. The deity looked over his records and found that there was a certain Ch'ing-t'i who had been in hell for three years. He sent out runners to look for Ch'ing-t'i. Mu-lien fol-lowed them, and when they arrived at the banks of the Nai River they saw many tormented people there. (Here the manuscript stops.)

Stein 2614 goes into much greater details about the interview between Mu-lien and his father concerning the fate of his mother. (In this manuscript, the fruit of arhatship won by Mu-lien is written errone-ously as *a-nan-kuo* several times instead of the correct *a-lo-han-kuo*.) After being told by his father to search for a certain A-niang in the various hells, Mu-lien commences his journey. The account gives de-tailed descriptions of the hells visited, the hell of the rakshas, the hell with mountains of knives, the hell with horse-headed demons, etc. Finally Mu-lien finds his mother in the seventh level of Avīci, suffering from all kinds of tortures and with blood flowing from all her pores.

The popularity of the *Yü-lan-p'en-ching* was accentuated by the significant commentary written by the famous Hua-yen and Ch'an master Tsung-mi. Already conversant with Confucian literature[28] Tsung-mi put his considerable literary talents to an exposition of the main theme of the sutra, filial piety, primarily for the edification of the Confucian literati. One might say that Tsung-mi was consciously making an attempt to bring Confucianism and Buddhism closer together by claiming that both systems emphasize filial piety as the highest of virtues. In the very beginning of the commentary, Tsung-mi boldly wrote: "That which began during the primordial chaos and now saturates heaven and earth, unites man and deity, connects the high and the low, and is revered alike by the Confucians and the Buddhists, is none other than filial piety."[29]

This theme is elaborated further in the first portion of the commentary. In the process of stressing filial piety, Tsung-mi made some startling assertions. For instance, he wrote that "Prince Siddhārtha did not assume the kingship, but left family and country because he wished to cultivate the Way and become enlightened, so as to repay for the love and benefactions of his parents."[30] Siddhārtha thus becomes a filial son entirely acceptable to the Chinese. Furthermore, Tsung-mi contended that Mu-lien joined the monastic order with the same motive in mind. "Because Mu-lien was filial and wished to convert his parents in payment for their efforts in bringing him up, he left the household life to become a monk, and be-

---

With the help of the Buddha, Mu-lien manages to rescue his mother from her tortures, only to have her reborn as a hungry ghost. In this state, whatever food was given her became a ball of fire. Again with the help of the Buddha, she forsook her rebirth as a hungry ghost to be reborn as a black dog in Rājagaha, then as a woman, and finally as a deva in Trāyastriṁśa Heaven. In its main outline, Stein 2614 resembles Pelliot 2319.

Two other manuscripts, Pelliot 3107 and Pelliot 4988, contain fragments of the story.

[28] For his biography, see *SKSC* 6, *T* 50.741c-742a.
[29] *T* 39.505a.   [30] *Ibid.*

came foremost in the exercise of extraordinary powers. With his divine eyes, he saw that his deceased mother was reborn as a hungry ghost. He was unable to rescue her, and consequently he enlisted the aid of the Buddha. The master demonstrated to him the method of the *yü-lan-p'en* offering, and with the aid of this offering, Mu-lien rescued his mother from her dire straits."[31]

Tsung-mi recognized that in Confucianism, filial piety was considered as the highest of virtues. Emperors and scholars all established ancestral temples to honor the deceased ancestors. All the laws of the realm and the teachings of the masters stemmed from this virtue, which was regarded as the norm of heaven and the guiding principle of earth. In Buddhism, he wrote, "there are the sutras and the rules of discipline. The sutras manifest principles and wisdom, while the rules discourse on conduct. Although the rules of conduct number over 10,000, the essential one emphasizes filial piety."[32] To bolster his point, he then quoted a passage from the *Fan-wang-ching*:[33] "When Śākyamuni attained supreme enlightenment under the bodhi tree, he first formulated the bodhisattva *prātimoksha* rules[34] which call for filial piety and obedience to parents, teachers, monks, and the Three Jewels. When piety and obedience are developed to their highest perfection, then piety is designated as a moral precept."

Tsung-mi acknowledged that there existed some differences between the Confucian and Buddhist observance of

[31] *T* 39.505ab.   [32] *T* 39.505b.

[33] *Fan-wang-ching*, *T* 24.1004a, said to have been translated by Kumārajīva, although some scholars have questioned this. See Michihata, *Bukkyō to Jukyō rinri*, 155, where we are told that the work was probably compiled in China sometime during the Sung and Ch'i dynasties (420-502), and that it was based on such sutras as the *Hua-yen-ching*, *Nieh-p'an-ching*, *Jen-wang pan-jo-ching*, *P'u-sa ti-ch'ih-ching*, *P'u-sa shan-chieh-ching*, and *Yu-p'o-sai-ching*. The *Fan-wang-ching* is generally accepted as the *Vinaya* of the Mahāyāna Schools in China.

[34] The *prātimoksha* rules, numbering 227 in the Pāli *Vinaya*, and over 250 in the Tibetan and Chinese versions, are the basic rules of conduct for the Buddhist monks.

filial piety. For instance, he pointed out that the pious Confucian was mainly interested in leaving behind a good name for posterity, whereas the Buddhist was more concerned with assistance to others in this life. Again, he noted that the Confucians sacrificed while observing memorial services for departed ancestors, while the Buddhists were concerned with preserving life. However, he contended that the similarities in observing filial piety far outweighed the differences. In both instances, the filial son was most respectful to his parents while they were living, most joyful in supporting them, greatly worried over their illness, deeply grieved at their death, and utterly solemn at the sacrifices.[35]

This commentary by Tsung-mi on the *Yü-lan-p'en-ching* represents the most serious attempt on the part of a Buddhist monk to convince the Confucians that Buddhists were just as filial as they were. The *Yü-lan-p'en-ching* provided a suitable vehicle for Tsung-mi to express his ideas, and it must be admitted that he was a bold and articulate advocate. His contention that Śākyamuni left the household life to become a monk in order to repay the love and affection of his parents and that the Buddhists were just as earnest and sincere as the Confucians in their practice of filial piety furnish good evidence of his willingness to take new positions to make Buddhism acceptable, even though in the first instance it meant rewriting Buddhist history. It could be that Tsung-mi felt his own life was a good example of religious accommodation. Born into an aristocratic family and educated in his youth in the Confucian classics, he was converted to Buddhism and rose to eminence as a Hua-yen master, yet he still considered himself a filial son true to his Confucian heritage.

Owing to the wide acceptance of the *Yü-lan-p'en-ching* among the populace, the *Yü-lan-p'en* festival became one of the popular celebrations during the T'ang dynasty. During such celebrations, the religious connotations appear to have been forgotten, and the people regarded the occasion chiefly

[35] *T* 39.505c. It will be remembered that these sentiments are exactly those expressed in the *Hsiao-ching*.

as one for everybody to have a good time. Such an attitude is reflected in the following passages in the *T'ai-p'ing kuang-chi*: "After the T'ien-pao era (742-755) there was a certain Mr. Chang who was regional commander of the Chien-nan area. On the fifteenth day of the seventh month, he ordered all the monasteries in the surrounding areas to display their treasures for the sightseeing public to enjoy."[36] "[During the Chen-yüan era, 785-804] on the fifteenth day of the seventh month, many of the people in Canton display their rare treasures in the Buddhist monasteries and assemble all kinds of amusements in the K'ai-yüan monastery."[37]

Witness of these celebrations is furnished by the Japanese Ennin, who traveled in China during the years 838-847. In the detailed diary which he kept, he described the celebration which he personally observed. For the festival in 840, when he was in T'ai-yüan in Shansi, he recorded: "We were invited by the head of the Ssu-chung-ssu and went with the mendicant to the monastery to have our forenoon meal, after which we went to the Tu-t'o-ssu and worshipfully observed the All-Souls' Festival. We also went into the prefectural headquarters and saw the Dragon Spring. Next we went to the Ch'ung-fu-ssu and went around paying reverence to the Buddha Hall, Balcony, and other cloisters. All had arranged displays. Their lustrous beauty was dazzling, and the displays were most wonderful. Everybody in the whole city had come to look respectfully at them."[38] In 844 he was in Ch'ang-an and his description there reads as follows: "On the fifteenth day of the seventh moon, the various monasteries of the city made offerings for the All-Souls' Festival. The monasteries made flowery candles, flowery cakes, artificial flowers, fruit trees, and the like, vying with one another in their rarities. Customarily they spread them out as offerings in front of the Buddha halls, and people of the whole city go around to the monasteries and perform adoration. It is a most flourishing festival."[39]

[36] *TPKC*, ch. 122 (Peking 1959), 2.860.   [37] *Ibid.*, ch. 34, 1.216.
[38] E. O. Reischauer, *Ennin's Diary* (New York 1955), 268-269.
[39] *Ibid.*, 344.

Not only did the populace participate in this Buddhist festival, but the T'ang imperial house also took an active interest in the proceedings. This interest was manifested in the support which the central government gave to different monasteries and temples to celebrate the festival. A passage in the Buddhist encyclopedia, *Fa-yüan chu-lin*, reads as follows: "If it is a national monastery such as the Hsi-ming or Tz'u-en monasteries in Ch'ang-an, all the expenses for the celebration, beyond what is provided for by income derived from the manorial lands granted by the imperial house and the personal share land, are furnished by the state. Therefore, every year, musicians, porters carrying vessels filled with all sorts of articles, and government officials to present such vessels come in great numbers."[40]

The imperial interest was also manifested by direct participation in celebrations held within the imperial precincts. The celebration held during the year 768 was noted in a number of sources. In the Buddhist annals, we read: "During the seventh month, a *yü-lan-p'en* celebration was ordered by imperial decree. Ancestral tablets for seven generations back, beginning with Kao-tsu, were carried over from the T'ai-miao to the chapel within the imperial precincts, accompanied along the streets by pennants, flowers, and musical instruments. At the chapel, the tablets were welcomed by numerous officials. This was an annual celebration."[41]

The same occasion was recorded in the dynastic history as follows: "On the fifteenth day of the seventh month (of the year 768) Tai-tsung had vessels made for the celebration of the *yü-lan-p'en* festival in the imperial chapel. These vessels were decorated with gold and jade, and were worth over a million cash. Ancestral tablets for seven generations back, beginning with Kao-tsu, were also created, covered with pennants and dragon parasols, and on the pennants were inscribed the names of the ancestors. These tablets were carried out from the imperial precincts to be displayed in the

[40] *T* 53.750b.   [41] *FTTC*, ch. 41, *T* 49.378c.

monasteries. On that day, the host of officials with their paraphernalia were arrayed at the Kuang-shun Gate to await the
tablets and the vessels. With the multitudes carrying pennants and flowers, dancing and shouting on the streets, the
celebration was an annual affair."[42]

The foregoing, with the exception of Tsung-mi's commentary, constitute in the main the important Buddhist sutras
stressing the theme of filial piety. To be sure, other sutras also
touched upon the virtue. For instance, in the *Fan-wang-ching*
there are passages to the following effect: "We should be
filial, obedient, and compassionate toward our parents, our
brothers, and other relatives." "If we are children of the Buddha, we should constantly entertain the earnest wish of being
filial and obedient to our parents, teachers, monks, and the
Three Jewels."[43] Chinese Buddhists also like to point to the
sutra, *Fo sheng T'ao-li-t'ien wei-mu shuo-fa-ching* (*Sutra on
the Buddha ascending to Trāyastrimśa Heaven to preach to
his mother*), translated by Dharmaraksha,[44] as one which describes the filial piety of the Buddha. According to the Buddha legend, Māyā, mother of the Buddha, died seven days

---

[42] *CTS* 118.6b. In the *Tzu-chih t'ung-chien* 224.16b-17a, the festival
for the same year is noted: "On the *ping-hsü* day of the seventh month,
the emperor donated vessels containing offerings to the Chang-ching
Monastery. The ancestral tablets for the seven preceding emperors were
prepared, and their names inscribed on pennants. The host of officials
waited to receive them at the Kuang-shun Gate. From this date on,
it became an annual affair." Hu San-sheng of the Yüan dynasty com-
menting on this passage wrote: "In the *Yü-lan-p'en-ching* of the
Buddhists, the monk Mu-lien, upon perceiving that his deceased mother
was reborn among the hungry ghosts, said to the Buddha, 'On the
fifteenth day of the seventh month, let tasty food and fruits be placed
in vessels and offered to the Buddhas of the ten directions on behalf
of those parents and ancestors for seven generations back who are in
dire straits.' "
The Chang-ching Monastery mentioned here was erected by the
eunuch Yü Ch'ao-en in honor of the deceased empress Chang-ching,
wife of Emperor Su-tsung, reigned 756-762. See *CTS* 184.12a; *TFYK*
927.6b.

[43] *T* 24.1006a, 1007b.   [44] *T* 17.787b-799c.

34

after giving birth to the child. This sutra informs us that after the Buddha attained enlightenment, he ascended to Trāyas-triṁśa Heaven and remained there for three months, preaching the law to his mother. With this filial duty completed, he descended to earth again to resume his mission among men. Later, when Confucians criticized the Buddha and Buddhists as being unfilial, the Buddhists often referred to this sutra to refute the Confucian charge.

In the British Museum there are two versions of an *Erh-shih-ssu-hsiao ya-tso-wen* composed by a monk, Master Yüan-chien,[45] wearer of the yellow robe (Stein 3728 and P I), that praises in flowery language this virtue of filial piety. In the Pelliot collection it is 3361. The entire piece consists of 107 lines of seven characters each, with the 108th line consisting of eight characters. In the text, mention is made of several individuals renowned for their acts of piety, Mu-lien, Emperor Shun, Wang Hsiang, Kuo Chü, and Lao-lai-tzu. Of these individuals, the pious deeds of Mu-lien, Kuo Chü, and Wang Hsiang have already been mentioned. Emperor Shun is usually presented as a paragon of piety, while Lao-lai-tzu is said to have entertained his aged parents, even at the age of seventy, by donning multicolored robes and performing children's games.[46]

Filial heart is the true bodhisattva,
Filial conduct is the great arena of the *Tao*.
Filial conduct is the sun or moon shining on a dark street,
Filial heart is the ship crossing over the sea of misery.
Filial heart eternally resides in the land of Mañjuśrī,
Filial conduct constantly dwells in contented and joyful villages.
Filial conduct is no different from the rains of spring,
Filial heart is the same as the fragrance of the hundred flowers.

[45] Concerning this *ya-tso-wen* and Yüan-chien, see Michihata, *Bukkyō to Jukyō rinri* 129-132.
[46] *Shih-chi* 61.3a.

Filial heart is as broad and extensive as the canopy of
clouds,
Filial conduct is as clear as the rays of the sun.
Filial conduct can rescue one from the myriad disasters,
Filial heart can release one from the thousand
misfortunes.
Filial piety is the gem amidst all the treasures,
Filial piety is the king of the thousand virtues.
In Buddhism, piety is the basis for becoming the Buddha,
In all matters, one must be filial toward one's parents.
By being in accord with piety in our present life, we can
avoid rebirth in the future,
Filial piety can dissolve all the calamities of life.
If we practice filial piety toward our aged parents,
This is the equivalent of opening (and reading) the
sutras all day.
If we can cause our loving parents to be happy with our
virtuous words,
What need is there for our parents to urge us to furnish
them with delicacies?
If we wish to emulate the upright characteristics of the
Buddha, then there is nothing that can surpass filial
piety.

We come now to the second type of response by the Buddhist to the criticism that Buddhism is unfilial, namely, the
forging of sutras stressing filial piety as the central theme.
The most important of these responses is the *Fu-mu en-chung
ching (Sutra on the importance of parental love)*. A large
number of manuscripts of this forged sutra have been found
in Tun-huang. In the Peking Metropolitan Museum are eleven
manuscripts of this work, varying in length from 39 to 122
lines,[47] while in the British Museum twenty copies are to be
found.[48] Three versions are in the Bibliothèque Nationale:

[47] *Tun-huang i-shu tsung-mu-lu so-yin* (Shanghai 1962), 395; Ch'en
Yüan, *Tun-huang chieh-yü-lu* 507ab.
[48] *Tun-huang i-shu tsung-mu-lu so-yin* 395, 414.

Pelliot 2285, 2418, 3919. One of the versions in the Stein collection, Stein 2084, is reprinted in *T* 85.1403b-1404a. The sutra appears under various titles, *Fu-mu en-chung-ching, Fo-shuo fu-mu en-chung-ching, Fu-mu en-chung-ching chiang-ching-wen, Fu-mu-en-chung su-wen.*

It is not known who composed this work. The date of composition is probably early T'ang. The title is not found in Tao-hsüan, *Ta-T'ang nei-tien lu*, finished in 664, but it does appear in the *Ta-Chou k'an-ting chung-ching mu-lu* completed by the monk Ming-ch'üan in 695. However, this does not mean that the text did not exist before 664, for as a matter of fact, it was mentioned as early as the first year of Wu-te, or 618.[49] The title is also found in the section on forged sutras in Chih-sheng, *K'ai-yüan shih-chiao lu*, where a note is added that the text refers to the filial exploits of three famous men of antiquity, Kuo Chü, Ting Lan, and Tung Yen.[50] The present Tun-

[49] Michihata, *Tōdai bukkyō shi no kenkyū* 309.

[50] *T* 55.673a. Kuo Chü lived during the period of the Later Han and was a native of Ho-nei. His family was rich, and when the father died, the family fortune was divided into two portions and given to the two younger brothers of Chü. Chü himself claimed nothing, taking only his mother so that he could support her. He, his wife, and his mother moved into a haunted house and lived there in poverty. Later when a son was born, Chü worried that the additional mouth would take food away from his mother, and consequently he and his wife decided to kill and bury the child. As he was digging the grave, he uncovered a cauldron made of gold, and inscribed with the following words: "Heaven has bestowed this golden cauldron to Kuo Chü. Let no official seize it, and let no other person take it away." Kuo took the cauldron to the owner of the haunted house, but the owner refused to take it. Later the government officials heard about the case, and insisted that Kuo keep the find. In this manner, Kuo was able to support both his mother and his child. See Liu Hsiang, *Hsiao-tzu-chuan*, 1 ab, in *Shih-chung ku-i-shu*; Chao Meng-chien, *op.cit.* See also *FYCL* 49, *T* 53.658c; Giles, *Chinese Biographical Dictionary*, no. 1059.

Ting Lan, first century A.D., was also a native of Ho-nei. After his mother died, he made a wooden statue exactly like her, and attended the statue as if it were a living person. One day, a neighbor Mrs. Chang came over to borrow some object from Mrs. Ting. Mrs. Ting

huang version of the *Fu-mu en-chung-ching*, however, makes no mention of these three individuals, and one must conclude that these names have been erased by later copyists. Undoubtedly the text was very popular during the T'ang dynasty for it was the source of many different versions, illustrated texts, and popular stories. The following is a translation of the main portion of the work:

The Buddha said, "In this world our parents are closest to us. Without parents we would not be born. We are lodged in our mother's womb for ten months, and when the time is ready, the child is born and falls on the mat. The

---

as usual first sought the opinion of the wooden statue. This angered Mrs. Chang, and she threw something at the statue. The statue immediately assumed the appearance of displeasure, whereupon Mrs. Ting refused to lend the object to Mrs. Chang. When Mr. Chang heard about the matter, he became exceedingly angry and stormed over to the Tings' residence to revile the statue. Ting returned shortly afterward and saw the statue in an unhappy mood; when he learned what had happened he took his sword, rushed over and killed Mr. Chang. Ting was of course seized by the officials, and as he took leave, the wooden statue shed tears. The officials now freed Ting and congratulated him for his filial piety. See Morohashi Tetsuji, *Dai Kanwa Jiten* 1.78b, quoting from Sun Sheng, *I-shih-chuan*. See also Giles, *op.cit.*, no. 1937. The account of Ting Lan as found in the Buddhist work *FYCL* 49, *T* 53.658c is a little different. Here we are told that Mrs. Ting one night accidentally burnt the face of the wooden statue, and for this act she lost all her hair. Ting now moved the statue to the main road, where it was worshiped by Mrs. Ting for three years. One night the statue suddenly returned to the Tings' residence. Whenever neighbors came to borrow objects, the Tings would lend if the statue appeared affable, but not if the statue appeared otherwise. See also Liao Yung-hsien, *Shang-yu-lu* 11.36 ab, 1617 ed.; Chao Meng-chien, *op.cit.*

Tung Yen, also of the Han dynasty, was a grandson of the sixth generation of the famous Confucian Tung Chung-shu. He was famous for his filial conduct toward his mother. The mother of a neighbor, Wang Chi, once chided Chi for his attitude toward her, and compared him unfavorably with Yen. This displeased Chi very much, and in a jealous rage he insulted Yen's mother. Yen became exceedingly angry over this, and when his mother died, he killed Chi and then surrendered himself voluntarily to the authorities. The emperor, however, pardoned him. See Liao, *Shang-yu-lu* 13.38a.

child is nurtured by the parents and put to sleep in the cradle. Embraced by the parents, he makes all kinds of noises, and smiles even though he does not talk.

"When he is hungry and needs food, only the mother will feed him, and when he is thirsty, only the mother will suckle him. When the mother is hungry, she swallows her bitterness and gives out sweet words; she allows the baby to sleep in the dry place while she herself occupies the wet spot. Only the father will love him, only the mother will nurture him. The loving mother goes back and forth to the cradle, and of her ten fingers, her forefinger is never clean (because of her always tending the child).[51] . . . Vast and boundless indeed is the love of a mother for her child. How can one repay such a loving mother?"

Ānanda said to the Buddha, "May the Blessed One tell us how the loving care of parents is to be repaid?"

The Blessed One replied to Ānanda, . . . "If a filial, obedient, and loving son would prepare sutras and thus create blessings for his parents, or prepare a *yü-lan-p'en* offering to the Buddha and the monks on the fifteenth day of the seventh month, thereby receiving boundless fruits, such a son would be repaying for the love of his parents. If there is also a person who copies this sutra and circulates it among the people, so that it would be read and recited, that person would be repaying for the love of his parents.

"At times, the parents might go to a neighboring village to draw water or gather kindlewood or turn the millstone and would not return on time. On such occasions, the child at home would cry and think about his mother.[52] When she returns home, the child in the cradle would see her coming

[51] The next few lines are faulty, and it appears that something is missing. In Pelliot 2418 and Peking *Ho* 12, there is a passage which reads: "The child sleeps on the dry spot, while the mother sleeps on the wet spot. For the duration of three years, he drinks the white blood of his mother." See Yang, *op.cit.*, 2.681,699.

[52] In Tsung-mi, *Yü-lan-p'en-ching su* 2, *T* 39.508b, the quotation is slightly different: "The mother would suddenly be frightened, and her breast would flow. She then knows that her child at home is thinking of her, and she immediately hurries home."

from the distance, and at this sight, he would shake his head back and forth, or crawl toward his mother to welcome her. The mother would bend down, stretch out her hands to wipe away the dust from his face, and kiss him. Then she would offer him her breast to feed him. The mother is happy upon seeing the child and the child is likewise glad upon seeing the mother. There is really nothing that can surpass such mutual expressions of loving care and compassion.

"At the age of two or three, the child would learn how to walk. During mealtimes, he would become better acquainted with his father.

"Again, the mother might go to a party elsewhere, where she might obtain some sweetmeats and cakes; instead of eating them herself, she would take them home to give to her child. In nine cases out of ten, she would return with something, and everybody would be happy. . . .

"If there are faithful sons and daughters who would, for the sake of their parents, recite one sentence or one verse in this *Mahāprajñāpāramitā-Sutra on the loving care of parents,* they would be able, as soon as they have done so, to wipe out without any trace all offenses against their superiors,[53] to listen constantly to the words of Buddha, and to attain emancipation rapidly."

Ānanda arose from his seat, threw his robe over his left shoulder, knelt down, clasped his hands, and spoke to the Buddha, "Blessed One, how shall we name this sutra? How shall we receive it?"

The Buddha replied, "Let this sutra be named *Fu-mu en-chung-ching.* If there are living beings who are able to create blessings for their parents, prepare sutras, burn incense, adore the Buddha, make offerings to the Three Jewels, or feed the assembly of monks, then you should know that these people are repaying for the loving care of their parents."[54]

[53] Heaven, earth, prince, parents, and teachers.
[54] *T* 85.1403b-1404a.

The purpose of this forged sutra is obvious, namely, to make Buddhism popular among the common masses of Chinese who are imbued with the spirit of filial piety. One might say that the sutra was designed to appeal especially to the hard-working farming masses, not the well-to-do upper classes. The atmosphere of the farming village, of peasants at work in the fields, of simple earthbound family relations and pleasures, pervades the entire work, not the atmosphere of those families with servants and wet-nurses.

However, though the sutra was designed for the edification of the peasants, it was read by the educated clergy. Even Tsung-mi, the highly educated cleric, saw fit to include passages of this sutra in his commentary on the *Yü-lan-p'en-ching*. We have already quoted one such passage. Another quotation reads: "Embraced by the parents, the child smiles even though he does not talk, and makes all kinds of noises. When he is hungry and needs food, only his mother will feed him, and when he is thirsty, only his mother will suckle him."[55]

It appears that the Pure Land master Shan-tao also read the forged sutra. Though no direct quotations can be found, there are certain passages in his commentary on the *Kuan wu-liang-shou-ching* that appear to be related to contents of the *Fu-mu en-chung-ching*. For example, Shan-tao wrote: "If there were no father, that which is able to procreate is lacking. If there is no mother, that which gives birth is missing. If both of these are missing, then there is no place for life to be entrusted. Only when parents are present can there be a place to receive this body. Since there is a desire to receive this body, then one's own karma is the internal cause, and the essence and blood of the parents are the external cause. With the harmonious union of these two, the body is formed. Because of this, the love of our parents is indeed profound."[56]

In the last sentence, the words are *fu-mu en-chung*, exactly as in the title of the forged sutra. The entire passage appears

[55] *T* 39.508b.　　　　[56] *T* 37.259ab.

to be an elaboration of the opening sentences in the forged sutra: "Without parents, we would not be born." Furthermore, Shan-tao wrote: "When the child grows up, he shifts his love to his wife and children and harbors ill-feeling toward his parents."[57] In the *Fu-mu en-chung-ching*, there is a passage that reads: "When the son searches for and finds a wife, and rears his own sons and daughters, then the relations with the parents gradually become distant."[58]

Besides pointing to Buddhist sutras that emphasize filial piety, and forging sutras which stress the same theme, the Buddhists also attempted to win Chinese approval by claiming that their conception of piety was superior to that of the Confucians. In so doing, they developed some interesting ideas about filial piety. For instance, they contended that the Buddhist concept was superior in that the filial son aimed, not just at attending to all the needs of the parents, as the Confucians did, but at converting the parents to Buddhism, so that the latter would enjoy all the benefits that come with being followers of the Buddha. This idea was put forth at an early date by the Buddhists. In *Mou-tzu*, the interrogator criticized the action of Hsü-ta-na (Sudāna)[59] in giving away his father's wealth—including his wife and children and the sacred white elephant that produced rain—to strangers. Such action was inhuman and unfilial, he charged. Mou-tzu answered that Sudāna recognized the impermanence of worldly pleasures and so he gladly practiced charity in order to realize the *Tao*. As a result of his actions, "his parent's kingdom received auspicious signs, enemies were not able to invade the land. When he became the Buddha, his parents and his brothers all attained deliverance. If this is not filial piety and humanity, then what is piety and humanity?"[60] Hui-yüan (344-416), the famous cleric and sage of Lu-shan, expressed the same idea when he wrote that if one person leaves the household life

[57] *T* 37.259b.　　　　　[58] *T* 85.1403c.

[59] The Buddha in one of his previous rebirths. See *Liu-tu-chi-ching 2, T* 3.7c-11a. For Pāli, see *Vessantara-jātaka.*

[60] *T* 52.4a.

and becomes virtuous, then all the six relationships (father and son, older and younger brother, husband and wife) would be benefited.[61] Sun Ch'o (ca. 300-380), describing the Buddha in his treatise *Yü-tao-lun (Elucidation of the way)* likewise wrote that the Buddha "then returned and illuminated his native country, and widely spread the sounds of the doctrine. His father, the king, was stimulated to understand, and likewise ascended the place of enlightenment: what act of filial piety could be greater than such a glorification of his parents?"[62]

However, this theme is best expressed in a short text, entitled *Fo-shuo hsiao-tzu-ching (Sutra on a filial son)*, said to be translated during the Western Chin period, with name of translator lost. The content of the sutra is such that one is inclined to think it was composed by a Chinese, and not a translation of a foreign text. The following is a translation of this text:

> The Buddha said to the monks, "A mother bears a child in her womb for ten months, and during this period, her body is heavy with sickness. On the day of birth, it is difficult to describe the dangerous plight of the mother and the fright of the father. After birth, the mother gives the dry place to the baby while she occupies the wet spot.[63] In her utmost sincerity, her blood turns to milk for the baby. She rub and wipes and bathes the baby, she clothes, feeds, and teaches him. She instructs him to be courteous toward teacher and friend, and respectful toward elders. If the child is happy and kind, the parents are pleased, and if the child is miserable, the parents are distressed. When the child leaves home, the parents are worried, and when he returns, they inquire about his welfare; they are alarmed

[61] *T* 52.30b.

[62] *T* 52.17c, translated in E. Zürcher, *The Buddhist Conquest of China* (Leiden 1959), 284.

[63] This sentence is always used to denote the perfect example of maternal love for her child.

that he would go astray. The love and affection of the parents being thus, how can the child repay them?"

The monks answered, "To express his gratitude for the loving care of his parents, the child should respect them to the utmost, and serve them with a compassionate heart."

The Buddha replied, "If a son attending his parents should satiate their tastes with delicious foods, please their ears with heavenly music, adorn them with the choicest raiments, and carry them on his shoulders over the four seas to the end of his life, would all these be considered filial piety?"

The monks answered, "There is no greater example of filial piety than these acts."

The Buddha replied, "No, these could not be called piety. If the parents are ignorant and obstinate and do not adore the Three Honored Ones, if they are cruel and tyrannical, robbing at random and misbehaving promiscuously, if they use false language to criticize the teachings, if they are addicted to disorder and confusion and opposed to what is upright and true, if they are violent and truculent, then the son should admonish them and try to awaken them. If they are still in the dark and do not see the light, then in order to convert them, he should resort to concrete action. For example, he should lead his parents to the royal prison where the criminals are being punished, and say to them that these are rebellious criminals whose bodies are covered with poison and who bring death upon themselves. After death, their spirits would be tethered to mountains where they would be buffeted by scalding waters and seething fires and myriads of other tortures, with no one to rescue them. Because of their evil careers, they would encounter such calamities. If the parents still do not mend their ways, then the son should weep and wail and resort to fasting. Though the parents do not understand, they love their son and, fearing for his state of health, they would be forced to yield somewhat to honor the *Tao*. If the parents should now reform and take refuge in the Buddha and the five cardinal precepts, then they would be benevolent and not kill, be honest and yielding and not steal, be pure and not commit adultery, be trustworthy and not deceitful, be filial and not intoxicated. As a result, within the clan the parents will be loving and sons filial, husbands upright and wives chaste, the families harmonious and the servants obedient. . . . Only this is piety in a world without piety, that is, to lead the parents to forego evil for good, so that they would embrace the five precepts and resort to the threefold refuge. . . . If one cannot convert the parents with the aid of the Three Jewels, then even though one supports his parents with piety he would not be considered to be filial."[64]

One might say that this thesis of the Buddhists, i.e., that conversion to Buddhism enables one to convert his parents, was the strongest argument against the charge of unfiliality. In the eyes of the Confucians, leaving the household life to become a monk, thus cutting off all ties with parents and terminating the family line, was an unfilial act to be condemned. The Buddhists argued, however, that this was not so: by joining the monastic order, the monk was now in a position to convert his parents to Buddhism, so that they would attain salvation and escape repeated misery in the endless cycle of transmigration. This was the greatest boon that a monk could confer on his parents, and surely this must be acknowledged as filial.

The Chinese Buddhists pursued this line of argument still further by contending that the Buddhist monk aims not merely at salvation for his parents, but at salvation for all living creatures. In this role, he would be fulfilling what the Chinese Buddhists call the *ta-hsiao*, or great filial piety. This great filial piety is considered to be far superior to the Confucian piety, which is confined to one family and limited to serving only one's parents, whereas the Buddhist piety is universal and all-inclusive, and embraces all living creatures, some of whom might well be our ancestors in different forms.

[64] *T* 16.780bc.

According to the Buddhist theory of rebirths, living beings are continuously revolving in the various modes of existences, as deities, men, or animals. It is therefore possible that the father in one life may be the son in another, and that the ancestors may be the friends around us. This was what Fa-lin had in mind when he wrote, "All forms of life in the six modes of existences may be my parents. Within this cycle of rebirth, how can we distinguish between enemies and loved ones?"[65] Upon assuming the monastic robe, the Buddhist looks upon all beings as equal, and he vows to deliver all of them from misery to the other shore of enlightenment. When he accomplishes this goal, he is confident that some of his own ancestors and the ancestors of others are included in the group who are emancipated. The Buddhist writers in China argue that such an achievement in bringing about universal salvation can only be characterized as great.

As early as the fifth century, Hui-yüan had written that when one individual is converted, his beneficial influence would flow throughout the world.[66] After Wei Yüan-sung[67] had attacked Buddhism in a memorial presented in 567, a Buddhist layman, Wang Ming-kuang, wrote a refutation which contained the following paragraph: "As for the piety of monks, first, they obey the various Buddhas; next, they repay for the loving care bestowed on them by their parents, living beings, the ruling prince, and the Three Jewels; finally, they work on behalf of all sentient beings. When these three endeavors are carried out ceaselessly and tirelessly, then they are considered as expressions of great filial piety."[68]

During the early years of the T'ang dynasty—in 621, to be exact—a Taoist Fu I presented a strong anti-Buddhist memorial in which he charged the Buddhists with negligence in serving their parents.[69] He was answered by a monk Ming-

[65] *Pien-cheng-lun*, T 52.529b.   [66] *T* 52.30b.
[67] See Yü Chia-hsi, "Pei-Chou hui-fo chu-mou-che Wei Yüan-sung," *Fu-jen hsüeh-chih* 2.2 (1931) 1-25; K. Ch'en, *Buddhism in China* (Princeton 1964), 187-194.
[68] *KHMC* 10, T 52.158c.   [69] See n. 13, above.

chi who wrote: "It is said that if one wishes to seek loyal ministers and filial sons, one needs only look among those who read the *Classic on filial piety* and the two chapters in *Lao-tzu*, there is no need to consider those who read widely in the Buddhist sutras. If we examine the *Classic on filial piety* and *Lao-tzu*, we find that they throw light only on worldly loyalty and piety, and do not touch upon loyalty and piety beyond this world. How is this? Those who remain in the world do their best to cultivate the fields and serve their parents. Those who leave the household life practice the way and honor the law in order to promote loving compassion. Those who do their best to serve their parents are merely repaying for some immediate small favors, while those who promote loving compassion are requiting for some great virtue in the future. Even though the latter may for the moment appear to be deficient in reverence and contemptuous of their parents, in the end they are able to save and to rescue them. This is really the great filial piety."[70]

In outward behavior, Ming-chi admits that the conduct of the monk is contrary to the usual practice of piety, but in reality, he is pursuing a course that will result in the greatest benefit to his own parents and others, namely, their salvation. This theme is also expressed by Fa-lin in his *P'o-hsieh lun (Treatise on the destruction of heresies)*: "Although in outward appearance the monk may appear to be lacking in deference to parents, within his bosom he is filial to them. In the ceremonies, he may be deficient in his obedience to the ruler, but in his heart he shelters the imperial favor. With his beneficial influences embracing enemies and relatives, he completes the great obedience."[71] In another text, the *Pien-cheng lun (Treatise in defense of the upright)*, he wrote: "Buddhism teaches filial piety in order that its followers will reverence all parents under heaven. It teaches loyalty in order that its followers will reverence all the ruling princes under heaven. To civilize the myriad countries, that is the highest form of benevolence in the enlightened ruler. To serve as an example

---

[70] *KHMC* 12, *T* 52.175b.   [71] *T* 52.489bc.

within the four seas, that is the greatest piety of the sage-king. . . . The Buddhist sutra says that when ignorance covers the eye of wisdom, living beings continuously revolve in the cycle of rebirth, committing all sorts of deeds, so that fathers and sons interchange positions, enemies become friends and friends become enemies. Therefore, the monk abandons secular life to pursue the true religion . . . and considers all sentient beings as equal to his own parents." And further on in the same treatise, he wrote: "To broaden benevolence and to rescue widely, these are also the acme of loyalty and filial piety."[72] Here Fa-lin clearly stresses the point that the aim of the Buddhist is not merely to serve his own parents, but to benefit all other parents and sentient beings, that is, to lead all of them to salvation, and this he considers to be the highest form of filial piety.

During the Sung dynasty, the Neo-Confucianists attacked Buddhism even though they borrowed ideas and concepts from the Indian religion. To answer such attacks, Ch'i-sung (1007-1072) wrote a treatise entitled *Fu-chiao-pien (Essay supporting the religion)*, one portion of which dealt with filial piety from the Buddhist viewpoint. In the preface to this section he wrote, "As for filial piety, all the religions honor it, but Buddhism accords it special honors, even though its explanations are not known to the world."[73] Ch'i-sung then proceeds to devote some twelve sections to the consideration of filial piety, for the purpose, as he puts it, to discover and make known the profound principles and hidden meanings of the great filial piety of the sages. This is probably the sole Buddhist treatise devoted entirely to the discussion of piety.

For Ch'i-sung, filial piety is one with the moral precepts or *sīlas*; in fact, it stands at the forefront of the precepts. That which produces all the good and meritorious deeds are the moral precepts. If one slights the moral precepts, how can one produce good deeds, and if one slights piety, where would the moral precepts originate? He concludes, therefore, that piety is the virtue that would hasten one to the attain-

[72] *T* 52.529b, 531b.   [73] *T* 52.660a.

ment of the incomparable and true way. One of the moral precepts is nonkilling of living things. Ch'i-sung argues that this nonkilling must be considered as one aspect of piety, for in the endless cycle of transmigration, it is conceivable that our ancestors are reborn as animals, and to kill an animal would involve the possibility of killing one of our ancestors. Rather than face such a prospect, the Buddhist resorts to nonkilling and seeks to protect the life of even the tiniest living thing.

In Ch'i-sung's mind, filial piety stems from the good, and every man has a good heart. If Buddhism does not broaden this good heart, then goodness will not grow and piety will diminish. Buddhism as a religion teaches man to look upon the parents of others as our parents, and to protect the lives of all beings as our lives. Consequently, to manifest goodness, the Buddhist cherishes even insects and worms; to be filial, he even exhorts all the demons and deities. To rely on piety while living in the world, he will bring peace to the world and eradicate strife. To rely on goodness and leave this world, he will bring about mercy and compassion to reform the world.[74]

In some of these passages, Ch'i-sung does not depart radically from the Confucian viewpoints in his treatment of filial piety. For example, he agrees with the idea expressed in the *Classic on Filial Piety* that piety consists of glorifying one's parents and ancestors. In another passage, however, he refers to the *ta-hsiao* of Buddhism. "The world considers Confucius, but not the Buddhists, to be filial, I say that the Buddhists are filial. . . . The Confucians merely safeguard piety, but the Buddhists extend it. The Confucians humanize piety, but the Buddhists spiritualize it. . . . Supreme and great indeed is Buddhist piety."[75] What Ch'i-sung meant here is that the Confucians think of filial piety entirely in terms of human relations on this earthly level, between father and son. The Buddhists, on the other hand, consider piety in terms of something spiritual which extends into the future. When the

[74] *T* 52.661c.   [75] *T* 52.661b.

faithful Buddhist converts his parents, his ancestors, and the ancestors of others, he makes it possible for them to attain at least rebirth in one of the Buddhist heavens if not nirvana. Herein lies the difference between the Confucian and Buddhist filial piety, and this difference constitutes the basis of the Buddhist claim that its conception of piety is superior to that of the Confucians.

Let us now summarize. From its inception in China, the Buddhists were attacked by the Confucians as being unfilial. The Buddhists counterattacked by pointing first to the numerous Buddhist sutras which stress the virtue of filial piety. They also referred to the example of Buddha himself, who manifested his piety by going to the Trāyastriṁśa heaven to preach to his mother after his enlightenment. In addition to these sutras, the Buddhists also forged a body of apocryphal literature emphasizing piety. In these endeavors, the Buddhists sought to prove that they were not only filial, but were just as filial as the Confucians. The next stage in the Buddhists' attempt to win approval for their religion was their development of a new concept of filial piety. They admitted that monks may, by leaving the household life, appear to be unfilial, but in truth, the monk by his acceptance of Buddhism transforms himself into a vehicle for the conversion and salvation of his parents. By so doing, he is expressing his filial piety to his parents, though in a different way from that of the Confucians. Carrying this one step further, the Buddhist argues that by converting not only his parents but all other living beings, the monk is exercising the utmost in filial piety. In other words, the Buddhist practices the great filial piety which is far superior to the Confucian concept.

ANCESTRAL WORSHIP

Closely related to filial piety is ancestral worship, and here, too, the Buddhists made significant accommodations to Chinese practices. To the Chinese, ancestral worship is the epitome of filial piety. As the *Chung-yung* puts it, "To serve the dead as one serves the living, to attend to the departed as one would those present, that is the highest of filial piety." As soon as the father dies, there is a period of mourning that normally lasts twenty-seven months. Upon the termination of this period, the soul of the departed becomes the spirit of the ancestor, a tablet is placed in the ancestral temple, and sacrifices are now offered to it. Such sacrifices are carried out on memorial days. In spite of having left the household life, the Chinese monks in T'ang China often participated in these memorial services. This was especially true in the case of the national commemoration days held in memory of the deceased emperors.

So far as we know, there are no notices of clerical participation in these memorial services prior to the T'ang. In the T'ang-hui-yao, there is an entry which reads that during the second year of Chen-kuan (628) an imperial decree called for the celebration of memorial days in the Chang-ching Monastery in Ch'ang-an as an annual affair.[76] If this entry is correct, then this is the earliest notice of Buddhist participation in the national memorial services. However, this entry is open to question, for in 628 the Chang-ching Monastery had not yet been constructed, and it was not until 767 that the eunuch Yü Ch'ao-en[77] petitioned for the erection of the monastery to honor the memory of the deceased Empress Chang-ching, wife of Emperor Su-tsung, who reigned during 756-762.[78]

Aside from this notice in the T'ang-hui-yao, there are other indications of participation by monks. In 706, during the reign of Chung-tsung (684-709) a memorial service was held in the imperial precincts with monks participating in a vege-

[76] *THY* 49.5b, Wu-ying-tien chü-chen-pan.

[77] Died 770. For biography, see *CTS* 184; *HTS* 207.

[78] *THY* 48.6ab. It is possible that the Chen-kuan in the 628 decree is a mistake for Chen-yüan, one of the *nien-hao* for Emperor Te-tsung, the successor of Tai-tsung and who reigned from 780 to 804. There is also the possibility that such a decree was in fact issued in 628, but that the celebration was not held in the Chang-ching Monastery but in some other place.

tarian feast and incense-burning ceremony.[79] Beginning with
the reign of Hsüan-tsung (713-755) such memorial services
were held not only in the capital but also in the districts and
departments all over the empire. This is indicated in the following passages in the *T'ang liu-tien*: "On national memorial
days, two Taoist and two Buddhist monasteries in each of the
two capitals are selected to hold vegetarian feasts. Taoist
priests and priestesses, and Buddhist monks and nuns all assemble at the site of the feast. Civil and military officials
of the fifth rank and above in the capital and pure lofty officials
of the seventh rank and above all assemble to present incense
and then withdraw. In each of the outlying departments, one
Taoist and one Buddhist establishment are selected to stage the
vegetarian feasts. In all, the officials of some eighty-one departments and districts present incense and prepare vegetarian feasts."[80]

Concerning the memorial service held in Yang-chou in 838
to honor Emperor Ching-tsung, the Japanese monk Ennin has
preserved a detailed description for posterity. The service
was held in the K'ai-yüan temple, with some 500 monks in attendance. Also present were the leading civil officials of the
area, including the minister of state and governor-general of
Yang-chou, Li Te-yü. During the service, Sanskrit hymns
were chanted, incense burnt, and prayers uttered, all on behalf of the spirit of the departed emperor. After the service
the vegetarian feast was held within the temple.[81]

It is clear from such notices that Buddhist monks and nuns
actively participated in such memorial services held in the
monasteries on behalf of the deceased imperial ancestors. For
instance, in the memorial service held in 773 in honor of T'ai-
tsung, some 4,000 monks were present,[82] while 1,000 monks
were present at the memorial service held to honor the memory of Wen-tsung in Ch'ang-an in 841.[83] Such memorial serv-

[79] *FTTC* 40, *T* 49.372b.   [80] *TLT* 4.17a.
[81] Ennin, *Nittō guhō junrei gyōki* 1.14-15 (*Dainihon bukkyō zensho* [Tokyo 1918], vol. 113).
[82] *TFYK* 52.578a, Chung-hua Shu-chü, ed. (1960).
[83] *Ennin* 3.83.

ices really have nothing to do with Buddhism, but the imperial house encouraged clerical participation, presumably to ensure that Buddhism would be enlisted to overcome whatever evil forces might threaten the throne and the empire. The important thing to note, of course, is the participation of the monks in what are really services connected with ancestral worship.

Much more important is clerical participation in what can genuinely be called services on behalf of their ancestors. In the Confucian ceremonies, even during the period of mourning, some memorial services are held. Such services are called *hsiao-hsiang*, held after one full year of mourning, i.e., during the thirteenth month after the death of the ancestor, and the *ta-hsiang*, held one full year after the *hsiao-hsiang*, i.e., during the twenty-fifth month after the departure of the ancestor. In Buddhism, there are a number of such memorial services held during the period of intermediate existence.

According to the Buddhists, the soul of a person who has died goes to an intermediate existence and stays there for seven days, or seven times seven days, before being reborn into another mode of existence. During this period, the soul is in a state of suspense, so to speak, not certain as to what form it would take in the next rebirth. In the *Fo-tsu t'ung-chi* we are told that "when a person dies, his soul goes to the intermediate state. If it has not yet obtained the karma to be reborn, it would remain in this state for the full seven days. If at the expiration of the seven days, it still has not obtained the karma for rebirth, it will die and then come to life again to continue for another seven days. In this fashion, dying and reviving until the end of forty-nine days, then it will certainly be reborn in another form."[84]

If during this period of intermediate existence, there is no one to produce merits on behalf of the deceased, and if the deceased during his lifetime had not accumulated meritori-

---

[84] *FTTC* 33, *T* 49.320c; Hsüan-tsang, tr., *Yü-chia shih-ti-lun* 1, *T* 30.282a.

ous karma, then he is bound to be reborn in hell.[85] It was this idea that the living could do something for the benefit of the soul in the intermediate state that gave rise to the Buddhist memorial services known as the Seven-seven Feast. On the seventh day, and on every seventh day after that until the forty-ninth day, services would be held for the welfare of the departed spirit, and the merits accruing from such services would enable the soul to avoid being reborn in an evil state of existence—such as that of an animal, hungry ghost, or denizen of hell—and, instead, to be reborn as a man or deity.[86]

Besides these Seven-seven Feasts, the Buddhists also held memorial services on the hundredth day, on the anniversary, and on the third year after the death of the ancestor. There is no Confucian equivalent for the Buddhist hundredth-day service, but the annual and triennial services would appear to correspond to the Confucian *hsiao-hsiang* and *ta-hsiang*. In fact, it was this correspondence that led Chih-p'an, compiler of the *Fo-tsu t'ung-chi* to write: "Confucius said that a child three years after birth leaves the bosom of his parents, hence there is the three years of mourning to repay for this care. The Buddhist sutras say that an individual should be able to emerge from his intermediate existence only after forty-nine days, and therefore the Seven-seven Feasts are arranged. As for those people at present who perform Buddhist ceremonies on the hundredth day, the *hsiao-hsiang*, and *ta-hsiang*, even though such ceremonies follow the Confucian writings on mourning, still they provide opportunities for the cultivation of merits in Buddhism. Should we not have faith in them?"[87] According to this, Chih-p'an believed that the

[85] Śikshānanda, tr., *Ti-tsang p'u-sa pen-yüan-ching* 1, T 13.779a.

[86] Tao-ch'eng, *Shih-shih yao-lan* T 54.305b; also Tsung-chien, *Shih-men cheng-t'ung* 4, in *Hsü Tsang-ching* II/3/5.404a-405a. See also *Kuan-ting-ching* 11, T 21.529a: "One who has died becomes like a child in the intermediate state. If his offenses and blessings are not definitely settled, then his descendents should cultivate merits for his benefit, and pray for his rebirth in one of the immeasurable Buddha-lands in the ten quarters. Upon receiving such merits, he is certain to be reborn there."

[87] T 49.320c.

Buddhist observance of the annual and triennial memorial services followed the Confucian mourning rites of *hsiao-tsiang* and *ta-hsiang*. If Chih-p'an is correct, then we have here a very good example of the Buddhists taking over an important Confucian practice as part of its campaign to refute the charge of unfiliality.

The Confucians say that the mourning rites and sacrifices carried out by the descendants of the deceased were to express the gratitude and piety of the children for the care and love bestowed on them by their parents. In the case of Buddhism, the Seven-seven memorial services were primarily for the purpose of getting the soul in the intermediate state to be reborn in a better mode of existence. Likewise, the hundredth-day, annual, and triennial ceremonies were also performed for the welfare of the departed spirits. At such ceremonies, sutras were recited or copied and vegetarian feasts arranged, and the merits accruing from such deeds were then assigned to the stock of merits of the deceased ancestor, so that he might be reborn in a higher state. As all these memorial services were carried out by the Buddhists for the welfare of their ancestors, the Buddhists in China could justly claim that they were just as filial to their departed ancestors as the Confucians were.[88]

THE FIVE SĪLAS AND THE FIVE NORMS

Besides claiming that they were filial like the Confucians, the Buddhists made another attempt to harmonize their practical ethics with those of the Confucians; this was the corelation of their five cardinal precepts with the five norms of the Confucians.[89] The five cardinal precepts in Buddhism are not to kill, not to steal, not to commit adultery, not to tell lies, and not to drink intoxicating liquor. The five norms in Confucian-

[88] For a discussion of clerical participation in ancestral worship, see Michihata, "Chūgoku bukkyō to sosen sūhai," *Bukkyō shigaku* 9.1.9-11.

[89] See Michihata, *Tōdai bukkyōshi no kenkyū* 357-376; *Bukkyō to Jukyō rinri* 133-154; *Chūgoku bukkyōshi no kenkyū* 262-265.

ism are human-heartedness, righteousness, propriety, knowledge, and trust.

During the Northern Wei dynasty, there appeared a text entitled *T'i-wei Po-li-ching*[90] in two *chüan*, forged ca. 460 by a monk named T'an-ching. The sutra acquired a wide follow-

[90] *Sutra on Trapuśa and Bhallika.* In *Vinaya* 1.4, translated by I. B. Horner, *Book of Discipline* (London 1951), 4.5-6, we read that the Buddha during the eighth week after enlightenment was resting under a tree, experiencing the bliss of enlightenment. Two merchants, Tapussa and Bhallika (according to the *Theragāthā Commentary* 1.48, the two were brothers) while on their way from Ukkala to Rājagaha saw the Buddha at the foot of the tree. A tree deity who was a blood relation of the two urged them to offer barley-gruel and honey-balls to the Blessed One, saying that this would be a source of happiness and blessing for a long time. The merchants did as the tree deity suggested. After the Buddha had eaten the offerings, the merchants approached him and asked to be accepted as lay disciples. Thus the two became the first lay disciples of the Buddha. The two merchants are also mentioned in *Aṅguttara* 1.26, where they are recorded as being the first lay disciples of the Blessed One. The episode is also mentioned in *Jātaka* 1.80.

In the Pāli canon, there is a *Tapussasutta* in *Aṅguttara* 4.438-448, translated in E. M. Hare, *Gradual Sayings* (London 1935), 4.293-295. According to this sutta, the Buddha was taking the noonday rest at Uruvelakappa. Tapussa approached Ānanda and said that he was a householder given to the pursuit of pleasure. Yet he heard that there were young monks who had renounced the pleasures of life and having done so, became calm and steadfast. He appeared to be much puzzled by this. Ānanda took Tapussa to the Buddha and reported the conversation to him. The Buddha replied that before he became enlightened, his mind was not calm and steadfast, for he had not yet seen the perils of pleasure and was not inclined to give it up. But after he had passed through the nine trances (the four form *jhānas*, the four formless *jhānas*, and the cessation of perception and consciousness), then he became wholly awakened and his mind became calm and steadfast.

In the Chinese canon, there is no counterpart of this sutta. However, the meeting of the merchants and the Buddha is mentioned in a number of places: *Ssu-fen-lü* 31, *T* 22.781c; *Wu-fen-lü* 15, *T* 22.103a; *Jui-ying pen-ch'i-ching* *T* 3.479a; *Pen-hsing chi-ching* 32, *T* 3.801a; *P'u-yao-ching* 7, *T* 3.526b. For a discussion of the forged *T'i-wei Po-li-ching*, see Mochizuki, *Bukkyō daijiten* 4.3193c-3195a; Tsukamoto Zenryū, *Shina bukkyōshi kenkyū Hokugi-hen* (Tokyo 1942), 293-353;

ing among the populace as it was written in the simple popular language. A text of this forged sutra was discovered in Tun-huang, and portions of it are preserved in quotations found in later works. One of the points stressed is the equation of the five precepts with the five norms.

In the *Chin-kuang-ming-ching wen-chü* of Chih-i the famous T'ien-t'ai master, we find the following quotations taken from the *T'i-wei Po-li-ching*: "Not to kill is paired with human-heartedness, not to steal is paired with righteousness, not to commit adultery is paired with propriety, not to drink intoxicating liquor is paired with knowledge, and not to tell lies is paired with trust."[91] In his *Jen-wang-ching su*, Chih-i returns to this same equation, again basing it on the *T'i-wei Po-li-ching*: "Concerning the teachings, there are the five precepts. Not to kill is paired with the east, the east is wood, and wood is based on human-heartedness. The meaning of human-heartedness is to preserve life. Not to steal is paired with the north, north is water, and water is based on knowledge. The one who knows does not steal. Not to commit adultery is paired with the west, west is metal, and metal is based on righteousness. The one who is righteous does not commit adultery. Not to drink intoxicating liquor is paired with the south, the south is fire, fire is based on propriety, propriety means to be protected against committing faults. Not to tell lies is paired with the center, the center is earth, earth is based on trust. The one who tells lies is cunning and perverse, and double-headed, he is not in conformity with rectitude. The one who is upright is not biased or perverse."[92] It will be noticed, however, that though these two quotations are made from the same source, they do not coincide as far as the equations are concerned.

Makita Tairyō, "Tonkōbon Daii-kyō no kenkyū," in *Bukkyō-daigaku Daigakuin kenkyū kiyō*, 137-185. The Tun-huang version of the sutra is Stein 2051, in the British Museum.

[91] *T* 39.51b.

[92] *Hsü Tsang-ching* I/40/4.376ab. Essentially the same passage is quoted by Chi-tsang (549-623) in his *Jen-wang-ching su*, *Hsü Tsang-ching* I/40/3.239a.

During the early T'ang dynasty another work appeared, quoting from the *T'i-wei Po-li-ching* concerning the five precepts and the five norms; this was the *Pien-cheng-lun* of Fa-lin. The equations here follow those given by Chih-i in the *Jen-wang-ching su.*[93] In the *Chih-kuan fu-hsing ch'uan-hung-chüeh* 711-782 by Chan-jan, the T'ien-t'ai master wrote without quoting any source: "To have compassion and not kill is human-heartedness; to be clear-minded and perspicacious and not steal is righteousness; to be careful and not commit adultery is propriety; to be steadfast and not drink intoxicating liquor is knowledge; not speak what is wrong is trust."[94] It is interesting to note that in this passage, Chan-jan makes the same equations as those found in Chih-i, *Chin-kuang-ming ching wen-chü.* Similarly, Tao-shih in the *Fa-yüan chu-lin,* c. 88, *T* 53.926c, and Tsung-mi in his *Yüan-jen-lun, T* 45.708c, make the same equations of the five precepts with the five norms. One is at a loss as to how to account for the differences in the equations, as the quotations are all made from the same source, the *T'i-wei Po-li ching.*

The above are the attempts of the Buddhists to prove that Buddhism and Confucianism are close to each other in their observance of some fundamental ethical concepts and practices and thus gain the support of the Confucian writers. One indication of the measure of this support may be found in the writings of the Confucians. Yen Chih-t'ui (b. 531) of the Northern Ch'i dynasty has a passage in his work, *Yen-shih chia-hsün, kuei-hsin-p'ien* which reads: "The introductory portions of the Buddhist scriptures establish five prohibitions which agree with the five norms in the secular literature. Thus human-heartedness equals the injunction not to kill, righteousness is not to steal, propriety is not to commit adultery, knowledge is not to drink intoxicating liquor, trust is not to tell lies."[95] Likewise, Wei Shou (506-572), compiler of the official *Wei-shu,* wrote in the *Treatise on Buddhism and Taoism*: "There are also the five precepts, which are to abstain

[93] *T* 52.494c.　　　　　　[94] *T* 46.341c.
[95] *Yen-shih chia-hsün* 5.12a, *SPPY* ed.

from killing, stealing, adultery, falsehood, and intoxicating liquor. In general these may be equated with human-heartedness, righteousness, propriety, knowledge, and trust. Only the terminology is different. One who observes them will be reborn in the superior state as deity or man, while one who commits these offenses will descend to the world of misery as demons and animals."[96]

The chart below indicates how nine different sources equate the five precepts with the five norms.*

Source	no killing	no stealing	no adultery	no drinking	no lies
Chin-kuang-ming ching wen-chü (Chih-i)	I	II	III	IV	V
Fa-yüan chu-lin (Tao-shih)	I	II	III	IV	V
Yüan-jen-lun (Tsung-mi)	I	II	III	IV	V
Yen-shih chia-hsün (Yen Chih-t'ui)	I	II	III	IV	V
Wei-shu (Wei Shou)	I	II	III	IV	V
Chih-kuan fu-hsing (Chan-jan)	I	II	III	IV	V
Jen-wang-ching su (Chih-i)	I	IV	II	III	V
Jen-wang-ching su (Chih-tsang)	I	IV	II	III	V
Pien-cheng-lun (Fa-lin)	I	IV	II	III	V

*I = human-heartedness; II = righteousness; III = propriety; IV = knowledge; V = trust.

In this discussion we have sought to provide a clue to answer the question of why Buddhism was finally accepted by the Chinese despite features in Buddhism which were un-

[96] *Wei-shu* 114.2b.

satisfactory to the Chinese. According to our findings, we are convinced that one of the primary reasons why Buddhism alone was able to gain a wide following among the Chinese was that it was able to adjust itself to Chinese ethical practices and beliefs. Nowhere is this better illustrated than in the Buddhist attempts to demonstrate its adherence to the cardinal Confucian virtue of filial piety and ancestral worship. By presenting an image of itself as conforming to Chinese social and ethical values it was able to convince the Chinese that it was no longer a foreign and Indian religion but had become Chinese.

Yü-lan-p'en. This term is usually Sanskritized as *ullambana*. See J. Eitel, *Handbook of Chinese Buddhism* (Hongkong 1888), 185; B. Nanjo, *Catalogue of the Chinese Translation of the Buddhist Tripiṭaka* (Oxford 1883), 78. St. Julien, *Méthode pour déchiffrer et transcrire les noms Sanscrits* (Paris 1861), 65 has suggested *avalambana*. The former term is, however, a hypothetical word, for it is not found in the Sanskrit dictionaries.

The word *ullambita*, a past participial form of *ud-lamb*, does exist (see Monier-Williams, *A Sanskrit English Dictionary*, 219), meaning suspended, as does *avalambana*, which means hanging down, support. The Japanese scholar J. Takakusu has suggested *ullumpana*, a Pāli word meaning salvation, saving, full of mercy, and derived from *ullumpati*. See P.T.S. *Pāli-English Dictionary*, 156. For Takakusu's theory, see E. Ashikaga, "Notes on Urabon," *JAOS* 71 (1951), 72. J. Rahder has made a similar suggestion. (See M. W. de Visser, *Ancient Buddhism in Japan* [London 1935], 65.) The form *ullumpati* is found in the *Sumaṅgalavilāsinī* (1.177: Buddhaghosa's commentary on the *Dīghanikāya*) where the Buddha is said to be "indifferent to worldly pleasures, mild-mannered, with a mind full of mercy." Again, in the *Paramatthadīpanī* (35: Commentary to the *Petavatthu* by Dharmapāla), we read *ullumpana-sabhāva-saṇṭhitā*, of helpful disposition, full of mercy. Iwamoto Yutaka in his latest study *Mokuren densetsu to urabon* (225-231), however, argues that neither of these two terms is acceptable.

According to Hsüan-ying (seventh century), who compiled

a *I-ch'ieh-ching yin-i* in 25 *chüan*, the transcription *yü-lan-p'en* is wrong, and that it should be *wu-lan-p'o-na*, which means hanging upside down. Deceased ancestors, if guilty of some offense and with no descendants to sacrifice to them, would suffer the misery of hanging upside down among the hungry ghosts. Offerings made to the Buddha and the monks on the first day of the rainy season would rescue these ancestors from their state of suspense and misery. He concluded that the interpretation of this term as a vessel to hold foodstuff is wrong. (See *T* 54.535b.)

If Hsüan-ying is correct, then there is no idea of a vessel involved at all in the term, since the whole term is a transcription of a foreign word. Be that as it may, the tradition that the term is connected in some way with a vessel cannot be dismissed so easily. Dharmaraksha's translation, the *Yü-lan-p'an-ching*, makes it clear that a vessel is meant, for the passage reads: "to put all the sweet and beautiful things in the world inside a vessel." Tsung-mi in his commentary on the term wrote: "*Yü-lan* is a term of Central Asiatic origin and means to hang upside down. *P'en* is a Chinese word meaning vessel. If we follow the colloquial, we would say that the entire term means a vessel for rescuing those in a state of suspense" (*T* 39.506a).

Notices in various other sources record the making of vessels: *FYCL* 62, *T* 53.750a, *tsao fo p'en*; *CTS* 118.6b, *tsao yü-lan-p'en*; *Tzu-chih t'ung-chien* 224.16b-17a, *li ch'u yü-lan-p'en*. The commentary by Hu San-sheng on the last passage has the following: "assemble all kinds of food and fruits and place them inside the vessels."

A writer of the Sung dynasty adds a still further explanation of the term. According to Yü-jung in his *Yü-lan-p'en-ching-su hsiao-heng-ch'ao*, c.1, *Hsü Tsang-ching*, I/87/4.375a, "The term *yü-lan-p'en*, according to the translators of the Sung dynasty, is a wrong abbreviation of a Sanskrit word. The correct reading is *wu-lan-p'o-na*, which means filial piety, obedience, offering, affection, hanging upside down, or a state of suspense. The character *p'en* is also a wrong abbreviation, for the old reading was *p'en-tso-na*. The new reading is *men-tso-lo*, also *men-tso-nang*. In Chinese this means a rescue vessel. The meaning of the entire expression should be a vessel for saving those in a state of suspense."

Now the Chinese term *men-tso-nang* or *men-tso-lo* could be a transcription of *muñcana* or *muccana*, but these words do not mean vessel, they mean release or deliverance. However, if we take the old reading *p'en-tso-na*, then we can find a good Sanskrit and Pāli word, similar in sound and meaning a vessel or receptacle, *bhājana*. (See Monier-Williams, *Dictionary*, 752; P.T.S. *Pāli English Dictionary*, 125.) J.J.L. Duyvendak, "The Buddhist Festival of All-Souls in China and Japan," *Acta Orientalia* 5.1 (1926), 39-48, referred to an article by M. W. de Visser, "Het Buddhistische Doodenfest in China en Japan," *Mededeelingen der Koninklyke Academie van Wetenshappen Afdeeling Letterkunde*, deel 58, Série B, no. 5 (Amsterdam 1924), 89-128, which noted such references in Sung literature. Unfortunately I have not been able to consult this article. I am inclined to think that the Sung writers referred to in this article are the same as those mentioned in his book, *Ancient Buddhism in Japan*, 61-65.

Let us now recapitulate. Hsüan-ying defined *wu-lan-p'o-na* as hanging upside down, suspended. Tsung-mi considered only *yü-lan* to be the transcription of a foreign word, and defined it also as hanging upside down. Yü-jung of the Sung dynasty did likewise. All these explanations would connect the word with a derivative, either *avalambana* or *ullambita*, from the root *ud-lamb*, to hang. Takakusu and Rahder would connect the term with *ullumpana*, derived from *ud-lump*, to save, to rescue. The Pāli form *ullumpati* is found in *Vinaya* 2.279; *Dīghanikāya* 1.249: *ullumpatu bhavaṃ Gotamo Brahmaṇiṃ pajan*, "Let the Blessed Gotamo rescue the Brahman world." See also *Mahāvyutpatti* 8704, *ullumpatu māṃ*, and Edgerton, *Buddhist Hybrid Sanskrit Dictionary*, 149. Thus, *ullumpana*, rescue or deliverance, would appear to be preferable to *ullambana* or *avalambana*, hanging upside down, as the original purpose of the service carried out by Mu-lien was to rescue his mother. The use of the Chinese character *lan* for *lum* in *ullumpana* does not present too great a problem. St. Julien, *op.cit.*, cites two examples: no. 1718 *t'an* and no. 1730 *t'an* for the *dum* in *udumbara*. In Oda, *Bukkyō daijiten*, 1783, we find *lan* for the *lum* in Lumbini.

It is true that Hsüan-ying and Tsung-mi included the idea of rescue in their discussions of the term, but Hsüan-ying did not say that *wu-lan-p'o-na* included this idea. Tsung-mi linked the idea of rescue with the character *p'en*, saying it was a vessel for deliverance.

In view of what is said, I would propose the following suggestion as a solution to the problem. First of all, I am inclined to think that the idea of suspended or hanging upside down probably represented a mistaken reading by the Chinese, who confused some form of *ud-lamb* (to hang down) with *ullumpana*, rescue or deliverance. It might well be that when Dharmaraksha made his translation, he used *yü-lan-p'en* for *ullumpana*. However, with the passage of time, the Chinese Buddhist monks, upon reading the term *yü-lan-p'en*, thought it referred to some form derived from *ud-lamb*, such as *avalambana* or *olambana*, and hence interpreted it to mean hanging down, suspended upside down. Both Hsüan-ying and Tsung-mi thought that this was so. As vessels were used to hold the offerings during the service, some Chinese, not knowing the origin of the term *yü-lan-p'en*, mistakenly interpreted *p'en* to be a separate character meaning vessel. Hsüan-ying protested against this, saying that *p'en* was not a separate character but was part of the whole transcription, and he said that the correct transcription should be *wu-lan-p'o-na*. In spite of Hsüan-ying's objections, Tsung-mi persisted in considering *p'en* as a separate Chinese character meaning vessel. In this, it appears that Tsung-mi was in error. Moreover, there also exists the possibility that *p'en* is an abbreviation of *p'en-tso-na*, *bhājana*, mentioned by Yü-jung, and here again, *p'en* cannot be considered as a Chinese term.

If there were a Sanskrit or Pāli original for the Chinese *yü-lan-p'en*, I am inclined to think that it could well be *ullumpana bhājana*.

64

THREE

POLITICAL LIFE

In India, the Buddhist saṅgha considered itself to be a community beyond the authority of the secular rulers. It claimed to be an organization consisting of members who had renounced the involvements and attachments of family, society, and the state to live the religious life of the recluse. By joining the Buddhist saṅgha and undertaking the vows of celibacy, poverty, subsistence on alms, and the cultivation of monastic discipline, the Buddhist monk no longer felt bound by the norms of political and social conduct that governed the lives of ordinary people. Specifically, he claimed that he was no longer obliged to reverence and render homage to the secular rulers of the state. And so it happened in India that it was the ruler who paid homage to the monk. Scattered through the Buddhist canon are instances of the Indian ruling princes, such as Bimbisāra and Ajātasattu of Magadha and Pasenadi of Kosala bowing before the Buddha and the assembly of monks. Probably the most famous instance of such an attitude on the part of a secular ruler was the behavior of King Harsha, emperor of all India, who, upon learning that the eminent Chinese monk Hsüan-tsang had arrived in the vicinity of the imperial camp, hurried over to where Hsüan-tsang was instead of waiting for the Chinese cleric to come to him, and rendered homage to him by bowing to the ground and kissing his feet.[1]

In the *Sāmaññaphalasutta* of the *Dīghanikāya*, there is recorded an interesting dialogue between Ajātasattu, king of Magadha, and the Blessed One over this very problem of the homage due a monk by a ruler. The Buddha asked Ajātasattu

---

[1] *T* 50.247a; R. Grousset, *In the Footsteps of the Buddha* (London 1932), 206.

what he would do if one of his slaves should don the yellow robes and be admitted into the order. Would he force the man to come back and be a slave again?

Ajātasattu's answer states in no uncertain terms that the ruler should pay homage to a monk, even though that monk was a runaway slave formerly in his employ: "Nay, Lord, rather should we greet him with reverence, and rise up from our seat out of deference toward him, and press him to be seated. And we should have robes and a bowl, and a lodging place, and medicine for the sick—all the requisites of a recluse—made ready and beg him to accept of them. And we should order watch and ward and guard to be kept for him according to the law."[2]

Not only did the Buddhist monks feel that they were under no obligation to pay homage to the ruler, but it also appears that they regarded kings in an unfavorable light, as unworthy of reverence. Numerous passages may be found referring to kings as an ever present danger, along with thieves, fires, waters, beasts of prey, creeping things, and nonhuman beings.[3]

In other passages, the greed of kings is mentioned. One such passage reads: "Now by what means may neither kings nor thieves take away my possessions, nor fire burn them, nor water carry them away, nor those whom I do not like take them away?"[4] This greed is also cited in the following passage of the *Milindapañha*: "Kings are grasping. The princes might, in the lust of power, subjugate an extant country twice or

---

[2] *Dīghanikāya* 1.60-61, translated in T. W. Rhys Davids, *Dialogues of the Buddha*, 1.76-77.

[3] *Mahāvagga* 2.15.4, translated in I. B. Horner, *Book of the Discipline* 4.148. See also the same list of dangers in *Mahāvagga* 4.15.7, translated in Horner, *Book of Discipline*, 4.222; *Cullavagga* 9.3.4, translated in Horner, *op.cit.*, 5.342.

[4] *Majjhimanikāya* 1.86, translated in I. B. Horner, *Middle Length Sayings*, 1 (London 1954), 113. See also the same idea in *Aṅguttaranikāya* 4.282, translated in E. M. Hare, *Gradual Sayings*, 4.188; "Now how can I arrange so that rajahs may not get this wealth of mine, nor thieves filch it, nor fire consume it, nor water carry it off, nor ill-disposed heirs make off with it?"

thrice the size of what they had, but they would never give up what they already possessed."[5]

Finally, the tyranny of kings was something that the monks feared. Again in the *Milindapañha*, King Milinda asked Nāgasena the Buddhist monk why he had joined the order. Nāgasena replied that he had joined to the end that all sorrow might perish, and no further sorrow might arise. When the king pressed the matter and asked whether this was the reason for all members of the saṅgha, the monk replied, "Certainly not, sire. Some for these reasons, but some have left the world in terror of the tyranny of kings, some have joined us to be safe from being robbed, some harassed by debts, and some perhaps to gain a livelihood."[6]

It is probable that such passages concerning kings were in the minds of those monks compiling the *Mahāvaṁsa* when they wrote: "Thus, reflecting that Sovereignty, being the source of manifold works of merit, is at the same time the source of many injustices, the man of pious heart will never enjoy it, as if it were sweet fruit mixed with poison."[7] Hence it is no surprise to find a Burmese proverb to the effect that a person serving a king, like one in poverty, or in sickness, or in debt, is as good as dead.[8]

When this Indian religion, Buddhism, was introduced into China during the Han dynasty, it was confronted with an entirely different political atmosphere. The Chinese political system was based on the concept of a strong central authority embodied in the person of the emperor, who was assisted in the administration of this authority by a complex network of bureaucratic organs in the capital and the provinces. The ideology behind the system was Confucian, and one of the principal features of this ideology was the concept of *li*, or proper conduct, according to which order, stability, and har-

---

[5] *Milindapañha* 4.2.2, translated in T. W. Rhys Davids, *The Questions of King Milinda*, 1.203.

[6] *Milindapañha* 2.15, translated in Rhys Davids, *op.cit.*, 1.50.

[7] W. Geiger, *The Mahāvaṁsa* (London 1912), 266.

[8] E. Sarkisyanz, *Buddhist Backgrounds of the Burmese Revolution*, 78.

mony in the empire would be achieved if every member of society performed correctly the various functions that he as a member of that society was supposed to perform. In other words, it was the duty of the ruler to rule, the ministers to minister, the father to behave as a father should, and sons to conduct themselves as sons should. Moreover, it was the duty of every Chinese to render proper homage to the emperor, because it was the emperor in his capacity as the Son of Heaven who gave life to all his subjects and whose virtues were equal to those of the creative powers of nature.[9]

In the administration of his imperial authority, the emperor was assisted by a body of officials who had successfully passed the civil examinations based on the Confucian classics. These officials were the experts on what was considered to be the proper conduct for all the component parts of Chinese society, and together with the emperor they constituted the ruling class. Bureaucratic officials, ancient and modern, have certain features in common, one of which is insistence on precedents as the justification for any course of action. For Chinese officials, the best source for such precedents would, of course, be the Confucian classics or previous Chinese history.

It was this Chinese imperial state governed by a bureaucracy steeped in Confucian ideology that Buddhism met head on after its introduction and spread in China. Unfortunately for the Buddhists, there had never existed in China prior to the introduction of Buddhism the idea of a community of monks as a separate and special social group. When the Buddhist community of monks in China attempted to assert its special and independent status as the saṅgha did in India, it was inevitable that conflict between the saṅgha and the imperial bureaucracy should arise. The saṅgha's insistence that it be governed by its own monastic laws was anathema to the official bureaucracy who held that the concept of *li* was binding on every Chinese. In the end the imperial bureaucracy triumphed; the saṅgha abandoned its claim as a special, in-

[9] E. Zürcher, *The Buddhist Conquest of China,* 233.

dependent group and submitted to the state. As a result, the lives of monks in China were not regulated solely by monastic law but also by secular law, while the affairs of the saṅgha were controlled and supervised by the proper organs in the imperial government. However, it must be emphasized that the Buddhists in China did not submit to this bureaucratic control without putting up a long and spirited struggle. The rest of this chapter will be concerned with the story of this conflict and eventual adjustment.

The initial blast in this conflict between the saṅgha and the imperial authorities was fired in 340 by Yü Ping,[10] a member of the powerful Yü clan that dominated court politics of the Eastern Chin dynasty during the third, fourth, and fifth decades of the fourth century. The focal point of the controversy was whether or not the Buddhist monks should pay homage to the emperor just as any other Chinese subject did. Yü Ping, who had acted as regent since the emperor Ch'ing was young, started the controversy by issuing an edict on behalf of the emperor, in which he advocated that the monks should reverence the ruler. In the beginning, he pointed out, the ancient rulers had some definite reasons for prescribing the acts of reverence. It was not a case of their merely rejoicing at the sight of their subjects bending the knees and bowing. Rather, such acts of reverence were instituted for the purpose of preserving law and order and stability in the realm. Just as a son should show respect to his father, so should the subject show respect to the ruler. Since there were definite reasons for the veneration of rites and ranks, there was no justification to depart from them. The doctrine of Confucianism, which was the backbone of these rites of veneration, had had a long history and had been faithfully adhered to by a hundred generations. It was unthinkable that such a system regulating the conduct of all loyal subjects should be disregarded by the present dynasty. The Buddhist monks were the subjects of the Chin dynasty and did not differ from the rest of the population so far as their capacities and intelligence were concerned. "But

[10] 296-344. Biography on *Chin-shu* 73.7b-9a.

if they, on account of the abstruseness of their theories, use their apparel to commit insubordination, to arrogate to themselves the haughty behavior of a foreign lord, and to stand upright before the Lord of Ten Thousand Carriages [the emperor]—that again is something I cannot accept."[11]

The Buddhist response to this edict was presented by the president of the Department of Affairs of State Ho Ch'ung (292-346), a Buddhist layman and the leader of the court faction opposed to the Yü clan. In this response he was joined by a number of his followers. Ho's main argument was that the Buddhists in observing the five precepts (abstention from killing, lying, stealing, sexual relations, and drinking intoxicating liquor) were actually assisting the ruler in his civilizing influence. Furthermore, even though the religion, introduced during the Han dynasty, had had its periods of development and decline, it had never harbored any evil or false doctrines. Now, if we should order the monks to pay homage to the ruler, it would certainly destroy their teaching, thus leading to the abandonment of meritorious practices and the appearance of vulgar deeds.[12]

Yü Ping kept the controversy alive by issuing another edict on behalf of the emperor. In this second edict, Yü contended that although the hundred rulers of the past had enunciated rules and regulations, none of them had ever permitted alien practices to become mixed with Chinese customs. As for the five Buddhist precepts, these were but trifles compared to the virtues of the Confucian relationships. The *li* or rites were indeed important and reverence great. All principles of government were contained in them. "If there was no clear manifestation between high and low, then there would be no unity in the kingly teaching. If there were no unity, then there would be confusion."[13]

In response to this second edict, Ho and his followers ar-

---

[11] *HMC* 12, *T* 52.79bc, translated in Zürcher, *op.cit.*, 161; *CSM* 1. *T* 52.444a.
[12] *CSM* 1, *T* 52.444ab; *HMC* 12, *T* 52.80a.
[13] *HMC* 12, *T* 52.80a; *CSM*, 1, *T* 52.444b.

gued that monks and Buddhist laymen had always complied with the imperial laws and had never attempted to sow confusion within the ranks of the Confucian relationships. Ever since Han times, no one had argued for changes in the status of monks, yet somehow there had been no detriment to the regulations and the distinctions between inferior and superior. "We notice that when the Chinese monks burnt incense and uttered their earnest wishes, they always gave first consideration to the ruler, and wished him abundance of blessings and prosperity. Their sentiments for the ruler were really without bounds."[14]

In this last reply Ho Ch'ung and his followers reassured Yü Ping and the ruler that the monastic order was not a rebellious group bent on sowing confusion and disruption within the Confucian society, but that it was just as concerned with maintaining order and respecting the position of the emperor. To a certain extent, they succeeded. The controversial issue was submitted to the Board of Rites and after an extended discussion, the scholars on the Board agreed with the position taken by Ho Ch'ung. On this initial confrontation, therefore, the Buddhist viewpoint prevailed, and the suggestion of Yü Ping was not acted upon.[15]

In these arguments and counterarguments, we can already see the issues clearly defined. Yü Ping represented the Confucian imperial bureaucracy and stated the case for the supremacy of the secular government over religion. The world of human relationships as exemplified by the Confucian concept of *li* should never be determined by what lies beyond this world. The ruler is supreme; his laws and regulations must be binding on all alike. If the monastic orders were to claim special and separate treatment, there would be disorder and confusion in human relationships.

Ho Ch'ung and his followers sought to rely on the absence of historical precedents. Monks had never reverenced the rulers in the past, why change now? Moreover, the Buddhists were loyal, law-abiding subjects benefiting the empire

[14] *HMC* 12, *T* 52.80b.   [15] *HMC* 12, *T* 52.79b, 80b.

71

through their observance of the five cardinal precepts: they were actually assisting the ruler by not killing or stealing or behaving immorally and by their solicitous concern for the ruler in their prayers.

The next confrontation between the Buddhists and the state establishment occurred in 400. During the previous year, Huan Hsüan[16] had rebelled against the Chin emperor and set himself up as an independent satrap in south China. Although Huan was a man of culture and familiar with the current trends of Buddhist and Taoist thought of his age, he was at heart a military man suspicious of the role played by the Buddhist monks in court circles. His anticlerical attitude was manifested in two measures that he proposed: first, that the saṅgha should be purged of undesirable elements, and second, that monks should pay homage to the rulers.

In 400, charging that the saṅgha was harboring extravagant, immoral monks as well as evaders of tax and labor services, and that the monasteries in the towns and cities had become the gathering place of bullies and vagabonds, Huan proposed a purging of the monastic community. Only those monks who could read and explain clearly the meaning of the sutras, who practiced diligently the moral precepts, and who lived in retirement in mountain hermitages without dabbling in vulgar practices, would be allowed to retain their status as monks; all others would be defrocked and laicized. There was one exception, however. The community of monks at Lu-shan led by Hui-yüan[17] was exempted from this purge because he considered them to be models of exemplary conduct.[18]

Hui-yüan responded to this proposal in a letter to Huan Hsüan, the first portion of which acknowledged that the saṅgha had become infiltrated with degenerate and impure elements, and that there was a need to purge such undesira-

[16] 369-404. Biography in *Chin-shu* 99.1a-15b; *Wei-shu* 97.1a-13a.

[17] 334-416. Biography in *KSC* 6, *T* 50.357c-361b, translated in Zürcher, *op.cit.*, 240-253.

[18] *HMC* 12, *T* 52.85a.

ble features from the religion. If this purge were accomplished, false monks would be driven out while true believers would then be able to follow the religion without fear of criticism. However, he warned that though the objectives of the proposal were admirable, their execution would be difficult. In Buddhism there are three kinds of activities: meditation, reciting the sutras, and performing meritorious deeds. These three are different, but they are all rooted in the rules of discipline. There may be some who perform meritorious deeds but who are not living in mountain hermitages. There may be some who read the sacred literature diligently but who are not eloquent in expounding their meaning. There may be some who are too advanced in age and hence unable to perform meritorious deeds but who have not committed any wrong. All such monks would be suspect under the proposed tests. Activities are easy to investigate, but truth and falsehood are difficult to ascertain. If cases involving monks in the cities and towns were submitted to Huan Hsüan for judgment, there would be no problem and (Yüan) would abide by Huan Hsüan's decision. But there is danger that inferior officials in the country and border regions, who are not familiar with Buddhism, would render improper judgments against pious and meritorious monks, and this is something that he (Yüan) is greatly concerned about. Yüan therefore proposed that in cases where the local officials are not certain, such cases should be submitted to higher, more enlightened, officials in the cities. At the end of the letter, Yüan made a plea for sons of good families who had professed the religion for generations to join the saṅgha and become monks. If this were done, he concluded, the saṅgha would not then be plagued with the problem of harboring undesirable or impure elements.[19] Evidently Huan Hsüan was moved by the cogency of Hui-yüan's arguments, for he did not take any action against the saṅgha at the time.

Early in 402 Huan Hsüan attempted to resurrect a measure first advanced by Yü Ping, i.e., that monks should bow before

[19] *HMC* 12, *T* 52.85bc. See also Zürcher, *op.cit.*, 260.

the emperor. He did this by addressing to his ministers a letter in which he contended that Yü Ping, while respectful toward the emperor, had not argued his case fully. Even Buddhism, Huan said, was based on respect, respect for the Blessed One, respect for the masters of the law, and hence was no different from Chinese practices. The ruler, along with heaven and earth, possessed the virtue of giving life to all beings, so that even monks benefited from the ruler's activities. This being the case, why should the monks reap the blessings of the ruler but neglect to pay homage to him? He concluded his letter by calling upon the ministers to state their opinions.[20]

The ministers responded with a number of letters. One by Huan Ch'ien,[21] a general of the Army of the Interior, quite frankly admitted that Buddhist monks were different from the Chinese in their behavior, for they shaved their hair, abandoned their families, and destroyed all desires. In other words, they deviated from all that are emphasized in the rites, and hence a case could be made to allow them to deviate from the normal codes of behavior.[22]

The most prolific correspondent was Wang Mi,[23] president of the Department of Grand Secretariat, president of the Ministry of Functionaries, and an ardent lay supporter of Buddhism, who submitted seven letters in all to Huan. His main contentions were that although the monks bore a reverential attitude toward the ruler and agreed with the activities of other subjects, their aspirations transcended the affairs of the ordinary human world. In foreign lands, for instance, the rulers invariably reverenced the monk, on the assumption that it was the Way that was valued, and not the relative position of the man. For four hundred years, Buddhism had flourished in China without being subjected to limitations, mainly because the religion was beneficial to the state.[24]

[20] *HMC* 12, *T* 52.80b.   [21] Biography in *Chin-shu* 74.
[22] *CSM* 1, *T* 52.445a; *HMC* 12, *T* 52.80ab.
[23] 360-407. Biography in *Chin-shu* 65.8ab.
[24] *HMC* 12, *T* 52.80c-81a; *CSM* 1, *T* 52.445ab.

In a series of answers, Huan Hsüan refuted all these arguments advanced by Wang Mi. First, since monks did pay respect to their spiritual masters, why not also to the ruler, whose creative powers bestowed beneficial results even on the monks?[25] As for the veneration of monks by foreign rulers, Huan contended that this was because such foreign rulers and their subjects were uncivilized barbarians who were frightened and awed by the superstitious Buddhist hierarchy of spirits and their doctrine of retribution. The situation in China was different. If it were the Way that was valued, then indeed this was all the more reason why the ruler should be revered, since it was the ruler who personified the highest Way of the Sage.[26] Moreover, in refuting Wang's contention that there had been no limitation on Buddhism during the previous four hundred years, Huan countered with the argument that historical circumstances had changed drastically. Whereas previously Buddhism was followed only by the foreigners in China, now it was practiced even by the rulers, and Chinese rules of conduct should therefore take precedence over foreign customs.[27]

After receiving these responses from his ministers, Huan was apparently not entirely satisfied, and now he sought the opinion of the Buddhist monk whom he admired greatly, Hui-yüan, saying that he, Hui-yüan, would certainly have something to contribute which would clarify his doubts. Hui-yüan answered this request in 402 with a letter[28] that contained the gist of the arguments which he was to elaborate further in his treatise, *Sha-men pu-ching wang-che lun* (*A Treatise on the monk not paying homage to the ruler*).[29]

[25] *HMC* 12, *T* 52.81a; *CSM* 1, *T* 52.445b.
[26] *HMC* 12, *T* 52.81bc; *CSM* 1, *T* 52.445bc.
[27] *HMC* 12, *T* 52.81b; *CSM* 1, *T* 52.445c.
[28] Preserved in *HMC* 12, *T* 52.83c-84b; *CSM* 1, *T* 52.447c-448b, portion translated in Zürcher, *op.cit.*, 258-259.
[29] This treatise, finished very likely early in 404, has been translated into English by L. Hurvitz, "Render Unto Caesar," in Early Chinese Buddhism, *Sino-Indian Studies* (1957), 5.3-4.96-114. See also Zürcher, *op.cit.*, 237-238, 258-259. For Chinese text, see *HMC* 5, *T* 52.29c-32b.

In the initial letter as well as in the treatise, Hui-yüan presented a cogent statement of his contention that the saṅgha and the secular state should be clearly delineated, basing this conclusion on the very nature of the Buddhist dharma. He argued that in Buddhism there are two levels, the laymen who follow the teachings of the master but who still remain at home, and the monks who leave the household life to cultivate the Way. For the former, there is no problem, for the devout laymen still cherish the relations of family and society, they respect their parents and their elders, and they observe the proper methods of paying homage to the rulers. In this respect, they are no different from the rest of the Chinese in their loyalty to the emperor and in their piety to their parents.

With the other class, the clergy, however, the situation is entirely different. The monk has terminated all ties to family and society, he is a stranger to the world of human relations. The teachings of the master tell him that he must flee from the world with all its attachments if he wishes to destroy suffering and sorrow and attain the bliss of emancipation. Having fled the world, he transcends the codes of conduct that govern the people of the world, and therefore should not be restricted by such codes of conduct. However, while inwardly he deviates from the norms of natural relationships in the family, he is not opposed to filial piety, and while outwardly he is negligent in reverencing the ruler, yet he has not lost his respect for him. The benefits emanating from one monk who is virtuous will extend to the six relationships as well as to all under heaven. Such a monk should be free to work out his own salvation, free from the limitations of secular restrictions. After all, one should not wear the clerical robe at an imperial audience, and one should not use a begging bowl in the palace. Chinese and barbarians should not be intermingled, and if those who shave their heads and mutilate their bodies are suddenly entangled with the rules of China, this would be an indication of different species becoming mutually involved, something that Hui-yüan said he would be uneasy about.[30]

From Hui-yüan's biography, we learn that Huan Hsüan hesitated as to what he should do upon receipt of Hui-yüan's letter, and after he had usurped the throne in 404, he issued an edict which stated: "The greatness of the Buddhist doctrine is something which We cannot fathom, but on account of [the monk's natural] feelings of respect for the ruler, We [decide] to let them have their [own way of] being reverent. . . . [Henceforward] the monks shall no more be made to pay respect."[31]

After Huan Hsüan rendered his decision, it seems that two of his ministers, Pien Ssu-chih and Yüan K'o-chih still protested, and in their statements, they argued: "In the whole realm there are none who are not the king's subjects. For those who turn toward the civilizing influence of China, and wear the monastic robe to oppose the rites toward the ruler, this is something my stupid feelings are uneasy about." "What the monks believe in may be unique, but it does not transcend the world. How is it possible for them to differ from ordinary people?"[32]

In these two episodes concerning Yü Ping and Huan Hsüan, we see the Buddhist monks courageously asserting their independent and separate status under the Southern dynasties. They claimed what amounted to extraterritorial status: i.e., that their lives were to be regulated by monastic law, not by secular codes, and hence they were not required

[30] In Hui-yüan's biography, we find a synopsis of the treatise. See KSC 6, T 50.360c, translated in Zürcher, op.cit., 251.

[31] Zürcher, op.cit., 251. See HMC 12, T 52.84b; CSM 2, T 52.451b. The testimony of Wang Chien (452-489) is of interest here. He wrote that during the Chin dynasty, monks called themselves p'in-tao (poor cleric) and sat in the presence of the emperor. Yü Ping and Huan Hsüan attempted to make the monks render the proper respect for the emperor, but on account of the disagreement among courtiers, these attempts were not successful. The Liu Sung emperors also tried to get the monks to conform, but they likewise failed. See KSC 13, T 50.411a.

[32] HMC 12, T 52.84c; CSM 2, T 52.451bc.

to pay the homage to the Chinese emperor required of other subjects.

During the centuries between the Chin and the T'ang dynasties, this controversial issue continued to occupy the attention of some rulers in both north and south China. In the ninth month of 462, during the reign of Emperor Hsiao-wu of the Liu Sung dynasty, a proposal was presented calling for the monks to render the proper homage to the emperor, which the emperor accepted but which the monastic community disregarded.[33] One of the barbarian rulers of the short-lived Hsia Kingdom in north China, Ho-lien-po-po claimed around 409 that he was a Buddha among mankind, had an image of the Buddha painted on his back, and called upon all the monks in his kingdom to worship the image, thereby worshiping him at the same time.[34] It is not known whether the clergy actually did so or not, but since he was a cruel tyrant who never hesitated to execute people, it is more than likely that the monks did. Emperor Yang (reigned 605-616) of the Sui dynasty wanted to change the practices of former dynasties and in 607 ordered the clergy to pay homage, but the clergy refused to comply.[35]

We come now to the T'ang dynasty founded by the Li clan, and by virtue of this fact, the ruling house claimed descent from the sage Lao-tzu, who was also surnamed Li. This, of course, redounded to the benefit of the Taoists, and in official functions Taoism was accorded a favored position on grounds of filial piety.

The first move made by a T'ang emperor occurred early in 662, when an edict issued on the fifteenth day of the fourth month proposed that Taoist priests and priestesses and Buddhist monks and nuns should pay the proper homage to the emperor, empress, and the crown prince, as well as to their parents, and called upon his officials to discuss the issue.[36]

[33] *CSM* 2, *T* 52.452a.
[34] *CSM* 2, *T* 52.452a; 3, *T* 52.456c.
[35] *CSM* 3, *T* 52.457a; *KHMC* 25, *T* 52.280c.
[36] *KHMC* 25, *T* 52.284a; *CSM* 3, *T* 52.455b.

This was the signal for a flurry of memorials presented by Buddhists, all arguing against the proposal. On the twenty-first day of the fourth month, a throng of over 200 monks assembled to discuss the issue, and on the fifteenth of the fifth month, a grand congregation of over 1,000 civil and military officials of the ninth rank and above, officials of prefectures and districts, and some 300 monks led by the famous cleric Tao-hsüan gathered for another debate on the imperial proposal.

Prior to this meeting, Tao-hsüan had on the twenty-fifth and twenty-seventh days of the fourth month presented statements to a number of officials and to the mother of the empress, setting forth his position against the imperial proposal. His main argument is contained in the following passage: "In his manner of living, the monk has no regard for wealth and sensuous beauty and is not shackled by honors and emoluments. He considers mundane matters as floating clouds, and his form and life as a bright flame. Therefore he is proclaimed as one who has left the household life. One who has done so no longer embraces the rites of one who remains in the family, one who has forsaken the world is no longer immersed in the practices of the world. Such a principle is self-evident, and is the unchanging model for a hundred generations."[37]

To support his position, Tao-hsüan quoted from the Buddhist scriptures. From the *Fan-wang-ching* he extracted the following passage: "It is the teaching that those who leave the household life do not reverence the ruling prince, the parents, or the six relationships."[38] From the *Nieh-p'an-ching* (*Nirvāṇasūtra*) came the following: "Those who have left the household life should not reverence the householder."[39]

As for the members of the faction in favor of the imperial proposal, they contended that all living within the four seas are subjects of the emperor and hence should pay homage to him. All subjects enjoy the benevolent rule of the emperor,

---

[37] *CSM* 3, *T* 52.457ab; *KHMC* 25, *T* 52.286a.
[38] *T* 24.1008c. [39] *T* 12.399c.

and it therefore behooves every subject to repay that benevolence by acts of reverence. The ruler, the *Tao*, heaven, and earth are the four great ones (see *Tao-te-ching*, ch.25), and for the monks to reverence the *Tao* but not the ruler is indeed contradictory. As for the Buddhist claim that monks should not reverence a layman, the imperial supporters countered with a reference to the *Vimalakīrtisūtra*, where monks paid homage to Vimalakīrti, who was himself a layman.[40]

After some discussion, the assembled officials requested the monks to withdraw from the meeting, since the imperial decree had called for deliberation by officials. In the absence of the clergy, the assembled officials took a vote, with the result showing 539 against the clergy paying homage, and 354 for the proposal.[41]

In view of the unfavorable vote cast by a majority of the officials, Kao-tsung issued a decree in the eighth day of the sixth month, 662, in which he declared that there was no need for the clergy to pay homage to the ruler, but since parents played such an important role in bringing up children, the clergy should prostrate themselves before parents to pay homage to them.[42]

It is interesting to note that while the debate was going on, two officials, Ts'ui An-tu and Shen Hsüan-ming sought to effect a compromise by suggesting that venerable monks who excelled in virtue be exempted from paying homage, while beginners who were deficient in training and lacking in virtue should pay homage.[43] Nothing came out of this novel proposal, however.

The imperial edict of 662 was a partial victory for the Buddhists in that they were no longer required to reverence the ruler. They were, however, still required to reverence their parents, and this decree angered the monks, who bombarded the officials with another flurry of protests.[44] As the contents

[40] These statements are gathered in *CSM* 5, *T* 52.464c-470b.
[41] *CSM* 6, *T* 52.472a; *KHMC* 25, *T* 52.289bc.
[42] *KHMC* 25, *T* 52.290a; *CSM* 6, *T* 52.472c.
[43] *CSM* 5, *T* 52.465b; *KHMC* 25, *T* 52.288c-289a.
[44] For these protests, see *CSM* 6, *T* 52.472c-473c.

of these protests involve issues other than those concerning our main theme, we shall have to lay them aside.

There was another issue which neither the *Kuang-hung-ming-chi* nor the *Chi-sha-men* mention, but which must have stirred some discussion at the time. It will be recalled that in India, the practice was for monks to receive homage from rulers and parents. Such a practice would be unthinkable in Chinese society. However, to prevent the emergence of such a request by the clergy, the throne in 657 decreed that the Buddhist and Taoist clergy were not to receive homage from their parents and seniors.[45] After the imperial decree of 662, the controversy appears to have subsided, although the question of paying respects to parents was still alive.

While the Buddhist saṅgha might be said to have won the battle in the sense that the proposal to make the monks pay homage to the ruler was defeated, in the long perspective of history it must be said that the monks lost the war, for while they were arguing and writing in defense of their position, the state in the form of the imperial bureaucracy was taking other steps to deprive the community of monks of its independent status. The ordination of monks, which was strictly a matter of concern only to the individual and the saṅgha in India, came under increasing supervision by the state in China. Monks had to be registered, their numbers limited, and their ranks purged of undesirable elements from time to time by the imperial authorities. Instead of their conduct being regulated solely by monastic law, the monks faced increased control under secular laws during the T'ang dynasty. The construction of temples and monasteries likewise was subjected to increasing government supervision.

Such a loss of special status by the saṅgha of course did not occur suddenly under the T'ang; its beginnings could be traced back to the period of the North-South dynasties. Previously we have pointed out that by and large the saṅgha was able to maintain its position as a special group under the Southern dynasties in the south. This was not so in north

[45] *FTTC* 39, *T* 49.367a; *THY* 47.11a.

China under the Northern dynasties, especially under the Northern Wei. Immediately after the establishment of the dynasty, Emperor T'ai-tsu (reigned 386-409) decided to appoint a *tao-jen-t'ung* or chief of monks to preside over a government bureau which would exercise jurisdiction over the monastic community. For this office he appointed Fa-kuo. This move immediately placed the cleric in a dilemma. As a subordinate member of the imperial bureaucracy he was of course obliged to reverence the emperor, but as a monk he had to be mindful of the passages in the Buddhist canon forbidding such a practice. Fa-kuo extracted himself from this dilemma by resorting to a clever stratagem. He said, "T'ai-tsu, being intelligent and wise and liking our doctrine, is a present day Tathāgata. It is fitting that monks should pay him full honors. . . . Since he who can spread the doctrine is the prince among men, I have not bowed to the emperor, but have merely paid my respects to the Buddha."[46] By this clever appointment the emperor asserted his control over the saṅgha and the monks reacted by submitting to the imperial authority. On the basis of this control over the saṅgha the Northern Wei dynasty carried out a number of restrictive measures pertaining to monks.

Among these was a measure calling for investigation of unregistered monks. In 472, the following edict was issued:

> For many years now, monks have not been living within the monasteries but have been wandering around the countryside and consorting with lawless elements. We command the people to form groups of fives for mutual protection and not harbor these monks. As for the unregistered monks, they should be thoroughly investigated, and if they are found to exist, they should be handed over to their provincial garrisons. Those in the vicinity of the capital should be sent back to their local monk office. Those in the outlying regions who have to travel about to reach and convert

[46] *Wei-shu* 114.8b-9a, translated in J. R. Ware, *Wei Shou on Buddhism, TP* 30 (1933) 129.

people for the sake of the Three Jewels should bear a document from their provincial *wei-na*, while those in the capital should bear a document from the capital *wei-na*. Any violation of this shall be punished.[47]

Such an edict carried the implication that monks had to be registered, although there is no indication in the *Shih-lao-chih* about the inception of such registration. Further indication of such registration is contained in a memorial presented in 486.

It was decreed formerly that at the beginning of the census, ignorant people, trusting to luck, falsely called themselves followers of the Way, hoping thereby to evade the imposts, and that unregistered monks and nuns were to be unfrocked and laicized. Again, it was decreed that the abbot and *wei-na* should conduct an examination of their respective monasteries concerning those monks and nuns under investigation. Those who are zealous in their observance of the Way should be permitted to carry on, but those who are coarse, whether registered or not, should be laicized. In accordance with this decree, 1,327 monks and nuns were laicized in the various prefectures.[48]

Besides requiring registration, the state also restricted the number of ordinations, as for example in 492, when a decree was issued permitting large prefectures to ordain only 100 monks and nuns on the eighth day of the fourth month (Buddha's birthday) and the fifteenth day of the seventh month (the Buddhist All-Souls' Feast), a middle-size prefecture to ordain 50, and a small prefecture to ordain 20.[49] The method of choosing the candidates to fill this quota was also carefully regulated in a decree issued by Empress Dowager Ling in 517: in the large prefecture, the allowable ordinations were to be chosen from a list of 300 candidates; in a middle-size prefecture, from 200 candidates; and in a small prefecture from 100 candidates. Monastic and secular officials in the pre-

[47] *Wei-shu* 114.18b.   [48] *Ibid.*, 114.20ab.   [49] *Ibid.*, 114.20b.

fectures were to conduct the examination and make the choice to fill the quota. If there were not enough candidates of strict behavior and conduct, then the quota was to be left unfilled. If unwise choices were made, then secular officials such as the governor, prefectural chief, and district magistrate were to be pronounced guilty and punished for violating the imperial decree. As for monastic officials, they were also to be punished, with the chief of monks and the *wei-na* banished 500 *li* to another prefecture and reduced in rank to that of a common monk. A similar penalty was to be levied on those monks and nuns who ordained slaves and on those who raised children of slaves to be ordained when they became of age.[50]

In 509, Chief of Monks Hui-shen presented a memorial which contained the following statement:

> There may be monks who do not live within the monastery but who roam about among the populace. Such are the monks who commit offenses and bring confusion to the doctrine. If there are offenders, they should be unfrocked and returned to lay life. If monasteries are to be built, the complement of monks in them should be limited to fifty or more, and permission to build should be granted only after a petition has been presented. Anyone who builds a monastery without obtaining permission should be punished for violating an imperial decree, and the community of monks should be banished to distant provinces.

These proposals of Hui-shen were accepted by the emperor.[51]

It is obvious that under the Northern Wei, the sangha was no longer the independent community of monks that it claimed to be. The chief of monks in the imperial bureaucracy and the monks had to pay homage to the emperor; all monks and nuns were required to be registered, and ordination was limited by secular laws. It was this tradition of secular control over the sangha that was carried over to the T'ang dynasty.

[50] *Ibid.*, 114.24b-25a.   [51] *Ibid.*, 114.22b.

First, the registration of monks was regularized and made official. In the seventeenth year of K'ai-yüan, or 729, Emperor Hsüan-tsung issued a decree calling for the registration of monks and nuns and the compilation of such a registry every three years.[52] In other sources, we are told that three copies of such a monk's registry were made, one copy was kept in the local prefecture, one sent to the Tz'u-pu (Bureau of National Sacrifice), and one kept by the local community of monks.[53]

The registration called for by the edict of 729 revealed that there were 75,524 monks and 50,576 nuns, and 5,358 temples and monasteries. Japanese and Korean monks who had gone to China to study Buddhism were not counted in the census, but if they did not return to their native countries within nine years, then they were required to be registered.[54]

Registration of monks was something that was condemned in the Buddhist sutras. On this point, one of the Buddhist sutras, the *Jen-wang-ching* was very specific:

> If my disciples, the monks and nuns, were to be registered and employed by government officials, then they are not my disciples. That would be the way of soldiers and slaves. If government officials would be appointed to oversee the saṅgha and regulate the registration of monks, if great and small chiefs of monks were to assist each other to keep the saṅgha under bondage, then that would be like the way of prisoners, soldiers, and slaves. At such a time, the law of the Buddha would not last long.[55]

[52] *FTTC* 40, *T* 49.374b. However, in the *T'ang-ling shih-i* edited by Niida Noboru, section on *tsa-ling*, p. 859, the date for this decree is given as the seventh year of K'ai-yüan, or 719. Regardless of which date is correct, one thing is certain, the compilation of such a monk's registry occurred during the reign of Hsüan-tsung.

[53] *TLT* 4.16ab; *HTS* 48.9a.

[54] *THY* 49.10a; *HTS* 48.9a.

[55] *Jen-wang-ching*, *T* 8.833c, Kumārajīva's translation. Some Japanese scholars have argued that this is a Chinese forgery. See Mochizuki, *Bukkyō daijiten* 4106bc.

What is most interesting is that in the translation made by Amoghavajra during the T'ang dynasty, this passage has been altered considerably. Here the reading is: "If in the future all ruling kings of the country, the crown princes, and the ministers should order an illegal registration of my disciples and appoint officials to regulate it, or if great and small chiefs of monks should unreasonably employ my disciples as servants, then you should know at that time, the law of the Buddha would not last long."[56] During Amoghavajra's time in China (746-774), the T'ang government was already registering monks and employing them in the palace chapels and national monasteries to hold services and pray for the welfare and protection of the empire. Amoghavajra, who was on good terms with Emperors Su-tsung (756-762) and Tai-tsung (763-779) could not very well disavow official policy, and could not write, therefore, that any monk who was registered or employed by the government was not a disciple of the Buddha. In order to avoid any attack or criticism of current T'ang policy, he wrote about illegal registrations and unreasonable employment. Of course, government practices were not illegal or unreasonable, but Kumārajīva's version, however, contained no such qualifications.

The second area in which the state sought to impose its control over the saṅgha involved the ordination. Ordination, generally speaking, should be a private concern; the individual should be free to apply for admission to the saṅgha if he so desired, and the saṅgha after investigation and examination would accept him into the order through the regular ordination procedures. Ordination was therefore a private concern of the individual and the monastery, with the state playing no role at all.

In China during the T'ang dynasty, it is obvious that such a conception of ordination was no longer possible. By mid-T'ang, the state had become thoroughly involved in the process of ordination by its practice of issuing a certificate to all those who were ordained. Such a certificate was issued by the

[56] *Jen-wang-ching, T* 8.844a, Amoghavajra's translation.

Bureau of National Sacrifice, a government bureau which in 694 was first given jurisdiction over Buddhism by Empress Wu Tse-t'ien. Prior to this time, even as early as during the period of the North-South dynasties, monks were required to carry a sort of identity card, giving their names and native places, used mainly to facilitate travel. It is not possible to ascertain just when this ordination certificate was first issued. In Japan such an ordination certificate was already in vogue in 720[57] and, since the Japanese took over the practice from China, it is clear that the Chinese had been issuing certificates before that date.[58]

A monk became eligible for an official ordination, at which time he received his certificate, through a number of methods. One was through an examination, which usually consisted of testing the candidate's ability to recite a minimum of leaves from a sutra, or to read and explain a text. The first recorded instance of this type of examination took place in 705, when,

[57] Michihata Ryōshū, *Tōdai bukkyōshi no kenkyū*, 66.

[58] According to the *Seng-shih-lüeh* T 54.246b, such an ordination certificate was first granted by the Bureau of National Sacrifice in 747. However, this must be a mistake by Tsan-ning, compiler of the *Seng-shih-lüeh*. For a detailed discussion of this error, see Michihata, *Tōdai bukkyōshi no kenkyū*, 60-66. The gist of Michihata's argument is that Tsan-ning misread a passage in the *T'ang-hui-yao* 49.5b: "In the fifth month of the sixth year, it was ordered by the emperor that monks and nuns shall as before revert to the control of the commissioners of meritorious works of the two streets and shall no longer be subject to the Bureau of Guests. The Bureau of National Sacrifice is ordered to grant certificates to those who are ordained." The date here, sixth year, refers to the Hui-ch'ang era. Tsan-ning, however, interpreted this to refer to the T'ien-pao era. This is impossible, for in the T'ien-pao era, the offices of the commissioners of meritorious works in Ch'ang-an were not yet established. During the fifth year of Hui-ch'ang, 845, the control of the saṅgha was shifted from the offices of the commissioners of meritorious works to the Bureau of Guests, and now in the sixth year, there was another shift from the Bureau of Guests back to the offices of the commissioners. The use of the characters *i-ch'ien*, as before, is most meaningful here, for this refers to a situation in the previous year, when the saṅgha was under the control of the commissioners of meritorious works.

in pursuance of an imperial decree issued that year, a young postulant Ta-i in the Ling-yin Monastery recited passages from the *Lotus Sutra* and ranked first.[59] The important point to note is that the examination was carried out under the supervision of the local military governor named Hu Yüan-li. During 757, it was decreed that any layman who could recite 700 leaves from a sutra would be eligible to be ordained.[60] The next year, 758, another decree reduced the number of leaves to 500.[61] The number of leaves was still further reduced in 825, when it was decreed that if a male postulant could recite 150 leaves, and a female postulant 100 leaves, then they would be eligible for ordination.[62] Certificates of ordination were also conferred on those postulants who could pass an examination on the three baskets of the canon.[63] If a candidate passed the examination successfully, he was certified by the secular authorities in charge as being qualified for ordination, after which he went to his spiritual preceptor for the final ceremony.[64]

Besides passing an examination, an individual might also obtain the certificate of ordination through what is known as *en-tu*, or ordination by the grace of the emperor. On certain occasions, such as the official recognition of a monastery by the state, on imperial birthdays, or memorial days in honor

[59] *FTTC* 40, *T* 49.371b; *SKSC* 15, *T* 50.800a.
[60] *SKSC* 15, *T* 50.803c. Biography of Tao-piao.
[61] *FTTC* 40, *T* 49.376a.
[62] *FTTC* 42, *T* 49.384c; *TFYK* 52, Chung-hua Book Co. ed. 1.580.
[63] *FTTC* 41, *T* 49.379a.
[64] We have referred to postulants for a few times. This category, called *t'ung-hsing* in Chinese, was established during the T'ang dynasty in the belief that before a person could become a novice, he must undergo a period of training and study. As a postulant, he must observe the five cardinal precepts, but he did not shave his head. His duties embraced study of the scriptures, and the performance of such menial tasks as attending to the abbot or monastery guests. As a postulant he was not exempted from the customary tax and labor services. After one year he was eligible for an examination to determine whether or not he was qualified to become a novice. See *Ch'an-yüan ch'ing-kuei* c. 9, *Hsü-tsang-ching* II/16/5.464a-465a.

of deceased emperors and empresses, or on imperial visitations to a newly established monastery, abbots of monasteries would present the names of qualified postulants to the local government offices, which in turn would recommend them to the Bureau of National Sacrifice. No examination was required; ordination was permitted as a favor of the emperor. This type of ordination had existed even before the T'ang, but under the T'ang it became more prominent. The earliest instance of it during the T'ang dynasty occurred in 635, when Emperor T'ai-tsung issued an edict calling for the ordination of 3,000 monks and nuns. The reason for this step, according to the edict, was that the recent warfare had left many monasteries and temples without their quota of the clergy. The edict called upon the local officials to select energetic, sincere, and virtuous candidates regardless of age, and recommend them for ordination.[65]

In 648, there was an even larger number of ordinations by imperial grace. Emperor T'ai-tsung in a conversation with the famous Hsüan-tsang asked the latter what should be given first priority in spreading the law. Hsüan-tsang replied that the most important step was to ordain more monks. Accordingly the emperor decreed that every monastery in the capital and commanderies should each ordain five monks. It is recorded that in all over 17,500 monks and nuns were ordained.[66] In the same year, when the crown prince established the Tz'u-en Monastery to honor Empress Wen-te, 50 famous monks of great virtue were selected to live in the monastery, and each one was allowed six novices to serve him.[67] In 738, Emperor Hsüan-tsung ordered that whenever

[65] FTTC 39, T 49.364b; CTW 5.17b.
[66] FTTC 39, T 49.366b. In the biography of Hsüan-tsang, compiled by Hui-li, Ta-tz'u-en-ssu san-tsang fa-shih chuan 7, T 50.259a, a few more details are to be found. The Hung-fu Monastery in the capital which T'ai-tsung had erected in 634 to honor the memory of the Queen Mother Mu (See THY 48.4b) was accorded special treatment and permitted to ordain fifty instead of just five monks. In all, as there were 3,716 monasteries in the land, a total of more than 18,500 monks were ordained.
[67] FTTC 39, T 49.366c.

monasteries were without clergy, such monasteries should, according to their sizes, ordain six or seven monks, the candidates to be selected from those outstanding in learning and discipline and recommended by their local communities.[68] Again in 747, he issued another edict calling upon every monastery in the empire to select postulants of pure conduct and recommend them for ordination, with each prefecture being permitted to have three such ordinations.[69] In 768, during the first month, when the emperor Tai-tsung went to the Chang-ching Monastery to burn incense, a total of 1,000 monks and nuns were ordained, and in the next year, during memorial services honoring Empress Dowager Chang-ching, a total of 400 monks and nuns and Taoist priests were ordained.[70]

The foregoing are but random selections culled from the Buddhist historical records, but they are sufficient to indicate the nature of this method of obtaining ordination.

Finally one could also obtain the certificate of ordination by purchasing it. This practice started in 757. The suppression of the An Lu-shan rebellion, which broke out in 755, had depleted the imperial treasury, with no funds left to buy supplies for the army. To replenish the imperial coffers, the government embarked on a scheme of selling ordination certificates to anyone able to pay 100 strings of cash for one. The scheme was successful, for we are told that people in the two capitals of Ch'ang-an and Lo-yang flocked to take advantage of the purchase. In all, over 10,000 Buddhist monks and Taoist priests were ordained by this method, and the imperial treasury was richer by about a million strings of cash.[71]

[68] *CTW* 24.4a.

[69] *FTTC* 40, *T* 49.375c; *SKSC* 15, *T* 50.802c.

[70] *TFYK* 52, Chung-hua ed. 1.576,577. This Chang-ching Monastery was located just outside the T'ung-hua Gate of Ch'ang-an, and was constructed in 767 by Chief of Intendance of the Inner Palace Yü Ch'ao-en to honor the memory of Empress Dowager Chang-ching. See *THY* 48.6ab. For Yü Ch'ao-en, who died in 770, see *HTS* 207.4b-6a; *CTS* 184.7a-8a.

[71] *FTTC* 40, *T* 49.376a; *FTLT* 13, *T* 49.598bc; *HTS* 51.4b; *CTS* 48.2a. Prices in the two capitals immediately after the rebellion were highly

This scheme of selling ordination certificates to raise revenue was in the nature of a temporary expediency, and it was apparently discontinued by the state once the economic crisis was over. However, once the practice was started, it was difficult to stop it, and local officials resorted to it to raise revenue. There was a certain Wang Chih-hsing in Anhui who in ca. 824 sold more than 100 certificates daily to anyone able to pay 2,000 cash for one. Later on, during the Sung dynasty, the sale of ordination certificates became part of a national policy to raise revenue for the imperial treasury.[72]

Thus we see that there were three ways to become officially ordained in T'ang China: to pass an examination on the scriptures, to be the recipient of imperial favor, or to buy the ordination certificate; control over every one of the three methods rested with the state. This was indeed a far cry from practices in India, where the state kept aloof from ordination procedures.

Not only did the state claim supremacy over the saṅgha by the right to ordain monks, but it also exercised the power to defrock them. Periodically during the T'ang dynasty, the imperial authorities carried out what is known as selecting monks, literally purging the saṅgha. The reasons behind such purges were usually the desire of the government to rid the saṅgha of degenerate monks or rebellious elements in the guise of monks, and the necessity to reduce the number of people who had taken refuge in the monasteries to escape taxation and the labor services. The unmentioned reason is more

inflationary, with the price per *tou* or peck of rice around seven strings. (One string consists of 1,000 cash.) This would mean that each certificate of ordination costs about the equivalent of fourteen *tou* of rice. See *HTS* 51.5a.

[72] For the Sung policy, see Tsukamoto Zenryū, "Sō no zaiseinan to bukkyō," in *Kuwabara Hakushi kanreki kinen Tōyōshi ronsō* (Tokyo 1934), 549-594; Yüan Chen, "Liang-Sung tu-t'ieh k'ao," in *Chung-kuo she-hui ching-chi-shih chi-k'an* 7.1 (1944), 42-101; 7.2 (1946).1-78; K. Chen, "The Sale of Monk Certificates During the Sung Dynasty," *Harvard Theological Review* 49.4 (1956), 307-327. For Wang Chih-hsing, see *CTS* 174.4a; *CTW* 706.1b-2a.

likely to be the fundamental Confucian antagonism to the saṅgha as a social group opposed to so many aspects of Chinese culture. Such purges had already been ordered by rulers in previous dynasties. For instance, Shih Hu (reigned 335-349), in ordering a purge of the saṅgha, complained that in the saṅgha there were scoundrels and vagrants who were avoiding the labor services, as well as some misfits who did not behave like monks.[73] In a previous discussion on Huan Hsüan, we referred to his criticism of the monastic community, i.e., that "[the monks] in the capital compete with each other in extravagance and lewdness. . . . Evaders of labor service crowd together from a hundred miles [around]; tax evaders fill the temples and monasteries."[74]

Such conditions in the monastic community were undoubtedly what the first emperor of the T'ang had in mind when in 627 he issued his edict calling for the defrocking of all those monks and nuns who did not observe the religious discipline. Those who were energetic and zealous in the practice of their religion, however, were ordered to move to large monasteries, where they would receive adequate shelter, clothing, and food. Within the capital, three Buddhist monasteries would be permitted to exist; in the outlying areas, one in each prefecture.[75]

In 714, President of the Department of the Grand Secretariat Yao Ch'ung presented a memorial charging that since the Shen-lung era (707-709), imperial princesses and members of the empress's family had been conducting private ordinations and expending private fortunes to construct monasteries. As a result, evasion of labor services, lewdness, and immoral conduct had become rampant. The Buddha taught people, the memorial continued, to develop love and compas-

[73] KSC 9, T 50.385c.
[74] HMC 12, T 52.85a, translated in Zürcher, op.cit., 260.
[75] FTTC 39, T 49.363a; CTW 3.6a-7b. This edict was issued during the fifth month of 627. The very next month, the prince of Ch'in or Li Shih-min was installed as crown prince, and to celebrate the occasion a general amnesty was proclaimed, which included the suspension of the purge of the monastic community.

sion and to act for the benefit of others, thus bringing about peace to all beings; why should this unregulated ordination of wicked people be allowed to defile the law? The emperor agreed with this view and immediately ordered his officials throughout the empire to purge the saṅgha of bogus monks and undesirable elements. Altogether some 30,000 monks were laicized.[76]

In another attempt to screen out unqualified monks from the community, Hsüan-tsung in the sixth month of 724 ordered his officials to examine the monks to see how well they were acquainted with the canon. All monks under sixty were required to recite 200 leaves of sutras during an examination to be held once every three years, and all those who failed would be laicized.[77] A similar attempt to screen out unworthy monks was ordered by the emperor in the seventh month of 835, following the advice of the premier Li Hsün (d. 835). Monks were now required to read fluently 500 leaves of Buddhist texts, and within these 500 leaves, to be able to recite 300 leaves. After the decree was issued, monks in the capital were given three months to prepare for the examination. Anyone who failed the tests would be laicized. Certain groups were exempted: those monks over fifty who were mentally senile, the deaf, the dumb, the lame, and recluses who were acknowledged by all to be perfect in religious conduct.[78]

In 731 Emperor Hsüan-tsung recalled that for some twenty years no official ordination had been allowed, but now he heard that there were monks below the age of twenty in the empire. He therefore called upon all local officials to investigate the matter, assign the responsibilities for this situation, and impose the proper punishment.[79]

[76] *THY* 47.11b. In the *FTTC* 40, *T* 49.373b, the number defrocked is put at 12,000 instead of 30,000.

[77] *THY* 49.6b.

[78] *CTW* 74.13b; *FTTC* 42, *T* 49.385b. This edict, however, was observed for but a short period, for when Li Hsün was executed in the eleventh month for complicity in trying to kill eunuchs, the edict was rescinded.

[79] *THY* 49.6b.

We come now to the best-known case in T'ang history of such purging of the saṅgha, the Hui-ch'ang persecution of Buddhism. The actual decree calling for suppression was issued in the eighth month of 845, but long before this, measures had already been taken to defrock monks. At this critical juncture in the history of T'ang Buddhism, we are indeed fortunate that a very observant Japanese monk, Ennin, was in Ch'ang-an, and in his diary we are given a detailed account of the measures taken by the state. As early as the third month of 842, an edict was issued which dismissed nameless monks (those not properly registered) and forbade the enrollment of postulants and novices.[80] In the tenth month another edict specified that all the monks and nuns of the empire who practiced alchemy or mystic incantations, who had escaped from the army, who had scars and tattoo marks on their bodies, who had been committed to hard labor for offenses, who maintained wives or indulged in sexual intercourse, and who did not observe the rules of discipline should be laicized. The edict goes on to say that those monks who possessed wealth and wished to retain it should also return to lay life and pay the necessary tax. Taking advantage of this stipulation, 1,232 monks from the left half of Ch'ang-an and 2,259 from the right half returned to lay status.[81]

This was followed in the ninth month of 843 by another imperial order calling for the defrocking of all those monks in the capitals and the provinces whose names were not in the public registers. Ennin reported that over 300 monks who had recently wrapped their heads (because they had been shaved) were executed.[82] The next year, in the tenth month of 844, in connection with the destruction of small monasteries, the monks and nuns in the destroyed monasteries were all forced to return to lay status. In all, Ennin reported thirty-three such monasteries destroyed and the monks defrocked.[83]

The most serious blows were to fall in 845. First, all those

[80] *Ennin* 3.87.
[82] *Ennin* 3.94.
[81] *Ennin* 3.90.
[83] *Ennin* 4.98.

monks and nuns under thirty were returned to lay life, then those under forty, finally all those under fifty. By the fifth month of 845, Ennin reported that all the monks in the capital had disappeared. Next, all those over fifty who lacked the proper documents issued by the Bureau of National Sacrifice were defrocked.[84] In the eighth month of 845, the axe fell on the saṅgha; all the monks and nuns in the empire, numbering some 260,500, were ordered to return to lay life.[85]

With the state exercising the power to ordain monks on the one hand and to take away their clerical status on the other, the saṅgha in China had in fact lost another battle in its long struggle to maintain itself as a special group within the Chinese political system. We turn now to yet another phase of this process, the regulation of the conduct and movement of the monks in accordance with secular laws. It will be remembered that the strongest argument adduced by Hui-yüan was that monks, by leaving the household life, had transcended society and were no longer bound by secular laws. In the T'ang dynasty, such an argument no longer had any effect, and in such legal works as the *T'ang-liu-tien* or the *T'ang-lü su-i*, we find examples of secular laws promulgated by the state to govern the saṅgha.

Besides the *Vinaya* controlling the conduct of the Buddhist clergy, the basic code governing Buddhist and Taoist monks and nuns during the T'ang dynasty was the *Tao-seng-ke* (Rules concerning Buddhist and Taoist clergy), formulated during the Chen-kuan era, probably in 637.[86] This *Tao-seng-ke* is no longer extant, however, but the Japanese work *Sōni-ryō*, which governs the conduct of the community of monks and nuns in Japan, was based on it. Therefore a study of the *Sōni-ryō* would give us a good idea of the contents of the *Tao-*

---

[84] Ennin 4.101.

[85] For the edict of suppression, see *CTW* 76.9b-10b; *FTTC* 42, *T* 49.386a; *CTS* 18A.14a-15a; *THY* 47.16b-17b.

[86] See Takigawa Masajirō, "Ryō no shūge ni mieru Tō no hōritsu sho," *Tōyō Gakuhō* 18.35-41; Moroto Tatsuo, "Tōsho ni okeru bukkyō kyōdan no tōsei," *Bunka* 16.6 (1952), 66ff.

seng-ke.[87] While it is not possible to find the equivalent of every article of the *Sōni-ryō* in the T'ang laws as found in the *T'ang-liu-tien* or the *T'ang-lü su-i*, we do find similarities in many cases, thus reinforcing the assumption that the contents of the twenty-seven articles of the *Sōni-ryō* were modeled largely after T'ang examples. We shall refer to some of these cases where the provisions of the T'ang codes superseded the monastic code and called for penalties for offenses which went beyond those specified in the *Sōni-ryō* or the Buddhist *Vinaya*.[88] Before we do this, however, it is necessary to summarize the penalties imposed for violations of the secular laws. Such penalties consist of five categories:

1. *ch'ih* (beating with bamboo). This is divided into five grades: beating with 10, 20, 30, 40, or 50 strokes.
2. *chang*, same as the first category, but more strokes, again divided into five grades: 60, 70, 80, 90, and 100 strokes.
3. *t'u* (imprisonment at hard labor), also five grades: one, one and a half, two, two and a half, and three years.
4. *liu* (banishment to distant places). Three grades according to distance: 2,000, 2,500, 3,000 *li*.
5. *ssu* (death by strangulation or beheading).[89]

Our first example concerns food taken by monks. In the *T'ang-liu-tien* there is a long passage pertaining to the food,

---

[87] The *Sōni-ryō* may now be found in a work, *Ryō no shūge*, compiled by Koremune Naomoto, of which a modern edition exists in two volumes, ed. Hayakawa Junzaburō (1912-1913). In this edition, the *Sōni-ryō* is in vol. 1, pp. 224-280. It is also found in the *Kokushi taikai*, edited by Kuroita Katsumi, vol. 23, pp. 206-255. In all it consists of twenty-seven articles. For a study of this Sōni-ryō, see Miura Hiroyuki, *Hōseishi no kenkyū* (Tokyo 1919), 1113-1132.

[88] This situation is mentioned in the biography of Hsüan-tsang, where it is stated, "In the sixth year of Yung-hui (665) an imperial edict was issued to the effect that when Taoist and Buddhist clergy commit offenses the details of which are not clear, then they shall be judged by secular laws." *Ta-tz'u-en-ssu san-tsang fa-shih-chuan* 9, T 50.270a.

[89] *TLSI* 1.19b-22b.

clothing, and behavior of monks. Concerning food, the passage specifies that if a monk drinks intoxicating liquor, eats meat, or prepares food with the five strong-smelling plants, he shall be sentenced to hard labor.[90] Let us examine what the Buddhist *Vinaya* says about these offenses. The rule covering liquor-drinking is Pācittiya 51, which stipulates that the penalty for drinking intoxicating liquor can be removed by mere confession before the assembly of monks.[91] This is indeed a far cry from the penalty of hard labor prescribed in the T'ang code.

As for eating meat, the Buddhist code is even more lax. In the *Mahāvagga* 6.31.14 we read that meat can be considered pure, that is, fit for consumption by monks, if the monks did not see the meat prepared, did not hear of the preparation, and did not suspect that it was prepared specifically for them. As can readily be seen, these three qualifications opened the doors wide for monks to eat meat. Moreover, since the laity ate the meat of cows, sheep, deer, fowls, and fish, it is reasonable to assume that such meats were sometimes offered to the monks for alms. Monks were supposed to accept whatever was offered to them, and for the monks to accept one kind of food and refuse another would be disrespectful to the donor and would deprive the laity of the opportunity to acquire merits through their acts of charity.

Finally, concerning the five strong-smelling plants—which in the Buddhist texts are given as garlic, three kinds of onions, and leeks—the Buddhist Pāli *Vinaya* specifies that the offense of eating garlic is simply a wrongdoing which may be removed merely by confession.[92]

[90] *TLT* 4.16b.

[91] Horner, *Book of the Discipline*, 2.385.

[92] Horner, *op.cit.*, 3.245; 5.196. In the Chinese Buddhist literature, the five strong smelling plants are called *wu-hsin*. Concerning their prohibition, the *Fan-wang-ching*, T 24.1005b reads: "Disciples of the Buddha should not eat the five strong smelling plants." *Ta-pan nieh-p'an-ching* 11, T 12.432c-433a: "The five *hsin* are strong smelling and should not be eaten." See also *Chu-ching yao-chi* 20, T 54.189ab; *Mahāvyutpatti* 5731-5734, 5815.

The reasons given in the Chinese Buddhist literature against eating these strong-smelling plants make very interesting reading. In the *Ta-fo-ting shou-leng-yen-ching*,[93] we read:

> ... all those sentient beings who practice meditation should refrain from eating the five strong-smelling plants. These five when eaten cooked serve as aphrodisiacs, and when eaten raw will increase anger. Suppose a man should eat these strong-smelling plants, even though he may be able to explain the twelve divisions of the sutras, still the deities of the ten directions would object to his foul odors and would keep a safe distance from him. On the other hand, whenever he eats these items, hungry ghosts will come and lick his lips. His blessings will gradually disappear and he will always be without benefits. Though he practices meditation, the bodhisattvas, the heavenly deities, and the virtuous spirits of the ten directions will not come to protect him. ... After death he will join Māra's family, and bewitched by Māra, his blessings will be exhausted and he will descend into Avīci hell.

If the Japanese *Sōni-ryō* is a faithful echo of the *Tao-seng-ke*, then it appears that the penalties even in the Chinese monastic code were heavier than those in India. In Article Seven of the *Sōni-ryō*[94] we are told that those monks and nuns who drink liquor and eat meat, and who use the five strong-smelling plants shall be sentenced to thirty days at hard labor. Such a penalty conforms to that inflicted by the T'ang secular code.

Turning next to clothing, one passage in the *T'ang-liu-tien* reads: "Taoist priests and priestesses [and Buddhist monks and nuns] shall wear saffron, dark green, black, yellow, or dark faded color robes. If they should wear lay attire, or robes made of silk, ... they shall be laicized."[95]

[93] Ch. 8, *T* 19.141c.
[94] Hayakawa, *Ryō-no-shūge* 1.242-243.
[95] *TLT* 4.16b.

On this point, the *Sōni-ryō*, Article Ten, specifies that those monks who wore robes other than the colors specified or robes made of silk should be sentenced to ten days of hard labor, while those who wore lay attire should be penalized by a hundred days of hard labor.[96] These penalties are in contrast with that specified in the T'ang code, which declared that a monk should be defrocked for the same offenses. As in previous instances, the Pāli *Vinaya* provides that violations of the rule concerning the color of the monastic robe is an offense requiring expiation only, that is, confession before the assembly of monks.[97]

This problem concerning the color of the monastic robe is a complicated one. What were the colors allowed to the Buddhist clergy? The *T'ang-liu-tien* is not entirely clear on this point, for it mentioned only Taoist priests and priestesses and not Buddhist monks and nuns. But it is abundantly clear from the rest of the passage that Buddhists were included, for we find references to the Three Jewels and the *san-kang*, the three officials of the Buddhist monastery. Since the approved colors in the *T'ang-liu-tien* were for both Taoists and Buddhists, it is not certain which colors were to apply to the Buddhists and which to the Taoists. In general, the principle followed by the Buddhists in China was that the robes should not be of the primary colors, but should be of colors produced by a combination of them. The mixed or faded colors produced by the combination were called *huai-se*. In such Chinese *Vinaya* texts as the *Ssu-fen-lü* 16, *T* 22.676c, *Shih-sung-lü* 15, *T* 23.109b, and *Wu-fen-lü* 9, *T* 22.68a, the permissible mixed colors were dark green, mud-colored, or saffron. If a monk were to receive a robe of the primary color, then he should discolor it to the acceptable mixed color. Such a practice was already specified in the Pāli *Vinaya*. In Pācittiya 58,[98] we read; "When a monk obtains a new robe, any one mode of disfigurement must be undertaken; either dark green, or mud-colored, or black." However, it appears that

---

[96] Hayakawa, *op.cit.*, 1.247.   [97] Horner, *op.cit.*, 2.406-408.
[98] *Ibid.*

the rule concerning colors was not strictly observed. In the
She-li-fo wen-ching, *T* 24.900c, we are informed that the
Mahāsaṅghikas wore yellow; the Dharmaguptikas, red; the
Sarvāstivādins, black; the Kāśyapiyas, saffron; and the
Mahiçāsakas, dark green. A slightly different version is found
in the *Ta-pi-ch'iu san-ch'ien wei-i*, *T* 24.925c-926a, where we
read that the Dharmaguptikas wore black; the Sarvāstivādins,
red.

In the Pāli *Vinaya*, one of the four great offenses that result
in expulsion from the order is stealing, the other three being
killing, sexual intercourse, and lying about the extraordinary
faculties. In the *T'ang-liu-tien* there is a passage: "One who
steals and destroys an image of the Buddha or Lao-tzu shall
be imprisoned for three years. If the offender is a Taoist
priest or priestess or a Buddhist monk or nun, there shall be
the additional punishment of labor and banishment. If the
image involved is that of the perfect sage of the Taoist or a
bodhisattva of the Buddhist, then the punishment shall be decreased by one grade."[99]

It is obvious that for the offense of stealing, the T'ang code
called for much harsher punishment. Instead of mere expulsion, the monk or nun was subjected to three years of imprisonment, hard labor, and banishment. This penalty was in fact
much heavier than that imposed on a layman for the same offense, i.e., imprisonment for three years. The commentary on
this particular offense states that the heavier punishment inflicted on a Taoist or Buddhist monk arose from the charge
that the clergy was stealing and destroying an object of his
own religion.

The T'ang code *T'ang-lü-su-i* makes a distinction between
robbery that involves force or pressure and petty thievery
with no use of force. If one committed robbery with the use
of force, even if the robber did not obtain anything, he was
to be penalized by imprisonment at hard labor for two years.
If he actually stole something, then the penalty increased in
accordance with the amount or value of the objects stolen. If

[99] *TLT* 19.7b-8a.

he injured someone in the act of stealing, he was to be strangled, and if he killed someone, he was to be beheaded.[100]
When petty thievery was committed with no force used, then
the penalty was lighter. If the thief did not succeed in stealing
anything, he was to be bambooed fifty strokes. If he stole as
little as a foot of something, he was to be bambooed sixty
times. The penalty increased with the amount of goods stolen,
going up to imprisonment and banishment.[101] As for killing,
the T'ang code concerning this crime states that anyone guilty
of plotting murder must be imprisoned for three years. If he
injured the victim, he must be strangled, and if he succeeded
in killing the victim, he must be beheaded.[102]

Did the monastic community in China come under the
jurisdiction of these laws covering stealing and killing? If we
accept the conclusion that the *Sōni-ryō* in Japan is a faithful
model of the *Tao-seng-ke* in China, then we shall have to answer the question in the affirmative, for in the first article of
the *Sōni-ryō* it is clearly stated that monks committing robbery and murder must be turned over to government officials
and punished according to law.[103]

Concerning prognostication, fortune telling, divination, and
healing, the T'ang codes contain some pertinent passages. In
the *T'ang-lü-su-i*, we read that those who create weird books
and magic incantations must be strangled, and those who
transmit such books and incantations to deceive the public
must also be strangled.[104] In another passage we are told that
private families could not possess astronomical instruments
and books or books on divination. Offenders must be imprisoned for two years.[105] Furthermore, there is the imperial decree of 653 which forbade the Taoist and Buddhist clergy to
heal and practice divination.[106] Finally there is the passage
in the *T'ang-liu-tien* specifying that any clergy practicing
divination and fortune-telling must be laicized.[107]

---

[100] *TLSI* 19.12a-13b. [101] *TLSI* 19.14a.
[102] *TLSI* 17.11b. [103] Hayakawa, *op.cit.*, 1.228-230.
[104] *TLSI* 18.12b-13a. [105] *TLSI* 9.17b.
[106] *THY* 50.19ab. [107] *TLT* 4.16b.

The very first article in the *Sōni-ryō* specifies that monks
and nuns who falsely predict calamities and good fortunes by
looking at the heavenly signs and who cunningly deceive the
multitudes with them shall be turned over to government officials and punished according to law.[108] Note here that there
is no mention of the penalties, except that the offenders were
to be turned over to the government and punished according
to law. The law according to the T'ang code clearly stated the
penalties for the offenses named: strangulation for producing
and transmitting weird books and incantations to deceive the
multitudes; two years' imprisonment for possessing books on
divination; return to lay status for practicing divination and
fortune telling.

In the case of monks healing people, there is no mention in
the T'ang code about the penalty imposed, whereas the *Sōni-
ryō*, Article Two, specified that any monk who relied on fortune-telling and sorcery to cure people must be laicized.[109]

Another offense was the possession of military books. In the
first article of the *Sōni-ryō*, we read that any monk guilty of
reading military books must be punished according to the
laws of the government. The law applicable in this case is
clearly stated in the *T'ang-lü-su-i* 9.17b, where we learn that
possession of military books was prohibited and anyone
breaking the law must be imprisoned for two years.

In one section of the *T'ang-liu-tien*, there is a long passage
relating to the behavior of the Taoist and Buddhist clergy. As
most of the practices mentioned are also found in the *Sōni-
ryō*, I shall list them here and indicate the penalties specified
in both sources.

T'ang-liu-tien 4.16b	*Sōni-ryō*
1. riding on horses (return to lay status)	1. not listed
2. quarreling while intoxicated (return to lay status)	2. quarreling while intoxicated (return to lay status) Hayakawa, *op.cit.*, 1.243

---

[108] Hayakawa, *op.cit.*, 1.226-230.

[109] *Ibid.*, 1.234-235.

3. soliciting guests (return to lay status)	3. not listed
4. presenting religious goods to government officials (return to lay status)	4. presenting religious goods to government officials (hard labor for 100 days) *Ibid.*, 1.236
5. forming questionable cliques (return to lay status)	5. forming questionable cliques (hard labor for 100 days) *Ibid.*
6. going from door to door teaching religion (hard labor)	6. not listed
7. marrying (hard labor)	7. not listed. (It is understood however that any married monk would be expelled from the order, for he would be guilty of sexual intercourse with women.)
8. indulging in music, gambling and dramatic performances (hard labor)	8. indulging in music, gambling, and dramatic performances (hard labor for 100 days) *Ibid.*, 1.236ff
9. abusing monastery officials (hard labor)	9. abusing monastery officials (hard labor for 100 days)
10. insulting elders (hard labor)	10. insulting elders (hard labor for 100 days) *Ibid.*

As far as the Pāli canon is concerned, it must be noted that in offenses similar to the above, the penalty imposed is in every instance much lighter. For example, if one monk abuses another and falsely accuses him of having committed one of the four great offenses resulting in expulsion from the order, he is merely put on probation and temporarily suspended from the order.[110] If he insults another monk, he is guilty of just a pācittiya offense, which requires mere confession.[111] A monk guilty of forming cliques and fomenting division in the saṅgha is absolved of the offense by being tem-

[110] Saṅghādisesa 8, Horner, *op.cit.*, 1.281.
[111] Pācittiya 2, Horner, *op.cit.*, 2.173.

porarily suspended from the order.[112] Finally, for a monk to engage in singing, dancing, and playing music was simply to commit an offense of wrongdoing, a very minor offense.[113]

The list of offenses listed in the *T'ang-liu-tien* furnishes one of the best commentaries on how restrictive the secular laws had become concerning the activities of the Buddhist monks. For instance, the prohibitions against riding on horses, soliciting guests, and going from door to door to teach the religion are not found in the *Sōni-ryō* or in the Pāli canon. Such restrictions are also mentioned in the imperial decrees and in the regulations of the government bureau having supervision over Buddhism. According to the regulations of the Court of State Ceremonials, monks could not dwell for more than three nights in a private family; if they intended to go beyond that, they had to inform the proper officials, and then the limit could be extended to seven days at the most. If they planned to go on a journey, they had to obtain a travel permit from the prefectural or district office.[114]

Such restrictions on the movement of monks were also decreed on the third month of the fifth year of K'ai-yüan (717) and on the fifth month of the twelfth year of K'ai-yüan (724) when monks were not permitted to reside in houses where they were not allowed.[115] In 714, on the thirteenth day of the seventh month, there was another imperial decree that read:

---

[112] Saṅghādisesa 10, Horner, *op.cit.*, 1.299-300.

[113] Cullavagga 5.2.6, Horner, *op.cit.*, 5.145.

[114] *HTS* 48.9a. In this connection, we may refer to Ennin's experience. When he wanted to travel from Yang-chou to T'ai-chou to visit the famous Kuo-ch'ing Monastery on Mt. T'ien-t'ai, he wrote to Li Te-yü (787-849, biography in *HTS* 180.1a-9a; *CTS* 174.1a-14a), the governor-general of Yang-chou, as follows: "The scholar monk Ennin, the novices Ishō and Igyō, and the sailor Tei Yūman. The above ask to go to the Kuo-ch'ing-ssu of T'ai-chou to seek teachers, and, on leaving T'ai-chou, to go to the capital" (Reischauer, *Ennin's Diary*, 27). The petition was never granted, and Ennin was not able to visit Mt. T'ien-t'ai.

[115] *TFYK* 63, Chung-hua ed. 1.708, 710.

We have heard that many families of officials keep monks, nuns, Taoist priests and priestesses as their protégés, and their wives and children mingle with them without fear of gossip. Such clerics offer the deceitful pretext that they are practicing meditation, or they falsely predict blessings and disasters. Such affairs carry the implication of heresy, and they heavily damage the great plans. Henceforth, families of officials are not allowed to keep monks and nuns in their households. If such families wish to prepare vegetarian feasts for some auspicious or unlucky events, they should report to the local prefectural or district officials, indicating the number of monks, nuns, priests, and priestesses they wish to invite from a designated monastery, and then only the specified number may be permitted to go.[116]

The same year, on the twenty-ninth day of the seventh month, another edict was issued forbidding the saṅgha from carrying out certain kinds of business in the city.

We have heard that within the streets of the city wards, monks have opened shops to copy sutras or to cast images of the Buddha. From now on, such businesses are prohibited in the streets and markets of the cities. If one wishes to reverence the Buddha he should go to the temple for the services of worship. If one desires sutras, he should buy them from the temples. If the sutras are scarce, then let monks copy them within the temples. This shall be the case in the prefectural temples also.[117]

So far we have confined ourselves primarily to the problem of the relationship between the saṅgha and the state, the gradual erosion of the independent special status claimed by the monks, and the increasing absorption of the monastic community into the body politic of the imperial state. We might illustrate this gradual absorption with some further examples, first to show how closely identified with the state the

[116] *THY* 49.6a.   [117] *Ibid.*

105

sangha had become, and how far it had gone from its claim as a special group which had transcended the affairs of society.

First of these examples is the *nei-tao-ch'ang*, or the palace chapel.[118] The term was first used during the reign of Emperor Yang of the Sui dynasty, but such a chapel within the precincts of the imperial palace had existed long before the Sui dynasty. As early as 425, there is mention of a chapel established by Emperor T'ai-wu of the Northern Wei dynasty, and during the revival of Buddhism after the persecution of 574-577 under the Northern Chou dynasty, seven virtuous monks were assembled in 579 in the imperial palace to hold a Buddhist service. It was during the reign of Empress Wu Tse-t'ien that the institution flourished, owing mainly to the patronage she dispensed. Such palace chapels were established not only in Ch'ang-an but also in the eastern capital Lo-yang, with the chapels staffed by numerous monks. Succeeding emperors continued to support the institution, with Emperor Tai-tsung one of the most fervent. The monks who participated in the services were conveyed into the chapel by horses furnished by the emperor. Ennin in his diary describes a palace chapel in operation: "Buddhist images and scriptures have been placed since early times in the place of ritual inside the Ch'ang-sheng Hall, and three sets of seven monks who are versed in devotions have been drawn from the monasteries of the two halves of the city and assigned in rotation to perform devotions there each day without cease, both day and night."[119]

One very useful function served by these palace chapels was that they provided Buddhist worship services which could be attended by the royal family, especially the ladies in the imperial household. However, the chapel also played a political role, i.e., that of reciting sutras for the protection of the state from evil, natural calamities, and foreign invasion.

[118] The following account is based largely on Tsan-ning, *Seng-shih-lüeh*, T 54.247bc.
[119] Reischauer, *op.cit.*, 341-342.

This is stated specifically in the *Seng-shih-lüeh*, where we are told that whenever the Tibetans encroached upon the border regions, the emperor ordered the monks in the palace chapel to recite the *Jen-wang-ching*.[120] For the Chinese rulers, the most important portion is Section 5, entitled "Section on the Protection of the State." In this section we read that the Buddha told the various assembled kings what they should do to protect their kingdoms against threats of internal and external dangers. For instance, if the kingdoms were faced with internal rebellions, external invasions, banditry, fires, floods, and windstorms, they should assemble a hundred images each of Buddhas, bodhisattvas, and arhats, and place them on elaborately decorated high seats. Then a hundred masters of the law should be invited to recite and explain the *Jen-wang-ching*. Hundreds of variegated lamps, incense, and flowers should be presented as offerings to the Three Jewels. If the sutra were to be recited twice a day, accompanied by all these arrangements, then all the spirits in the kingdom would come forth to protect the country. Not only would such a service protect the country, but it would also bring about blessings. If one desired prosperity, high officialdom, sons and daughters, wisdom, intelligence, and rewards from the deities, he could obtain all of them by reciting this sutra in accordance with the above instructions. Furthermore, recital could also ward off evil. The misery of sickness would be eradicated, the shackles of bondage from chains and cangues would be broken. Even if one were to commit the four great crimes entailing expulsion from the order (killing, stealing, sexual intercourse, boasting of one's extraordinary powers) or the five crimes against one's superiors (heaven, earth, ruler, parents, teacher), or break all the commandments, or practice the six heretical teachings, he would be able to escape the inexhaustible demerits and misery resulting from these deeds by merely reciting this sutra.[121]

[120] *T* 54.247b. For the two translations of the *Jen-wang-ching*, see *T* 8.825a-834a and *T* 8.834a-845a. The sutra belongs to the *Prajñāpāramitā* class.

[121] *Jen-wang-ching*, Kumārajīva's translation, *T* 8.829c-830a.

A specific instance of such a ceremony is recorded for the tenth month of the first year of Yung-t'ai, or 765: "During the tenth month, the Tibetans crossed the borders and threatened the capital. The emperor ordered two cartloads of the *Jen-wang-ching* to be delivered to the Hsi-ming-ssu and other monasteries, and an imperial edict called on Amoghavajra to install a hundred high seats and to lecture on the sutra. The emperor himself was present to offer incense, pay homage, and listen to the lecture. Within a short while, the invaders were pacified."[122]

In the *Fo-tsu t'ung-chi* we read further that after the Tibetans were pacified, an imperial decree was issued that read: "The support of the *Jen-wang-ching* is to protect the country. The translation made in the former period is not entirely accurate." The emperor therefore called on the Master of the Tripitaka Amoghavajra, the monks Fei-hsi and Liang-pen, and others to retranslate the sutra in the Nan-t'ao Garden of the Ta-ming Palace. The emperor personally read and compared the translations, and even though the doctrines of the new and old were alike, he declared the new translation to be superior in style and meaning. He thereupon wrote the

---

[122] *FTTC* 41, *T* 49.377c-378a. Apparently there was another recitation of the *Jen-wang-ching* during the previous month, which is recorded in the *Ts'e-fu yüan-kuei* 52, Chung-hua ed. 1.576. This account indicated that in the ninth month of the first year of Yung-t'ai, a hundred high seats each were established in the Tzu-sheng and Hsi-ming Monasteries for lectures on the *Jen-wang-ching*. The sutras were loaded into two royal carriages which were lifted out from the royal palace by strong men clad in golden armor. Festoons of various colors, depicting bodhisattvas and spirits, were carried on carts drawn by goats, deer, and cows, and paraded before the hundred officials arranged in their proper places according to rank and salary. Such offerings lasted through two periods of seven days each. Officials above certain ranks were also ordered by imperial decree to supply incense and prepare vegetarian feasts, and play music at the Hsi-ming Monastery for one full day. Soon after, when the Tibetans encroached on the borders, the lecture sessions on the *Jen-wang-ching* were suspended. However, such lectures were resumed in the tenth month, in the Tzu-sheng Monastery, and this is very likely the session described in the *FTTC*.

preface and promoted Amoghavajra to become president of the Court of State Ceremonials.[123]

By participating in the services within the palace chapels, and by reciting the *Jen-wang-ching* in the chapels and in the monasteries of the capital for the protection and welfare of the empire, the Chinese monks subordinated their own interests to those of the state, they cast aside their attitude of aloofness from secular affairs and became thoroughly involved as a good Chinese subject would in the political fortunes of the government. Just as the imperial armies served as the military arm, and the imperial bureaucracy as the political arm, so the saṅgha served as the religious arm of the government to ensure that the spiritual forces of the universe would work for the benefit of the empire and not bring about any spiritual mishap. This spiritual function was also exercised by the Buddhist clergy in the national monasteries established by the imperial government. Such national monasteries were supported in large part by the imperial treasury, and were charged with the celebration of those aspects of the imperial cult connected with the royal birthday, anniversaries, and memorial services for departed ancestors. Such celebrations had nothing to do with Buddhism, and the fact that Buddhist monks participated in them is another indication of how closely now the saṅgha had become identified with the state. The monks living in such national monasteries did not have to worry about their livelihood; they were in a certain sense part of the national bureaucracy, for their daily needs were subsidized by the state.[124] The memorial services

[123] *FTTC* 42, *T* 49.378a. I think we know the reason why the emperor wanted a new translation, for as we pointed out previously, the Kumārajīva version contained passages saying that those monks in the employment of the state were not true disciples of the Buddha. At a time when monks were actively working for the interests of the state, such passages would naturally be unacceptable to the ruler. Amoghavajra made some changes in the reading of those pertinent passages to render them acceptable.

[124] For a detailed study of the origins of these national monasteries, see Tsukamoto Zenryū, "Kokubunji to Zui Tō no bukkyō seisaku

and birthday celebrations held in these monasteries were also supported by the imperial treasury. For instance, to honor the memory of Emperor Ching-tsung, who was assassinated in 826, a commemoration was held in the K'ai-yüan Monastery in Yang-chou on the eighth day of the twelfth month, 838, witnessed by Ennin, and he entered in his diary: "A national commemoration day. Fifty strings of cash were donated to the K'ai-yüan-ssu to arrange a vegetarian feast for 500 monks."[125] On the sixth day of the sixth month, 840, Ennin was visiting the Ta-hua yen-ssu on Mt. Wu-t'ai and he recorded in his diary: "An imperial emissary arrived at the monastery, and the assembly of monks all went forth to meet him. It was the rule that each year clothing, alms bowls, incense, flowers, etc., were sent by imperial order. The emissary sent to the mountain presented to the twelve great monasteries 500 fine robes, 500 packages of silk floss, 1,000 pieces of cloth for the Buddhist *kashāya*, dyed in dark color, 1,000 ounces of incense, 1,000 pounds of tea, and 1,000 hand towels. At the same time he went around the twelve great monasteries arranging, with imperial permission, for vegetarian feasts."[126] If such provisions were made for those great monasteries on Mt. Wu-t'ai which were not national, it is reasonable to expect that similar provisions would be made available for the great national monasteries.

It appears that this practice of establishing national monasteries began with Emperor Wen of the Sui dynasty, who ordered the construction of the Ta-hsing-shan Monastery in 584.[127] However, it was under the T'ang that such national monasteries began to assume prominence. During the reign of Empress Wu Tse-t'ien, the Ta-yün Monasteries were established in the two capitals and in all the prefectures of the realm. The name of the national monastery was taken from a sutra bearing the same title, *Ta-yün-ching*, or Great

---

narabi ni kanji, *Nisshi bukkyō kōshōshi no kenkyū* (Tokyo 1944), 1-47.

[125] *Ennin* 1.14. [126] *Ibid.*, 3.70. [127] FTTC 39, T 49.359c.

cloud sutra, translated by Dharmakshema in the first part of the fifth century. This sutra was specially useful to the empress for a very important reason. According to the Confucian political system, women were not permitted to assume the position of head of state, so when the empress usurped the throne in 683, she had to find some justification for her action outside of Confucianism. The Buddhist *Ta-yün-ching* provided her with just the source needed, for in Chapter Four of the Dharmakshema translation, there is a conversation between the Buddha and a female deity in which the Buddha predicted that because of merits earned through listening to the *Mahāparinirvāṇasūtra* and to the teachings of the Buddha, she would be reborn in a future age as a universal monarch. A similar prediction is to be found in Chapter Six, to the effect that 700 years after his death, a girl would be chosen ruler after the death of her father.[128] These passages were seized upon by a crafty monk, Huai-i, and presented to the public as justification of Wu Tse-t'ien's assumption of imperial power, together with the claim that the empress was none other than a reincarnation of Maitreya, the Future Buddha. The empress was overjoyed by this discovery and she had the *Ta-yün-ching* circulated throughout the empire. In 690 she took the further step of establishing the official Ta-yün-ssu.[129]

The monks living in these empire-wide Ta-yün-ssu carried out the propaganda campaign, i.e., that the empress was the reincarnation of Maitreya. In many cases, the Ta-yün-ssu were not newly constructed monasteries but were established institutions whose names were merely changed. Indicative of the geographical scope of these Ta-yün-ssu is the fact that when Hui-ch'ao was traveling in Central Asia during the K'ai-yüan era (713-741) he found them in far-away An-hsi or Parthia and Kashgar.[130]

[128] *T* 12.1098a, 1107a.
[129] *HTS* 4.5a; *CTS* 6.3b. For Hsüeh Huai-i, see biography in *CTS* 183.13a-14a.
[130] W. Fuchs, "Huei-ch'ao Pilgerreise durch Nordwest-Indien und Zentral-Asien um 726," *Sitzungsberichte der Preussischen Akademie*

Though Emperor Hsüan-tsung reversed the policy of Wu Tse-t'ien and favored Taoism over Buddhism in the state ceremonies, he did not pursue a repressive policy against Buddhism, and during his reign, Buddhist monks continued to be closely associated with state activities. In line with this attitude, he decreed in 738 that national monasteries be established in all the prefectures of the empire, to be called K'ai-yüan-ssu,[131] and in 739, he issued another decree calling for the celebration of imperial birthdays in these monasteries, with the memorial celebrations for deceased ancestors to be held in another national monastery, the Lung-hsing-ssu established by his predecessor.[132] Again, it appears that what took place was the designation of existing monasteries to become K'ai-yüan-ssu in the different prefectures. These monasteries retained their names through succeeding reigns, for we learn that when Ennin reached Yang-chou in 838, he took up residence in the K'ai-yüan-ssu of that city.[133]

There is still another area where we can see this close relationship between the saṅgha and the state, and this is the

der Wissenschaften, Phil.-hist. kl., 30 (1938), 456-457; P. Pelliot, "Une bibliothèque médiévale retrouvée au Kansou," BEFEO (1908), 8.512. For the Chinese, see T 51.979b, which reads as follows: "Furthermore, in An-hsi, there are two monasteries administered by Chinese monks, who practice the Great Vehicle and do not eat meat. The chief of the Ta-yün Monastery is Hsiu-hsing, who is skilled in oratory and who was formerly a monk in the Ch'i-pao-t'ai Monastery in the capital. The tu-wei-na of the Ta-yün Monastery is named I-ch'ao, skilled in explaining the Vinaya. He was formerly of the Chuang-yen Monastery in the capital. The abbot of the monastery is Ming-hui, who is esteemed for his religious conduct, and like the others he is also from the capital. . . . There is also a Ta-yün Monastery in Kashgar, administered by a Chinese monk who is a native of Min-chou."

[131] FTTC 40, T 49.375a; THY 50.20b.

[132] FTTC 40, T 49.375a: "In the twenty-seventh year of K'ai-yüan (739) it was decreed that on memorial services for deceased emperors, the Buddhist and Taoist monks shall go to the Lung-hsing-ssu to hold services and prepare vegetarian feasts. On imperial birthdays, the services to pray for the longevity of the emperor shall be held in the K'ai-yüan-ssu." See also THY 50.21a for the same decree.

[133] Ennin 1.7.

actual participation of monks in politics during the T'ang dynasty. There is no better example of this than the life and activities of Hsüeh Huai-i, the monk closely associated with Empress Wu Tse-t'ien. Hsüeh was originally a commoner surnamed Feng who made his living peddling cosmetics. Impressive in appearance and possessed of extraordinary strength, he was able to worm his way into the imperial precincts and become the favorite of Empress Wu Tse-t'ien. To facilitate his entry into the palace without attracting undue attention, Empress Wu ordained him a monk, and appointed him abbot of the famous Pai-ma Monastery in Lo-yang. As the favorite of the empress, he held a number of important commissions, such as building the imperial ancestral hall, and leading expeditions to repel the Turks who had invaded the border regions. He was also instrumental in finding scriptural passages from the Buddhist scriptures to justify Empress Wu's accession to the throne. For these accomplishments, he was awarded various honors and titles by the grateful empress: *Tso wei-wei ta-chiang-chün* (grand general of the imposing guards of the left); *Fu-kuo ta-chiang-chün* (grand general sustaining the state); *Chin-yu-wei ta-chiang-chün* (grand general of the right guards); *Liang-kuo kung* (duke of Liang) and wearer of the purple robe.

Because of his close connections with the empress, he was arrogant and haughty, and his underlings repeatedly committed crimes which no one dared to protest. His underlings once set upon a censor, Feng Ssu-hsü, who had dared to initiate impeachment proceedings against Hsüeh, and almost beat him to death. On another occasion, when he found that the imperial physician was enjoying imperial favor, he became so angry that he burned down the ancestral hall that he had constructed. In the end, however, Empress Wu, incensed over his arrogance and imperious attitude and also over rumors that he was plotting against the throne, had him seized and strangled and his followers banished to distant regions.[134]

[134] *CTS* 183.13a-14a.

We have now traced at some length the struggle between the Buddhist saṅgha and the imperial state over the status of the clergy, and the slow but inexorable process in which the monks moved away from the original Buddhist contention of noninvolvement in society and politics to a position of active support for and participation in the political program of the government. What was nominally a saṅgha affair in India, the ordination of monks, became a process in which the imperial government bureaucracy took an active interest. After the monk was ordained, he was subjected to considerable control over his behavior and his movement. In some cases, he willingly consented to pray and work actively in the palace chapels and the national monasteries on behalf of the state and the ruling class, and for this contribution he was subsidized by the imperial treasury. All in all, therefore, what we see here is a gradual deemphasis of the saṅgha as a special religious group devoted mainly to religious matters, and an increasing tendency for the clerics to become just like any other Chinese subject in the empire. This process of Sinicization of the monastic community may also be seen in the techniques of bureaucratic control over the saṅgha which evolved in China. It was inevitable, given the bureaucratic nature of the imperial system, that sooner or later the government would establish the proper official organ to deal with affairs connected with the saṅgha. Here again we see the assertion of the Chinese principle that a religious association must be subordinate to the imperial bureaucracy, that there is no such thing as a separation of church and state.

The earliest example of a governmental organ established to control the saṅgha occurred during the early years of the Northern Wei dynasty. According to the *Shih-lao-chih*: "Formerly an Office to Oversee Blessings was established, later changed to the Office to Illumine the Mysteries, manned by officials and charged with supervision over monks and nuns."[135] To head this bureau, Emperor T'ai-tsu of the Northern Wei appointed a monk named Fa-kuo and conferred on

[135] *Wei-shu* 114.21b.

him the title of *tao-jen-t'ung*, or chief of monks. The account in the *Shih-lao-chih* on this appointment reads as follows: "Formerly, in the period of Huang-shih (396-398), there was in the prefecture of Chao a monk named Fa-kuo whose practice of the commandments was exact to the extreme, and who explained books on the doctrine. When T'ai-tsu heard of his fame, he commanded that he be respectfully invited to the capital. Later he made him chief of monks."[136] Later in the dynasty, the name of the office was changed to *Chao-hsüan-ssu* or (Office to Illumine the Mysteries) while that of the head was changed to *sha-men-t'ung*.[137]

Under the chief of monks in the government bureau there was a subordinate called *tu-wei-na*, a term that is difficult to translate.[138] In the prefectures throughout the empire, local offices of the *Chao-hsüan-ssu* were established, called *seng-ts'ao*, or Monk's Office, staffed by a *chou-sha-men-t'ung*, or prefectural chief of monks, and a subordinate called *wei-na*.

This bureaucratic setup of the Northern Wei was inherited by the Northern Ch'i (550-577), and then by the Sui (581-618).[139] According to the *Po-kuan-chih* of the *Sui-shu*, the *Chao-hsüan-ssu* now consisted of one great chief, one chief,

[136] *Ibid.*, 114.8b, translated by Ware in *TP* 30.128-129, with slight changes. This entry furnishes some indication of the time that the Office to Oversee Blessings was established, sometime in 396-398. The *FTTC* 38, *T* 49.353c recorded that the event took place in 397.

[137] The change from *tao-jen-t'ung* to *sha-men-t'ung* was made with the appointment of T'an-yao to the office in the Ho-p'ing era (460-465). As for the time of the change in the name of the office, this is uncertain. L. Hurvitz in his translation, *Wei Shu, Treatise on Buddhism and Taoism* (Kyoto 1956), 83, wrote that the change was made after the capital was moved to Lo-yang in 494. However, in the *FTTC* 38, *T* 49.355a, the name *Chao-hsüan-ssu*, or Office to Illumine the Mysteries already appeared in an entry dated 460.

[138] *Wei-shu* 114.22a. The term *wei-na* is usually considered to be a combination of the final syllable of the Sanskrit *karmadana*, the official in charge of life in a monastery, and the final character of the Chinese expression *kang-wei*, guiding principles. For a discussion of this interpretation, see Hurvitz, *op.cit.*, 76. We might therefore render *tu-wei-na* as the *wei-na* of the capital.

[139] *Sui-shu* 27.1a.

and three *tu-wei-na*.[140] The office itself was under the jurisdiction of the *Ch'ung-hsüan-shu* (Office for the Exaltation of Mysteries) in the *Hung-lu-ssu* (Court of State Ceremonials). The holders of the office of great chief of monks were still famous clerics appointed by the throne. One of the most eminent was T'an-ch'ien, who was appointed by Emperor Wen in 587 and after that was chiefly responsible for that emperor's favorable policy toward Buddhism. It was T'an-ch'ien who persuaded the emperor to erect the 111 stupas throughout the empire in 601-604 to store the relics of the Buddha, a move designed to contribute toward the ideological unification of the empire.[141]

Beginning with the T'ang dynasty, the situation changed. Supervision over the sangha passed into the hands of government offices headed by lay officials. During the early years of the T'ang dynasty, this jurisdiction was vested in the Office for the Exaltation of Mysteries, located within the Court of State Ceremonials. The Court of State Ceremonials was charged with general supervision over foreign guests and the ceremonies involved in their audiences before the throne, and the gifts exchanged. In addition, the court also had charge over the funeral rites. Buddhism was placed under the jurisdiction of this office because it was of foreign origin. The court was staffed by a president who was a mandarin of the third degree, second class; two vice-presidents of the fourth degree, second class; and two assistants of the sixth degree, second class.[142] As for the Office for the Exaltation of Mysteries, the chief was a mandarin of the eighth degree, second class, aided by two assistants who were mandarins of the ninth degree, second class.[143]

In these descriptions of the two organs we see a significant departure from previous practices. Whereas the Office to Illumine the Mysteries heretofore had been headed by monks, now the T'ang bureau was headed by civilian mandarins.

[140] *Ibid.*, 27.7b.
[141] *FTTC* 39,49.359c; *HKSC* 18, *T* 50.571b-574b.
[142] *HTS* 48.11ab.   [143] *HTS* 48.9a.

This situation remained unaltered despite numerous shifts in the controlling bureaus.

The first shift occurred in 694, when Empress Wu Tse-t'ien transferred jurisdiction from the Court of State Ceremonials to the *Tz'u-pu* (Bureau of National Sacrifice), one of the organs in the *Li-pu* (Ministry of Rites).[144] The transfer was made by the empress, who was a devout follower of Buddhism, to show that she favored Buddhism and that she no longer considered the religion to be foreign. Another move to show her favor was her decree placing Buddhism above Taoism in all court ceremonies.

In the Bureau of National Sacrifice, the staff consisted of a senior secretary—a mandarin of the fifth degree, second class—and an auxiliary secretary—a mandarin of the sixth degree, second class. They were charged with supervision over sacrifices, offerings, astronomy, clepsydra, memorial services for deceased emperors and empresses, taboo names, divination, medicine, and monks and nuns. In connection with monks and nuns, the bureau was responsible for taking the census of the monastic community and compiling a registry of monks once every three years, administering the examinations to candidates who sought to be ordained, and granting of certificates of ordination.[145]

In 736, during the reign of Hsüan-tsung, the ministers of the Department of Grand Secretariat and the Imperial Chancellery presented a memorial arguing that since Buddhism originated in the western regions, it should be treated as a foreign religion and placed under the jurisdiction of the Court of State Ceremonials. This proposal was accepted by the emperor. However, in the very next year, this action was reversed, and Buddhism again reverted to the jurisdiction of the Bureau of National Sacrifice,[146] and there it remained until the reign of Tai-tsung, 763-779.

[144] *THY* 49.4b; *FTTC* 39, *T* 49.369c-370a; *SSL*, *T* 54.245c.
[145] *TLT* 4.11ab, 16ab; *HTS* 46.9a; 48.9a.
[146] *THY* 49.4b; *FTTC* 40, *T* 49.375a. In the *SSL*, *T* 54.245c, we are told that these two events took place in the fourteenth and fifteenth

Under Tai-tsung, there appeared a new official on the bureaucratic horizon to assume supervision over the Buddhist community, the commissioner of meritorious works, *kung-te-shih*. The emergence of this office is closely related to the flourishing state of Buddhism under Tai-tsung. Counted as fervent followers of Buddhism were some of the most powerful officials and prime ministers of the period, such as Wang Chin,[147] Tu Hung-chien,[148] Yüan Tsai,[149] and Yü Ch'ao-en.[150] As ardent followers of Buddhism, these men and others were greatly interested in the meritorious works that the religion encouraged, such as the construction of monasteries, erection of statues, holding religious assemblies for discussions and dissemination of the law, copying sutras, preparing vegetarian feasts, building bridges and roads, setting up dispensaries, etc. Such activities were actively promoted by one of the most illustrious monks of the period, Amoghavajra,[151] who felt that such meritorious works would alleviate suffering and calamities and bring blessings to the empire, the dynasty, and the people. Under such conditions, Ch'ang-an during the reign of Tai-tsung was a most flourishing center of Buddhism, with the throne, the officials, and the saṅgha led by Amoghavajra collaborating in promoting welfare activities and altruistic projects. It was under these circumstances that the office of commissioner of meritorious works was established during the reign of Tai-tsung, sometime prior to 774. The full title, *Kou-tang ching-ch'eng chu-ssu-kuan hsiu-kung-te-shih* (commissioner of meritorious works in charge of the Buddhist and Taoist temples in the capital), first appeared in a document dated 774,[152] with the incumbent being a lay

year of K'ai-yüan, or 726 and 727. However, this is erroneous, and may be ascribed to Tsan-ning's mistake in copying.

[147] 700-781. Biography in *CTS* 118.5a-6b; *HTS* 145.3b-4b.

[148] 709-769. Biography in *CTS* 108.5b-6b; *HTS* 126.6b-7b.

[149] D.777. Biography in *HTS* 145.1a-3a; *CTS* 118.1a-4b.

[150] See n. 70.

[151] Died 774. Biography in *SKSC* 1, *T* 50.712a-714a, translated by Chou I-liang in *HJAS* 8 (1945) 284-307.

[152] *T* 52.851a.

disciple of Amoghavajra named Li Yüan-tsung (d. 776). Amoghavajra described him as one who had been his protégé for thirty years, energetic, sincere, and diligent in his study of Buddhism.[153] After Li died, his successor in the office was Liu Ch'ung-hsün.[154]

What is significant here is that both these men, Li and Liu, were eunuch generals in the Imperial Guards and hence were powerful and influential elements in court politics. Such figures so close to the emperor as commissioners of meritorious works, responsible for Buddhism in the capital, very likely began to encroach upon and to usurp some of the Bureau of National Sacrifice's powers over the Buddhists, and there was very little that the bureau could do about it.

When Tai-tsung died in 779, his successor Te-tsung, taking cognizance of the confused situation created by two offices claiming jurisdiction over the saṅgha, and also of the fact that eunuch generals were serving as commissioners of meritorious works, abolished the post of commissioner. In his decree ordering the dissolution, the emperor gave his reasons for so doing. He declared that the task of the Imperial Guards was to be on strict guard morning and evening as agents of the ruler, while Buddhism stressed the cultivation of conduct. Since the two were so different, they should be separated. For a general to be in charge of Buddhist activities would not be appropriate. Moreover there already existed central and local officials to regulate the affairs of Buddhism.[155]

Besides these considerations, there probably are some financial factors involved. The numerous meritorious activities promoted by Tai-tsung must have made quite a dent in the imperial treasury, and Te-tsung felt some retrenchment was necessary. There exist some intriguing hints about such cutting back of meritorious works. For example, in 780, in the

---

[153] See *Pu-k'ung piao-chih-chi* 3, T 52.844b.

[154] See *Chen-yüan hsü-k'ai-yüan-lu*, T 55.761c. See also the important article by Tsukamoto. "Tōchūki irai no Chōan kudokushi," *Tōhōgakuhō* 4 (Kyoto 1933). 368-406.

[155] *Chen-yüan hsü-k'ai-yüan-lu*, T 55.761c-762a.

fourth month, someone presented a gilt-bronze image of the Buddha, but the throne rejected it, saying, "What merit is there? This is not for me." And in the seventh month, he suspended celebrations of the All-Souls' Feast in the palace.[156]

Ten years later, in 788, Te-tsung reestablished the office of commissioner of meritorious works. Instead of one, he created three positions, commissioners of meritorious works for the left and right halves of the capital and for the eastern capital.[157] These officials not only concerned themselves with meritorious works, but also appropriated some of the functions hitherto held by the Bureau of National Sacrifice. Again, the positions were held by powerful eunuch generals of the imperial guards. We may refer to one of these as an example.

Tou Wen-ch'ang[158] was the commissioner for the left half of the capital after 789.[159] In the imperial guards he held the title of commander of the protective army of inspired strategy of the left (*tso-shen-ts'e hu-chün chung-wei*). His influence was said to be pervasive throughout the empire, for most of the military and civil officials in the capital and provinces were his protégés. As commissioner of meritorious works, he was involved in the translation of sutras, and his name is specifically linked with the translation of the *Hua-yen-ching* (*Avataṁsakasūtra*) in forty chapters made by the monk Prajñā during 796-798.[160] In another Buddhist source we are informed that Tou used the income derived from manorial lands granted to him by the emperor to prepare huge vegetarian feasts for 10,000 monks on Mt. Wu-t'ai to celebrate the imperial birthdays.[161]

Up to 807, it is not clear whether the control of the com-

[156] *CTS* 12.5ab.

[157] *Chen-yüan hsü-k'ai-yüan-lu*, *T* 55.756b, 763a; *Chen-yüan hsin-ting shih-chiao mu-lu* 17, *T* 55.892a; *Tzu-chih t'ung-chien* 237, entry for the fourth year of Yüan-ho (809), commentary by Hu San-sheng; *HTS* 48.9a.

[158] Biography in *HTS* 207.6ab; *CTS* 184.8b-9a.

[159] *Chen-yüan hsü-k'ai-yüan-lu*, *T* 55.764b.

[160] *Chen-yüan hsin-ting shih-chiao mu-lu*, *T* 55.895a-896b.

[161] *Kuang-ch'ing-liang-chuan* *T* 51.1116a.

missioners extended beyond the capitals of Ch'ang-an and Lo-yang to the rest of the empire. From the contents of the texts, it appears that their jurisdiction covered only the capitals, while the Bureau of National Sacrifice still exercised control in the provinces. In 807, however, an imperial edict placed the entire saṅgha under the control of the commissioners of meritorious works and decreed that the Bureau of National Sacrifice need no longer memorialize on the matter. Not only the Buddhists but also the Taoists were included.[162]

There was one further change during the T'ang dynasty. In 845, at the height of the Hui-ch'ang anti-Buddhist persecution pushed by Emperor Wu-tsung, the Grand Secretariat presented a memorial proposing that since Buddhism came from India, it was not a Chinese religion and should therefore be placed under the jurisdiction of the Bureau of Guests in the Ministry of Rites. This proposal was approved by the emperor.[163] However, in the very next year, this move was rescinded and the Buddhist community was again placed under the jurisdiction of the commissioners of meritorious works.[164] This was the last change in bureaucratic control over the saṅgha during the T'ang dynasty.

It may be of some value to see how the office of the commissioner operated in actual practice. Here again we turn to the Japanese monk Ennin for an eye-witness account. After Ennin arrived in Ch'ang-an in the fifth year of K'ai-ch'eng

---

[162] *THY* 49.5a; 50.23ab; *SSL, T* 54.245c; *HTS* 48.9b.

[163] *THY* 49.5b; *SSL T* 54.245c. For the functions of the Bureau of Guests, see *HTS* 46.9b-10a, translated in Robert des Rotours, *Traité des Functionaires et Traité de l'Armée, Traduits de la Nouvelle Histoire des T'ang* (Leiden 1947), 1.92-96. The *HTS* 48.9b account that this shift was made in the second year of Hui-ch'ang, or 842, must be considered erroneous.

[164] *THY* 49.5b; *HTS* 48.9b; *SSL T* 54.245c. The *THY* passage reads: "In the fifth month of the sixth year, it was ordered by the emperor that monks and nuns shall as before revert to the control of the commissioners of meritorious works of the two streets and shall no longer be subject to the Bureau of Guests. The Bureau of National Sacrifice is ordered to grant certificates to those who are ordained."

(840), he went on the twenty-third day of the eighth month to the office of the commissioner of meritorious works of the left half of the city (since he was lodged temporarily in the Ta-hsing-shan-ssu which was to the east of the central thoroughfare) to request permission to reside in Ch'ang-an for the purpose of receiving instruction in the law. His party at the time included, besides himself, his two disciples Ishō and Igyō, and his attendant Tei Yūman. On the twenty-fourth day he was taken to the office of Commissioner Ch'iu Shih-liang,[165] who was, in addition to being the commissioner, also a commander of the protective army of inspired strategy of the left. Upon arrival at the commissioner's office, he was asked in detail about the reasons for his coming to Ch'ang-an, and he presented a document setting forth the necessary data about his arrival in Yang-chou, his residence there, his pilgrimage to Mt. Wu-t'ai to visit the sacred mountain, and finally his arrival in Ch'ang-an. "They now request to be permitted to reside provisionally in the monasteries of the city, to seek teachers, and listen to their instruction, and to return to their homeland. Respectfully stated in full as above. They humbly request a decision."[166] Because Ch'iu was not in his office that day, the document could not be presented. On the twenty-fifth day, a messenger from the commissioner's office summoned the Japanese to go there, and when he arrived, he received the document, which stated that he and his party were to stay provisionally in the Tzu-sheng-ssu in the northeastern part of the city.[167]

On the twenty-fifth day of the fifth month of 842, Ennin received a document from the commissioner's office, asking for information about foreign monks, what country they came from, when they arrived in the city, the monasteries they resided in, their names, ages, and accomplishments. In response,

---

[165] 779-841. Biography in *HTS* 207.8b-10a.

[166] Reischauer, *Ennin's Diary*, 286-287.

[167] *Ennin* 3.81. It must be noted that the Commissioner's office responded to Ennin's request with remarkable alacrity; only one day was needed to complete the transaction.

the Japanese made the following statement on the twenty-sixth day:

> The Japanese monk Ennin of the Tzu-sheng-ssu, aged fifty, expositor of the *Lotus Sutra*, and his disciples, the monk Ishō, aged thirty, and the monk Igyō aged thirty-one; also expounders of the *Lotus Sutra*....
>
> The said Ennin and the others, for the purpose of copying missing sutras and treatises and transmitting this work back to their country, arrived in Yang-chou with a Japanese tributary embassy in the seventh month of the third year of K'ai-ch'eng (838). They arrived at this city on the twenty-third day of the fifth year of K'ai-cheng (840), and, receiving permission from the commissioner, resided provisionally in the Tzu-sheng-ssu and received instruction.[168]

In other entries, Ennin noted that the commissioner carried out an edict issued by the emperor on the ninth day of the tenth month, 842, which called for the defrocking of monks and nuns who practiced alchemy, incantation, or the black arts; who had fled from the army, who bore scars and tattoo marks on their bodies; who maintained wives and committed sexual offenses.[169] On the thirteenth day of the ninth month, 843, the Japanese entered in his diary that the commissioner was ordered by the throne to force all unregistered monks to be laicized.[170] Then on the first day of the fourth month, 844, he wrote that the commissioners were to see to it that monks and nuns were not to be on the streets at the time of the noon-day meal, and that they were not allowed to stay overnight in another monastery.[171] In the entry for the fifteenth day of the seventh month, 844, we learn that the commissioners called upon the Buddhist monks to read the scriptures and to pray for rain.[172]

Ennin's account indicates how close a supervision the commissioner's office in Ch'ang-an exercised over the foreign monks in the city. As soon as he arrived, he had to ask for

[168] *Ibid.*, 3.89.   [169] *Ibid.*, 3.90.   [170] *Ibid.*, 3.94.
[171] *Ibid.*, 4.96.   [172] *Ibid.*, 4.97.

123

permission to reside in the capital, and when permission was granted, a specific monastery was designated. After taking residence in the Tzu-sheng-ssu, Ennin was still required to furnish more data about himself. His activities and movements were closely supervised. It would be misleading to generalize just from the experience of one foreign monk, but it does appear from Ennin's report that the commissioner's office kept close watch on what was going on in the monastic community, and that on the whole it functioned efficiently and expeditiously.

We have gone at some length to describe the government bureaus which had jurisdiction over the Buddhist community of monks during the T'ang dynasty. This account makes it unmistakably clear that the saṅgha accepted and came to terms with the prevailing Confucian ideology of the supremacy of the state over any religious association within its borders. The first portion of this study discussed the shift in the position and attitude of the monks themselves. Instead of being individuals who claimed to be above and beyond the secular state, they became part of the political system, they obeyed the laws of the state, and they served the state in various capacities. Viewed in the perspective of Chinese history, we may say that these developments in the positions of the saṅgha and the monks in China represent but still another aspect of the gradual acculturation of Buddhism to the Chinese scene. The Buddhist monk became a Chinese subject, the monastic community a Chinese religious organization subject to the jurisdiction of the imperial bureaucracy. Buddhism had become Sinicized politically.

FOUR

ECONOMIC LIFE

BUDDHIST temples and monasteries were established primarily for religious purposes. They served as the place where ritual worship of the Buddha might be practiced, where monks and nuns could follow the religious discipline prescribed by the Buddha, where the clergy could preach the teachings to all those who came, and where pious laymen could acquire some knowledge of Buddhism and deepen their faith in the Buddha. However, when a temple or monastery became rich and powerful, then it began to widen its scope of activities. Thus we find the Buddhist saṅgha in T'ang China occupying an important role in the economic life of the Chinese through its ownership of land, operation of industrial installations, and commercial enterprises. In this chapter we shall discuss these activities, considering first the problem of temple lands, then the industrial installations such as the water-powered mills and oil presses, and then such commercial operations as lending goods or money, the Inexhaustible Treasury, and temple hostels.[1]

TEMPLE LANDS AND THEIR CULTIVATION

Even before the T'ang, Buddhist monasteries had received land from devoted donors, the income of which was to be used for maintenance of the monasteries. For instance, as early as 420, an official named Fan T'ai built a Ch'i-huan Monastery and then donated sixty *mou* of fruit and bamboo

[1] The bibliography on the economic and commercial activities of the Buddhist saṅgha in China is very extensive, and for a fairly complete and selective list of the important studies made so far by the Oriental and western scholars, the reader is referred to my work, *Buddhism in China*, 523-526.

groves to it.[2] Emperor Wen of the Sui dynasty donated a hundred *ch'ing* of land to the Shao-lin Monastery at the foot of the sacred Mt. Sung.[3] By mid-T'ang so much land had passed into the hands of the Buddhist monasteries that they were attacked by the memorialists as being among the major landowners of the empire. Very likely these charges were exaggerated, yet it is entirely possible there is some degree of truth in them. As will be discussed in detail later, the rich and powerful landowners often entrusted land to the Buddhist institutions as a subterfuge to escape taxation. It is not clear how much land was involved in such operations, but the amount must have been considerable, large enough to arouse the ire of the memorialists.[4]

Just how much land did the Buddhist monasteries own? Unfortunately, there is no precise information on this point. The only indication is that *shu-ch'ien-wan-ch'ing* of fertile lands and fine fields belonging to the Buddhist saṅgha were confiscated in the 845 suppression of Buddhism. How is this figure to be interpreted? Interpreted in one way, taking the character *shu* as modifying *ch'ien-wan*, one would arrive at the figure, several ten millions of *ch'ing*. Such a figure however is patently erroneous, for it would exceed the total area under cultivation in China at the time. According to Tu Yu,

[2] *KSC* 7, *T* 50.368c.

[3] *CSTP* 77.16b. One *ch'ing* of land consists of 100 *mou*. One *mou* is roughly one-sixth of an acre.

[4] Evidence of such land held by the monasteries is quite numerous: (a) Biography of Tao-ying (d. 636), *HKSC* 25, *T* 50.654b, in which we read that the P'u-chi Monastery in P'u-chou (present-day Shansi) established three estates, consisting of fields devoted to hemp, wheat, and millet.
(b) *FTTC* 42, *T* 49.384c, Lung-hsing Monastery in Hang-chou, raised funds from devoted followers to establish an estate of 1,000 *ch'ing*.
(c) E. O. Reischauer, *Ennin's Diary*, 131, Fa-hua Cloister in Mt. Ch'ih, Teng-chou, Shan-tung, owned an estate that provided 500 *shih* of rice annually.
(d) *Ibid.*, 321, decree of emperor on the ninth day of the tenth month, 842: "If the monks and nuns possess . . . fields and gardens, these are to be confiscated by the state."

the arable land during the T'ien-pao era (742-755) was only 14,303,832 *ch'ing*.[5] However, there is another way of interpreting the figure.[6] According to this interpretation, we should read the expression as *shu-ch'ien* (several thousand) up to a *wan* (ten thousand), thus making the area confiscated as several thousand, up to ten thousand, *ch'ing*. If we interpret the expression in this fashion, the area confiscated becomes much more plausible.

How did the monasteries acquire their large land holdings? In general, we may distinguish the following methods:

A. Donations

Examples of such donations have already been mentioned. They were made by members of the imperial family, the nobility, and the rich families of the realm. Since the ruling emperors and their families were often favorable to Buddhism, they made generous donations to temples and monasteries in the vicinity of the capital. For instance, after Hsüan-tsang returned from his pilgrimage to India, the Hsi-ming Monastery in Ch'ang-an, which served as his translation headquarters, received from the emperor 100 *ch'ing* of fields and gardens, 100 families of tillers of the soil, 50 carriages, and 2,000 bolts of cloth.[7] However, the most generous donors by far were the nobility and the rich families. Contemporary literature contains numerous references to donations of large estates and buildings to the saṅgha. A well-known instance of such a donation is the one by the eunuch Yü Ch'ao-en who in 767 presented the estate he had formerly received from the emperor to the saṅgha, to serve as the site of the Chang-ching Monastery in honor of the deceased empress Chang-ching. This

---

[5] *T'ung-tien* 2.15c-16a.

[6] This was suggested by Prof. L. S. Yang of Harvard University.

[7] *CTW* 257.2a. Other instances of such imperial donations were: (*a*) T'ai-tsung of the T'ang dynasty donated forty *ch'ing* of land to Shaolin Monastery on Mt. Sung in Honan. See *CSTP* 77.17b, 74.1a; (*b*) Hsüan-tsung donated one thousand *mou* of land to the Ta-sheng-tz'u Monastery in Ch'eng-tu when he was there in 757. See *FTTC* 40, *T* 49.376a.

estate was located just outside the Tung-hua Gate of Ch'ang-an, and was acclaimed as one of the most attractive sites in the capital. In constructing the Chang-ching Monastery, Yü spared no wealth. He regarded the timber obtainable in the vicinity of the capital as lacking in the quality required for the grand and magnificent structure he had in mind, and he had the material imported from far-away Szechuan for the purpose. Just the cost of construction was said to have exceeded a billion cash.[8] Another well-known case concerns one Li Teng, the owner of so much land that he was said to have the land itch. During the turmoil attending the An Lu-shan rebellion he donated his land to the Hui-lin Monastery in Lo-yang.[9]

The act of donating the land was, of course, closely connected with the Buddhist concept of earning merits; it was a meritorious act ensuring a more desirable rebirth in the future. The saṅgha in Buddhism is acknowledged as a great field of merit, and any donation which will provide food, clothing, or shelter to the community of monks will earn merits for the donor. For this reason, some donors expressly wrote in their will that they "hereby donate this twenty *mou* of personal-share land to the shrine and cloister, to provide for all the monks from the various quarters, and to give them a permanent abiding place."[10] By this meritorious deed of donating land to the saṅgha, the donor hoped for a better rebirth or salvation in the future for himself, and for blessings to befall his ancestors, parents, and family.

This practice of the rich in donating land to the saṅgha became so prevalent that complaints were soon lodged by the Confucian memorialists. One official charged that the rich and fertile lands in the vicinity of the capital were largely in the hands of the Buddhist monasteries.[11] Another official,

[8] *CTS* 184.7a-8a; *TFYK* 927.6b.

[9] *HTS* 191.6b-7b; *SKSC* 20, *T* 50.839c.

[10] D. C. Twitchett, "Monastic Estates in T'ang China," *Asia Major* 5.2 (1956) 128.

[11] *CTS* 118.6a.

Hsin T'i-fou went so far as to complain in 711 that the Buddhist monasteries controlled 70 to 80 percent of the wealth of the empire.[12] Such complaints led the throne to take some action.

Emperor Jui-tsung (710-712) prohibited further donations of land to monasteries by officials and commoners, and anyone violating the decree would have his land confiscated and given to the poor and to needy farmers.[13] Emperor Hsüantsung in 713 forbade certain categories of officials and nobility from establishing temples and monasteries on their manorial estates.[14]

B. *Purchase or Appropriation of Land by Monasteries*

According to T'ang land regulations, sale of property was prohibited except under certain circumstances.[15] If the owner were poverty-stricken at death, then it was permissible for the family to sell land for funeral expenses. Again, if the land were needed as the site for a residence, water-powered mill, or a storeroom, or if the owner moved from a small and remote village to a larger village, then sale was permissible.[16] These circumstances really permitted quite a wide range of latitude and opened the door for the sale of land in spite of governmental prohibition. Moreover, it appears that land was leased or offered as mortgage for loans. The net result was that there was a considerable flux in the ownership of land during the dynasty.

The plight of the peasant in all countries and all ages is certainly not an enviable one. He is virtually on the edge of bankruptcy and starvation at all times, and when natural calamities such as floods or drought or man-created disorders such as wars and banditry strike, he is pushed over the brink.

[12] *THY* 48.12b. [13] *THY* 48.12b. [14] *Ibid.*, 50.19b.

[15] *TLSI* 12.14b: "Those who sell one *mou* of personal share field shall receive ten strokes of the bamboo." In the *Shih-huo-chih* of the *HTS* 51.3b, the passage reads: "At first, during the Yung-hui era (650-656) buying and selling of land held in perpetuity and personal share land were prohibited."

[16] *HTS* 51.1b-2a; *TLSI* 12.15a.

Faced with debts and taxes, he has no recourse but to sell or mortgage his land. During the T'ang dynasty those who were in a position to take advantage of the financial plight of the peasants were the rich families and the Buddhist monasteries with their large financial resources. Once the peasant mortgaged his land, he had practically lost it, for the mortgage was almost certain to be foreclosed because of his financial condition. As a result, the peasants lost whatever land they had, and the estates of the rich families and the Buddhist monasteries increased in size. The iniquities of the practice led to repeated imperial decrees. In 735, the throne decreed that "buying, selling, or mortgaging land is prohibited,"[17] and in 752, another imperial edict was issued stating that "henceforth it is not permitted to buy or sell *yung-yeh* or *k'ou-fen* fields in contravention of the laws."[18]

In spite of these prohibitions, however, land continued to change hands. In one contemporary source we read: "Although this system [of prohibition] is in effect, observance of the regulations has become lax since the K'ai-yüan (713-741) and T'ien-pao (742-755) eras, so that the evils of consolidation of land in the hands of the few surpass those during the reigns of Emperors Ch'ing (32-7 B.C.) and Ai (6-1 B.C.) of the Han dynasty."[19] Also of interest on this point is the testimony of Lu Chih (754-806), the eminent T'ang statesman. He wrote that, as a result of the laxity in observing the land regulations, "those who are rich acquire land to the extent of tens of thousands of *mou*, while the poor do not even have homes in which to rest their feet. These poor depend entirely upon

[17] *TFYK* 495.21c.

[18] *CTW* 33.4a. Under the equal-field system in vogue during the first half of the T'ang dynasty, all male adults between twenty-one to fifty-nine years of age received from the state 100 *mou* of land, 80 *mou* of which were to be considered as *k'ou-fen-t'ien* or personal-share land, and 20 *mou* as *yung-yeh-t'ien* or land held in perpetuity. The personal-share land was to be returned to the state after the death of the recipient.

[19] *T'ung-tien* 2.16b, translated in K. Chen, *HJAS* 19 (1956), 74.

the powerful and rich, becoming in fact their private possessions. They borrow their seedlings and food, they pay rent for
their land and dwellings. Throughout the year they toil and
sweat continually without a day of rest. . . . Those who own
land, however, lead leisurely lives, living on the income of
their land. Such is the unbridgeable gap between the rich and
the poor."[20]

Here and there in the literature may be found evidence of
the Buddhist monasteries buying land. One instance concerns
the An-kuo Monastery in Ch'ang-an which bought some land
for 138½ strings of cash.[21] Another instance involved the
Ch'an master Shan-chien who by astute commercial transactions gained a profit of 300 strings of cash, of which 280 were
used to buy an estate and the remainder a vegetable garden.[22]
We read also of one monk, Nan-ts'ao, who solicited enough
funds to buy ten *ch'ing* of land for the Lung-hsing Monastery
in Hang-chou.[23] There is also the case of another monk, Ming-
yüan, who in 813 arrived at the Ling-chü Monastery in Yang-
chou, and within a short while was able to raise enough funds
to reclaim some 3,000 *ch'ing* of land which had previously
been mortgaged.[24] Finally, a monk, Wen-chü, during the T'ai-
ho era (827-835) purchased twelve *ch'ing* of land for the
Kuo-ch'ing Monastery on Mt. T'ien-t'ai.[25] One further passage
which concerns a monk named Hui-chou of the Ch'ing-ch'an
Monastery needs to be noted here. In his biography we read
that after forty years of tireless efforts, he built up a manorial
estate complete with thriving forests and vegetable gardens,
fertile irrigated fields, warehouses and granaries filled with
grains, and numerous water-powered mills. The estate sur-
passed even those of the very rich in the capital.[26] Hui-chou
was born in 596 and died in 667. Unfortunately we are not

---

[20] *Lu Hsüan-kung chi* 22.15a, *SPPY* ed.; also *TFYK* 495.24ab.
[21] *CSTP* 114.1a.   [22] *CTW* 455.6b.
[23] *CCC* 59.7b.   [24] *CTW* 745.18b.
[25] *SKSC* 16, *T* 50.808b; *FTTC* 22, *T* 49.246b.
[26] *HKSC* 29, *T* 50.697c.

told how he built up his estate, but it is a fair guess that purchase of land was one of the means.[27]

C. Grants of Land by the State to Monks and Nuns

Buddhist literature refers to two categories of land, that allocated to the monks and nuns by the state, and the *ch'ang-chu-t'ien*, or permanent property of the monastery.[28] The relationship between the two categories is by no means clear. One of the interesting features of the former, known as the equal-field system, was the stipulation that "all Taoist priests are to be granted thirty *mou* of land, Taoist nuns twenty *mou*. Buddhist monks and nuns are to be treated likewise."[29] The date for the inauguration of this startling innovation is in doubt. Such T'ang sources as the *T'ang-hui-yao*[30] indicate that the practice was initiated during the early years of the K'ai-yüan era, sometime around 725. However, there is some reason to believe that the granting of land to Taoist and Buddhist clergy was already in vogue during the Chen-kuan era (627-649), even though the official decree was not issued until the early K'ai-yüan years.[31]

The wording in the original decree granting the land to the Taoists and the Buddhists would suggest that the measure was originally intended to benefit the Taoists. This is understandable, for the T'ang emperors, whose surname was Li, claimed descent from Lao-tzu, the first sage of Taoism, also

---

[27] The following are further bits of evidence of land acquired by the monasteries: (*a*) *CTW* 19.3b, decree of Jui-tsung: "Buddhist and Taoist monasteries have occupied land and water-powered mills on a broad scale." (*b*) *CTS* 118.6a, biography of Wang Chin: "In the vicinity of the capital, the rich and fertile lands, together with the handsome profits derived from them, are mostly in the hands of Buddhist and Taoist monasteries."

[28] *Shih-shih yao-lan* B, *T* 54.302c-303a: "The term permanent property refers to the dwelling places, utensils, wooded areas, fields, gardens, servants, animals and grains belonging to the sangha. . . . These may be used by the sangha, but they are not to be divided and sold."

[29] *TLT* 3.10b.   [30] *THY* 59.18b.

[31] *CKC* 3, *T* 52.386b; *FYCL* 55, *T* 53.708a.

surnamed Li. However, it must be admitted that the emperors were not antagonistic toward Buddhism; in fact, they consciously and assiduously participated in services within the Buddhist temples in order to ensure that the protective and beneficent powers of Buddhism would also descend upon them. The two religions are invariably mentioned together in T'ang literature; hence, it is not surprising that any favors granted by the emperors to the Taoists would also be extended to the Buddhists.

However, there appears to be another aspect to this issue of land grants, namely, that the grants were probably made for the purpose of limiting the property held by monks and nuns.[32] If it is correct that monks and nuns since early T'ang had owned private property, then there was about a century during which monks could buy and sell land, receive land as security for loans, or claim land when the loans were not paid. Such activities could have resulted in some monks amassing a considerable amount of property. To prevent such a tendency from getting out of hand, the dynasty promulgated the rule that monks and nuns were to receive a definite amount of land in the hope of limiting the area owned by each person.

Regarded in this light, the contents of an edict issued the tenth year of K'ai-yüan or 722 becomes understandable. This edict reads as follows: "K'ai-yüan tenth year, first month, twenty-third day, edict to the Bureau of National Sacrifice. All the land held by Buddhist and Taoist monasteries, in excess of that legally granted according to the number of monks, nuns, and Taoist priests, shall be taken back through legal processes and given to destitute male adults who lack land. As for the permanent property of the monasteries, this may be constituted by the land returned from the Buddhist monks and nuns, and Taoist priests and priestesses. A monastery with more than a hundred resident monks must not

[32] This point is discussed by Mori Keirai in his article, "Tō no kindenhō ni okeru sōni no kyūden ni tsuite," *Rekishigaku kenkyū* 4 (1935), 1.53-59.

possess more than ten *ch'ing* of land, one with more than fifty monks must not have more than seven *ch'ing*, and one with fewer than fifty must not have more than five *ch'ing*."[33]

In this edict, two different categories of land are clearly delineated, that which is open to appropriation by the state and distribution to the poor, and that known as the permanent property of the monastery. The former category would appear to involve that which could be taken away and this could well have some reference to the grants of thirty and twenty *mou* of land to monks and nuns respectively. Such land could be used by the monks and nuns for their support only during their lifetime. According to the edict, any land in excess of that legally granted would then be appropriated by the state and distributed to the needy.

The second part of the edict refers to the permanent property of the monastery and contains the very puzzling expression, "This may be constituted by the land returned from Buddhist monks and Taoist priests." Just what is this land returned by the clerics? Surely it could not be the same as the land referred to in the previous portion, that which is appropriated and distributed to the poor. It must have reference to some other land held by the monks and nuns. Yet what this land is remains unclear. A possible explanation could be that this refers to the allotment of land that each monk and nun was legally entitled to, the thirty and twenty *mou* of personal-share land respectively. Instead of the individual monk or nun holding this land, he could return it to the state, and the state would then grant this land to the temple or monastery to become the permanent property of that institution. However, this practice raises another problem: if a hundred monks turned over to their monastery the thirty *mou* of land each was entitled to, the total of 3,000 *mou* or thirty *ch'ing* would be far in excess of the ten *ch'ing* of land which the edict permits a monastery with a hundred monks to own. Of course the problem would cease to exist if one assumed that the edict was never fully enforced, and by and large this is a

---

[33] *THY* 59.18b.

fair assumption. For example, a certain T'ien-chu Monastery in Hang-chou established an estate from which it harvested annually over 10,000 *shih* of grains.[34] Now it is estimated that the average yield per *mou* during T'ang and Sung times was between one and one and a half *shih*, depending on the quality of land. Any estate that yielded 10,000 *shih* would therefore range from 6,700 to 10,000 *mou*, or from sixty-seven to a hundred *ch'ing*. Another example is the Ta-hsiang Monastery in Lung-chou, Shensi, which owned over fifty-three *ch'ing* of land, of which forty-five were fertile fields.[35]

During the T'ang dynasty, it was also the practice for the state to support the grand monasteries of the state, such as the Ta-yün or K'ai-yüan Monasteries in various parts of the empire, or the Hsi-ming Monastery in Ch'ang-an. These imposing institutions were maintained by the state and were entrusted with the responsibility of protecting the spiritual welfare of the state. To support these grand monasteries, the state usually granted them large tracts of land. The following passage illustrates this: "In the case of a grand monastery of state such as the Hsi-ming or Tz'u-en Monasteries in Ch'ang-an, the state grants manorial fields to it in addition to the personal share fields that it already possesses. Everything necessary for maintenance is furnished by the state."[36]

Financial Responsibility of the Monastic Estates

With the Buddhist clergy owning land and the Buddhist monasteries playing the role of landlord, what financial obligations to the state did they have to assume? In previous dynasties, monks generally were exempted from taxes and labor services. Under the Northern Wei, for instance, the saṅgha grew to tremendous proportions—over two million monks, according to the *Shih-lao-chih* in the *Wei-shu*—primarily because many people wanted to escape from the onerous tax

[34] *SKSC* 15, *T* 50.803c.
[35] *CSTP* 113.48b; see also Twitchett, "Monastic Estates," *Asia Major* 5.138.
[36] *FYCL* 62, *T* 53.750b.

and labor burdens imposed by the state.[37] During the Northern Chou dynasty, one of the charges leveled against the sangha by the renegade monk Wei Yüan-sung was that the monks were exempted from taxation.[38] However, there were instances when the clergy were taxed. Hou-chu of the Northern Ch'i, who reigned from 565-576, decreed that the clergy must carry the same tax burden as other people.[39] In 450, when the Northern Wei was invading Sung territory in the south, the Sung authorities levied a tax on monks and nuns.[40] It appears, however, that these levies were temporary expedients and were not permanently fixed in law.

Under the T'ang, the favored position of the clergy was affirmed by legal provisions. Whenever the census of the empire was compiled, monks and nuns were entered, not in the regular household registers, but on a separate list designated as the *seng-chi* or monk's register. The preparation of this register was started in 729. Copies of this monk's register, which was drawn up every third year, were sent to the offices of the prefectures and to the Bureau of National Sacrifice in the central government. Significantly no copy was sent to the Bureau of Finance, which prepared the annual budget and the tax levies. This meant that the monks and nuns were not included in the register of taxpayers in the realm. In this connection, one of the measures decreed by Emperor Wu-tsung in the persecution of Buddhism in 845 is of interest. Besides confiscating the land of the Buddhist monasteries, he also forced 260,500 monks and nuns to return to lay life, so that they would be subjected to the biennial tax.[41]

Sometimes the tax-free status of the clergy was stressed in particular decrees of the emperor. We have one source which indicated that Emperor Hsüan (847-859) personally went to Wan-shou Monastery to present the imperial tablet to it, together with a donation of 260 *mou* of land. At the same time he ordered the ordination of 120 monks, each one to receive

---

[37] *Wei-shu* 114.31b.   [38] *KHMC* 7, *T* 52.132b.
[39] *T'ung-tien* 11.63a, Commercial Press ed.
[40] *Ibid.*, 11.62c.   [41] *CTS* 18A.15a.

a certificate of ordination and to be exempted from governmental services.[42]

Very naturally the privileged position of the clergy made ordination as a Buddhist monk a very attractive and lucrative proposition. When the sale of monk certificates was inaugurated officially in 757 by the central authorities as an expedient to raise funds for the imperial coffers, many individuals took advantage of the opportunity to buy certificates, not to become monks, but primarily to enjoy the financial privileges associated with the clergy, the chief of which was exemption from taxation. At the same time, local officials began also to sell certificates and to arrange for private ordinations. Such practices gave rise to clerical groups referred to in contemporary literature as bogus monks (*wei-lan-seng*), lay monks (*pai-hsing-seng*), or landlord monks (*ti-chu-seng*).[43] Such bogus monks led lives exactly like ordinary laymen—they had families, engaged in gainful pursuits, and lived in society— but because they purchased ordination certificates or were ordained privately, they enjoyed the privileged status of monks. In a document which Pelliot brought back from Tunhuang, the two terms *pai-hsing-seng* and *ti-chu-seng* were used to designate a certain Ling-hu Fa-hsing who rented eight *mou* of land to a layman named Chia Yüan-tzu.[44]

This practice of rich laymen taking refuge in monastic life to escape taxation came under repeated attacks in memorials. Hsin Ti-fou, in a memorial presented in 711, wrote: "At present those who are able to put up wealth and rely on their influence have become *śramaṇas*. Those who wish to avoid the labor services and to practice deceit have all become converted. Only those who are poor and virtuous have not been ordained."[45] On another occasion, he complained that "the

[42] *CSTP* 118.2a.

[43] See Naba Toshisada, "Chūban Tōjidai ni okeru giransō ni kansuru ichi kompon shiryō no kenkyū," *Ryūkoku-daigaku Bukkyō-shigaku ronsō* (Tokyo 1939), 129-140.

[44] See Pelliot 3153. Also Niida Noboru, *Tō-Sō hōritsu bunsho no kenkyū* (Tokyo 1937), 351.

[45] *CTS* 101.14b; *THY* 48.12b.

ordination of monks goes on increasingly, so that those who are exempted from the tax in produce or labor services number several tens of thousands. Thus, while the national expenditure is increased several times, the national income is decreased several times."[46] Li Ch'iao wrote: "The national economy and defense are both dependent on the adult population. Now the adults are all leaving family life, potential soldiers are all entering monastic orders. How are we to fulfill our military obligations and tax levies?"[47] Finally, there is the testimony of Yang Yen when he advocated passage of the biennial tax system. "When rich families have many adults, such adults generally become officials or monks, or render special services to claim exemption from the levies of adults. The poor, on the other hand, have no such refuge to turn to, but retain their status as taxed adults. As a result, in the case of the upper classes the tax burdens are avoided, but for the lower classes the burden is increased."[48]

As for the land owned by the temples and monasteries, it appears that legally they are not exempted from taxation. The best-known documentary evidence to support this conclusion is the request by the Buddhists in 811 to obtain tax exemption for their estates and water-powered mills. "First month, sixth year of T'ien-ho. The monks in the capital petitioned the government to exempt their estates and water-powered mills from taxation. The prime minister Li Chi-fu memorialized, saying: 'There is always a fixed quota in the amount of money and grains taxed. It is not permissible to be lenient toward the Buddhist saṅgha, whose resources are more than enough, and force the poor who have no means to make up the difference.' The throne followed this advice."[49] If the Buddhist institutions had enjoyed exemption privileges, there would have been no cause for such a request. Again, there exist numerous literary passages which describe special privileges bestowed on certain monasteries, thus implying that others did not enjoy the same privileges. For instance, the ten

[46] CTS 101.15b.
[48] THY 83.13b-14a.
[47] HTS 123.2b.
[49] THY 89.5b.

138

monasteries on Mt. Wu-t'ai in Shan-si were exempted from taxation by Emperor T'ai-tsung as a special mark of imperial favor after he had subdued the area.[50] Again we read that in 888 a donation of 800 *mou* of land made to the Nan-shan Ch'an Monastery was exempted from taxation.[51] If monastery lands enjoyed exemption, why was it necessary for the throne to specify this privilege as a favor? One can only conclude that legally monastery lands were subject to taxation.

In actual practice, however, the situation appears to have been different. Rich and powerful monasteries were often able to obtain special privileges—and among these privileges was tax exemption of their land—from the government through the intercession and protection of powerful and influential families and officials. To obtain these special privileges, the monasteries often sought to be designated as officially recognized institutions. Some high official or rich influential layman, or someone in the church hierarchy, would want to enhance the status of his favorite monastery, and would attempt to obtain a tablet inscribed with characters written by the emperor himself. If he were fortunate enough to obtain such a tablet, he would present it to the monastery with appropriate ceremonies, and henceforth the monastery would be designated as an officially recognized establishment. Once this status was obtained, then the particular monastery could claim special financial privileges. It was this preferred status of such a monastery that led the rich and powerful families to establish some connections with it so as to enjoy tax exemption on their land.

Such connections could be established in several ways. The rich landowner could hand over his land to the monastery under the pretext of donating it. He could build a monastery on his land, or convert a manorial house into a monastery, then petition for the tablet inscribed with the imperial hand. Once this was obtained and the monastery officially recognized, then the landowner could transfer his land to the mon-

[50] Chang Shang-ying, *Hsü Ch'ing-liang-chuan* 2, *T* 51.1131b.
[51] *CTW* 793.10b-11a.

astery. Probably the most prevalent method was for the powerful landowner to establish his own family burial grounds and shrine, which would be called a *kung-te-yüan* (merit cloister) or *kung-te-fen-ssu* (merit cemetery cloister) within the limits of an officially recognized monastery, and in due course of time would claim the monastery as its own private burial grounds. All his land would then be transferred to the monastery and would then be exempted from tax burdens. Or he might construct a Buddhist monastery on his private burial grounds, and then petition for official recognition. The existence of a merit cloister is affirmed as early as 711.[52] After that it is mentioned in 727 and again in 767.[53] During the succeeding Sung dynasty, these merit cloisters were to become even more numerous.

Of considerable interest is the relation between the donating landowner and the merit cloister. Ordinarily, when a donor made his gift of land to a monastery, he specified that the donation was permanent and outright, with no strings attached. With the merit cloister, the situation becomes more complex. Ostensibly the landowner had donated his land to the merit cloister, but the merit cloister in the first place was his own creation; it was, in other words, a dummy organization which he had established for a very definite purpose, to evade the tax obligation. The land which he had donated to the merit cloister could be regarded as monastery land as far as the state was concerned, but since the merit cloister was a private establishment, all land belonging to it was still considered a private family property. Moreover, the family also possessed the right to appoint cloister officials and administrators of the property, and this placed the appointed officials under the domination of the landowner, ready to comply with his desires at all times.

The following account describes one such merit cloister. A certain Liu Fen, who was active in putting down the rebellion of Huang Ch'ao in south China, obtained eight hundred *mou* of land in 886, and in 888 donated it to a Ch'an cloister which

[52] *FTTC* 40, *T* 49.373a. [53] *Ibid.*, *T* 49.374a, 378a.

he established on the land. Because he was brave in the field of battle and filial to his forefathers at home, all his land was exempted from taxation. He invited five Ch'an monks to live in the cloister. The monks were very industrious in cultivating the land. In addition to the performance of their duties, the monks were expected not to visit houses of ill-repute or to drink intoxicating liquor or to steal any cloister property with intentions to sell it. All their daily needs were fully provided for. Liu's family were also not permitted to frequent the cloister and ask for food and drink. During the spring and autumn sacrifices, only two or three members of the family were permitted to go to the cloister to participate in the ceremonies of ancestral worship, and they were not allowed to linger around after the completion of the ceremonies or to disturb the property of the cloister. Finally, Liu insisted that if any of the monks should disregard or disobey his words, they would be reprimanded immediately and forced to leave the cloister.[54]

Financially, therefore, the merit cloister performed a very useful function on behalf of the rich and powerful landowners. They provided the medium through which the landowners could avoid taxes on their land. They also served as means of investments through which the owners could accumulate gains to acquire more land by purchase or by appropriation.

Started during the T'ang dynasty, the movement to establish merit cloisters accelerated during the Sung, so that many officially recognized monasteries were converted to merit cloisters. Faced with this situation, devoted followers of Buddhism and monks frequently complained to the throne. In 1137, an official named Ch'en Kung-fu asked the throne to prohibit government officials from seizing officially recognized monasteries and converting them to private merit cloisters.[55] Another memorial in 1250 charged that "in recent years whenever scholars or the gentry joined the government, they would formulate new practices. They would appropriate and convert famous monasteries to private merit cloisters,

---

[54] *CTW*, 793.17a-18b.   [55] *FTTC* 47, *T* 49.425b.

and seize the fields and products to form a monastic estate."[56] In the same year a monk, Ssu-lien, complained bitterly that the important ministers of the government, after having "forcibly appropriated monastery lands to serve as burial grounds, would further occupy several monasteries and convert these into merit cloisters. They take possession of everything within the monasteries. One day the monasteries must present rice, the next day tea and bamboo shoots, the next day firewood and charcoal, and after that bamboo and timber. They are even asked for monthly presents of the rarities of land and water. As soon as a monk dies, invariably these people secretly take over his belongings and include them in their private possessions."[57]

In view of the rather considerable amount of land exempted from taxation and the consequent loss of tax revenues, the central authorities made some attempts to curb such grants of lands to monasteries. Jui-tsung (710-712) issued a decree prohibiting officials and commoners from donating land to monasteries; anyone who did so would have his land confiscated and distributed to the poor. The next emperor Hsüan-tsung in 713 forbade those below the ranks of dukes and imperial princes from establishing their manorial residences on monastery lands.[58] In all probability these were futile attempts to stem a practice that had become too widespread through the manipulations of powerful officials and rich laymen.

Cultivators of Monastery Lands

Since the monks themselves did not cultivate the land owned by the monasteries, who did the cultivation? Generally speaking, these cultivators fell into three main classes, temple slaves, tenant farmers, and the novices and probationers.

Temple slaves were already in existence during the Period of Disunity. In the list of objects donated by Fu Chien of the Former Ch'in dynasty (351-394) to the cleric Seng-lang,

---

[56] *Ibid.*, 48, *T* 49.431c.　　[57] *Ibid.*　　[58] *THY* 48.12b; 50.19b.

three slaves were included, to be used for sweeping and cleaning monastery grounds.[59] During the Northern Wei period, Chief of Monks T'an-yao had criminals freed on condition that they serve as slaves whose duties were to cultivate the fields and do the manual work within the monasteries.[60] The presence of such temple slaves during the reign of Emperor Wu of the Liang dynasty (502-549) may be seen in the memorial of Kuo Tsu-shen, who asked the emperor to prohibit monks from keeping *pai-t'u* and the nuns from having *yang-nü*. These were probably menials performing personal services for the monks and nuns.[61]

During the T'ang dynasty the number of such temple slaves increased greatly. Some of them were originally attached to the land when it was donated to the monasteries. Others were probably drawn from what was a considerable army of unemployed peasants whose lands had been absorbed by the powerful families and monasteries. Such people, in order to gain a livelihood, did not mind accepting the status of slaves to till the soil of the monasteries. Finally there were those who were so poverty-stricken and burdened with debts that they mortgaged themselves to the monasteries to become slaves. Among the documents found in Tun-huang there is one, now kept in the Bibliothèque Nationale in Paris and catalogued as Pelliot 3150 which tells about a certain Wu Ch'ing-shun who belonged to a family of three brothers. Because the family was so poor and debts so heavy, Wu agreed to mortgage himself to Abbot So of the Lung-hsing Monastery in the area in return for ten *shih* of wheat, one *shih* and six *tou* of flaxseed, three *shih* and two *tou* of *chun-mai*, and nine *shih* of millet. After the transaction, Wu was to be entirely under the disposition of the temple abbot, and not permitted to go elsewhere. (The document was dated tenth month, twenty-

[59] *KHMC* 28, *T* 52.322b.
[60] *Wei-shu* 114.17ab. The most authoritative work on the Buddha households is by Tsukamoto Zenryū, *Shina bukkyōshi kenkyū, Hokugi-hen* (Tokyo 1942), 165-213.
[61] *Nan-shih* 70.25ab.

eighth day, *kuei-mou*, which could be 835 or 895.) There is
no way of knowing how many such slaves existed during various periods of the T'ang dynasty, and the only figure available is that connected with the persecution of 845, when
150,000 slaves were manumitted. It is likely that this group
of slaves constituted the bulk of the cultivators of those monastery lands which were not too extensive.[62]

As for the large estates owned by the monasteries, these
were usually cultivated by tenant farmers known as *chuang-
k'e, chuang-hu, tien-k'e, tien-chia, tien-hu*, and *tien-min*. In
Buddhist literature they are sometimes called *ching-jen*, or
pure people, so called because they were the ones who performed certain deeds such as farming, handling gold and silver, or trading in goods, thus sparing the clergy such impure
acts.[63] Usually such tenants had left their native villages because of some catastrophe or unrest or because their own
land had been bought by rich landlords or because of oppres-
sion by local officials. They lived on the land they rented from
the monasteries, and were obliged to pay rentals to the monasteries for the use of the land. The amount of such rental is
not clear. In a memorial which Lu Chih presented, he wrote,
"In the vicinity of the capital, the official tax per *mou* was five
sheng of grain, while the rental collected by private families
amounted to one *shih* of grain per *mou*, which would be
twenty times that of the official tax. In the case of middle-
grade land, the rental would be halved, which would still be
ten times that of the official tax."[64] The standard practice during the T'ang was to set the rental at roughly one-half the harvest of each *mou*. Such being the case, if the rental were one
shih per *mou*, then the harvest per *mou* would be about two

[62] On the problem of temple slaves, see Michihata Ryōshū, "Chūgoku
bukkyō to dorei no mondai," in *Tsukamoto Hakushi shōju kinen bukkyō shigaku ronshū*, Kyoto, 1961, 764-783. See also his *Chūgoku bukkyōshi no kenkyū*, 9-58, for a much more exhaustive discussion.

[63] *Shih-shih yao-lan* B, *T* 54.303b, "They are called pure people because they perform pure deeds for the monks, so that the monks may
avoid committing offenses."

[64] *Lu Hsüan-kung tsou-i* 15.7b.

shih, a yield which could be produced only in very fertile land. The average yield was more likely to be about one *shih* per *mou*, with the rental on such fields being five *tou* or half a *shih*.[65]

Fan Chung-yen during the Sung dynasty wrote that "for each *mou* of middle-grade land, the harvest in unhusked grain would be about one *shih*."[66] Another bit of information is furnished by Lo Ta-ching of the Sung dynasty, who wrote that "in ordinary years 100 *mou* of land would yield 50 *shih* of rice, but in a bountiful year the yield would be around 100 *shih*."[67] Ordinarily to produce one *shih* of rice, a little more than two *shih* of unhusked grain would be required.[68] When Lu Chih wrote that private families were collecting one *shih* as rental, he must have been referring to unhusked grain, not rice. Besides cultivating the fields, these tenants were also called upon from time to time to render other labor services for their landlords. Such services were not definitely specified, but were of a temporary nature. In one instance, the tenants were called upon to repair a wall that had collapsed, and in another, they served as porters to carry oil.[69]

From their landlords, the tenants borrowed the seedlings for the new crops, the farming implements, and the draught animals to work in the fields. Their houses were also provided by the landlords. The condition of these tenants must have been very difficult indeed, for Lu Chih described them as toiling and sweating without rest all year round, and barely having enough food and clothing.[70]

Finally there was the third group of cultivators, the novices

[65] Niida, *Tō Sō hōritsu*, 402.

[66] Fan Chung-yen, *Wen-cheng-kung chi* 8.20a, *SPTK* ed.

[67] *Ho-lin yü-lu* 7.7a; see also Chu Li, *Han-T'ang shih-chien hou-chi* 6. 8b-9a.

[68] Chu Li, *op.cit.*, 6.9a: "To produce fifty *shih* of rice, one would require about 120 *shih* of unhusked grains."

[69] *Yu-yang tsa-tsu* 8.7b; 15.6a, *SPTK* ed.

[70] *Lu Hsüan-kung chi*, 22.15a. For a good discussion of the condition of these tenant farmers, see Kato Shigeshi, *Shina keizaishi kōshō* (Tokyo 1952), 1.233-245.

and probationers within the monastery. Even though these were members of the saṅgha, they were called upon to work in the fields. This was a practice long in vogue within monastic circles. For instance, when Tao-an the famous cleric (312-385) first entered the order, he was forced to work in the fields for three years before he was given a sutra to study.[71] Only after the novice had undergone the rites of ordination to become a full-fledged monk was he exempted from manual labor in the fields.

This prohibition against farming activities by monks is clearly stated in the Buddhist *Vinaya*, or *Rules of discipline*. According to Pācittiya, No. 10, some monks at Āḷavī had occasion to dig the ground while repairing a shrine, thus harming some living things in the soil. People criticized the monks for this action and reported it to the Buddha. The Buddha scolded the monks, and then laid down the rule: "If a monk digs the ground, or has it dug, he is guilty of an offense to be expiated."[72]

On another occasion, the same monks were cutting some trees while repairing a shrine, and in the process of cutting, they injured the son of a tree deity residing in the tree. The deity reported the matter to the Buddha, whereupon the latter enunciated the following rule: "For destruction of vegetable growth, there is an offense to be expiated." In defining vegetable growth, the text goes on to say, vegetable growth means "what is propagated from roots, propagated from stems, propagated from joints, propagated from cuttings, and fifthly, what is propagated from seeds."[73] Such a rule effectively barred monks from harvesting any grain grown from seeds.

Finally, there was the rule against watering vegetables. The same monks at Āḷavī used water to sprinkle grass, even though they knew that the water contained living forms. The Buddha rebuked them for so doing, and ruled: "If monks,

[71] *KSC* 5, *T* 50.351c.
[72] I. B. Horner, *Book of the Discipline*, 2.223.
[73] *Op.cit.*, 2.226-229.

knowing that the water contains life, sprinkle grass or clay, or have them sprinkled, they are guilty of an offense to be expiated."[74]

If monks were prohibited from digging the soil, harvesting the grains, or watering the vegetables, then they could not engage in any argicultural labor in the fields. In Chinese Buddhist literature, this prohibition is clearly stated in the translation by Kumārajīva, entitled *Fo-i chiao-ching*: "Those who adhere to the five precepts are not permitted to engage in commercial transactions, cultivate fields, build residences, keep slaves, and raise animals. All sorts of plantings and cultivation as well as all wealth and gems should be scrupulously avoided. . . . They are also not permitted to cut grass and trees, till the soil, or dig the good earth."[75] So popular was this text that the Emperor T'ai-tsung of the T'ang ordered it to be copied and distributed to officials in the capital and the provinces.[76]

These pācittiya rules against farming were also made known to Chinese Buddhists through the translations of the various *Vinayas*. In the *Ssu-fen-lü*, for instance, we read: "If a monk digs the soil or has another person dig, that is a pācittiya offense."[77] The rule against cutting vegetable growth is found also in the *Ssu-fen-lü*,[78] as is the rule against sprinkling.[79] As for the fear that farming might harm living things which reside in the soil, trees, or grass, it is expressed in a number of places.[80]

In the *Eihei shingi* of Dōgen, the famous Japanese Zen monk, it is specified that one of the responsibilities of the overseer in a Zen monastery was to see that monks did not engage in the four heretical acts, one of which was agricultural labor. Farming involved the killing of insects and worms in

[74] *Op.cit.*, 2.261.   [75] *T* 12.1110c.
[76] *FTTC* 39, *T* 49.365b.   [77] Ch. 11, *T* 22.641b.
[78] Ch. 12, *T* 22.641c; ch. 24, *T* 22.734c.
[79] Ch. 12, *T* 22.646c; ch. 24, *T* 22.735a.
[80] *Wu-fen-lü* 6, *T* 22.41c; *Shih-sung-lü* 10, *T* 23.74c-75a; *Seng-ch'i-lü* 14, *T* 22.339a; *Ken-pen yu-pu* 27, *T* 23.776ab.

the soil, and Buddhist monks were not to commit such deeds.[81]

However, some monks in the monastic community felt that this avoidance of agricultural labor was not entirely appropriate, for it shifted the burden of labor to others. Consequently, we read in Chinese Buddhist literature of monks working in the fields. A critic of Buddhism in the sixth century wrote: "Monks till the soil and cultivate the fields and gardens side by side with the farmers; they trade in goods to seek wealth, competing with the traders for profits."[82] Strictly speaking, however, such practices were by no means prevalent and were the exceptions rather than the rule. Because of this, the monastic community was often criticized as being parasites of society who had to be fed and clothed by others.

Within this general context, there was one school, the Ch'an School, which deviated from this practice of avoiding agricultural labor. The Ch'an School abided by the slogan "one day no work, one day no food." In other words, Ch'an monks had to perform some manual labor each day, otherwise they would not be served with food on that day. We must therefore ask ourselves how this sanction of agricultural labor originated, in spite of *Vinaya* prohibition of such work.

If we examine the *Recorded Sayings* of the Ch'an masters, we shall find that the slogan "one day no work, one day no food" originated with Huai-hai, who compiled the *Pai-chang ch'ing-kuei*, the basic rules regulating the deportment of Ch'an monks and the organization and administration of Ch'an monasteries.[83] In the *Recorded Sayings* of this master we read: "Whenever the master worked, he always exerted himself far more than his group. His followers could not tolerate this, and so one day they hid his working implements and entreated him to desist from his strenuous efforts. The master said, 'I have no special virtues, and therefore I strive to work together with people.' He searched everywhere for his implements but could not find them, and in the process he

---

[81] *T* 82.338c.　　　　　　　　　[82] *KHMC* 8, *T* 52.143a.
[83] For this work, see *T* 48.1109c-1159b.

forgot about eating. Thus the slogan 'one day no work, one day no food' became popular in the world."[84]

Such a divergence from accepted practices required some justification, and this the master provided again in his *Recorded Sayings*. One of his disciples asked him whether there was any punishment involved in such deeds as cutting grass, chopping wood, digging wells, and tilling the soil. The master replied: "It is not possible to say there is punishment, nor is it possible to say there is no punishment. This question of punishment or no punishment depends on the person involved. If a person is greedy and tainted by considerations of possessions and nonpossessions, and has a mind interested in seizing this and abandoning that, and if he cannot avoid mentioning such things within the course of three sentences, then that person is certainly to be punished. But if he exceeds three sentences without mentioning such considerations of gain or loss, and if his mind is empty and detached and does not entertain any thought of emptiness and detachment, then that person will not be punished."[85]

In this reply, one sees Huai-hai taking his stand on a basic Buddhist belief, that the intention behind the deed and not the deed itself determines the nature of the karma produced. If the monk decides that his performance of agricultural work is entirely for the benefit of the Three Jewels and not for any personal gain, then the manual labor is perfectly appropriate and permissible. In describing such manual labor in the fields and gardens, Huai-hai used a special term, *p'u-ch'ing*, collective participation. By this term, Huai-hai meant that all the monks in the saṅgha would work together on a basis of equality to achieve a common goal.[86] So deep was his belief in the propriety of *p'u-ch'ing* that even in his old age he insisted on working in the fields against the advice of his fellow monks.

[84] *Hsü Tsang-ching* II/24/5.410b.
[85] *Pai-chang ta-shih Ch'an-shih yü-lu* in *Ku-tsun-su yü-lu* ch. 1, *Hsü Tsang-ching* II/23/2.84b-85a.
[86] *SKSC* 10, *T* 50.77c; *Pai-chang ch'ing-kuei* 6, *T* 48.1144ab; *Hsü Tsang-ching* II/16/3.273ab.

This Ch'an tradition of monks working in the fields was carried over into Japan, and we find the following section in one of Dōgen's works: "The task of the head gardener is difficult and most arduous. . . . He is always in the garden, constantly planting and raising his crops. . . . He is no different from the peasant, for all day long he is tilling the soil and hoeing with his hoe and rake, or carrying human wastes for fertilizers."[87]

In the eyes of the Ch'an School, this *p'u-ch'ing*, or collective participation, was much more than mere working in the fields for some common goal, it was also considered a form of religious practice, as the following passage clearly indicates:

> In those instances of collective participation, all should exert equal effort regardless of whether the task is important or unimportant. No one should sit quietly and go contrary to the wishes of the multitude. While performing his duties, one should not indulge in ridicule or laughter, or boast about one's talents or ability. Rather, one should concentrate his mind on the *Tao*, and perform whatever is required by the multitude. After the task is completed, then one should return to the meditation hall and remain silent as before. One should transcend the two aspects of activity and nonactivity. Thus, though one has worked all day, he has not worked at all.[88]

It is clear from this passage that the Ch'an monk was to regard agricultural labor in the same light as *tso-ch'an*, or sitting in meditation, and since it was part of the spiritual cultivation of the monk, the labor was considered appropriate and acceptable.

In this insistence on the part of Huai-hai that Ch'an monks must do their share of work in the fields, we see another ex-

[87] *Eihei shingi*, *T* 82.336a.
[88] *Huan-chu ch'ing-kuei*, Yüan-Ming ed., in *Hsü Tsang-ching* II/16/5.499a. See also *Ch'an-yüan ch'ing-kuei* 9, *Hsü Tsang-ching* II/16/5.464b-465a.

ample of the independent and Chinese feature of Ch'an Buddhism. Instead of being bound by the *Vinaya* rules against manual labor, he made some accommodation to the prevailing Chinese work ethic, that every able-bodied adult should perform some productive work. By so doing, he was able to counteract the criticism that the monks were parasites on society. As he himself wrote, "I combed the Mahāyāna and Hīnayāna *Vinayas* extensively, and arrived at a happy medium by establishing rules of conduct that aimed at goodness. I therefore decided not to follow the traditional *Vinayas* but to establish a separate Ch'an tradition of life."[89]

Before we close this discussion of temple lands, it is only proper that something be said about their role in the temple economy. Through gifts, purchases, and foreclosure of mortgages, the Buddhist establishment became one of the great and powerful landowners during the T'ang dynasty. Unlike other landowners, the officialdom and the rich families who had to divide their holdings upon the death of the head of the family, the Buddhist monastery was a permanent establishment maintaining its holdings as a unit, and even increasing them with the passage of time, with no need of division among heirs. This feature gave the Buddhist monastery certain advantages which private individuals did not possess. Out of the income received from these extensive holdings, the Buddhist monasteries were able to establish industrial and commercial enterprises which were productive of even more income and which in turn added to the wealth of the saṅgha.

INDUSTRIAL ENTERPRISES

A. *The Water-powered Mills*

One of the most profitable enterprises established by the Buddhist monasteries was the water-powered mill (*nien-wei*), the function of which was to produce flour. The Chi-

[89] *SKSC* 10, *T* 50.770c, biography of Huai-hai.

nese *nien-wei* or mill consisted of two pieces of stone, one on top of the other, with the top piece movable and the bottom stationary. Furrows were chiseled on the faces which ground against each other, and this grinding movement pulverized the grains. The power that moved the upper stone was furnished by horses, oxen, or water. Water, of course, provides the cheapest and most convenient source of power, since it can function continuously and requires no food. During the T'ang dynasty, most of the mills in operation were powered by water, and this fact created problems that required government action.

To transmit the flowing water into energy to turn the mill, some special equipment was necessary. Such equipment required considerable capital, which only the few could provide. As a result only rich and powerful families and the Buddhist monasteries were able to establish and own water-powered mills. Moreover, the use of water for the mills meant that water normally intended for irrigation would have to be diverted from the farmlands to those areas where the mills were located. Whenever this diversion occurred conflict between the farmers and the mills arose. As China always considered agriculture its primary industry, the government often took steps to regulate the establishment of water-powered mills, or to prohibit their operation at certain months of the year when water was needed for irrigation. In some areas, however, where the owners of the mills were all-powerful, such governmental regulations proved futile and the farmers suffered.

In the *T'ang-liu-tien* 7.9b, there is the following stipulation: "Whenever water is needed for irrigation, the water-powered mills are not permitted to compete for its use." The commentary to this passage added: "From the lunar sixth month until the second month of the following year, all the gates [controlling the water to the mills] shall be closed, and only if there is a surplus may the mills use it." From this we may conclude that the government considered irrigation to be of primary, and the mills of secondary, importance. In another document, found in Tun-huang and now reposing in Paris, the mills were granted the use of water from the first of the ninth month to the end of the year. "Every year, after the thirtieth day of the eighth month, and before the first day of the first month, [the mills] are permitted to use water. During the other months, we shall rely on the proper officials to seal the gates channeling water to the mills. . . . The irrigation needs of the people must first be served. If rainfall is sufficient and no irrigation is needed, then the gates may be opened."[90]

If one examines these two sources carefully, he will find that the period of water usage permitted to the mills varies. Both sources agree that the mills could not use water during the first, second, sixth, seventh, and eighth months. The *T'ang-liu-tien* indicates that usage is permitted during the third, fourth, and fifth months, while the Tun-huang document gives the ninth, tenth, eleventh, and twelfth months but not the third, fourth, and fifth months. How to reconcile the differences in the two versions remains unsolved, except that regional and climatic differences, the amount of rainfall, and the differences in the farmers' planting seasons might have been responsible.

Scattered here and there in the printed sources are notices concerning these water-powered mills. One such notice tells about a certain Yang Su (d. 606) who was so rich that his household contained several thousand servants, and that the water-powered mills he owned were beyond count.[91] In the biography of Kuo Tzu-i, we are told that in 778 over eighty such mills were ordered to be destroyed by imperial decree because they deprived the farmers of water needed for irrigation.[92] Then there was the official in the Ho-hsi area (now Kansu) who established water-powered mills as a means to

---

[90] See Pelliot 2507. The document, entitled *T'ang-tai shui-pu-shih*, is reprinted without pagination in Lo Chen-yü, *Ming-sha shih-shih i-shu*.
[91] Li Jung, *Tu-i-chih* 1.15, *TSCC* ed. *Sui-chu* 48.12b.
[92] *CTS* 120.14a.

earn income which he used to help the needy and the famished in his area.[93]

As these mills were profitable enterprises, rich and powerful families, as well as the Buddhist monasteries, vied with one another to establish them wherever water was available. By far the best sources of information concerning these monastery-owned mills are the Tun-huang documents.[94] Very often these documents are the financial reports rendered to the assembly of monks in a certain monastery by a monastery official whose responsibilities correspond to that of an accountant. Such reports were usually presented at the end of the old year or the beginning of the new one. The Japanese monk Ennin was present at one such session in the Tzu-sheng Monastery in Ch'ang-an on the twenty-fifth day of the twelfth month, 840, when the accountant rendered his report.[95] In such reports, the income received by the monastery from various sources as well as the expenses incurred during the year are listed.[96] For a detailed picture of the economic activities of Buddhist monasteries, these reports are unrivaled in their importance, for they contain data about the income derived from the operation of oil presses, water-powered mills, interest from loans, rental from land, and donations. Such income was always in the form of products, various grades of wheat, flour, husked rice, oil, beans, hemp, cotton, or cloth.

As we are interested mainly in the operation of the water-powered mills here, let us take just one example, extracted from the accountant's report for 885 on income derived from mills owned by the Ching-t'u Monastery in Tun-huang.

[93] *HTS* 111.3a, biography of Wang Fang-i.

[94] These documents bearing on the mills, which I examined in the autumn of 1969, have been subjected to an extensive study by Naba Toshisada in his article, "Chūban Tōjidai ni okeru Tonkō chihō bukkyō jiin no tengai keiei ni tsuite," *Tōa keizai ronsō* 1 (1941), 549-577, 847-874; 2 (1942), 535-556.

[95] Reischauer, *Ennin's Diary*, 296.

[96] Examples of such reports may be found in Naba, *op.cit.*, 1.552-565; Gernet, *Les Aspects Économiques*, plates III, IV, V.

Products	Amount	
wheat flour	40 *shih*	spring mill income
wheat flour	12 *shih*	spring mill income
wheat flour	20 *shih*	2nd spring mill income
wheat flour	6 *shih*	mill income
3rd grade wheat flour	6 *shih* 8 *tou*	spring mill income
wheat flour	6 *shih* 8 *tou*	autumn mill income
wheat flour	60 *shih*	spring mill income
2nd grade wheat flour	6 *shih* 8 *tou*	spring mill income
2nd grade wheat flour	3 *shih* 8 *tou*	autumn mill income
2nd grade wheat flour	3 *shih* 6 *tou*	autumn mill income
bran	18 *shih*	mill income
wheat flour	44 *shih* 4 *tou*	spring mill income
2nd grade wheat flour	3 *shih* 5 *tou*	spring mill income
2nd grade wheat flour	3 *shih* 9 *tou*	mill income
bran	10 *shih*	spring mill income.[97]

From this document, as well as others found in Tun-huang, it is clear that wheat flour constituted the main item in the revenue derived from the mills.

Though the mills were owned by the monasteries, they were not operated by the monks but by lay families known as *wei-hu* (miller families) chosen from among the tenant farmers on the monastic estates. Besides the millers, there were also maintenance men referred to as *wei-po-shih* who were very likely technicians or skilled workers responsible for keeping the mills in good running order.

Strictly speaking, the miller's function was to provide flour to feed the monks in the monastery. It must be kept in mind that we are dealing with people in north China, whose main staple is not rice but flour. To produce this flour, the miller received grains from the monastery, which the monastery had obtained as rental from monastic land or as interest from loans. The miller provided the labor, the monastery provided the raw materials and the mill. Sometimes the flour made by the miller exceeded the amount needed for food by the monks, in which case the surplus flour was sold to the public by the monastery for a profit.

[97] Pelliot 2040.

155

Besides milling the flour for the monastery, it was also possible for the miller to carry on his own milling business with the monastery-owned mill. With his own resources he could purchase grain and convert this into flour, which he could then sell to the public to earn a profit. Since the mill he used was not his own, but the monastery's, he was obliged to pay a certain tax to the monastery for his operation. In the monastery accounts, this tax was entered as income from the mill (*wei-ju*) and constituted an important source of revenue. For the miller, this was a lucrative business, for the monastery-established mill was probably the only mill in the area, and he enjoyed what virtually amounted to a monopoly in the milling business. Furthermore, the miller might also mill flour for those people who brought grains to him. For such services he charged a certain fee, a portion of which was also turned over to the monastery.

In this manner, the monastery and the miller mutually benefitted from the operation of the mill. The monastery had its flour manufactured for food or for sale, and also received a considerable income from the miller for his private business. The miller enjoyed the protection of the monastery and had nothing to fear from outside competition. He also had the mill to manufacture flour needed by his own family.

Oil Presses

In the Tun-huang documents, two terms are frequently mentioned, *liang-hu* and *liang-k'e*. After an exhaustive study of the use of these terms, Naba concluded that the first referred to the families operating the oil presses, and the second to the tax paid by the oil pressers to the monastery. He also wrote that the two terms were derived from the expression *liang-tzu*, the piece of wood used to press the oil out of the seeds.[98]

Oil was an almost indispensable item for the monasteries. It was used for cooking and also as fuel for the countless lamps in a monastery. In the Tun-huang financial reports,

[98] Naba, "Ryō-ko-kō," *Shina bukkyō shigaku* 2.1 (1938), 1-40; 2.2.27-68; 2.4.30-82.

the list of expenditures frequently included entries that read: "oil three *tou*, for the use of the ever-burning lamps."[99] Consequently, the manufacture of oil was an important commercial enterprise for the Buddhist monasteries. To manufacture it, the monastery would establish oil presses in the family of a lay tenant; such a family would then be called a *liang-hu*. The relation between the oil pressers and the monastery was one of mutual interdependence, as in the case of the millers. The monastery granted to the oil pressers the concession of manufacturing and selling oil, and it also furnished the equipment for the operation. In payment for this concession, the oil presser had to manufacture all the oil needed by the monastery. The raw material needed for this operation was supplied by the monastery; hence, in the financial reports, one would read an entry for "hempseed, two *shih* eight *tou*, delivered to the oil presser to be pressed into oil," or "hempseed, four *shih* three *tou*, delivered to the oil presser to be pressed into oil."

Besides manufacturing the oil needed by the monastery, it appears that the pressers, for the privilege of using the presses, had to pay an oil tax known as the *liang-k'e*, usually in a certain quantity of oil and oilcakes. The latter were made from the residue of the seeds after the oil had been extracted, and could be used as fodder for animals. For this procedure, the presser had to furnish his own raw materials. It appears that the monastery sometimes established more than one press, and the oil tax was assessed on the group as a whole, with each individual presser then paying his share. This oil tax frequently shows up in the annual financial report of the monastery accountant.

After fulfilling the oil needs of the monastery, it was permissible for the presser to do some business of his own. With his own resources, he could purchase hempseed, manufacture oil, and sell this product in the open market. Most of the profits he derived from this operation were his own, but he had to turn over a certain portion of them to the monastery. In

[99] See Pelliot 2032, 2040, 2049.

this instance, however, the payment was not in oil but in goods such as grains, flour, cloth, or beans. As in the case of the miller, the oil presser enjoyed certain advantages arising from the support and protection of the monastery. The monastery was usually the dominant institution in the area, and its protection assured the presser unusual opportunities for the marketing of his products. In turn, the more oil the presser sold on his own, the more income the monastery received.

As stated in the beginning of this discussion, the terms *liang-hu* and *liang-k'e* are found only in the Tun-huang documents and not elsewhere. From this we may conclude that the terms were applicable only to the oil pressers of that area. The question as to whether the conditions pertaining to the manufacture of oil in Tun-huang were also in existence in other parts of China during the T'ang dynasty, is one that must remain unanswered for the present.

Inexhaustible Treasury

Before the rise of a modern economy with its complicated financial system, a commercial transaction usually involved three elements: coins, goods, and buying and selling for profit. The Buddhist rules of discipline, according to the Pāli version, specifically prohibit monks from handling gold and silver and from buying and selling goods. The *Vinaya* of the Sarvāstivādin School, however, takes a more conciliatory attitude. In the Chinese version of this *Vinaya*, there is a passage telling about some merchants who were on the point of departing for some distant land to trade. Before they left, they deposited some goods, which they had donated to the saṅgha, with the monks, and instructed them to loan these goods out for interest, and thus earn a profit. The monks replied that they were not authorized to do so by the Buddha, but went ahead and reported the matter to the Blessed One. Upon hearing of the proposal, the Buddha gave permission to accept the goods, and authorized the *ching-jen* or pure people within the monastery grounds to carry out the commercial transactions for gain, such gain to be used for the benefit of the dhamma and saṅgha.[100]

In the *Mahāsaṅghikavinaya*, we read that if goods donated to the saṅgha were not consumed by the monks and nuns, then such surplus could be sold or loaned out to earn a profit, with such profits to be used for matters pertaining to the Buddha and the saṅgha.[101] In the *Vinaya* of the Mūlasarvāstivādins, there is also an account describing practices among Indian monastic circles whereby the saṅgha could accept and store goods presented by devoted followers and loan them out for gains, provided such gains were to be used for worship services, or for repair work in the monasteries.[102] It is clear then that in India the saṅgha was already engaged in commercial transactions for gains, provided that such gains were for the promotion of the Three Jewels. The goods which formed the basis of the transactions were designated as inexhaustible wealth (*wu-chin-ts'ai*) because they could be used indefinitely and earn interest continuously.

Scriptural evidence therefore exists to justify the establishment and the maintenance of the commercial institution known as the Inexhaustible Treasury in China. Such treasuries had existed even prior to the T'ang dynasty. During the Liang dynasty, Emperor Wu (502-549) established thirteen such treasuries during his reign.[103]

There is some discussion as to whether the term *wu-ching tsang* in China was derived from the *Vinaya* tradition as found in the literature of the Mahāsaṅghika and Sarvāstivādin Schools. Some writers do not think so and have contended that the term was derived from Mahāyāna sutras such as the *Vimalakīrti* and *Avataṁsaka*.[104] The relevant passages in the *Avataṁsaka* states that the bodhisattva, thanks to his Inex-

[100] *Shih-sung-lü* 56, T 23.415c.
[101] *Mo-ho-seng-ch'i lü* 10, T 22.311c.
[102] *Ken-pen-shuo i-ch'ieh yu-pu p'i-nai-ya* 22, T 23.743bc.
[103] KHMC 19, T 52.237c; CSTCC 12, T 55.93b.
[104] Yabuki Keiki, *Sangaikyō no kenkyū* (Tokyo 1927), 508; Gernet, *Les Aspects Économiques*, 211.

haustible Treasury, presents gifts to the Three Jewels,[105] while in the *Vimalakīrti*, we are told that the bodhisattva institutes the Inexhaustible Treasury to help those who are destitute.[106] According to this interpretation, the term *wu-chin-tsang* originated from this idea of the inexhaustible stock of merits possessed by the bodhisattva which he offers to the Three Jewels above and to the poor below.

The Inexhaustible Treasury served as the mechanism through which the Buddhist saṅgha carried out many of its financial transactions. For this purpose it used the goods stored in the treasury. Such goods were acquired in a number of ways. The most common method was through donations by the faithful, who hoped to gain by such acts meritorious karma that would benefit their future rebirths. Such donations might have been originally intended for the consumption of the saṅgha; if such donations were not excessive, they would be consumed entirely with no leftover as surplus. But it often happened that the saṅgha could not consume all the goods donated; in this case the surplus was added to the stock of the Inexhaustible Treasury. In other instances, the powerful and the rich made outright gifts to the saṅgha, specifically as stocks for the treasury. In return for these donations, the saṅgha made the gift of the law to the faithful donors. Strictly speaking, therefore, there was the idea of an exchange of commodity. Still another common method was to replenish the stock of the treasury with the revenues received by the monasteries from their extensive land holdings. One well-known example concerns a monastery with sufficient land to yield 10,000 *shih* of grain annually, which were placed in the Inexhaustible Treasury of that particular monastery to be used for the benefit of the saṅgha.[107] Equally well-known is the case of Li Teng, who donated his entire family fortune to the Hui-lin Monastery near Lo-yang to serve as the inexhaustible wealth of that monastery.[108]

What did the Inexhaustible Treasury in a monastery do

[105] *T* 9.437c.
[106] *T* 14.550b.
[107] *SKSC* 15, *T* 50.803c.
[108] *Ibid.*, 20, *T* 50.839c.

with the goods it possessed? For one thing, it could lend such articles out to borrowers and charge an interest of 4 or 5 percent per month, which was the rate authorized by T'ang regulations.[109] Very likely some sort of security was required. Such security could be in the form of immovable objects, i.e., land, house, flour mill, etc., or movable objects as clothing, utensils, animals, etc. If the debtor defaulted on his payment, the security in the form of immovable objects could be utilized for the benefit of the creditor, but the latter could not take possession of it. Ownership of the property remained with the debtor even though he did not pay his debt. The situation was different with reference to movable property. If the debtor could not pay his debt, then the property could be sold by the lender to recover the debt. Frequently peasants living in the vicinity of the treasury would borrow grains in the spring, with the understanding that the amount plus interest would be repaid in the fall after harvest. Sometimes the goods in the Inexhaustible Treasuries were sold and the proceeds used for the promotion of the dhamma and saṅgha.

Of the numerous Inexhaustible Treasuries in existence during the T'ang dynasty, the most famous was the one found in the Hua-tu Monastery which belonged to the School of the Three Stages.[110] A very detailed and interesting description of this treasury is given by a T'ang writer, Wei Shu, in a work entitled *Liang-ching hsin-chi*. This description is translated in full in the following:

In the third year of K'ai-huang (583), Kao Chiung, duke of Ch'i and vice president of the Office of State Affairs, gave up his private residence and memorialized that it be converted into a monastery. At the time a monk named Hsin-hsing arrived from Shan-tung and was put up in the monastery established by Kao Chiung. He compiled a *San-chieh-chi* consisting of some thirty *chüan*. In gen-

[109] TLT 6.13b; THY 88.21a.
[110] For the most exhaustive study of this school, see Yabuki Keiki, *Sangaikyō no kenkyū*.

eral, he emphasized perseverance, hard work, and tolerance. He said that man may be divided into three classes:
the wise, the stupid, and the ordinary. Since he taught this
idea, his teaching became known as the School of the Three
Stages.[111] He was apparently successful in his work of conversion, hence the monastery became known as the Hua-
tu Monastery.[112]

Within the confines of the monastery there was an Inexhaustible Treasury established by Hsin-hsing. After this,
the donations from residents in the capital gradually increased, and by the end of the Chen-kuan era, the money,
silk, and golden embroidery piled up in the treasury was
beyond calculation. Famous monks were often deputed to
oversee the treasury, the proceeds of which were used to
repair monasteries in the realm. People from as far away
as Yen (Szechuan), Liang (Kansu), Shu (Szechuan), and
Chao (present-day Hopei) all came to the treasury to borrow. The volume of daily loans was beyond measure. Regardless of whether or not the loans carried interest, nothing was put in writing, but when the loans were due, they
were repaid.

During the Chen-kuan period, a certain P'ei Hsüan-chih,
whose conduct was well regulated, entered the monastery
to serve as janitor for more than ten years. The people in
the monastery observed that his character was without
flaw, and consequently entrusted him with the task of
guarding the treasury. He secretly pilfered gold from the

[111] If we accept Wei Shu's explanation that the term *san-chieh*
refers to the three classes of people, then we should translate the term as
School of the Three Degrees. However, the term as used by the school
refers to the three stages in the duration of the law, that of the pure
law, counterfeit law, and decline of the law, and the particular types of
teachings suitable for each stage. Hence I have used the translation
Three Stages. See Tsukamoto Zenryū, "Shingyō no sangaikyōdan to
mujinzō ni tsuite," *Shūkyō kenkyū* 3.4 (1926), 66-67; Yabuki, *op.cit.*,
193-198.
[112] The Monastery to convert and to ordain. For the history of the
Hua-tu Monastery, see Yabuki, *op.cit.*, 112-116.

treasury, but the amount he stole was never ascertained. In fact, the monastery people did not even know about the pilferage. Suddenly he left without returning. Surprised, the monastery officials then searched his sleeping quarters and found the following verse left behind.

> You release a sheep before a wolf,
> You place a bone before a dog.
> Since I am not an arhat,
> How could I resist stealing?

They never found out his whereabouts.

Empress Wu Tse-t'ien transferred the treasury to the Fu-hsien Monastery in Lo-yang, but in the new location business did not flourish, and in the end, the treasury returned to the old site. During the first year of K'ai-yüan (713) an imperial decree called for the dissolution of the treasury. The valuables stored therein were distributed to the various monasteries to pay for repairs which were needed. In this manner, the institution was closed.[113]

Some additional information about this Inexhaustible Treasury in the Hua-tu Monastery may be found in the *T'ai-p'ing kuang-chi*, where we read that the earnings of the treasury were divided into three portions: one was earmarked for repairs to temples and monasteries in the empire, one was used to alleviate the sufferings of the famished and the destitute, and one for offerings to the Buddha. We are also told that faithful devotees vied with one another to donate goods and wealth to the treasury, bringing them by the cartloads and then disappearing without leaving behind their names.[114] The official reason given for the dissolution of the treasury

[113] Wei Shu, *Liang-ching hsin-chi* 2.15ab; *Yüeh-ya-t'ang ts'ung-shu* ed. v. 133. For the verse by P'ei Hsüan-chih, I have relied on the reading found in the *TPKC* 493.4048, which I consider to be better. There is some disagreement concerning the date of dissolution. Instead of 713, the *T'ang Liang-ching Ch'eng-fang-k'ao* of Hsü Sung, 4.25b, gives the ninth year of K'ai-yüan, or 721. From other sources it appears that 721 is the correct date.

[114] *TPKC* 493.4047 (Peking 1959).

in the Hua-tu Monastery was that it was guilty of fraudulent practices and that its affairs were not upright.[115] However, it is more than likely that the destruction was part of a wider movement to suppress the School of the Three Stages, which established the Hua-tu Monastery. Through its teachings, this particular school found itself at odds with the imperial authorities. For one thing, its viewpoint that the contemporary age was one of decay, corruption, and lawlessness implied criticism of the ability of the reigning authorities to rule. It further contended that in this age of decay, no government existed that was deemed worthy of respect. For advocating such views which reflected on the integrity and power of the ruling dynasty, the school was branded as heretical by Empress Wu Tse-t'ien, and its literature proscribed by Hsüan-tsung, the emperor who ordered the dissolution of the treasury and the monastery in 721. Finally in 725, Emperor Hsüan-tsung dissolved all the monasteries belonging to the School of the Three Stages.

We have devoted considerable attention to this Inexhaustible Treasury in the Hua-tu Monastery primarily because it was the best known of this type of commercial institution managed by the saṅgha. From its inception to the final dissolution in 721, the Inexhaustible Treasury enjoyed over a century of flourishing commercial activities, with the income of these activities being used for a wide variety of altruistic

[115] *TFYK* 159.15a. The date of the decree of dissolution is given here as 721, fourth month: "We have heard that the School of the Three Stages has established an Inexhaustible Treasury in the Hua-tu and Fu-hsien Monasteries. Every year during the fourth day of the first month, faithful devotees donate their wealth to the treasury. They say this is for the protection of the law and for the succor of the poor and weak. The treasury frequently, however, indulges in fraudulent practices and its affairs are not upright. It should therefore be abolished." This was followed by another edict in the sixth month, which stipulated that "the animals, manorial fields, and wealth of the Inexhaustible Treasury of the Hua-tu Monastery are to be distributed to the Buddhist and Taoist monasteries and temples in the capital. The wealth is to be used first to repair broken images of the Buddha and damaged buildings and bridges. If there is any left over, then this should be added to the permanent property of the monasteries."

projects. It must be added here that besides loaning out goods, these Inexhaustible Treasuries also served other commercial functions. One was that of the pawnbroker. Another was to serve as a repository where the patrons in the vicinity could deposit their wealth for safekeeping. For this service the treasury charged a fee.

Besides the data on commercial activities found in contemporary T'ang literature, a flood of evidence has been provided by the documents discovered in Tun-huang. In these documents may be found the most detailed description of the amount of goods borrowed by individuals from the monasteries, and the interest they had to pay. These documents are in the form of contracts negotiated between the monastery and the individual, covering loans which are usually in the form of products such as grains, cloth, silk, and in rare cases, money. The following are some examples of such contracts.

I. LOANS OF SEEDLINGS

A. *Yu* year, first day, third month. Commoner Ts'ao Mou-sheng of the lower village, owing to lack of seedlings, borrowed one *shih* and eight *tou* of beans from Monk Hai-ch'ing (of the Ling-t'u Monastery). The beans must be returned before the thirtieth day of the eighth month. If he disregards this contract and does not pay at that time, then he shall have to pay double the amount. His diverse belongings shall be seized to pay for the value of the beans. If he should disappear, then the guarantors shall repay the loan for him. If there should be an amnesty during the interval, it shall not affect the stipulations stated here. This contract is drawn up because of the fear that there would be an absence of trust. Both parties mutually consider it to be fair and clear, and attach their fingerprints to record it. Borrower, Ts'ao Mou-sheng, age 50. Guarantor, male novice, Fa-hui, age 18. Witness, Monk Tz'u-teng.[116]

[116] Stein 1475. In other portions of this same document, there are further samples of such loans. (1) Fifteenth day of the fourth month, Yen borrowed three *shih* of wheat from the Ling-t'u Monastery, with

B. *Wei* year, third day, fourth month, contract of Wu Chiung-ch'iu, who borrowed eight *shih* of millet for food from monk of Yung-shou Monastery. The millet must be returned by the end of the eighth month this autumn. If he does not repay on time, then his diverse belongings shall be seized to pay for the full value of the loan. If he should disappear during the interval, then the guarantors shall bear the responsibility for payment. This contract is drawn up because of the fear that there would be no faith. Borrower, Wu Chiung-ch'iu.

Guarantor, male Ssu-tzu.

"   Monk Ling-chun.

"   male Hsi- ? .[117]

II. LOAN OF SILK

A. Teng Shan-tzu borrowing silk.

Chia-wu year, eighteenth day of eighth month. Teng Shan-tzu, needing some cloth, went to Abbot Teng and borrowed one bolt of silk from him. The bolt is 38 feet, 5 inches long, and 1 foot, 9 inches wide. He also borrowed another bolt of silk, length 39 feet, width 1 foot, 9 inches. They must be repaid by the eleventh month. If he passes this deadline without payment, then he shall pay interest according to rates prevalent in the area. Fearing that no one

---

repayment to be made at the end of the eighth month. If repayment is not made on time, he must pay double the amount borrowed. (2) First day of the second month, monk I-ying borrowed from Hai-ch'ing two *shih* and eight *tou* of wheat, to be returned during the eighth month. If not, he must repay five *shih* six *tou*. (3) Sixth day of the third month, monk Shen-chi being in debt, borrowed from Ling-t'u Monastery two *shih* six *tou* of wheat, with the promise to repay during the eighth month. If not, he must repay five *shih* two *tou*. (4) *mou* year, eleventh day, fourth month, the commoner, Ma Ch'i-lin, lacking seedlings, borrowed from Ling-t'u Monastery eight *shih* of wheat, with the promise to repay during the eighth month. If not, he must repay sixteen *shih*.

Pelliot 2686 records a loan of four *shih* of seedlings by Li Ho-ho from the Ling-t'u Monastery.

[117] Pelliot 3730.

would keep faith, the parties have drawn up this contract to serve as proof for the future.

Borrower of silk, Teng Shan-tzu.

Witness, Chang Tsung-chin, official.

Witness, Abbot Tsung-fu.[118]

B. Hsü Liu-t'ung borrowing silk.

By a remarkable coincidence, two contracts have been discovered concerning a rather complicated loan. An official Hsü Liu-t'ung, on the fifth day of the sixth month, *i-ssu* year, borrowed seven bolts of silk from Abbot Shen of the Lung-hsing Monastery. At first he returned two and a half bolts, with the understanding that the remaining four and a half bolts would be repaid within five years. Each bolt was calculated to be worth twenty-two *shih* of grain. Twenty months after signing the above contract, Hsü paid (on the thirteenth day of the third month, *ting-wei* year) another bolt, leaving three and a half bolts remaining to be repaid. The following year (the sixteenth day of the fourth month, *mou-shen* year), Hsü was dispatched as an official to Hsi-chou. Since he could not return within the five years specified for the repayment of the entire loan, another document was drawn up, which indicated that Hsü still owed three and a half bolts, and that his two brothers would bear the responsibility for repayment during his absence.[119]

These contracts contain no indication of the interest charged for the loans, only the penalty for default, which was payment of double the amount borrowed. Some contracts contain the phrase, "the interest is to be in accordance with rates prevalent in the area." Unquestionably, interest was charged, for in the financial reports of the monasteries, a very common item was income from interest. For instance, the re-

[118] Pelliot 3124.

[119] Pelliot 3004 and 3472. Some further examples of such loans of silk: (1) Pelliot 3453: Chia Yen-ch'ang borrowed one bolt of silk from Abbot Hsin-shan of Lung-hsing Monastery; (2) Pelliot 3051: monk Fa-pao borrowed one bolt of silk from San-chieh Monastery; (3) Stein 4445: Ho Yüan-te borrowed three pieces of coarse wool from Yung-an Monastery.

port of the Ching-t'u Monastery in Tun-huang for the year 884 contains the following entries:

Hempseed, one *tou*, received from So Yen-ch'i, interest
  "   four *tou*, " " Ch'en Hsi-tzu, "
  "   two *tou*, " " Liu Ssu-po, "[120]

In other documents, however, the rate of interest is clearly indicated. The following are some examples:

Ma Ting-nu, borrowed millet two *shih*, returned three *shih* in autumn.
Chang Chu-tzu, borrowed millet two *shih*, repaid three *shih* in autumn.
Ma Ting-nu, borrowed wheat seven *shih*, repaid ten *shih* five *tou* in autumn.[121]

From these entries of loans and payment, we may conclude that borrowing was done in spring and payment in autumn, with the interest rate at a uniform 50 percent for half a year. Specific data are given in another document dated 905:

First month, ninth day. Liang Che-li borrowed beans one *shih*, repaid one *shih* five *tou* in autumn.
First month, twelfth day. An Chi-tzu, borrowed beans four *shih*, repaid six *shih* in autumn.[122]

These entries in the financial reports, of which we have given but a few samples, furnish ample evidence that such transactions in wheat, millet, hempseed, and beans constituted a flourishing commercial enterprise and a lucrative source of income for the monasteries in the Tun-huang area. The wide variety of loans made by one monastery may be seen in the report of the Ching-t'u Monastery for the year 884 or 944, one cannot be sure, for only the cyclical year is given.[123] The goods borrowed—wheat, millet, silk, cloth,

[120] Pelliot 2032. The list is much longer. I have just picked out a few entries.
[121] Pelliot, 3959.   [122] Pelliot 2932.
[123] Pelliot 2032, copied in Naba, *op.cit.*, 165-168; also quoted in Gernet, *Les Aspects Économiques*, passim.

hempseed, beans—were all temple property, derived from donations, income from fields, and from payment of interest.

What percentage of the total income of the monastery did the income from interest represent? The report of the accountant of the Ching-t'u Monastery in Tun-huang for 924 may be of interest here. He indicated that in this particular year, 366.9 *shih* of grain were received by the monastery. Of this amount, 44.4 *shih* or 12 percent represented revenue from temple land, 200-plus *shih* or 55 percent represented interest, and 120 *shih* or 33 percent represented donations from the faithful.[124] For that one year, at least, the revenue from interest constituted more than half the annual income, and it is reasonable to assume that this was not an exceptional case.

So far, we have discussed only those loans involving goods. In Tun-huang at this period, transactions were carried out largely in kind, for a money economy was not yet in vogue. However, there are some instances of loans in money. A document found by the Japanese in Central Asia, dated 781, contains reference to such a monetary loan.

Ta-li sixteenth year, third month, twenty-first day. Yang San-niang, needing some money, went to Yao-fang Village, and borrowed 1,000 cash. The interest rate shall be 200 cash each month, and the loan with interest must be paid within six months. If Yang should disappear after receiving the money, then the guarantor shall repay for him. Fearing that no one would have trust, the two parties mutually agree that this contract is fair and clear and attach our fingerprints to record it.
Borrower, Yang San-niang, age 45.
Guarantor, Monk Yu- ? , age 57.[125]

Another instance of such a monetary loan is found in a document discovered by Aurel Stein in Khotan, dated 782. This one read:

[124] Pelliot 2049, summarized in Gernet, *op.cit.*, 187.
[125] Niida, *op.cit.*, 250-251. Here is an interesting example of people in the border regions not knowing of changes which had taken place

The strong young male Ma Ling-chih,[126] being in dire need of cash and unable to obtain it anywhere, went to monk Ch'ien-ying of the Hu-kuo Monastery and borrowed 1,000 cash from him. The interest rate at the beginning of the month shall be [?] hundred cash. [127] Should Ch'ien-ying need cash himself, then Ma is to repay the amount borrowed with interest. If Ma is unable to pay, then he should permit Ch'ien-ying to seize family belongings such as cows and other animals to make up the amount of the loan. If there is a remainder after repaying the loan, then Ch'ien-ying will not claim that. Fearing that no one would have faith, the parties have drawn up this agreement. Both sides agree that it is a fair and clear document, and record this with their fingerprints.

Owner of money

Borrower of money, Ma Ling-chih, age 20.

Mother of borrower, Fan Erh-niang, age 50.

Younger sister of borrower, Ma Erh-niang, age 12.[128]

In the two instances cited above, the interest on a loan of 1,000 cash was 200 cash each month, or 2,400 cash a year. This would mean an astronomical interest rate of 240 percent per annum, four times the rate of 5 percent per month or 60 percent per year approved by the government. One can only conclude that in faraway Tun-huang and northwest China, money was a very scarce commodity and hence commanded an exorbitant rate of interest. Or it may be that the financial

---

in the capital. This document is dated Ta-li sixteenth year, but the Ta-li era had already expired two years before.

[126] The last character in the name is uncertain and undoubtedly is an abbreviation of some other character. Naba thinks it should be *chuang* but Niida reads it as *chih*. I have followed Niida's reading here.

[127] A key character giving the amount of interest is missing here. From other documents, however, the missing character is probably "two." See Niida, *op.cit.*, 250, 252. Gernet, *op.cit.*, 179 did not notice the character missing before the character "hundred," and said that the interest was one hundred cash.

[128] Stein 5867. See also Niida, *op.cit.*, 253; Naba, *Shinagaku* 10.3.148-149; Gernet, *op.cit.*, 179-180.

policies never penetrated to the remote areas to influence commercial transactions there.

Monasteries as Hostels

Strictly speaking, Buddhist monasteries in T'ang China were not private institutions but were the permanent property of the saṅgha of the ten directions. They were built with donations from the public or with the financial assistance of the government. Consequently they were open to any monk or nun who happened to be traveling and needed a place to spend the night. Ennin, the Japanese monk who traveled in China during the years 838-847, was able to find lodgings in Buddhist monasteries wherever he went. In time, the monasteries in T'ang China served not only as hostels for the clergy but for all travelers on the road. This was another of the commercial enterprises operated by the Buddhist monasteries.

Of those monastery-operated hostels which opened their doors free of charge to travelers, the most famous are those in the vicinity of Mt. Wu-t'ai in Shansi, called *p'u-t'ung-yüan*, or common cloister. Ennin left some valuable data concerning the location and distance between the common cloisters. Following are some excerpts covering the itinerary during the fifth year of K'ai-ch'eng, or 840.

Fourth month, twenty-third day. Ate gruel in early morning, then went northwest for twenty-five *li* to Pa-hui-ssu of Mt. Huang. Noonday rest here, ate millet. Afternoon traveled twenty *li* to Liu-shih Common Cloister. Stopped for night.

Fourth month, twenty-fourth day. Traveled along mountain valley northwest for twenty-five *li*, reaching Liangling Common Cloister. Stopped for noonday meal. After meal, went twenty *li* northwest to Kuo-yüan Common Cloister. Stopped for night.

Fourth month, twenty-fifth day. Followed valley thirty *li* to west. Reached Chieh Common Cloister.

171

Fourth month, twenty-sixth day. Ate morning gruel, traveled twenty *li* to Ching-shui Common Cloister. Ate meal here. Traveled thirty *li* west to T'ang-ch'eng Common Cloister, then fifteen *li* west to Lung-ch'uan Common Cloister. Stopped for night.

Fourth month, twenty-seventh day. Traveled west for twenty *li* to Chang-hua Common Cloister. Ate noonday meal here. Went ten *li* to Ch'a-p'u Common Cloister, another thirty *li* to Chüeh-shih Common Cloister, spent night here.[129]

Ennin was on his way to Mt. Wu-t'ai in Shansi, the sacred mountain dedicated to the bodhisattva Mañjuśrī, and one of the most popular holy sites for pilgrims to visit. Now Shansi is a mountainous country, as Ennin's diary makes it abundantly clear, and travelers going over the mountains and valleys needed havens to rest and to spend the night. Ordinarily the traveler would be able to cover about sixty to seventy *li* in one day (roughly twenty to twenty-three miles). This fact appears to have determined the sites of the common cloisters established by Buddhist monasteries along the route, for according to Ennin, these cloisters were spaced usually from twenty to thirty *li* apart, just the right distance for the noonday break and the evening rest.

Ennin also furnishes valuable information about the conditions of these cloisters. In the entry for the twenty-third day of the fourth month, he wrote that the Shang-fang Common Cloister furnished lodgings and food (rice and gruel) to all persons who came there, regardless of whether they were clergy or laymen. Since the cloister was opened to all, it was called a common cloister. In this particular cloister, there were two monks, one pleasant and one dour. Concerning the Liang-ling Common Cloister, Ennin wrote that the master was not in, so they prepared their own meal. Owing to an epidemic of insects in recent years, the cloister did not have any provisions, so it had not served gruel or rice for a long time.

[129] *Ennin* 2.59-60.

As for the Kuo-yüan Common Cloister, the diary noted that because it was located deep in the mountains, no rice or gruel was served, only small beans. When the Japanese party reached the Chieh Common Cloister, they found a group of over a hundred monks, nuns, and women, on a pilgrimage to Mt. Wu-t'ai, sharing the cloister with them for the night. Further on, Ennin noted that the Chang-hua Cloister served gruel and rice, but the Chüeh-shih Cloister did not.[130]

From these scattered notices, we may visualize the common cloister as having two or three monks, one of whom was the master, to take care of the place. As these common cloisters were not commercial establishments but were simply rest houses, the traveler took his chances about finding food in one of them. Sometimes food was served, sometimes not; sometimes the guest had to furnish and prepare his own food. If the cloister were located in an area where the people could contribute some grains, rice and gruel were usually served, but if the area were poor, or if famine conditions existed, then the cloisters had no provisions. Some of the cloisters must have been quite large, for one was able to accommodate about a hundred guests for the night. These common cloisters, established during the T'ang dynasty, were still in existence during the Sung dynasty, as evidenced by a passage in the *Ta-Sung seng-shih-lüeh* of Tsan-ning (919-1001), which mentions "common cloisters, at present many of them in the Mt. Wu-t'ai area."[131]

Besides these common cloisters we have other evidence of the monasteries offering their quarters to the public without charge. During the T'ang period, competition for the *chin-shih* degree was very keen, and those scholars who were *chü-jen* flocked to the capital to take the examinations. Ordinarily the examinations took place during the day, but some candidates were permitted to stay until late at night. During the third year of Yüan-ho (808) a decree was issued by the throne, specifying that if a *chü-jen* finished his examination by nightfall and could not go back to his lodgings for the

[130] *Ibid.*   [131] *T* 54.237a.

night, he was to be put up in the Kuang-chai Monastery in the capital. The official examiners who waited for him to finish, and the retinue of the *chü-jen*, were to stay in the Pao-shou Monastery.[132]

This edict points to a situation that must have been quite prevalent during T'ang times. In the capital and in the important cities, the imperial authorities had established and maintained a number of national monasteries, whose function it was to provide spiritual protection to the emperor and state. Such grand monasteries of the state were therefore open to officials traveling on the road to assume their posts in the outlying provinces, or to the candidates for the civil service examinations on their way to the provincial or national capitals. The edict referred to above indicates that examination candidates could be installed for the night in some of the monasteries in the capital during examination periods. In such instances, it is unlikely that the candidate would have to pay for his lodgings.

As for traveling officials staying in monasteries, we have the following specific example. A certain Li Ao was appointed in 808 to a post in Ling-nan in south China, and started out from the capital Ch'ang-an in the first month of 809 with his family. On the twenty-fourth day of the second month, upon arrival in Chu-chou in Chekiang, his wife became ill, and the party lodged within a pavilion in the K'ai-yüan Monastery of the city. On the eighteenth day of the third month, the wife, while still living in the monastery, gave birth to a girl, and on the tenth day of the fourth month, the entire party resumed its journey to Ling-nan.[133] The account does not state whether or not Li Ao had to pay the monastery for the period that he stayed there. Since Li was traveling to Ling-nan to assume an official post, and since the K'ai-yüan Monastery was one of the national monasteries during the T'ang dynasty, it is reasonable to conclude that he was put up without charge.

There are also instances of monasteries renting out rooms

132 *THY* 76.19b.
133 Li Ao, *Lai-nan-lu* 18.147ab, *SPTK* ed.

on a long-time basis. For example we read that during the third year of Hsien-ch'ing, a certain Wang Chih of Ch'i-chou after serving a term as district magistrate in I-chou, stopped at a monastery on his way home, and there met a student who had been staying in the monastery for a long time.[134] In another source we read that "Yao Ch'ung did not have any settled living quarters, so he lived in the Wang-chi Monastery. When he was ill with malaria, the emperor dispatched emissaries to inquire about his daily condition. Every day dozens of carriages came."[135] Finally there is the story concerning a Cheng Kuang-wen who wanted to practice calligraphy but was too poor to buy paper. He heard that in the Tz'u-en Monastery there was an abundance of persimmon leaves. He therefore rented a room in the monastery and every day practiced calligraphy with the leaves.[136] In these instances, as in the previous case concerning Li Ao, there is no indication as to whether the occupants had to pay for the use of the monastery space. It is more than likely, however, that the long-time occupants had to pay something, since they were not on their way to examinations or to official posts.

The grand monasteries of the state and the common cloisters rendered a very valuable contribution to T'ang society in offering hostel services to certain categories of travelers. Other monasteries not in these categories, however, were not so civic-minded or altruistic, and frequently took in travelers for the income derived. Once the monasteries took in paying guests, they could not be selective in the choice of customers, and in the remote monasteries, such guests sometimes were undesirable characters or members of secret societies intent on fomenting rebellions and disorders. For such groups the monasteries were the perfect meeting and dwelling places. The presence of a large number of guests also disturbed the religious atmosphere of the monasteries, and disrupted the religious discipline of the monks living therein. Sometimes

[134] *FYCL* 75, *T* 53.852b.
[135] *Tzu-chih t'ung-chien* 211.20b-21a.
[136] Li Ch'o, *Shang-shu ku-shih TSCC* v.2739, p. 14.

such lay guests were so numerous that traveling clerics could not be accommodated in the monasteries. Concerning the K'ai-yüan Monastery in Teng-chou in Shan-tung, Ennin wrote, "The place was full of guests who were officials, and there were no spare rooms. When monks came, there was no place to put them."[137]

It is not possible to ascertain how extensive the practice of monasteries serving as commercial hostels was, but it must have been fairly widespread, so much so that the governing authorities felt compelled on several occasions to issue decrees prohibiting it. One such decree by Emperor Tai-tsung in 762 reads as follows: "I have heard that officials in the prefectures and subprefectures, in their public and private capacities, have often rented quarters in Buddhist and Taoist monasteries. Because this practice defiles the sacred quarters, it should be prohibited."[138] This prohibition was reiterated by Emperor Te-tsung in 789: "Buddhism and Taoism bestow blessings and benefits on all people. Their building and cloister walks should be revered and pure. Henceforth, the Buddhist and Taoist monasteries in the prefectural cities are forbidden to provide lodgings for guests."[139]

Buddhist sources have also preserved the texts of such prohibitions. One for the year 848 reads: "We have heard that many Buddhist and Taoist monasteries in the empire are inhabited by military and civil officials, who despoil and defile the sacred places and yet have no regrets over their misdeeds. Buddhist and Taoist monks are forced to go elsewhere, and the halls and living quarters are damaged. The guests sleep in the doorway, and do their cooking all over the corridors. When we think of this in our spare moments, we feel very sad. Henceforth, this practice should be absolutely forbidden."[140] In the very next year, the prohibition was affirmed: "P'ei Hsiu, the governor of Hsüan-chou, reports that many of the Buddhist and Taoist monasteries are trampled upon and defiled by officials and lodgers. From now on, lodg-

---

[137] *Ennin* 2.48.
[139] *CTW* 52.3a.
[138] *CTW* 46.12b.
[140] *FTTC* 42, *T* 49.387a.

ers should not be permitted in the monasteries, and any offender shall be heavily punished. The emperor gave his assent."[141]

It is unfortunate that we do not have more adequate information about the financial aspect of this particular activity of the monasteries, how much they charged their guests, the income derived from this source, and the ways in which the income was used. Likewise, we have very little data on some similar commercial activities carried out by the monasteries, such as the operation of warehouses, stores, and stations where one could rent carriages. If the annual financial reports of the monasteries in Ch'ang-an and Lo-yang were available, as they are in the monasteries in the Tun-huang area, we would have a much better picture of these minor commercial activities. Dynastic changes, with their attendant conflicts and destruction of Buddhist monasteries, and the unfavorable climate make this impossible.

SUMMARY

In the preceding pages, we have tried to describe the role which the Buddhist monasteries played in the industrial and commercial life of T'ang China. Such economic activities were quite considerable, and resulted in the Buddhist sangha's being included with the nobility and the rich and powerful families as the economic power structure of the empire. This economic power was mainly based on the sangha's possession of land. The income derived from the land, which the monasteries acquired through donations, purchase, and foreclosures of mortgages, enabled the Buddhist monasteries to carry on many of their commercial activities. This income, together with the goods donated by the faithful, constituted the capital for the Inexhaustible Treasuries established in many of the monasteries. The capital produced interest, the interest was added to the capital to produce further income; the process continued automatically. It is this feature that led

[141] *Ibid.*

French scholar J. Gernet to conclude that the Buddhist saṅgha was responsible for the introduction of modern capitalistic practice in China, with its productive use of capital and the automatic accumulation of interest.[142] However, he was careful to point out the religious origin of this innovation, the Buddhist theory of gifts to the saṅgha, which held that such gifts would be productive of meritorious karma for the donor. It was this theory that prompted the Chinese to donate land, oil presses, or water mills to the monasteries. The profits derived from these sources were then used by the monasteries for the furtherance of the law in China.

In their operation of these economic and commercial enterprises, the Buddhist monasteries acted no differently from the nobility and the rich and powerful families of the empire. As landowners, for instance, they required their tenants to pay the prevailing land rentals, and as lenders of goods or money, they exacted the same exorbitant rates of interest as did private individuals. By being an integral part of the economic power structure of the Chinese empire, the Buddhist monasteries with their economic and commercial activities represented yet another aspect of the process that took place in the acculturation of the saṅgha in China.

[142] Gernet, *op.cit.*, 223.

FIVE

LITERARY LIFE

IF ONE were to read the works of the T'ang poets, he would find that many of them, who were also officials in the government, were attracted to Buddhism because the religion offered an avenue of escape from the ills of the world. Such ills were usually taken to refer to the honors, power, prestige, and emoluments accruing from officialdom and political authority. These men had spent long years and arduous labor in preparing for the civil service examinations, and after having successfully passed them, had been appointed to office in the government bureaucracy. As literati and officials they were the ornaments of their families and the elite of Chinese society. Yet these men knew only too well that such honors and authority were so often dependent on the whims and vagaries of the persons at the top of the government structure. Time and again, officials had been demoted and banished to distant regions of the empire because of their involvement with chief ministers who had just been toppled from their offices by their rivals in the power struggle around the throne. In extreme cases, some of them had even been executed. During the ninth century, for instance, the political struggle between the Li clan (Li Chi-fu and his son Li Te-yü), Niu Seng-ju, Yang Ssu-fu, and P'ei Chi left their scars on the careers of numerous scholar-officials, including Po Chü-i, whom we shall discuss in greater detail later on. To these men, officialdom was indeed fraught with impending dangers and risks at all times, and it comes as no surprise therefore that in their poetry they expressed their desire to take refuge in Buddhism to get away from earthly struggles.

In one of his poems, Wang Wei (701-761)[1] wrote:

[1] *HTS* 202.10b-11a; *CTS* 190B.3a-4a.

Since I vowed to follow a vegetarian diet,
I have no more entanglements with worldly affairs.
I regard the fame and honor of officialdom as
superficial,
I live as I please, unshackled by external fetters.[2]

Or as Liu Yü-hsi (772-843),[3] expressed it: "Who does not
wish to be free from the fetters of rank and status?"[4]

When these poets wrote about withdrawal from earthly
struggles, they had in mind primarily the life of a recluse living in a Buddhist monastery far away from human habitation.
This was the ideal place to live, in the deep valleys of the high
mountains, amidst whispering trees and singing waterfalls,
with birds or wild animals as companions. Free from the attachments and the competition that entangle life in the
crowded cities, they could roam the mountains at will and let
their spirits wander with the clouds. Such sentiments are expressed in the following poems. Liu Yü-hsi, for example, in
a poem presented to the monk Yüan-chien wrote:

To you, who are like a solitary cloud coming out
freely from the mountain cavern,
Any famous scenic mountain serves as your refuge.[5]

Or Wang Wei again:

Monk Ch'ung-fan! Monk Ch'ung-fan!
You left in autumn to go to Mt. Fu-fu,
Now it is spring and you have not yet returned.
[You must be fascinated by] the bustling scene of
falling flowers and singing birds,
[You must be enjoying] the solitude, surrounded
by brooks and mountains just outside your door
and window.

[2] *T'ang Wang Yu-ch'eng chi* 4.15b, SPTK ed.
[3] HTS 168.3b-6a; CTS 160.9b-11b.
[4] *Liu Meng-te wen-chi* 7.4b, SPTK ed. Liu had served at various
times as governor of Ho-chou in Anhui, Ju-chou in Honan, and T'ung-
chou in Shensi.
[5] *Ibid.*, 7.14b.

Surrounded by hills, who cares anything about
the affairs of the world?
As the city dwellers gaze into the distance,
They see nothing but peaks covered with clouds.[6]

And another poem written by the same author while he was
at Kan-hua Monastery:

In this quiet valley one hears nothing but the
gentle sighing of pines,
In the recesses of the mountains there is no crying
of birds.
When one opens the door, one sees the snow-
covered mountains clearly delineated.
The singing of the golden brook permeates the
forest.[7]

Another poem, again by Wang Wei, describing a night spent
in the mountains:

In the secluded mountains, after a recent rainfall,
The air has the coolness of late autumn.
[You can see] the moon shining through the pine trees,
[You can hear] the clear spring water flowing over
the rocks.[8]

And another by Meng Hao-jan (689-765)[9] extolling the joys
of solitude and leisure which Monk Fu enjoys while living in
his retreat:

Where he lives is indeed most elegantly secluded,
And the people who live there have all attained
tranquility.
Dense groves of bamboo line both sides of the road,
The clear brook flows by the hut.
How free and relaxed is the monk,

[6] *T'ang Wang Yu-ch'eng chi* 1.12b.
[7] *Ibid.*, 5.19b.   [8] *Ibid.*, 3.10b.
[9] Biography in *HTS* 203.3ab; *CTS* 190C.2b.

Having abandoned all the worry and anxiety of the
    world,
The four meditations unite him with Suchness
So that he regards everything as illusory.[10]

These poems were usually written for monks living in their
mountain retreats, or after they themselves had enjoyed the
beautiful natural scenery of the secluded monasteries, watch-
ing the autumn moon rear its golden disk over the pine trees.
To these poets, life in the Buddhist monasteries exemplified
the spirit of solitude, leisure, and tranquility that they loved
so much but could not find amidst their official duties.

Among the T'ang poets mentioned above, Wang Wei enjoyed the closest connections with Buddhism. Wang was
famous as a poet and a painter, and the eminent literatus Su
Shih once said of him that in his poetry there is a painting,
and in his painting there is poetry. As an indication of his attachment to Buddhism, he took upon himself the *tzu* of Mo-
chieh, after the famous Buddhist layman Vimalakīrti, or Wei
Mo-chieh. After his wife died in 734, he refused to remarry
and chose to live a celibate life to exemplify his devotion to
Buddhism. Upon the death of his mother in 742, he converted
his villa and garden in Lan-t'ien to a monastery and donated
it to the saṅgha.[11] In the collection of his writings may be
found numerous pieces, such as memorials to the throne giving thanks for the imperial favor in bestowing inscriptions on
Buddhist monasteries, eulogies to the Buddha of the Western
Paradise, or biographical inscriptions of famous monks.[12]

We have already referred to examples of Wang's poetical
allusions to Buddhist monasteries. Other pieces are dedicated
to monks he met, or given over to expressions of sentiments
experienced in visiting famous monasteries. In his later years
he withdrew from society to while away the time in the leisurely company of monks and to immerse himself in Ch'an

[10] *Meng Hao-jan chi* 1.2b, *SPTK* ed.
[11] *CTW* 324.16a.
[12] For the eulogies to the Western Paradise, see *CTW* 325.15a;
325.17b.

meditation. Here is one example, entitled "Offering Food to a Monk from Mt. Fu-fu":

> Late in life I have come to know the principle of
>   purity and quietude,
> Daily I keep away from crowds of people.
> I am waiting for a monk from the distant mountains,
>   and have swept my hut beforehand.
> As expected, he actually came from his cloudy abode
>   to pay a visit to my isolated hut.
> I spread out the mat, and fed him with pine seeds,
> We burn incense and read the Buddhist books.
> When the day is almost done, we light our lamps,
> And in the evening, we strike the musical stones.
> Once we realize the joys of quietude
> We know that this life has more than its share of
>   tranquil leisure.
> What need is there to insist upon seeking refuge in
>   remote seclusion,
> For I as yet am one unaffected by worldly
>   involvements.[13]

Here is one written while he was visiting Hsiang-chi Monastery:

> Not knowing the location of Hsiang-chi Monastery,
> I walk several *li* over cloud-covered peaks
> And thru forests of ancient trees never treaded by
>   human feet.
> Whence come the peals of bells in the deep hills?
> The spring water gurgles as it is blocked by jutting
>   rocks,
> The sun shines, but it is cool in the shade of the
>   green pines.
> In the evening, by the side of the quiet pool,
> I sit in meditation, to drive away the poisonous dragon
>   (of disturbing thoughts).[14]

---

[13] *T'ang Wang Yu-ch'eng chi* 4.15a.
[14] *Ibid.*, 4.20a.

It would, of course, be a Herculean task to trace the role of Buddhism in the poetry and prose of the major T'ang literary luminaries, let alone the host of minor figures. For our purpose, I shall concentrate on one person, Po Chü-i (772-846), and let him stand as the best possible example of the role which Buddhism played in his literary output. I have chosen Po primarily because the literature on his relations with Buddhism is much more ample and readily available than it is with some of the other T'ang literary figures.[15] A recent study by the Japanese Hirano Kenshō, entitled *Haku Kyoi no bungaku to Bukkyō, Ōtani-daigaku kenkyū nempō* (Kyoto 1964), pp. 119-187, has been specially useful.

The details of Po's life and the times in which he lived have already been made known to western readers by Arthur Waley's work, *The Life and Times of Po Chü-i* (London 1949), and there is no need to repeat what Waley has so successfully done. However, it would be worthwhile to have a chronological table of the main events in Po's life, for such a table would assist considerably in following the events discussed in this chapter.

772 First month, twentieth day: born in Hsin-cheng, a small town in modern Honan.
776 At age 5-6: learned to compose poetry.
794 Fifth month, twenty-eighth day: father, Po Chi-keng, died in Hsiang-yang.
800 Passed *chin-shih* examination, ranked 4th among 17.
803 Passed a sort of placement examination known as *p'an-pa-ts'ui* together with another scholar named Yüan Chen, who became his closest friend.
803 Appointed collator of text in the palace library, at salary of 16,000 cash a month.
806 Resigned from post as collator, retired to Hua-yang Monastery with Yüan Chen to prepare for palace examination.
806 Passed palace examination, appointed director of administration at Chou-chih.
807 Member of Han-lin Academy.
808 Set subjects for essays in literary examinations.
808 Imperial censor of the left, salary 25,000 cash. Remained in post until 810. Very active in public affairs. Enjoyed support of Chief Minister P'ei Chi (765-813).

[15] For Po's biography, see *HTS* 119.4a-6a; *CTS* 166.9a-20a. See also E. Feifel, biography of Po Chü-i, *Monumenta Serica* 17 (1958), 255-311.

808 Married a girl surnamed Yang.
809 Daughter Chin-luan born.
810 Intendant of metropolitan finances, salary 40,000-50,000 cash a month. Held office until 811.
811 Mother died. Mourning period of three years spent at Hsia-kuei.
814 Assistant secretary to crown prince. Held office until 815.
815 Appointed marshal of Chiang-chou. Salary 60,000-70,000 cash a month, plus several hundred piculs of grains. Held office until 818.
817 Built grass hut in Lu-shan.
818 Appointed governor of Chung-chou in Szechuan.
820 Left Chung-chou to return to Ch'ang-an.
820 Assistant secretary in control of Customs Barriers.
820 First secretary in Bureau of Guests.
820 Received honorary title, grand pillar of state, which accorded him the status of an official of the second rank.
822 Appointed governor of Hang-chou, remained there until 824.
824 Returned to Lo-yang to become chief gentleman in waiting to the crown prince.
825 Appointed governor of Su-chou, remained in post until 826, when he resigned because of ill-health.
827 Went to Ch'ang-an to become president of palace library.
828 Became vice-president of Board of Punishments.
829 Returned to Lo-yang to become social secretary to crown prince. Remained in Lo-yang to end of life.
830 Appointed governor of Ho-nan. This was the title, but in reality, the post was like the mayor of Lo-yang.
833 Resumed post of social secretary to crown prince in Lo-yang.
835 Presented a collection of his writings to Tung-lin Monastery in Lu-shan.
835 Appointed governor of T'ung-chou, but declined, and was then appointed junior tutor to crown prince in Lo-yang, salary 100,000 cash a month.
836 Presented a collection of his writings to Sheng-shan Monastery in Lo-yang.
839 Completed library in Nan-ch'an Monastery in Su-chou, then presented a collection of his works to library.
840 Presented collection of works written in Lo-yang to Hsiang-shan Monastery in Lung-men.
841 Retired from civil service, retirement to take place officially at the beginning of the next year, with rank of president of the Board of Punishments.
846 Died in Lo-yang, buried in Lung-men. Posthumous title, vice-president of the Office of State Affairs.

As this study is concerned with the role of Buddhism in the literary life of the Chinese, we shall examine the relations between Po and Buddhist monks, what effects such relationships had on Po's poetry and his outlook toward life, and how this experience with Buddhism was manifested in Po's poetry.

The earliest indication of association with Buddhism is to be found in a poem sent to a monk acquaintance named Ming-chun.[16]

> After sunset the whole world is cool,
> And after a rain, mountains and rivers are clear.
> The prevailing wind comes from the west,
> The sounds of autumn are congealed in the
>   sounds of grasses and trees.
> I feel the rapidity of passing years,
> And lament the fading away of material things.
> Who would feel distressed
> Seeing how the seasons affect man's emotions?
> Let me ask the philosopher of the Gateway to
>   the Void.[17]
> What method is there to practice,
> Which will cause me to abandon the desires for
>   gain
> And not cause vexations to arise?[18]

This poem, composed in 800[19] expresses the universal emotion of melancholy evoked by the desolate autumnal scenery, and the agitations of the mind accompanying such melancholy. He is disturbed by the inevitable succession of autumns, and he seeks the help of a Buddhist acquaintance for some secret to quell these mental perturbations. I think we can safely assume that Po had already read about Buddhism, knew something of its teachings about the four truths of misery and the suppression of misery, and was tentatively searching in his own mind whether or not this was the religion for him. Probably of about the same time was another

[16] For some details concerning this monk, see *SKSC* 27, *T* 50.880c-881a.

[17] *k'ung-men*, a reference to the Buddhist doctrine of the transitoriness and evanescence of all life.

[18] *CCC* 9.13b, *SPTK* ed.

[19] On the dating of Po's poems, I have followed the chronology given in Hanabusa Hideki, *Haku Shi monjū no hihan teki kenkyū* (Kyoto 1960). For this poem, see 515.

peom that indicates Po's awareness of the transitoriness of life. This one is about poenies, and is addressed to a monk named Cheng-i.

> Today the red peonies in front of my steps,
> Some are beginning to fade, some are beginning to
>   bloom.
> When they bloom, I do not understand why they are
>   so beautiful,
> For when they fade, we realize that they are like
>   phantom bodies.
> How far is it from here to the Gateway to the Void?
> With these faded flowers, let me come and ask you.[20]

Here again, as in the poem mentioned previously, Po indicates that he has been thinking about the nature and meaning of man's life on earth and that he is looking toward Buddhism for some answers to his quest for salvation. In this quest, he was assisted by a monk named Ning-kung or Fa-ning of the Sheng-shan Monastery in Lo-yang, who gave him (ca. 800-801) eight characters considered to be the essence of the Buddhist discipline. So impressed was Po with this instruction that in 804, a year after Fa-ning's death, he composed a piece entitled *Pa-chien-chieh*, together with a preface which tells of his previous meeting with the monk. The eight characters are *kuan*, insight; *chüeh*, perception; *ting*, concentration; *hui*, wisdom; *ming*, understanding; *t'ung*, penetration; *chi*, salvation; and *she*, renunciation.

kuan

> With the inward eye looking at the external
>   world
> Where does the external world come from?
> And where does it disappear to?
> Looking at it again and again,
> One distinguishes between the inner and
>   outer world [between true and false].

[20] *CCC* 13.21a; Hanabusa, *op.cit.*, 525.

chüeh

Only the inner world [truth] is constant,
  but it is concealed by the outer world
  [falsehood],
If the true and the false are distinguished,
Then perception arises.
Without abandoning the external world
One grasps the real inner world.

ting

If the true inner world is not eradicated,
Then the false external world would not
  arise,
The source of the six senses
Is as clear as still water.
This is concentration
Which enables one to escape from *saṁsāra*.

hui

To enlighten with concentration
Then concentration would still have
  attachments.
To rescue with enlightenment
Then wisdom has no impediments.
It is like a pearl in a bowl.
When the bowl is still, the pearl shines.

ming

When concentration and wisdom are joined,
Then there is understanding.
When understanding illumines the outside
  world,
The world has nothing to conceal any more.
Just as a large round mirror
Reflects an image without being affected by it.

t'ung

With wisdom there is understanding,
This understanding is not obscure.
With understanding there is penetration,
This penetration is without obstacles.
Who is the one with unimpeded freedom?
He is the master of all change.

chi

The power of penetration is not constant
It changes in response to thought.
The characteristic of change is not existent
It appears in response to seekings.
When great compassion is manifested
Then one can rescue the many.

she

When all misery has been relieved,
Great compassion is also abandoned.
Since misery is not real
Then compassion is also false.
Therefore among all sentient beings,
There is really no one saved.[21]

In this work, Po outlines his interpretation of the various stages of mental cultivation. By cultivating insight, one becomes aware of the difference between the true and the false, between the external and the internal world. This awareness of the difference between the inner and outer world leads to the perception that the inner world alone is real and true. When this perception is attained, then there is concentration, which enables one to escape from the cycle of life and death. Concentration leads to wisdom, the wisdom that is like the gem in a bowl which shines forth when the bowl is still. With wisdom comes the understanding that is like a mirror, which

[21] *CCC* 22.10b-11b; Hanabusa, *op.cit.*, 559.

reflects all external objects without being affected by them. With understanding comes penetration, a mental state without impediments. With penetration comes salvation. The mind develops great compassion that aims at the salvation of the many from misery. However, after the mind has developed this compassion, it soon realizes that compassion and misery are both false, and that in the final analysis no one is saved. Po thus ends up in a state of equanimity or an impartial attitude toward the external world, which he considers to be false and nonexistent. He shows that he has learned the Mahāyāna and especially the Ch'an lesson by concluding that though sentient beings appear to be saved, in reality they are not saved at all because they are nonexistent in the first place. Though he comprehended this lesson intellectually, it appeared that he never achieved it in actual life, for up to the end of his life, he continued to show compassion for his fellow men, and emphasized this virtue in his poems.

In this poem we witness the determination of Po to gain greater understanding of Buddhism. At the same time, he was struggling through the competitive examinations to advance in officialdom. These two currents were to play important roles in the early period of his life.

Po Chü-i and his dear friend Yüan Chen (779-831)[22] decided to stand for the palace examination in 806, and to pre-

---

[22] Biography in *HTS* 174.2b-6a; *CTS* 166.1a-9a. Yüan was descended from the Tartar imperial family which ruled over north China during the Northern Wei dynasty (386-534). After the downfall of the dynasty, the family settled in Lo-yang and became thoroughly Sinicized. Yüan was a brilliant child who composed poetry at an early age and who passed the metropolitan examination when he was only fourteen, the earliest age that a candidate could come up for the examination. Ever since he and Po passed the placement examination in 803, the two formed a friendship which became one of the most famous in Chinese history. During his lifetime, Yüan served in various capacities as collator of texts in the palace library, inspecting censor, president of the Han-lin Academy, president of the Board of Rites, president of the Board of Revenues, and chief minister. Somewhat impulsive by nature, he antagonized many people in court and was exiled to distant posts a number of times.

pare for it, they went into retirement to the Hua-yang Monastery (Taoist) in Ch'ang-an. They lived in seclusion for several months, spending their time mostly in writing. In all, Po wrote seventy-five essays on contemporary problems. One of these essays discussed Buddhism and the clergy. It was written entirely from the viewpoint of a Confucian and contained some critical remarks against Buddhism and the conduct of monks.

As your minister humbly examines this religion [Buddhism], we may say that meditation and concentration are its roots, compassion and tolerance its base, rewards and punishments its branches, and vegetarian feasts and rules of discipline its leaves. There are some points in the religion which can attract people and assist in spreading the kingly way. However, your minister also considers that it is unacceptable for several reasons. Your minister has learned that the Son of Heaven receives the mandate from Heaven, and the myriad people receive the mandate from the Son of Heaven. When the mandates are in harmony, there is reason; when they are divided, there is confusion. If we interpose a foreign religion, wouldn't that create confusion even more? Moreover, our country uses force to pacify rebellions, and relies on the literary arts to rule the Flowery Kingdom. By grasping these two methods, we are able to regulate and control the people.

Now here comes this unimportant foreign religion which competes against the Son of Heaven. I am afraid that it will pervert the supreme culture without peer of our ancestors. Moreover, in our kingly teachings may be found all the roots, bases, branches, and leaves [of Buddhism]; why is it necessary for people to forego this and seek after that?

If one wishes to restore his nature through meditation and concentration, then the ancient sages taught the way of respectful quietude and nonactivity.[23] If one wishes to deepen his virtue with compassion and tolerance, then our

[23] Taoism.

191

ancient sages gave the instructions for loyalty, reciprocity, and commiseration.[24] If one wishes to prevent human perversities by a system of rewards and punishments, then our ancient sages had laws for punishing the evil and encouraging the meritorious.[25] If one wishes to suppress the sensual pleasures by vegetarian feasts and the rules of discipline, then our ancient sages had the ceremonies for avoiding the passions and pacifying the unorthodox.[26] Though we investigate Buddhism to the end, we find that its goals are the same as ours. It is probable that Buddhism can assist in spreading the kingly way, but since it appears under another name, then its foreign practices will breed divided loyalty. For this reason, I consider the foreign religion to be unacceptable.

Moreover, the monks and their followers are increasing and the Buddhist monasteries are getting extravagant with the passage of time. Man's labor is spent in the construction of monasteries, while people's profits are wasted in gold and precious adornments. The relations of prince and parent are transformed to that of disciple and master, husband and wife are separated by the rules of discipline. The ancients say that if one male does not farm, someone will be hungry; if one female does not weave, someone will be cold. Now the number of monks and nuns is countless, all depending on the farmer for food and the silk industry for clothing. My humble opinion is that the woes of the empire since the Chin, Sung, Ch'i, and Liang dynasties are in all probability due to this religion. I respectfully ask your Majesty to look into this matter.[27]

When Po wrote this critical essay against Buddhism in 806, he had already befriended several monks, written laudatory verses to them, and commenced his practice of mental discipline. Then why this two-faced attitude toward Buddhism?

[24] Confucianism.
[25] The Legalists.
[26] The Mohists.
[27] *CCC* 48.21a-22a; Hanabusa, *op.cit.*, 595.

The most plausible explanation appears to be that in writing this critical essay, Po was fulfilling the role of the Confucian official advising the emperor on state policy concerning the social and political problems of the times, and in this role had to repeat the standard arguments against Buddhism.

After passing the palace examination in 806, Po was appointed an official in the Chou-chih prefecture west of Ch'ang-an. He was now on his way up the bureaucratic ladder. In 807 appeared a poem addressed to the monk Wen-ch'ang, who traveled widely all over China preaching wherever he went. This monk hobnobbed with such leading literary figures as Han Yü (768-824),[28] and Liu Tsung-yüan (773-819),[29] and his poetry, which was concerned with the harmonization of Buddhism and Confucianism, was widely appreciated by the Chinese literati. In this poem, Po wrote that one who attains to the way of Buddhism is without attachment to external things, and that his mind becomes devoid of content when he sits in meditation during the night.[30]

Sometime around 808 or 809, Po wrote a farewell poem to a monk named Hsüan in which he compared the cleric to the lotus which grows out of the water but is not attached to the water, and praises him for his pure conduct and unsullied character.[31]

In 811, after the death of his mother, Po returned to Hsia-kuei to pass the period of mourning. Soon afterward, another misfortune struck when his only child, a daughter of three, died. In this period of grief, Po turned for solace to Buddhism and practiced Ch'an meditation under a master named Heng-chi. This master is mentioned in two poems written around 815. In one, Po wrote:

All my friends are scattered, and my acquaintances
   are getting fewer and fewer,
Such are the things that sadden my heart.

[28] Biography in *HTS* 176.1a-9b.
[29] Biography in *HTS* 168.6a-12a; *CTS* 160.11b-12a.
[30] *CCC* 13.15a; Hanabusa, *op.cit.*, 524.
[31] *CCC* 14.11a; Hanabusa, *op.cit.*, 528.

I practice meditation together with the Ch'an master,
And dispel all my worries and anxiety through
concentration.[32]

The other poem reads as follows:

Everyone is running away like mad to escape the
heat,
Only the Ch'an master does not leave his room.
It must be that no heat ever reaches the Ch'an room,
For as long as the mind is tranquil the body
will be cool.[33]

This period of grief coincided with misfortunes that befell
his closest friend, Yüan Chen. In 809, Yüan's wife died, and
in the same year, Yüan was exiled to a minor post in Chiang-
ling in Hupeh because of his political involvement in an incident concerning the mayor of Lo-yang.[34] After arrival in
Chiang-ling, Yüan wrote back to Po about his depressed
mood in the south. In answer to Yüan, Po wrote a long piece
consoling him, and suggested that he might find solace in
reading such Buddhist scriptures as the *Vimalakīrti, Saddharmapuṇḍarīka*, and the *Dhammapada*. He specifically
recommended that "if one wishes to eradicate grief and sorrow, one should read the Ch'an sutras. One should realize
that all things are empty, and not allow thoughts to be attached to anything."[35] In the same year, while attempting to
console Yüan, Po wrote another poem referring to Buddhism:

[32] *CCC* 15.9a; Hanabusa, *op.cit.*, 531.

[33] *CCC* 15.15b; Hanabusa, *op.cit.*, 533.

[34] It appeared that the mayor of Lo-yang had cast aspersions on the
character of a student, causing the latter to commit suicide. Yüan, who
was head of the Inspectorate Office in Lo-yang at the time, overstepped
his official powers and sought to remove the mayor from office. For
this, Yüan was ordered to leave Lo-yang and return to Ch'ang-an, and
after a few days in the capital, was exiled to Chiang-ling. See Waley,
Life, p. 70.

[35] *CCC* 14.21a; 24ab; Hanabusa, *op.cit.*, 530. This was written in 810.

Your tears shed at night melt away, known only to
   the moonlight shining thru the curtains,
Heart-broken while thinking of happiness in the past
   spent in the peony garden.
There is no medicine to cure such ills of the world,
Except reading the four chapters of the *Lankāvatāra*.[36]

In 811, while still in Hsia-kuei observing the mourning
period and weeping so much that his eyes suffered, Po again
referred to Buddhism.

> Though I am only forty years old,
> My mind is like that of a seventy-year-old.
> I have heard that in Buddhism,
> There is a gateway to emancipation,
> Where I can repose the mind, so that it
>   becomes like still water,
> And regard the body like floating clouds.

[36] *CCC* 14.3a; Hanabusa, *op.cit.*, 526.

The *Lankāvatāra* is one of the important texts of Mahāyāna Buddhism, and contains teachings which are generally attributed to the
Mind-Only School of Buddhism (*Wei-shih* in Chinese and Vijñānavāda
in Sanskrit). Lanka is usually identified as Ceylon, so that the title
means Descent into Ceylon. The sutra consists of a dialogue between
the Buddha and one of his chief bodhisattvas, Mahāmati.

Altogether four translations of the sutra have been made into Chinese.
The earliest was by Dharmaraksha; this translation is now lost. The
second was done by Gunabhadra in four *chüan*, completed in 443; the
third consisting of ten *chüan* was made by Bodhiruci in 513, and the
fourth in seven *chüan* by Śikshānanda in 704. All are still extant. When
Po Chü-i wrote of reading the *Lankāvatāra* in four chapters, he was
referring to the Gunabhadra translation.

The sutra emphasizes the doctrine of inner realization, which is
equivalent to enlightenment. In the case of one who has achieved this
inner realization, he is no longer subject to any dualistic thinking.
Dualism arises when the individual does not perceive the truth that all
things are empty, uncreated, and do not possess any individual characteristics. When the individual realizes the *śūnya* nature of all things,
he transcends mental discriminations and attains the absolute truth,
the absolute truth that is beyond words and analytical reasoning. See
D. T. Suzuki, *Studies in the Lankavatarasutra* (London 1957), ch. 1.

Shaking off my dust-covered clothing,
I will escape the rounds of rebirth.
Why should I be attached to this misery,
And still shrink from moving ahead to
  embrace Buddhism?
Thinking it over, I make a fervent wish,
I wish that this present body,
Will only reap the rewards of past karma,
And not serve as a future cause.
I vow that with the waters of wisdom and
  knowledge,
I will forever wash away the dust of passion.
I will not let this seed of loving passion,
Plant the roots of any more sorrow or grief.[37]

Po's sorrow over the death of his daughter is the subject of two poems written in 813. In one of these, he wrote:

The substance of form is originally not real,
Only the ether accidentally coalese to form the body,
Affection is fundamentally folly,
We are brought together temporarily by destiny to
  become relatives.[38]

The progress (or lack of it) Po made in the practice of Buddhism is described in a poem written in 814, while he was still at Hsia-kuei:

From the time I turned to the Way,
To the present it is already six or seven years.
I have forged the nature that is without comparison,
I have exhausted entirely the myriad of karmic causes.
Only the fire of affection is left,
Frequently harassing and burning me.
Could it be that the medicine is without effect?

---

[37] *CCC* 10.13b-14a. The expression *shih-shen ju fou-yün* (*a*) is very likely based on the passage *shih-shen ju fou-yün* (*b*) found in *Vimala-kīrti*, *T* 14.539b.
[38] *CCC* 10.9a.

Or is it that my vices are so numerous that they cannot
be totally cleansed?[39]

In these poems written during the period of mourning, we
get a glimpse of Po's views that the body is the root of all passions, that it is only a temporary aggregation of ether without
form or content, and that there is no use in mourning over the
death of such an entity. It is needless to point out that these
views are undoubtedly influenced by Buddhism.

Po returns to his practice of Ch'an meditation in another
very long poem addressed to two friends, Ch'ien Hui (755-
829) and Ts'ui Ch'ün (772-832), vice-president of the Board
of Rites, written in 814. At the very end of this piece,
he wrote:

Now I have more leisure to meet with my kindred
friends,
[But] on account of my sickness I serve the medicine
king.
To pacify my mental perturbations I take refuge in
meditation and concentration,
To preserve my spirit, I enter into the practice of
sitting and forgetting.
To cut off folly, I seek the sword of wisdom,
In order to save myself from misery and attain
salvation.[40]

This poem provides an interesting glimpse into the activities of Po during this period of mourning. Apparently he was
occupying himself with both Buddhist and Taoist practices
and literature, for his mention of the medicine king is a reference to the Buddhist deity Bhāishajyaguru, and his allusion
to the sword of wisdom cutting off ignorance and folly is a
standard Buddhist expression. The bodhisattva of wisdom,
Mañjuśrī, holds a sword in his hand. However, along with
Buddhist concentration, he also mentions the Taoist practice
of sitting and forgetting.

[39] *CCC* 10.14b; Hanabusa, *op.cit.*, 517.
[40] *CCC* 15.4b; Hanabusa, *op.cit.*, 530.

Upon the termination of the period of mourning, Po accepted a lowly post in the capital as assistant secretary to the crown prince, and moved back to Ch'ang-an in 814. In 815, when he was 44, he wrote a long poem to his friend Li Chien (764-821) giving some details about his outlook toward life at the time and his devotion to Ch'an Buddhism.

> I am at present extremely lucky,
> Luckier really than the former sages.
> I am already forty-four years old,
> And am an official of the fifth degree.
> This makes me feel a sense of contentment,
> I also have that which gives me security.
> In my early years
> I patterned my life according to the *Hsiao-yao*
>   chapter in *Chuang-tzu*.
> In recent years I have directed my mind
> Toward the meditation of the Southern School
>   of Ch'an.
> Without, I follow the practices of the world,
> Within, I escape the entanglements of my
>   immediate circle.
> Abroad, I do not dislike the court and public
>   places,
> At home, I do not crave for the company of men.
> Ever since I felt this way,
> Wherever I go, I am at peace.
> Physically I do not need to practice breathing
>   exercises to feel comfortable,
> Mentally I do not need to travel amidst rivers
>   and lakes to relax.
> When I am exhilarated, perhaps I drink some
>   wine,
> When I am unoccupied, I usually shut myself in.
> I sit silently until the depth of night,
> I sleep peacefully until the sun is high.
> In the autumn I do not consider the long nights
>   as misery,

In the spring I do not regret the rapid passage
   of years.
I transcend the considerations of age,
I am unmindful of the confines of birth and death.
Yesterday I talked together with you,
I feel we were so confiding with each other.
Now this Tao cannot be talked about,
But with you, I cannot help but say a few words.[41]

Po's excursion into Ch'an during these years is also noted in
a long piece written in 819, entitled *Ch'uan-fa-t'ang pei*. Here
he wrote that he received instructions on Ch'an under a master named Wei-k'uan (755-817) of the Hsing-shan Monastery
in Ch'ang-an. Wei-k'uan's master was Ma-tsu Tao-i (d. 788),
a disciple of Huai-jang, who in turn was a disciple of the sixth
patriarch Hui-neng. Wei-k'uan was already proficient in the
teachings of T'ien-t'ai before he came under the influence of
Ma-tsu. After embracing Ch'an, Wei-k'uan traveled extensively to preach before settling down in the capital. In his
travels, he is said to have tamed a tiger, received ordination
with a mountain spirit, and overcome a demon. In the capital,
his disciples numbered over a thousand, of which thirty-nine
were said to be excellent. It was when Po was assistant secretary that he received instructions from Wei-k'uan. The interchange between master and pupil is preserved by Po.

First question by Po: "Since you call yourself a Ch'an master, why do you preach?" The master answered, "The
highest enlightenment, when applied to the body, is called
the rules of discipline; when preached by the mouth, it is
called the doctrine; and when enacted in the mind, it is
called Ch'an. There are three applications, but in reality
they are one. It is like rivers and lakes with different names,
but the nature of the water is the same. The rules of discipline are the doctrine, the doctrine is not separated from
Ch'an. Why do you wrongly make a distinction between

[41] *CCC* 6.21ab; Hanabusa, *op.cit.*, 508. Po wrote the biographical inscription on the tombstone of Li Chien. See *CCC* 24.1b-4b.

them?" Second question by Po: "Since there is no distinction, then why do you cultivate the mind?" The master replied, "Originally there is nothing wrong with your mind, so why do you wish to cultivate it? You must never allow any thought to arise, regardless of whether it is tainted or pure." Third question by Po: "It is all right not to have tainted thoughts but is it wrong to have pure thoughts?" The master replied, "Nothing should be allowed to lodge in a man's eye. Gold dust is valuable, but when it is lodged in the eye, it is still painful." Fourth question by Po: "If I do not cultivate the mind and harbor no thoughts, then how am I different from an ordinary person?" The master replied, "The ordinary person is ignorant. The followers of the two vehicles (Hīnayāna and Mahāyāna) are bound to attachments. The true discipline is separated from these two defective ways. The one who practices the true discipline does not strive, nor does he cease mental action. Striving leads to attachment, and cessation of mental action ends in ignorance."[42]

In 815, political unrest shook the capital Ch'ang-an. Chief Minister Wu Yüan-heng was assassinated, and the memorial which Po presented to the throne demanding quick action to apprehend the assassins aroused the ire of his political enemies, with the result that he was exiled to the inferior post of marshal of Chiang-chou in Kiangsi.[43] This event was a major turning point in Po's life, and was responsible for a shift in his attitude toward the objectives of versifying. After years of active participation in government affairs right in the capital and vicinity, Po was now banished to a distant minor post in the provinces. To him, this was a demotion, and he must have felt discouraged over his failure in the political forum. His thoughts therefore turned to nature and the enjoyment of the leisurely life; he decided to treat his exile as a sort of semi-retirement from struggle in the political arena. In turn, this

[42] *CCC* 24.13ab.
[43] For an account of these events, see Waley, *Life*, 101-104.

affected his ideas concerning the role of poetry. Heretofore, he had been a fervent supporter of the Confucian ideal of poetry—i.e., the real value of poetry lies in its political and moral lessons hidden under the cloak of satire or allegory, lessons that should serve as the guide for virtuous rulers. Poetry should be concerned with the political and social grievances of the age, and should aim at reforming these grievances; it should, as he puts it, bring the suffering of the humble to the ears of the emperor.[44]

In Chiang-chou, far removed from the mainstream of events in the capital, Po concluded that it was futile for him to try to wield political and moral influence through his poems, and he wisely decided to versify on things that he could enjoy most in that area, leisure, mountains, waterfalls, the autumn moon, landscape, etc.[45]

The area surrounding Chiang-chou was admirably suited for this purpose, for not far away was Lu-shan, already famous for its superb sceneries and Buddhist monasteries. In these monasteries, where memories of the pure and simple lives of Hui-yüan and his followers were still preserved, Po found a congenial group of monks with whom he practiced Ch'an meditation and from whom he learned the Pure Land doctrines. To enjoy the beautiful landscape of Lu-shan to the utmost, he built a grass hut on the mountain to which he repaired whenever he could spare the time from his official duties in Chiang-chou.

In a letter to his friend Yüan Chen in 817, just after a housewarming party in his grass hut, Po wrote that after three years in Chiang-chou, his mind was completely at ease, and listed three reasons for this condition. First, he was enjoying good health and the company of his family and relatives. Second, his salary was sufficient to feed the large number of mouths in the family, and the food, especially fish and

---

[44] Such views concerning poetry are written down in a long letter by Po to Yüan Chen in 815. See *CCC* 28.2a-13a, parts of which are translated in Waley, *Life,* 107-114.

[45] See his piece, "Chiang-chou ssu-ma t'ing-chi," in *CCC* 26.1b-3a, written in 818.

wine, was excellent. Finally, he listed the pleasure of living in his grass hut in Lu-shan:

> where the clouds and water, fountains and rocks, are more lovely than at any other place in the mountain. The situation delighted me so much that I built myself a cottage there. There is a group of pine trees in front of it and a fine cluster of tall bamboos. . . . Every time I go there to be alone for a few hours, the visit tends to prolong itself to one of many days, for everything that has always given me most pleasure is to be found in this very place. I forget all about going home and would be content to stay here till the end of my days. . . . Wei-chih, Wei-chih, the night I wrote this letter I was sitting in my cottage under a window that looks out to the mountains. I let my brush run on as it would, setting down my thoughts at random, just as they occurred to me. And now, as I make ready to seal the letter, I suddenly find that dawn has almost come. Looking out I see only a few monks, some sitting, some asleep. From above comes the sad cry of the mountain monkeys, and from below the twittering of the valley birds. Friend of all my life, 10,000 leagues away, thoughts of our days together in the world's dusty arena rise before me and for a moment quite blot out this lovely scene.[46]

The stimulating effects of this grass hut in particular and Lu-shan in general on his versifying is described in the following poem, written in 817:

> Ever since I practiced assiduously the method
>   leading to the Gateway to the Void,
> I have dispelled the various kinds of mental
>   perturbation up to now.
> Only the demon of poetry is not conquered.
> Whenever the gay moment arises, I take pleasure
>   to chant.[47]

[46] Waley, *Life*, 120-121, with slight changes. Original in *CCC* 28.21a-22a.
[47] *CCC* 16.27b.

Here Po felt that his predilection for versifying might be an obstacle to his becoming a good Buddhist, for in his poems he was too emotional and sentimental, and strongly attached to the beauties of nature and the feelings of man. This being so, he was afraid that he would never achieve the state of equanimity so highly valued by the Buddhists.

In the poems composed during this period in Chiang-chou, Po writes freely of the joys and contentment he found in his excursions to Lu-shan, while at the same time revealing some of the lessons he had learned from his Buddhist studies and his association with Buddhist monks. One might say that he was living the life of a devout Buddhist layman. In a poem dated 817, he wrote:

> The guest at Hsün-yang is a layman.
> His body is like the floating cloud,
>   and his mind is like ashes.[48]

In another poem to a monk named Lang of the Tung-lin Monastery in Lu-shan, he wrote in 817 that he had pulled out a strand of hair from his head and noticed that it was white. What to do about it?

> Since I do not possess the powers of an immortal,
> How can I escape this fate of old age and death?
> There is only the gateway to emancipation,
> Which can carry one over this decrepit and painful
>   peril.
> I cover the mirror and gaze at the Tung-lin
>   Monastery,
> Subduing my mind, I thank the masters of
>   meditation there.
> Why complain about infirmity and white hairs?
> I shave them off but still I do not regret.[49]

---

[48] *CCC* 17.7a. The reference to floating clouds is taken from *Vimalakīrti, T* 14.539b. He likens his mind to ashes because it is no more consumed by the fires of passion.

[49] *CCC* 10.24ab; Hanabusa, *op.cit.*, 518.

Another poem dating from this period in Chiang-chou contains some further Buddhist expressions and a reference to the Western Paradise of Amitābha. This poem was written in 818 just after the death of a Ch'an master named Shen-tsou[50] and contains the following lines:

> Originally we were united in a society for
>   enlightenment and burning incense,
> Because we reject the passions and this body,
>   which are like lightning and bubble.
> We need not be disappointed and we follow our
>   master,
> He will first go and ask the Western Paradise to
>   be my host.[51]

In these poems Po gives some indications of the influence of Buddhist ideas in his thinking. He faces the problem of old age and death with equanimity, and he is confident that his belief in Buddhism will lead him to conquer the cycle of repeated rebirths. He is also cognizant of the illusory nature of the material body, that it is changing every moment and therefore it is not an object worth clinging to. Finally we see Po beginning to take an interest in the Pure Land School. This interest was to grow with the passage of time, until in his old age Po was solely concerned with rebirth in the Western Paradise of Amitābha. That this interest was aroused in Chiang-chou and Lu-shan is not surprising. Lu-shan was the famous Buddhist center associated with Hui-yüan, who dur-

[50] Also called Tsou-kung and Hsing-kuo shang-jen, after the Hsing-kuo Monastery in Chiang-chou. Died 817. See *CCC* 25.17b.

[51] *CCC* 17.10a. In the inscription composed by Po after the death of Tsou-kung, the reading of this poem is slightly different. In the second line, instead of *wei* the reading is *kung*, and in the third line, instead of *ch'ou ch'ang*, the reading is *lüan lüan*, longingly. See *ibid.*, 24.19a. The expression *tien-p'ao-shen* is taken from *Vimalakīrti*, *T* 14.539b, where we find such passages as *shih-shen ju p'ao pu-te chiu-li*: "This body is like a bubble which cannot last long"; *shih-shen ju tien nien-nien pu-chu*: "This body is like lightning, which is constantly changing every moment."

ing his sojourn on the mountain organized a Pure Land Society consisting of some of the outstanding literary figures of the period who met periodically to utter their earnest wish to be reborn in the Western Paradise. The memory of this society was still strong in Lu-shan when Po was there.

This blissful existence in Lu-shan and Chiang-chou came to an end in 818 when Po was appointed governor of Chung-chou in Szechuan. From Chung-chou, he was then called back to Ch'ang-an for a number of posts in the central government, and in 822, he was appointed governor of Hang-chou. On his way to Hang-chou he stayed at his grass hut in Lu-shan.

In Hang-chou, one of the favorite spots visited by Po was the Wu-lin Mountain, where the famous Ling-yin and T'ien-chu Monasteries were located. Po himself wrote that during the 600 or so days he was in Hang-chou, he went to Wu-lin Mountain twelve times chiefly to admire and enjoy the flowers there.[52] In one poem, after praising the beauty of the flowers in Ling-yin Monastery, he teased a monk in the monastery, saying that when the latter saw the flowers in bloom, he probably regretted he had ever left the household life.[53] In another poem he wrote that the exquisite flowers in the grounds of the Ku-shan Monastery were incarnations of heavenly apsaras.[54]

Among the monks whom Po befriended while in Hang-chou was the Ch'an master T'ao-kuang. In the *Hsien-ch'un-chih* 79.28a, there is this notice about him: "During the Ch'ang-ch'ing era (821-824) of the T'ang dynasty, a poetic monk who called himself T'ao-kuang built a shrine west of the Fa-an Cloister. He frequently recited poetry together with Lo-t'ien." Another friend was known as the Ch'an master of the Bird's Nest. This eccentric individual went about in tattered garments that were not changed all year round. He lived in the hills, near a tree with a magpie's nest, and this gave him his peculiar name. We are told that Po visited him

[52] *CCC* 53.13a.   [53] *CCC* 20.12a.   [54] *CCC* 20.13b.

in the mountain and asked him about Ch'an practices.[55] Still another was the expert on the *Vimalakīrti-sutra*, Yung-ch'üan, and in one poem, Po expressed the hope that in their future incarnations they would not forget their happy meetings in Hang-chou.[56]

So prolific was Po's versifying that he once asked a friendly monk in the Tung-lin Monastery in Lu-shan whether or not his poetic activities interfered with the vegetarian feasts held in the monasteries.[57] In another piece dated also in 824, he wrote that he must have been a versifying monk in his previous incarnation:

> The prose and verses (I have written) number
>   over a thousand,
> In mind and conduct I turn to the Mahāyāna.
> Sitting or resting on the bed of ropes, I fancy
> In my former life I must have been a versify-
>   ing monk.[58]

These poems written in Hang-chou are of great interest to us in that they summarize Po's deep and growing involvement with the Buddhist way of life. Concern for worldly problems is seldom expressed in them; indeed, one of the very few written in Hang-chou reads as follows:

> With disheveled hair on the temples, and with a
>   piece of cloth as scarf,

[55] *Hsien-ch'un-chih* 70.4b,16b. We read in the *FTTC* 42, *T* 49.384b that "when Po was governor of Hang-chou, he asked the Ch'an master of the Bird's Nest about the Buddhist way. The master replied, 'Never commit any evil and perform all the meritorious deeds.' Po Chü-i replied, 'Why, even a three-year-old child can say this.' The master retorted, 'Even though a three-year-old child can say it, an old man of eighty cannot practice it.' Po Chü-i agreed, saluted him, and left."

[56] *CCC* 20.22a. For a discussion of the poems written in Hang-chou and the places named in them, see Hiraoka Takeo, "Haku Rakuten no shi to Rinanshi-jiin wo chūshin toshite," in *Tsukamoto Hakushi shojū kinen bukkyōshigaku ronshū* 596-614.

[57] *CCC* 53.17b, dated 824. Hanabusa, *op.cit.*, 614.

[58] *CCC* 53.16b; Hanabusa, *op.cit.*, 614.

Early in the morning I traverse the cold mountain
    carrying firewood.
This group of girls on the banks of the Ch'ien-t'ang
    River,
Who are they, wearing red dresses and riding
    horses?[59]

From Hang-chou, Po was transferred in 824 to Lo-yang to
become chief gentleman-in-waiting to the crown prince. He
bought a house in Lo-yang and prepared to lead a leisurely
life devoted to his poetry. However, the Buddhist virtue of
compassion was so much a part of his life now that on the day
he moved into the house, he experienced a sort of guilt, living
the kind of life he desired the most while other less fortunate
living creatures were suffering. These feelings he expressed
in the following poem:

I have moved into my new house.
After quitting Hang-chou as governor, I have
    some extra wealth.
Now I can escape the heat and dampness,
And can also avoid worrying about cold and
    hunger.
Now I am recovered from my illness and my
    sick leave is not over.
My post is leisurely, being on detached assign-
    ment [in Lo-yang].
Happily there is the official emolument,
But no duties to tie me down.
In the early morning after cleaning up,
I open the studio and roll up the screens.
My household, together with the chickens and
    dogs,
They join me to make a happy crowd.
When I am in a happy mood, I drink some wine,

[59] *CCC* 20.19b, written in 823. This poem describes a poor hard-
working girl who asks why she has to slave, while other girls, presumably courtesans, wear fine dresses and ride horses.

Nothing relaxes me more than composing poetry.
Why practice the Way laboriously,
This is indeed nonactivity.
External attachments are indeed banished,
But in my bosom I frequently let my thoughts
 wander.
When they wander, how far they reach.
I sit silently and lower my eyebrows in
 meditation.
The prisoner held for over a decade,
The soldiers on expeditions tens of thousands
 of *li* away,
The birds in cages on spring mornings,
The turtle supporting the bed on winter
 evenings.[60]
The post horses galloping without rest,
with their four hoofs in ceaseless agonizing pain,
The mill ox with two eyes covered,
Who can fathom the dark world they live in?
Who can set them free,
To go as they please,
Each one following his own nature,
Just as I am doing this day and hour?[61]

After a brief interlude in Lo-yang, free from official duties and lolling in laziness, Po was appointed governor of Su-chou in 825; after assuming the post, he faced so much paper work that he had to work as he never had in the past. His predicament was compounded by the fact that his eyes were bother-

[60] In the *Shih-chi* 128.5b, *Kuei-ts'e-chuan*, there is a passage which reads, "In the south there was an old man who used a turtle to support his bed. After some twenty years, the old man died, and when the bed was moved, the turtle was still alive." In the *Pao-p'u-tzu* of Ko Hung, c. 3, this story is repeated. Here we read: "In the region between the Yangtze and Huai Rivers lived a man who during his childhood used a turtle to support his bed. After he died of old age, his family moved the bed and found the turtle still alive." Po Chü-i undoubtedly had this story in mind when writing this line.
[61] CCC 8.17b-18a.

ing him, for in 826 he wrote in a poem that he saw thousands of snow flakes floating before him in the air, and that objects appeared to him in a haze as if seen through a film of gauze even on a clear day. He continued:

The monks say that foreign defilements have entered
the eye,
The doctors say that the confused vision is caused by
a liver condition.
Curing the ailment from both ends, what improvement
is there?
The strength of the medicine is nebulous and the
power of the Buddha is remote.[62]

Po returns to his visual ailment in another poem written during the same year:

My eyes have been damaged for a long time
already,
The causes are deep and hard to remove.
The doctors all advise me to stop drinking wine,
My Buddhist friends mostly urge me to quit
official post as soon as possible.
On the table a copy of Nāgārjuna's treatise is
conveniently placed,
Within a box are kept some eye-healing pills.
Medicine prescribed by man must be useless,
I should have my eyes scraped by the golden
comb.[63]

[62] *CCC* 54.20a.

[63] *CCC* 54.20a. The treatise by Nāgārjuna mentioned in the poem is a reference to the *Treatise on the Eye*, and its mention here is of special interest, for it indicates the popularity of this Buddhist medical work in T'ang China. It is unlikely that the treatise is by the famous Buddhist thinker Nāgārjuna (second century A.D.); it could have been compiled by a doctor named Nāgārjuna, or it could have been attributed to Nāgārjuna because of the fame of the founder of the Mādhyamika system. The golden comb mentioned in the last line is also an Indian surgical instrument used for the removal of cataracts. The method of using the comb is described in such Buddhist sutras as the *Ta-pan*

When Po was in Hang-chou, he had heard about the existence of a Society for the Recitation of the *Hua-yen-ching*, and
became a member of it while he was in Su-chou. When he
was about to leave his post in Su-chou, the founder of the society, a venerable old monk named Nan-ts'ao, implored him
to write an account of it. This Po did in 826.

Monk Nan-ts'ao of the Lung-hsing Monastery in Hang-
chou during the second year of Ch'ang-ch'ing (822) invited
monk Tao-feng of the Ling-yin Monastery to lecture on the
Hua-yen sūtra. When he heard about Vairocana in the section on the Hua-tsang world,[64] Ts'ao became so elated that
he uttered an earnest wish, hoping that he could urge a
group of 100,000 people, monks and laymen, to recite the
Hua-yen sūtra. Each of the 100,000 people would in turn
urge a thousand others to recite one chapter of the same
sutra. The entire assemblage would meet together quarterly. Ts'ao carried out his earnest wish and organized the
group into a society, and regulated the proceedings
through quarterly vegetarian feasts. From the summer of
822 to the present autumn, fourteen such vegetarian feasts
have been held. At each feast, Ts'ao offered incense respectfully and knelt before the image of the Buddha, making the following supplication, "May I and every member
of the society be reborn before Vairocana in his paradise

---

nieh-p'an-ching 8, *T* 12.411a; 652c; *Ta-jih-ching-su* 9, *T* 39.699c. See
also *Hōbōgirin* 3.261 for illustrations of the golden comb. It is interesting to note that Po's very close friend Liu Yü-hsi also mentions the
golden comb in one of his poems:
> My eyes have become blind early,
> Although I am only middle age, I am like an old man.
> I look at vermilion and it resembles green.
> I am afraid of the sun and cannot stand the wind.
> You, my master, know the method of the golden comb.
> Can you help me see again?
>> *Liu Meng-te wen-chi* 7.51 *SPTK* ed.

[64] *Chüan* 8-10 in Śikshānanda's translation, *Ta-fang-kuang fo hua-
yen-ching*, *T* 10.39a-53c.

within the Golden Wheel of Precious Lotus, floating on the Great Ocean of Fragrant Waters in the Lotus-womb World [Padmagarbhadhātu]. Then I would be satisfied.

Ts'ao also solicited enough funds from the members to purchase an estate of ten *ch'ing* of land, the income from which was used to defray the expenses of the vegetarian feasts. When I was governor of Hang-chou, I heard that Ts'ao had uttered such an earnest wish. Now that I am governor of Su-chou, I see that Ts'ao had accomplished his objective. He has come from Hang-chou to Su-chou three times to request me to write this record. He said that he is now eighty-one years old and that he is rapidly nearing the end of his life. What he feared was that after his death, there would be no one to continue his original intention, so he begged me to write this account of the purpose of the society in order to prevent it from disintegrating. I am one of the hundred thousand members, so it is proper that I record this to extol Ts'ao.

I have heard that the merit of donating one strand of hair or one grain of rice will never be lost; how much greater is the merit gained in preparing with ceaseless energy the boundless offering of four vegetarian feasts annually, supplied by the income of a thousand *mou*? I have heard that the power of one earnest wish and the merit of one verse will never be lost; how much greater then is the merit accruing from a thousand mouths uttering the twelve divisions of the canon? Moreover, how much greater also when hundreds or thousands of ears are listening to myriads of sutras? I am sure that the disciples of Ts'ao will fulfill his earnest wish.

Here in this account we shall only preserve the spirit and meaning of the sutra. As for the names of the society members and the amount of wealth contributed, these will be preserved in another tablet. We shall only record the earnest wish that he manifested, to serve as the inspiration for future efforts.

Recorded by the former governor of Su-chou Po Chü-i
on the twenty-fifth day of the ninth month, second year of
Pao-li (826).[65]

After leaving Su-chou, Po returned to Ch'ang-an to assume
a number of posts that were outside the mainstream of political events swirling in the capital. This was Po's own choosing, for he considered that he was now entering the twilight
of his career and it would be much to his advantage not to
assume a sensitive post and run the risk of being banished to
remote regions. In 827 and 828, while in Ch'ang-an, he held
the post of head of the palace library, then vice-president of
the Board of Punishment. Among the Buddhist monks in the
capital with whom he renewed friendship was Tao-tsung, a
monk famous for his poetry. Tao-tsung did not write poetry
for the sake of poetry, he was mainly interested in versifying
as a means of communication with the literati with the intention of converting them to Buddhism. Some of his contem-
poraries thought that he hobnobbed with the literary men of
his time in order to gain secular honors and officialdom, but
Po was convinced that he was a pure monk interested only in
his religion. Previously, as early as 821, Po had temporarily
received ordination from Tao-tsung and had studied the
Hua-yen sūtra with him.[66] In a piece devoted to Tao-tsung
(written ca. 827-828), Po wrote that the Buddha uttered
psalms of praise, bodhisattvas wrote treatises, but that Tao-
tsung considered poetry to be the concern of Buddhism and
therefore wrote poetry. He would like the elite among the
people to know something about the highest truth of Buddhism, so he first attracted them with his poetical lines and
then introduced them to the wisdom of Buddhism.[67]

In an earlier piece written in Chiang-chou, previously referred to, Po felt that he was a good Buddhist, had success-

[65] *CCC* 59.7a-8b; *FFTC* 42, *T* 49.384c.
[66] *CCC* 60.11ab.
[67] *CCC* 51.20b-21a. The highest truth that Tao-tsung had in mind
was the truth without equal, based on the section entitled *Pu-erh fa-
men* in the *Vimalakīrti*.

fully absorbed the teachings of the master, but that he was not able to surmount the final barrier of suppressing all passions and emotions to achieve detachment because of his submission, as he puts it, to the demon of poetry. He could not help it, he felt, because versifying was his nature. Now in Ch'ang-an, under the influence of Tao-tsung, he arrived at a new conception of his role. He now believed it was possible to accommodate his own views of poetry with his acceptance of Buddhism. If his verses were taken up with such themes as the Mahāyāna virtues of skill-in-means or compassion or tolerance, they would assist in the conversion of people and thus would be of benefit to the religion.

In the poem devoted to Tao-tsung, referred to above, outwardly Po is praising the learned cleric for writing poetry to convert people, but beyond that, it appears that he is expressing his own new consciousness concerning the role of poetry. Hence in that same poem, he wrote, "Most people love your poetic lines, but only I understand your intention."

This kind of leisurely semiretired life in Ch'ang-an is referred to in a number of poems dated 827. In one of these, entitled *Hsien-yung* (Idle musings), we read:

> At night I sit mostly in meditation,
> Affected by the autumn atmosphere I chant.
> Thus leisurely, other than these two things,
> My mind does not dwell on anything else.[68]

In another poem, addressed to Monk Chih-ju of the Sheng-shan Monastery in Lo-yang, he wrote:

> Lazy and dull I know particularly what my destiny is,
> Though living alone I have gradually made some
>   friends.
> I do not open my door to uninvited strangers,
> But I welcome the Ch'an monks into my private study.
> We face the fire in early winter,
> Until midnight, the light is still in the lantern.

[68] *CCC* 55.4b.

Worry and toil are caused by knowledge and
 cleverness,
I am happy that I am utterly incompetent.[69]

Early in 829, while still in Ch'ang-an, Po wrote a series of
poems to his friend Yüan Chen and one of these contains a
good summary of his thoughts concerning Ch'an Buddhism.

Since you brought up the problem concerning past
 errors,
Let me offer the following observations on human
 affairs.
First, there is nothing like Ch'an,
Second, there is nothing like being drunk.
Ch'an can erase the difference between myself and
 others,
Drunkenness can cause one to forget glory and
 disappointment.
I will explain the matter to you in proper sequence,
So please pay a little attention to me.
Confucianism emphasizes ceremonies and regulations,
Taoism nurtures the spirit and breath.
Emphasis on ceremonies gives rise to ostentatious
 display,
One nurtures the spirit to avoid ill omen.
They are not as good as practicing Ch'an meditation,
For in it there is a profound meaning.
It is vast and undisturbed like the void,
Its crystal-clear awareness is better than sleep.
It eradicates all our silent memories,
It exhausts our never ending thoughts.
In the spring there is nothing to break the heart,
In the autumn there is no melancholy to cause tears.
I sit and achieve the joy of supreme truth,
As if the Prince of the Void has bestowed it on me.

[69] *CCC* 55.7b. This piece was written in 827, when Monk Chih-ju,
who ordinarily resided in Lo-yang, had gone to Ch'ang-an and visited
Po in his residence.

Since I have escaped from the toils of the world,
I am no longer subject to the sense of remorse.
After Ch'an there is drunkenness,
This kind of talk is not without reason.
With one cup all scheming is forgotten,
With three cups we feel that the world is as we like
    it . . .
I urge you, although you are now advanced in years,
When you come across wine, do not avoid it,
Otherwise, practice Ch'an,
The two roads lead to the same goal.[70]

Po felt that two years in the capital were enough and he
wanted very much to go back to his home and garden in Lo-
yang to spend the remaining years in retirement there. This
desire was no doubt aroused by the deaths of a number of his
close friends and political supporters in 828. And so in 829,
he was appointed adviser to the crown prince, with special
duties in Lo-yang. Since the crown prince was seldom if ever
in Lo-yang, the post was practically a sinecure. Until his
death in 846, Po was to spend all his time in the eastern capital. Now his real life of leisure and enjoyment began, with no
official responsibilities and with a sufficient government salary to maintain a comfortable living. Thus it comes as no surprise that just after settling in Lo-yang, he wrote:

I am now an official of the third rank,
Already aged fifty-eight.
Although my muscles and bones are already infirm,
I am still not feeble.
Though my wealth is not abundant,
Still I have enough to live.
I still have enough strength to climb mountains,
Whenever I have a chance to drink wine, I feel
    exhilarated.
The days and months are long when there is leisure,

[70] CCC 52.9b-10a.

Unrestrained, one can wander anywhere in the
    world.
I have a place to be comfortable in,
And I can do what I please without regard to
    seasonal ceremonies.
I loosen my belt to enjoy the breeze under the pine
    trees,
I carry my lute to play to the moon in the lake.
What mankind considers important,
Such as the seals of ministers and the battle-ax of
    generals,
These people are always scheming and worrying
    about their safety or insecurity,
Or the powers to control the life and death of people.
Such struggles cause distress of mind and a lifetime
    of misery,
And when they are successful, then other people will
    become jealous of them.
I doubt that in their hearts,
They are as happy as I am now.[71]

It was probably in this mood that he wrote in 830 a piece to
a monk named Yüan:

    The small pool is so clear that I can see the
        bottom,
    The idle guest sits with his robes loosened.
    I wonder whether or not the still water
    Is superior to one who is without thoughts?
    That pool is only clear and shallow,
    But this mind is tranquil and profound.
    Who can explain this meaning to me?
    Tomorrow I will ask the monk Tao-lin.[72]

One can imagine the scene that inspired this short piece.
Po was probably sitting beside the pool in his garden. The

[71] *CCC* 52.19ab.   [72] *CCC* 58.6a.

water in the pool was so still and unagitated that he could see the bottom. The stillness of the water led him to contemplate the tranquility of his own mind, attained through the practice of Ch'an meditation and no longer agitated by passions and attachments to worldly status and honor. So even in his leisure, his thoughts were constantly concerned with Buddhism.

In 831, Yüan Chen died. As his closest friend, Po was asked to present the funeral address. The remarkable feature of this address is that Po did not talk about the heart-broken grief he experienced at the death of his closest friend; instead he emphasized the long years of poetic exchange between them. Po accepted the death of Yüan as a fulfillment of their karma, and there was nothing he could do about it. In the end he said that according to the Buddhist sutras, "Whenever there is a conjunction of karmic streams, it must be because of the confluence of previous causes. Can one say that our relationship with each other is merely accidental? In numerous incarnations we have separated and met again. Now we have separated, but who can say we shall not meet again in the future?"[73]

Po was also asked by the Yüan family to write the biographical tomb inscription of Yüan Chen. According to the *Hsiu Hsiang-shan-ssu chi* (Account of the repairing of the Hsiang-shan Monastery), which Po wrote in 832, the Yüan family wanted to present him with Yüan Chen's personal belongings worth around 600,000 to 700,000 cash. Po repeatedly refused to accept the presents but, after the Yüan family persisted, he finally accepted them on condition that the entire sum be used to repair the building of the Hsiang-shan Monastery in Lo-yang. When monk Ch'ing-hsien said that the merits accruing from this gift were to be ascribed to Yüan Chen, Po replied, "As a result of this meritorious deed, who knows but that in a future kalpa Wei-chih and I shall meet again as friends in this land? As a result of our earnest wishes,

---

[73] *CCC* 60.17b.

who knows but that in another rebirth, Wei-chih and I would again visit together in this very monastery?"[74]

With the Hsiang-shan Monastery repaired and the monastery grounds beautified, Po began to frequent the place more often to enjoy the tranquility and leisure there. This mood is caught in a poem written in 832, the last lines of which read:

> The five sensual pleasures are dispelled, all worries
> extinguished,
> I am no longer tethered to anything in the world.[75]

His frequent visits to the monastery are indicated in the following:

> When I first arrived in Hsiang-shan, which became
> my home in old age,
> It was autumn and the white moon was full.
> From now on you are part of my home,
> Let me ask whether you are aware of this or not.[76]

From these poems we see that Hsiang-shan Monastery near Lo-yang began to play an increasing role in the leisurely and idle life of Po in the eastern capital. This idle life was shared by the Buddhist monks who were his companions in leisurely conversations. Four of these monks, Chao, Mi, Hsien, and Shih, are mentioned in the title of one of the poems written in 833.

> A white haired old man, wearing purple robes,
> I do not mix with the world but consort with the Tao.
> Three times I have been assigned to Lo-yang on
> special duty as an official,
> Half of my friends are among the monks.

[74] CCC 59.25b. The biographical inscription is found in ibid., 61.3a-7b. The Hsiang-shan Monastery near Lo-yang was one of the places Po loved to visit ever since he assumed the post of adviser to the crown prince in 829.

[75] CCC 58.24b.   [76] CCC 66.10b.

One must eventually withdraw from this wealth
  conscious world,
Long have I yearned for my karmic friends of the
  incense.
After the vegetarian feasts what can I offer you in
  return?
Only the springs, rocks, and the north wind in the
  western pavilion.[77]

The four monks mentioned here are all well known. Hsien
refers to the monk Ch'ing-hsien of the Hsiang-shan Monastery, who supervised the rebuilding of the monastery with the
funds donated by Po. Chao is the Ch'an master Shen-chao of
the Feng-kuo Monastery in Lo-yang. According to his biographical inscription which Po wrote in 839[78] he was one of
the skillful preachers of the day. Po also wrote a poem in his
honor,[79] and another one written in 834 described a night
they spent together in Lung-men:

The eighth year [of T'ai-ho], at the end of the
  second month,
The mountain pear trees were in full bloom.
In the Shui-hsi Monastery of Lung-men,
I met Yüan-kung in the evening.
We sat quietly facing each other,
Who knows the intimate conversations which
  we had?
The relation between before and after is
  terminated,
When one thought is not produced.[80]

[77] *CCC* 64.8a.
[78] *CCC* 70.13b-14a; Hanabusa, *op.cit.*, 673.
[79] *CCC* 57.23a.
[80] *CCC* 62.9b-10a, entitled *Shen-chao Ch'an-shih t'ung-su*. The last
two lines refer to the words spoken before Empress Wu Tse-t'ien by
the Hua-yen master Ch'ing-liang, "If one thought is not produced, then
the relation between before and after is terminated, and they exist
independent of each other. This is so with things as well as the ego."
See Chüeh-an, *Shih-shih chi-ku-lüeh* 3, *T* 49.833b.

As for Shih, he must be the Tsung-shih mentioned by Po in the poem entitled *Tsung-shih shang-jen*.[81] According to Po, Tsung-shih abandoned an official post and wife to become a monk, just as Gautama did. According to the biographical notice of Chao, both Ch'ing-hsien and Tsung-shih were his disciples. Mi undoubtedly refers to Tsung-mi (780-841), the renowned Ch'an and Hua-yen master, to whom Po dedicated the poem *Tseng Ts'ao-t'ang Tsung-mi shang-jen*.[82] Tsung-mi lived in the Ts'ao-t'ang Monastery in Mt. Chung-nan near Ch'ang-an, and probably met Po and the other three monks on a trip to Lo-yang.

In 835, Po gathered together his literary works in sixty *chüan* and presented the entire collection to the Tung-lin Monastery in Lu-shan. His own account of the donation stated that when he was marshal of Chiang-chou, he frequently read the works of Hui-yüan stored in the monastery, and his monk companions at the time requested that his collection of literary works also be deposited in the monastery there. Now, more than twenty years afterward, he put together the 2,964 pieces that he had written into sixty *chüan* and presented them to the monastery. He also hoped that in his future rebirths he might again visit the monastery. Finally he requested that the rules which applied to Hui-yüan's works also be made applicable in his case, namely, that his writings not be lent to visitors and that they not be taken from the monastery.[83]

The next year, 836, another collection of his works, this time totaling 3,255 pieces in sixty-five *chüan*, was presented to the Sheng-shan Monastery in Lo-yang, the reason being that in his early years, he had received instructions on Buddhism under the monks Ning and Ju-man of this monastery. The same stipulations concerning the use and circulation of the works were requested by Po.[84]

Po now felt the infirmities of old age overcoming him, and in 837, when he was sixty-six years old by Chinese counting,

[81] *CCC* 57.23ab.　　[82] *CCC* 64.7b, written in 833.
[83] *CCC* 61.21b.　　[84] *CCC* 61.22ab.

and had lost a couple of teeth,[85] he wrote a piece entitled "Sixty-six":

> I am now four years away from seventy,
> There is not much to boast about this life.
> Whenever I grieve over the passing away of people
>   I know,
> I rejoice that this body is still alive.
> How can I retain black hair permanently,
> Or prevent my vision from deteriorating?
> Old friends are lying in their graves,
> The servants now see their great grandchildren.
> I am so thin that I cannot support my own weight,
> I am so decrepit that I regret my white hair is
>   multiplying.
> How shall I face old age and sickness?
> I should entrust myself to the Gateway to the Void.[86]

In the following year, 838, Po gives a lively description of the kind of idle and lazy life of retirement he was living in Lo-yang in a piece entitled "Biography of a Master of Wine and Song," in which he imitated the style of T'ao Yüan-ming's "Master of the Five Willows." He says that the master of wine and song has forgotten his own name and does not know who he really is. After some thirty years of itinerant life as an official, he is now retired and settled in Lo-yang, in a site replete with a pool, bamboo, trees, and bridge. Though he may be poor, he is not cold or hungry, and though old, he is not yet a centenarian. He is most fond of drinking wine, playing the lute, and reciting poetry, and passes the time with friends with similar tastes. "In addition to these pleasures, he is addicted to Buddhism, and has penetrated into the doctrines of the small, middle, and great vehicles, and has as his religious

---

[85] *CCC* 61.29a.

[86] *CCC* 66.19a. The last two lines are a clear reference to the miseries that confront man in this world, miseries that led Śākyamuni to abandon the household life to become a recluse. Similarly Po writes that he seeks to escape from old age and sickness by taking refuge in Buddhism.

friend the monk Ju-man of Mt. Sung." The rest of the piece goes on to describe in greater details the joys derived from wine and verse. When he drinks, he becomes intoxicated; after getting over the intoxication he resumes his singing of poetry; after singing, he drinks some more and becomes intoxicated again. Intoxication and singing follow in a continuous cycle, hence he calls himself master of wine and song.[87]

For us, the interesting passage is, of course, that in which he places his interest in Buddhism alongside his favorite pursuits of wine and poetry. This indicates how deeply involved he was in the religion, studying the doctrines and meeting with Buddhist monks during his days of retirement in Lo-yang.

As further manifestation of his devotion to Buddhism, he made a third presentation of his works to a Buddhist monastery in 839, this time to the Nan-ch'an Monastery in Su-chou. When Po was governor of Su-chou, he had already planned to establish a library in the monastery. Now it was completed[88] and the collection of his works which he presented amounted to 3,487 items in sixty-seven *chüan*. In his account of the presentation, he wrote that he was a disciple of the Buddha, who, after hearing the teachings of the master, deeply believed in the doctrine of karma. In addition to a collection of his works stored at home, there are now, he said, three other collections. One is kept in the Sheng-shan Monastery in Lo-yang, the second in the Tung-lin Monastery in Lu-shan, and the third at Nan-ch'an Monastery in Su-chou. Why did he make these presentations? Because of an earnest wish he had made to the following effect: "May the worldly writings of my present life, with all their excessive words and ornate phrases, serve in future ages as the inspiration of hymns of praise extolling the Buddha's teachings, and to turn the wheel of the law forever."[89]

[87] *CCC* 61.30a-32b. Quotation from 30b.
[88] On the completion and the cost of this library, see Po's account in *CCC* 61.33a-35a.
[89] *CCC* 61.35ab.

One day before he wrote the above account, he composed
a stone inscription commemorating the completion of the library in the Nan-ch'an Monastery. Here he wrote that the
cost of construction and the sutras amounted to 3,600 strings
of cash, that the repository for the sutras was a revolving
octagonal structure which had 256 boxes holding 5,058 scrolls
of sutras.[90] Within the library there was also a refectory to
serve food to visiting monks and scholars. He wrote:

> Śākyamuni had said that all the Buddhas and all the
> dharmas issue forth from the sutras. Accordingly the
> dharmas depend on the sutras, the sutras depend on the
> library, and the library depends on the building. If the
> building is damaged, then the library will be destroyed. If
> the library is destroyed, then the sutras will fall into disuse.
> If the sutras fall into disuse, then the dharmas will be hid-
> den, and when the dharmas are hidden, then the incom-
> parable *tao* will expire. Alas, should not all the officials,
> leaders of *caityas*, and abbots reverence and protect this
> building? Should they not preserve and enlarge it if neces-
> sary? If some sutras are missing, let them be replaced, and
> if there are crevices in the library, let them be repaired,
> and if the building is damaged, let it be rebuilt. Those who
> act thus are the real disciples of the Buddha, and they will
> receive countless blessings, but those who act to the con-
> trary are not true disciples and they will be punished ac-
> cording to the rules of discipline.[91]

In 839, Po suffered what was most likely a minor stroke that
incapacitated his left leg. His mind was still clear, however,
and he wrote a number of poems describing his illness. In one
of these, he compared himself to the famous Buddhist layman Vimalakīrti. According to the Mahāyāna sutra of the

[90] See the illuminating article on the revolving library by L. C. Goodrich, "The Revolving Book Case in China," *HJAS* 7.2 (1942), 130-161.
[91] *CCC* 61.33a-35a. See S. Levi and E. Chavannes, "Quelques titres
enigmatiques dans la hiérarchie ecclésiastique du bouddhisme Indien,"
Journal Asiatique, 11th sér., 6 (1915), 307-309.

same name, Vimalakīrti was sick at home and the Buddha wanted to send one of his disciples to ask about his health. The disciples all begged off, giving as their reason that at one time or another in the past they had all been humiliated by the wise layman. Finally Mañjuśrī, the bodhisattva of wisdom, consented to go. This *Vimalakīrti-sūtra* was one of Po's favorite scriptures, for he referred to it very often in his poems. During his illness, the monk Ch'ing-hsien came to call on him. On this occasion, Po in his poem compares himself to Vimalakīrti and Ch'ing-hsien to Mañjuśrī.[92]

In his sickness, Po's thoughts turned to the Western Paradise of Amitābha, and in 840 he commissioned an artist named Tu Tsung-ching to paint a picture of that paradise with Amitābha in the center, flanked on the left and right by Avalokiteśvara and Mahāsthāmaprāpta. In the account which he wrote concerning this episode, he called himself a disciple of Śākyamuni and he put down some of his thoughts concerning this paradise. It is called the paradise of utmost bliss because the eight miseries[93] and the four evil destinies are missing there,[94] and it is called the Pure Land because the three poisons (lust, anger, and stupidity) and the five impurities are absent.[95] The Buddha is called Amitābha because his

---

[92] *CCC* 68.2a, 3a.

[93] Pa-k'u; birth, old age, sickness, death, separation from beloved ones, association with unpleasant persons and conditions, not getting what one desires, the five attachment groups. See *Dīghanikāya*, 2.305ff.

[94] The four evil destinies are rebirth as asura or titans, as animals, as hungry ghosts, and as denizens of hell.

[95] *pañcakashāyāh* or the five pollutions. These are:

kalpa-kashāya		pollution of the epoch, a time of war, pestilence, and disaster
dṛṣṭi-	"	pollution of views, a period when heresies flourish
kleśa-	"	pollution of the passions, a period when the passions of lust, anger, and delusions are strong
sattva-	"	pollution of beings, when men are mentally and physically weak and devoid of blessings
āyus-	"	pollution of life, when the duration of life is as low as ten years

See *Mahāvyutpatti* 2336-2340; *FYCL* 98, *T* 53.1005abc.

life is everlasting and his brightness is immeasurable. He went on to say that he paid the painter 30,000 cash for the picture, which measured 9 by 13 feet. When the painting was finished, he uttered the earnest wish that the merits accruing from this act would be transferred to all sentient beings, so that all those who were sick as he was would be relieved of misery and attain happiness, uprooted from evil to practice goodness, and be reborn in the Western Paradise in their next rebirth.

In the same year, he wrote that because of his illness and old age, his thoughts had turned to other beings in the evil states of existence, and he expressed the wish that they, like him, would escape from misery and attain bliss. To this end, he commissioned an artist to paint a picture of Maitreya's Tushita Heaven, using such colors as red, white, gold, and green to portray it. He also wrote that he had for a number of years now taken refuge in the Three Jewels, observed the eight precepts, and burned incense daily before the Buddha. He also indicated that he earnestly wished that all sentient creatures would be reborn in the Tushita Heaven, and from there follow Maitreya to be reborn on earth when that Buddha descends to the world to purify the religion, and under the ministry of Maitreya escape from the cycle of repeated rebirth to attain the incomparable *Tao*.[96]

In Lo-yang, Po referred to himself as the layman of Hsiang-shan Monastery. He always contended that he never could become a monk because of his attachment to literature. He had to express his emotions and feelings whenever they overcame him, and he could not suppress them as a monk should. Consequently, he always felt that he was a captive to the demon of poetry. Po felt a strong attachment to the Hsiang-shan Monastery, for it will be recalled that he contributed funds toward its rebuilding. The monastery served as the center of his interest and Buddhist activities during his life of retirement in Lo-yang. After the rebuilding was completed, he found that, while there were in the monastery

[96] *CCC* 70.10b.

images of the Buddha and a community of monks, there were no scriptures. So he began to collect scriptures from other monasteries, mending those which needed repairs, and completing those which were incomplete. In due time he was able to assemble 5,270 *chüan* of scriptures, which he classified into sutras, discipline rules, and treatises according to the *K'ai-yüan-lu*. With the canon now available, he then had some empty rooms in the northwest corner of the monastery renovated to serve as the library. When this was completed in 840, a celebration was held, accompanied by the burning of incense, feasting, and music, and with some 120 monks and laymen present. He then donated to the library all the poems he had finished since moving to Lo-yang in 829, altogether some 800 items in ten *chüan*. In making the presentation, Po again uttered the earnest wish that these poems might become hymns of praise to the Buddha in the future, and that he himself might in a future rebirth revisit the library to see his works in their new status.[97]

Po's infirmity resulting from his stroke apparently lingered on until 842, for he referred to it in a poem written that year to some of his clerical friends:

> The right eye is dim, the left leg infirm through
> rheumatism,
> The golden comb and the mineral water have been
> ineffective.
> It is far better to return to the joys of reciting the
> sutras of the three vehicles,
> There we realize that floating life and the numerous
> ailments are evanescent.
> I have no son to live with me in my grass hut,
> But I have a wife as my companion in old age in the
> arena of *Tao*.
> Why bother with asking monks to keep company,
> The moon just newly returned is the companion to
> the sick old man.[98]

[97] *CCC* 70.12b.
[98] *CCC* 69.28ab. Here again Po refers to the golden comb used by the

As the infirmities of old age and sickness gradually crept over Po, he knew that death was approaching, and in some of his poems written in 841 and 842 to monks, he expressed the hope that they might meet again in their next incarnation. One addressed to monk Fo-kuang written in 841, has the following lines:

> I am grateful for your troubles in accompanying me
>   down the mountain,
> Who knows of my sentiment at such a parting?
> I am already seventy, and the master is ninety,
> We should know that when we meet again, it will be
>   in other rebirths.[99]

Another addressed in 842 to monk Yün-kao of the Tung-lin Monastery in Lu-shan contains the following lines:

> Since we parted, I presume that you have made
>   much progress in your spiritual attainments,
> As you become older, how are you physically?
> Our karmic meeting in our next lives should not
>   be far off,
> Both of us have already passed seventy.[100]

It was in 841 that Po wrote six laudatory verses to honor the Buddha, dharma, saṅgha, sentient beings, repentance, and earnest wish. In the preface to these verses, Po wrote: "Lo-t'ien constantly has an earnest wish that the secular writings of this rebirth will in future rebirths become converted to hymns praising the teachings of the Buddha and turning the wheel of the law. This year I am already seventy. I am also old and sick. Because I am rapidly approaching the next rebirth, I have written six verses, which I recite while kneeling before the Buddha, dharma, and saṅgha. May they serve as the karma to bring about the blueprint of the future."

Buddhists for eye ailments. In referring to life as a fleeting cloud, he was echoing a sentiment which he expressed long ago while in Chiang-chou.

[99] *CCC* 68.17b.   [100] *CCC* 69.31b.

Verses praising the Buddha:

In the world of the ten directions, above and below
heaven,
I know absolutely now that there is no one like the
Buddha.
Grand and lofty, he is the teacher of gods and men.
Therefore I reverence his feet, praise him, and take
refuge in him.

Verses praising the dharma:

The myriads of Buddhas in the past, present, and
future,
All are manifested through the dharma which is
contained in the scriptures.
This is the great wheel of law, this is the vast treasury
of gems.
I therefore fold my hands and turn toward it with a
most devoted mind.

Verses praising the saṅgha:

The solitary Buddha and the hearers and all the
great monks,
Their cankers are exhausted, their fruits have
ripened, they are the Blessed Ones among sentient
beings.
Through cooperation they seek for the incomparable
Tao,
Therefore I bow my head before the precious monks
of Jambudvīpa.

Verses praising sentient beings:

Foolish people and ordinary beings,[101]

---

[101] *Mao-tao fan-fu. Fan fu* would be *pṛthagjana*, ordinary people. However, *mao tao* is puzzling. There appears to be a confusion here concerning two words, *bāla*, foolish, young; and *vāla*, hair. In Monier-Williams, *Dictionary*, 946 and 728, we are told that *vāla* is also written as *bāla*, and *bāla* as *vāla*. The two words therefore are often mixed.

All living beings in the house of fire,
Those who are born of womb, egg, sweat, and metamorphosis, all sentient beings,
If they plant roots of merits, they will certainly reap
the fruits of Buddhahood in the end.
I do not regard you lightly, you should not regard
yourself lightly.

Verses praising repentance:

From the beginningless aeon, all the evils that have
been created,
Some light, some heavy, regardless of their sizes,
I seek their characteristics, in the middle, inside and
out.
But they are unfathomable, this is repentance.

Verses praising earnest wish:

I wish to dispel all passions, I wish to abide in
nirvana.
I wish to ascend the ten stages (to bodhisattvahood),
I wish to rescue the four classes of beings.
When the Buddha appears in the world, I wish to be
close to him,
So that I would be the first to urge him to turn the
wheel of the law.
When the Buddha achieves nirvana, I wish to be
right there,
To offer the last offerings, and receive the seal of
bodhi.[102]

Almost up to the end of his life, Po continued to manifest
his concern for the welfare of less fortunate beings. On the I
River near Lo-yang, there was a narrow defile filled with

The original Sanskrit word must have been *bālapṛthagjana*, foolish,
ordinary people, but because *bāla* is sometimes written as *vāla*, hair,
whoever translated the term into Chinese used the characters *mao-tao*,
as if the reading was *vālapṛthagjana*.

[102] *CCC* 70.17a-18a.

treacherous currents and dangerous rocks which was the graveyard of ships trying to pass there. Po wrote that frequently in the depth of the winter nights, he had heard the anguished cries of shipwrecked sailors or the coolies who towed the boats through the defile. For a long time he had wanted to do something to alleviate conditions there. In 844, he enlisted the aid of compassionate monks to widen the defile and deepen the channel. The poor provided the labor, while the benevolent supplied the resources. Thus with one stroke, as Po puts it, the dangers of the past and the sufferings of the future were eradicated. To commemorate the event, Po wrote two verses, one of which reads as follows:

> A seventy-three-year old man like me, at the twilight of his life,
> Vows to change a dangerous defile into a free flowing thoroughfare.
> The ships passing here at night will no longer be overturned.
> In the early morning chill the people wading across from now on will suffer no more.
> Ten *li* of roaring rapids will become as peaceful as the milky way,
> The eight cold hells will be converted to sunny springs.
> Although my body will die, my spirit will live for a long time,
> Invisibly bestowing my compassion to all people after me.[103]

During the last few years of his life, Po witnessed the events leading to the most widespread persecution of Buddhism in China, the persecution of 845. Curiously enough, there does not exist a single poem during those years that referred directly to the measures taken by Emperor Wu against the religion he professed. Arthur Waley has suggested that

[103] *CCC* 71.4a. I am indebted to Professor L. S. Yang of Harvard for the correct rendering of the fourth line of the poem.

in one of the twelve fables about birds and beasts written during the years 842-846 there might possibly be an indirect reference to this episode. It reads as follows:

> The beast that is wounded by knife or spear will
> always bellow with rage.
> The bird that is caught in net or line twitters a doleful
> cry.
> How comes it that the little lamb, although it has a
> voice,
> Dies meekly at the butcher's gate, without one
> sound?[104]

Po managed to outlive the persecution. In the third month of 846, Emperor Wu died, and with his passing, the measures against Buddhism were no longer enforced. In the fifth month those measures were officially removed by the new emperor. Sometime during the eighth month of 846, Po died, and in the eleventh month he was buried in Lung-men, scene of the Buddhist temples that he loved so much.

Po's life may be conveniently divided into three phases. The first phase covers the period of preparation for the civil examinations and participation in officialdom. The second phase starts in 815 with his appointment as marshal of Chiang-chou, while the third covers the years 829-846, the period of semiretirement and finally retirement in Lo-yang.

During the first phase, Po was primarily interested in success as an official in the imperial bureaucracy, and directed his literary efforts and political talents toward that objective. Confucianism was the ideology that motivated him during this period. To him, the value of poetry lay in the political and moral lessons it could impart to the ruling emperors; consequently, poetry should concern itself with political and social grievances. As he himself puts it, poetry should influence

---

[104] *CCC* 71.16b-17a, translated in Waley, *Life*, 211. The silence of the lamb was thought to be a reference to the absence of any opposition to the persecution by the powerful patrons and the hierarchy of the Buddhist saṅgha in China.

public affairs.[105] During this period, Po was also beginning to take an interest in Buddhism through his contacts with Buddhist monks, especially Ning-kung and Ju-man of the Sheng-shan Monastery in Lo-yang and Wei-k'uan of the Hsing-shan Monastery in Ch'ang-an. This interest, however, was not yet strong enough to overshadow his preoccupation with the Confucian ideal of working for the welfare of the people through service with the emperor. In Buddhism, he was mainly interested in the teachings of the Ch'an school of Hui-neng, especially that aspect which had to do with the discipline of the mind. This interest was to continue throughout his life, for in his later poems he often referred to Ch'an meditation as one of his chief pastimes. However, during this early period of his life, he also wrote an essay attacking Buddhism as being detrimental to the welfare of the empire. It is questionable whether the sentiments expressed in this essay represented the real feelings of Po on the subject. The essay is one of some seventy-five written primarily to serve as guidance for those preparing for the imperial examinations, and it appears that Po was merely putting down the standard arguments against Buddhism to serve as models for later candidates.

With the assignment in Chiang-chou, Po started a new phase in his career. He interpreted this shift as a demotion, for now he was no longer close to the sources of power and was no longer an active participant in shaping imperial policy. This change in circumstances in turn affected his attitude toward poetry. No longer was his poetry concerned primarily with political and social problems. Now living in an area where the climate was milder than that in north China, and where the abundant rainfall produced lush valleys and luxuriant mountains, Po began to write more and more on the attractions of nature, mountains, landscapes, waterfalls, pine trees, the autumn moon, the things that he could enjoy at his leisure. Since he was no longer actively involved in the political intrigue in the capital, he decided to look upon his official

[105] Waley, *Life*, 10.

life in Chiang-chou (and later on, Hang-chou and Su-chou) as a sort of semiretirement, to enjoy the relaxed life of a poet-official with friends amidst congenial surroundings. This mood was greatly encouraged by his associations with monks at Lu-shan, the famous mountain retreat not far from Chiang-chou. It is likely that Po himself was now in a more receptive mood to welcome Buddhism. The loss of imperial favor and the demotion to a minor post were, of course, sources of disappointment to him, and in searching for causes responsible for his demotion, he very naturally began to examine the Buddhist doctrine of karmic retribution. This mood is well illustrated in a poem written in 818:

> Honor and rank are what people in the past have
>   mostly approved,
> But favor and disgrace come in an instant without
>   one's knowledge.
> Suddenly I lost the imperial favor and was at once
>   demoted,
> The customary three years have now passed but still
>   I have not been considered for transfer.
> The horn on the horse's head that you are looking for,
>   when will it grow?
> The light produced by the spark from knocking flint,
>   how long will it last?
> Since former circumstances and present lives are
>   like this,
> If you do not follow the Gateway to the Void, where
>   will you go?[106]

Under the influence of monks living in the Tung-lin Monastery of Lu-shan, Po gradually became more and more interested in Pure Land Buddhism and the Western Paradise of Amitābha, though he still maintained his deep interest in Ch'an Buddhism. He now called himself a Buddhist layman, but he frankly admitted that he had not yet attained the state of detachment so highly valued by the Buddhists, for he con-

[106] *CCC* 17.5ab.

233

sidered himself to be too deeply attached to the demon of poetry, and too addicted to the pleasures of the wine cup.

The third and final phase of his life was spent in Lo-yang, where he purposely lived to avoid the entanglements of court life in Ch'ang-an. Though he still held office during this period, he really had no official responsibility, so that in fact he was living the life of a retired official, receiving an adequate income but with no duties to perform. Now that he could live the life of detachment and noninvolvement in the affairs of the defiled world, he was contented with what he had. These were his karmic rewards, and he chose to abide by them. More and more during this period, his thoughts turned to the Western Paradise of Amitābha, and to the prospects of his future rebirths in which he hoped to meet the numerous friends who had already died. Consorting with Buddhist monks, discussing doctrinal matters with them, practicing meditation and invocation to Amitābha—these were some of the daily activities that claimed his attention. The focus of his Buddhist interest was the Hsiang-shan Monastery near Lo-yang, which he was instrumental in repairing and where he had deposited some of his writings. This preference for Buddhism is also stated in two poems written in 842:

> Recently someone returned from a voyage from
>   across the seas,
> Saying that he saw a castle deep within a mountain
>   in the ocean.
> Within were fairy shrines, one of which was vacant,
> It is commonly said that this shrine is waiting for
>   Lo-t'ien to come.

> I am studying the Gateway to the Void, I am not
>   studying to become a fairy.
> What you have just said is but empty talk.
> This ocean mountain is not the place I will go to,
> When I leave, I will go to Tushita Heaven.[107]

[107] *CCC* 69.31b-32a. The Tushita Heaven is the abode of Maitreya, the Future Buddha.

The background of these poems may be found in a story which is preserved in the *T'ai-p'ing kuang-chi*, c. 48, entry on Po Lo-t'ien. In this story, we are told that during the first year of Hui-ch'ang (841), when Li Shih-chi (Waley, *Life*, 197, has mistakenly read the name as Li Shih-leng) was inspector-general of Chetung, a merchant, sailing for about a month on a ship that was blown off course by a storm, finally came to a lofty mountain in the middle of the ocean, where the cloud formation, the strange flowers and weird trees, and cranes were all of such shapes and forms as never seen by man before. Then some people came down from the mountain to ask the merchant how he came, and after hearing his story, they invited him to land and to meet the heavenly master. They led him to a place that resembled a monastery. After entering a path, he came to the presence of a Taoist master with hair and eyebrows all white, and guarded by countless body-guards. The heavenly master told him that, since he was a man from the Middle Kingdom, it was his karmic destiny to reach this place, which the master said was the P'eng-lai Mountain. Now that he was already there, the master invited him to look around the place. The merchant readily agreed, and under the guidance of one of the master's attendants, toured the palace and the mountain. The jade terraces and jeweled trees dazzled his eyes as he traveled from court-yard to courtyard, each one with its special name. Finally he came to one that was locked, but he peeped in and saw that it was filled with a wide variety of flowers. The merchant asked the attendant about this courtyard and was told that it was the courtyard of Po Lo-t'ien, who was still in China and had not yet arrived to occupy it. The merchant noted every-thing seen and heard, and then took leave of the mountain. After he returned to Yüeh-chou, he reported everything to Li Shih-chi, who in turn informed Po of the whole episode. It was in response to this report that Po wrote the above two poems.[108]

Even when Po was still living, his poems had become so

[108] See also *FTTC* 42, *T* 49.386c.

popular that they were used as models in the literary examinations, performed by singing girls who recognized him wherever he went, inscribed in village schools, inns, monasteries, and boats, and recited by monks and women. This popularity even spilled across the sea to Japan, and during the ninth century and after, Japanese literature contained numerous references to Po's works. Lady Murasaki, author of the *Tales of Genji*, for instance, wrote that she and Her Majesty the Empress read the two books of ballads by Po, and in her novel she mentioned very often the works of Po and his friends Yüan Chen and Liu Yü-hsi. When Ennin returned to Japan in 847, he carried in his baggage a set of Po's works and a separate copy of the *Ch'ang-hen-ko (Everlasting sorrow).*[109]

Professor Ch'en Yin-k'o in his work, *Yüan Po shih-chien cheng-kao* (Shanghai 1958), 321-331, wrote that Po was at heart a Taoist, and that his interest in Ch'an meditation was but a façade. As evidence of this, he points to Po's lifelong interest in Taoist alchemy practices, such as refining the cinnabar pills to achieve immortality. This interest is mentioned, for instance, in a poem written in 817, which contains the following lines: "The alchemical process is not yet achieved, and the cinnabar is not willing to die";[110] in another poem written in Chiang-chou in 818, we read: "When the mercuric cinnabar is burnt, it immediately flies."[111] In a poem written to Yüan Chen in 825, he wrote: "The mercury has flown with the smoke."[112]

In his old age, however, Po appeared to have regretted this addiction to alchemy, for in a poem written in 840, we read:

> The years pass by rapidly,
> This world is but a tiny atom moving about
>   ceaselessly.
> Man's life enjoys but a limited span,
> But the love of life is endless.

[109] *T* 55.1078a.   [110] *CCC* 17.2b.   [111] *CCC* 17.16a.
[112] *CCC* 51.6a.

While a tender youth I admired middle age,
In middle age, I admired old age.
Now that I am aged, I crave for life,
And so I take drugs to attain immortality.
In the morning I swallow the essence of the sun,
In the evening I drink the morrow of the autumn
rock.
The blessings I prayed for have instead turned to
disaster,
There are numerous cases like me who have been
misled by medicine.
To use such medicine to aid lustful desires and to
extend the span of life,
I am afraid there is no such reward in the secret
merits of gods and men.[113]

According to Chen Yin-k'o, Po not only practiced alchemy, but he also embraced as his philosophy of life the Taoist idea of *chih-tsu*, to be content with what one has. Ch'en contends that this expression provides the key to an understanding of Po's attitude toward life. Because Po accepted this Taoist idea of *chih-tsu*, all his life he accepted what he considered to be his destiny and was satisfied with whatever conditions life had in store for him. Instead of striving and struggling, Po remained content with what he had, and took the easy path of enjoying nature and leisure, and this, according to Ch'en, exemplifies the Taoist negative attitude toward life.

It appears to me that Ch'en has downgraded too much the Buddhist influence on Po's attitude and conduct. That Po was a devout Buddhist disciple is beyond question. He himself wrote on one occasion that "Lo-t'ien is a disciple of the Buddha,"[114] and on another, "I have as my master the Buddha Śākyamuni."[115] We have seen that at least on two occasions, once in 829 and once in 842, he compared Taoism and Buddhism and declared in favor of the latter. Being a good Buddhist, he thoroughly understood the transitoriness and

---

[113] *CCC* 69.8a.   [114] *CCC* 61.35a.   [115] *CCC* 70.8b.

evanescence of life, for on several occasions he compared his body to a floating cloud or a bubble or a flash of lightning, lasting for just a moment and then disappearing. If life is like the fleeting cloud, then why be concerned with earthly honors and status, and why not just be satisfied with what one has? This is a perfectly reasonable attitude for a good Buddhist to hold to, especially when he considers that what he is, is mainly due to the rewards of karma over which he has no control. It is my contention, therefore, that Po's negative attitude toward life and his contentment with what he had could be satisfactorily explained on the basis of his Buddhist faith.

There is no question but that Buddhism played a dominant role in Po's poems. This is evidenced by the large number of poems addressed to Buddhist monks, or dedicated to Buddhist monasteries, and by the recurrent Buddhist themes that he inserts into his poetry. Foremost among these themes was his belief in karma and rebirth. Again and again, he signified his willingness to abide by his karma, and expressed the fervent wish that through its operation, he would meet his numerous friends again in future rebirths in the Western Paradise of Amitābha or the Tushita Heaven of Maitreya. Likewise, he referred on numerous occasions to the evanescence of life, using the favorite simile of the floating cloud to illustrate this point. He was familiar with a number of Mahāyāna sutras such as the *Saddharmapuṇḍarīka, Vimalakīrti, Avataṁsaka,* and the *Laṇkāvatāra.* When he was ill during his old age, he compared himself to the Buddhist layman Vimalakīrti. Buddhist technical terms are scattered throughout his writings. The list would be too long to repeat here, but the following are used time and again: *fan-nao,* the kleśas or passions; *k'ung-men,* gateway to the void; *liu-ken,* the six senses; *ch'an-ting,* concentration and meditation; *sheng-ssu-lun,* cycle of birth and death; *chung-sheng,* sentient beings; *chieh-t'o,* emancipation; *p'u-t'i,* enlightenment; *chih-hui,* wisdom; *hung-yüan,* fervent wish; *chen-ti,* the supreme truth. The repeated usage of Buddhist technical terms, the frequent references to

Buddhist doctrines and practices, the numerous allusions to Buddhist scriptures, and the favorable estimation of Buddhist monks by one of the most popular of T'ang poets furnish the best evidence of how far the Indian religion had traveled along the road of acculturation and acceptance by the Chinese.

EDUCATIONAL AND SOCIAL LIFE

AFTER centuries of steady growth[1] Buddhism during the T'ang dynasty had become the dominant faith of the masses of Chinese. It provided a philosophy and a system of thought for the educated and the elite, and it served as a religion of faith and salvation for the common people. Monks who had left society to lead the monastic life, hermits and recluses who had retreated from the cares of the world to seek solace and tranquility, the hard-working laymen who remained in society and sweated out their daily labors, women who were saddened by family losses, the high-born who desired something permanent in the world of change, the lowly and the humble who sought for a better rebirth in the future—all these people were drawn to the Indian religion, which by this time had infiltrated into all elements of Chinese society.

How did the religion reach such a diversified group in the Chinese world? What were the methods used by the Buddhists in propagating their religion? What were the instruments used in the campaign to spread the tenets and practices of the religion? These are some of the questions that will be considered in this chapter. Initially the discussion will center on the educational process or the techniques devised by the Buddhist saṅgha to put across its religious message.

The principal technique used to spread the message of the Buddha was through expositions of the sutras. These exegeses were delivered by a category of monks referred to in the Buddhist literature by a number of terms such as *ching-shih*, teachers of the sutras, or *chiang-shih*, master lecturers. In their expositions, they sometimes chanted the sutras, or they

---

[1] For a more extended discussion of this spread and the factors responsible for it, see my *Buddhism in China*, chs. 3-7.

recited the texts. Consequently, the Buddhist sources in discussing the qualifications of the *ching-shih* placed considerable emphasis on their vocal accomplishments as well as their literary abilities.[2]

In preaching, it was the practice of the Chinese masters to mount a high platform and lecture on their favorite text. Thus we read about a certain Pao-liang, who lectured on the *Nirvāṇasūtra* eighty-four times; the *Vimalakīrti*, twenty times; the *Śrīmālā*, forty-two times; the *Satyasiddhi*, fourteen times; and ten or more times on each of the following sutras: *Prajñā*-sutras, *Lotus, Daśabhūmika, Amitāyus, Śūraṅgama*, etc. The audience numbered more than 3,000 clergy and laymen. Such a lecturer would wander from temple to temple lecturing to large audiences of monks and laymen.

Sometimes the master would be assisted in the lecture by another monk designated as *fu-chiang-shih* (Repeat lecturer) or *tu-chiang* (Assistant lecturer). Such an individual became very useful when the audience consisted not only of learned monks and laymen, but also of the ordinary unlettered people who would not be able to understand the language of the written text. For instance, when Chih-tun lectured on the *Vimalakīrti*, Hsü Hsün served as his *tu-chiang*.[3] In the *Kuang-hung-ming-chi* we read: "Fa-yün of the Kuang-chai Monastery mounted the dais facing east in front of the Hua-lin Hall, while Hui-ming of the Wa-kuan Monastery mounted the dais facing west to become the *tu-chiang*. They recited the *Mahāparinirvāṇasūtra*."[4]

On such occasions, the master recited the text, then the *tu-chiang* explained what the master had recited in the vernacular language for the benefit of the unlettered members of the audience. However, the *tu-chiang* sometimes served other

[2] "What is valued is a combination of vocal and literary ability. If one possesses only a good voice but no literary talents, then the religious nature will not be awakened, and if there is only literary talent but no voice, then the ordinary sentiments will have no opening to enter" (*KSC* 13, *T* 50.415b).

[3] *KSC* 4, *T* 50.348c.   [4] *KHMC* 26, *T* 52.299a.

functions as well. After the master had finished his recital of the text, the *tu-chiang* had the privilege of questioning him on various points, and the master was obligated to answer. Thus Hsü Hsün questioned Chih-tun closely after his lecture on the *Vimalakīrti*.[5] Sometimes even members of the audience might question the master on debatable points. For instance, Fa-wei, a disciple of Yü Fa-k'ai, questioned Chih-tun repeatedly when the latter lectured on the *Aṣṭasāhasrikā*.[6] Occasionally the master would refuse to answer the questions put to him by the audience and call upon another monk to bear the burden. Thus we read that the monk Meng, after lecturing on the *Satyasiddhi*, pleaded illness and designated Tao-hui to answer the questions posed by Chang Jung from the audience.[7]

There is no question but that the master occupied a position superior to that of the *tu-chiang*. This superior rank is indicated by the fact that the master occupied the dais facing east or south, while the *tu-chiang* sat on the dais facing north or west.[8] Such a practice was in conformity with Chinese time-honored customs, in which the seats facing south and east were reserved for the honored guests.[9]

It is interesting to note here that the term *tu-chiang* is also found in Confucian circles, where the disciples likewise served as *tu-chiang* for the master. Thus we read in the *Hou-Han-shu*, "The teacher studied the *Spring and Autumn Annals* of the Ku-liang version under Fang Hsüan, the prefect of Chiu-chiang, and served as his *tu-chiang*."[10] Confucian and Buddhist practice and terminology appear to converge on

---

[5] *KSC* 4, *T* 50.348c: "Whenever Tun explained an idea, all the audience felt that Hsün would be unable to pose a problem, and when Hsün actually posed a problem, then the audience felt that Tun would be unable to explain it clearly. Thus sparring back and forth, both sides were not exhausted at all."

[6] *KSC* 4, *T* 50.350b. Biography of Yü Fa-k'ai.

[7] *KSC* 8, *T* 50.375b. [8] *KSC* 12, *T* 50.406c.

[9] See Ku Yen-wu, *Jih-chih-lu*, ch. 28, *tung-hsiang-tso-t'iao*. See also Chou I-liang, *Wei Chin Nan-Pei-ch'ao lun-chi* (Peking 1963), 377-78.

[10] *Hou-Han-shu* 26.9b. Biography of Hou Pa.

this point, and this raises the question whether or not there was any interchange between the two.

Beginning with the North-South dynasties, and extending through the Sui-T'ang period, another term was widely used to designate those who explained the dharma to the multitude; this was *ch'ang-tao-shih*, the master who preaches and enlightens. According to the Buddhists, "The one called *ch'ang-tao* proclaims the principles of the law for the purpose of enlightening the minds of the masses."[11] The passage goes on to explain that in the beginning of the transmission of the law, the audience merely repeated the name of the Buddha throughout the night. By morning, naturally, they were all tired and sleepy. To remedy the situation, virtuous monks were invited to sit on the dais and to lecture on the law. This the monks did with the aid of all sorts of stories and parables, and the interest of the audience was aroused and sustained. These monks became specialists in preaching and were given the designation *ch'ang-tao-shih*. Such *ch'ang-tao-shih* became popular during the Sui and T'ang dynasties and were in great demand among the populace. With their clever tongue, smooth language, and simple words, they were most effective in conveying the message of the Buddha to the popular masses. They traveled widely, hence they were sometimes also called *yu-hsing-seng* or *yu-hua-seng*.

The following passage presents a succinct description of the qualifications desired in a *ch'ang-tao-shih*: "In *ch'ang-tao*, four prerequisites are valued, voice, eloquence, talent, and profundity. If one has no voice, then he cannot arouse the multitude. If he is not eloquent, he cannot accommodate himself to circumstances. If he is not talented, he has no words that could be appropriated. If he is not profound, then his speech has no foundation to rest on."[12]

Apparently the clientele served by the *ch'ang-tao-shih* was quite diverse, for in the same source we read that if the master were preaching to those who had left the household life, he should emphasize such concepts as transitoriness of life

[11] *KSC* 13, *T* 50.417c.   [12] *KSC* 13, *T* 50.417c.

and stress clearly the need for repentance. If the audience consisted of kings, princes, and householders, then he should allude copiously to the secular literature and present it in beautiful literary language. If on the other hand the audience consisted of common people and country bumpkins, then he should use straightforward language based on experience; better still, he should resort liberally to local terminology and just describe good and bad karma.[13]

In the Buddhist biographies we read about a certain Tao-shun who during the early years of the K'ai-huang era (581-600) traveled about the countryside preaching the dharma and converting the village people. They gathered in droves to receive the law.[14] There is another Fa-tsang who traveled widely over such prefectures as Wan-nien, Ch'ang-an, Lan-t'ien, and Chou-chih.[15] Apparently the number of such traveling preachers rose alarmingly during the T'ang dynasty, with the result that the authorities promulgated regulations restricting their travels. For instance, such traveling preachers could not stay in a private family for more than three nights in succession; if they exceeded that limit, then they must inform the proper officials, in which case they would then be permitted to stay for seven nights. If they planned to go on a journey to distant places, then they must obtain permission to travel from the district or prefectural authorities.[16]

Whereas the *ch'ang-tao* monks were interested primarily in a general propagation of the dharma to the masses without relying on one specific text, another category of monks used a definite text or scripture as the nucleus of their instructions. These monks were called *su-chiang-seng*, popular lecturers, and to this category we shall now turn.[17]

[13] *KSC* 13, *T* 50.417c.   [14] *HKSC* 18, *T* 50.577a.
[15] *HKSC* 19, *T* 50.581b.   [16] *HTS* 49.9a.
[17] Numerous studies have been carried out by Chinese and Japanese scholars on this subject of *su-chiang* or lectures to the laity. The following are the more important ones: (*a*) Hsiang Ta, "T'ang-tai su-chiang-k'ao" *Yen-ching hsüeh-pao* 16 (1934), 119-132. (*b*) Hsiang Ta, "T'ang-tai su-chiang-k'ao," *Wen-shih tsa-chih* 3.9.10 (1944), 40-60. This article bears the same title as the previous one, but is in reality a new article,

There is still no consensus as to when the term *su-chiang* was first used. Hsiang Ta wrote that probably the earliest mention of the term in T'ang literature occurred in a work by Tuan Ch'eng-shih,[18] where reference is made to a *su-chiang-seng* named Wen-shu during the end of the Yüan-ho period (806-820).[19] However, in the *Hsü Kao-seng-chuan*[20] there is a passage which recorded that a certain monk Shan-fu was converted to Buddhism after having listened to a *su-chiang*, or popular lecture. The important point about this notice is that Shan-fu was said to have heard the lecture during the third year of Chen-kuan, or 629. If this notice is reliable, it would push back the earliest mention of the term a couple of centuries. There is some question, however, as to whether the term as used here is to be interpreted in the technical sense prevalent after the mid-T'ang period, and until there is some further corroborating evidence, we may have to hold to the view that the term came into vogue just before the Yüan-ho era. The term again appears in the *T'ung-chien*, where we are told that "Emperor Ching, on the day *ssu-mou*, sixth moon, 826, went to the Hsing-fu Monastery, there to watch the

---

containing considerable new data drawn from the Tun-huang documents. (*c*) Hsiang Ta, T'ang-tai su-chiang-k'ao, *Kuo-hsüeh chi-k'an* 6.4 (1950), 1-42. This is a reprint of (*b*), with the addition of two appendices. It is reprinted again in Hsiang's work, *T'ang-tai Ch'ang-an yü Hsi-yü wen-ming* (Peking 1957), 294-336. (*d*) Sun K'ai-ti, "T'ang-tai su-chiang chih k'e-fan yü t'i-ts'ai," *Kuo-hsüeh chi-k'an* 6.2 (1936), 1-52. (*e*) Sun K'ai-ti, "T'ang-tai su-chiang kuei-fan yü ch'i pen chih t'i-ts'ai," *Ts'ang-chou-chi*, vol. 1 (Peking 1965). (*f*) Chou I-liang, "Tu T'ang-tai suchiang-k'ao," *Wei Chin Nan-Pei-ch'ao lun-chi*, 377-386. (*g*) Naba Toshisada, "Zokkō to hembun," *Bukkyō shigaku* 1.2 (1950), 60-72; 1.3.73-91; 1.4.39-65. (*h*) Naba, "Chū Tō jidai zokkōsō Bunsho hōshi shakugi," *Tōyōshi kenkyū* 4.6 (1939), 461-484. (*i*) Kanaoka Shōkō, "To Godai hembun no igi, *Proceedings of the Okurayama Research Institute*" 1 (1954), 129-140. (*j*) Fukui Fumimasa, "Zokkō no imi ni tsuite," *Philosophia* 53 (1968), 51-64. (*k*) Fukui Fumimasa, "Tōdai zokkō gishiki no seiritsu wo meguru shomondai, *Taishō daigaku kenkyū kiyō*, 54 (1968), 307-330.

[18] *Yu-yang tsa-tsu hsü-chi* 5.11a, *Hsüeh-tsin t'ao-yüan* ed.

[19] More will be written about this monk later on.

[20] *HKSC* 20, *T* 50.602c.

monk Wen-hsü deliver a popular lecture."[21] Some very interesting data concerning the prevalence of *su-chiang* in the capital of Ch'ang-an during the T'ang dynasty is furnished by Ennin in his diary. To these entries we shall now turn.

The entry in the diary for the ninth day of the first month, 841, reported that an imperial decree was issued, calling for popular lectures to be presented in seven monasteries located in the left and right halves of the capital. In the left half, four monasteries were named: Tzu-sheng-ssu, where Master Hai-an of the Yün-hua Monastery lectured on the *Hua-yen-ching*; Pao-shou-ssu, where Master T'i-hsü lectured on the *Fa-hua-ching*; P'u-t'i-ssu, where Master Ch'i-kao lectured on the *Nieh-p'an-ching*; and Ching-kung-ssu, where Master Kuang-ying lectured, title of sutra not given. In the right half of the city three monasteries were designated. In two of the three sites, the Hui-jih-ssu and Ch'ung-fu-ssu, Ennin was not able to ascertain the name of the lecturers and the sutras, but for the third, Hui-ch'ang-ssu, the Japanese monk indicated that the monk of great virtue, wearer of the purple robe, Wen-hsü lectured on the *Lotus Sutra*, and that this monk "was the foremost among the monks in the capital who presented popular lectures."[22]

On the first day of the fifth month of the same year, Ennin again recorded that the imperial decree called for commencement of the popular lectures. In the two halves of the city, ten Buddhist monasteries would present lectures on Buddhism, while two Taoist monasteries would lecture on Taoism. A monk of great virtue, Ssu-piao of Tzu-sheng-ssu, lectured on the *Diamond Sūtra* in the Tzu-sheng-ssu, while Master of the Law Yüan-ching of Ch'ing-lung-ssu lectured on the *Nirvāṇasūtra*.[23]

Other notices in the diary concerning these lectures are as follows: "First day, ninth month (841). It was decreed that the various monasteries in the two halves of the city stage popular lectures." "Hui-ch'ang second year, first moon, first

---

[21] *Tzu-chih t'ung-chien* 243, *T'ang-chi* 59 (Peking 1957), 4.7850.
[22] *Ennin* 3.84. [23] *Ibid.*, 3.86.

day. . . . The various monasteries held popular lectures."
"Fifth moon. It was decreed that five sites in each half of the
city hold popular lectures."[24]

It will be noted that these popular lectures were held during the first, fifth, and ninth months of the year. There is a
reason for this. These months were the periods when the
Buddhists celebrated the three long months of fasting[25] and
it was thought that they were the proper occasions for the
popular lectures.

The procedural order of the popular lectures follows more
or less a set pattern. A Sung source lists the following nine
steps:

1. Reverence the three jewels.
2. Mount the dais.
3. Strike the chimes to quiet the crowd.
4. Chant the psalms.
5. Deliver the main lecture.
6. Proceed and stop according to circumstances, ask and
   listen in accordance with the law, and speak on what is
   delightful to hear.
7. After finishing the lecture, then ascribe the merits to
   others.
8. Repeat chanting the psalm.
9. Descend from the dais and finish the ceremonies.[26]

This passage gives some information about the procedure,
but the account is too condensed, and really does not furnish
an adequate picture. For a much fuller description, we must
look again to Ennin. In the fourth year of K'ai-ch'eng (839)
Ennin was in Wen-teng-hsien in Shantung, and was a guest
at a Korean monastery Ch'ih-shan-yüan in Ch'ing-ning village. While there he witnessed a popular lecture and wrote
down a detailed description of the procedure.[27]

24 *Ibid.*, 3.87-88.
25 Mochizuki, *Bukkyō daijiten*, 1618 abc.
26 Yüan-chao, *Ssu-fen-lü hsing-shih-ch'ao tzu-ch'ih-chi* 3, *T* 40.404b.
27 *Ennin* 2.39-40.

At 8 A.M. the bell announcing the lecture on the scriptures was struck, arousing the group, who slowly entered the hall. As soon as the audience had settled down, the lecturer entered the hall, and as he ascended the dais, the audience chanted the name of the Buddha in unison. The tune was Korean and did not resemble Chinese sounds. After the lecturer had ascended the dais, the chanting stopped. At the time a monk below the dais, following Chinese practices, chanted a line in Sanskrit, "how through this scripture," etc. When he reached the phrase, "we wish the Buddha would reveal to us the mysterious secret," the audience joined together in chanting, "the fragrance of the rules of discipline, the fragrance of meditation, the fragrance of emancipation." After the chanting was completed, the lecturer recited the title of the scripture, and then commenced explaining it in three parts. When this was complete, the *wei-na* came out, and in front of the dais, announced the reason for convening the meeting and recited the names of the patrons together with the things that they donated, after which he passed the document to the lecturer. The lecturer seized his chowry, read out the names of the patrons one by one, and uttered an earnest wish for each one. The discussants now took over, discussing doctrines and raising questions. When questions were raised, the lecturer lifted up his chowry, and after the questioner had finished, he would lower it and answer the question. Both the question and answer were recorded, as was the case in Japan, except that the procedure for raising objections was slightly different. After lowering his arms sideways three times and before he made his explanations, the questioner would suddenly shout his rebuttal in an enraged voice. The lecturer would accept the rebuttal and reply without offering any further refutation to the questioner.

When this procedure was completed, the lecturer then explained the scripture, after which the audience in unison uttered drawn-out praises. These praises included words

248

of blessings, ascribing the merits of the service to others. The lecturer now descended from the dais, while a monk chanted a verse to the effect that to abide in the world is like living in emptiness. The intonation resembled that in Japan. The lecturer then ascended the ceremonial platform, while a monk chanted the three refuges (the Buddha, the law, and the saṅgha.) The lecturer and the audience, singing in unison, now left the hall to return to their rooms.

Then the repeat lecturer, seated to the south of the dais, discussed what the lecturer had explained on the previous day. When he came to those sentences explaining the meaning of the text, the lecturer had written these on paper, which the repeat lecturer now read. After he had finished reading what was expounded the previous day, he then proceeded to the next text. Every day it was like this.[28]

Concerning the dais on which the lecturer mounted to speak, there is the following passage by Su E, *Tu-yang tsa-pien*: "The emperor (I-tsung) reverenced the Indian religion. During the winter of the twelfth year of Hsien-t'ung (871) he had two high daises made and presented to the An-kuo Monastery. One was called the Lecture Dais, and the other the Dais to Recite the Sutra. Each was two *chang* in height. Fragrant wood was polished to form the framework, which was lacquered. Gold and silver were worked into the shapes of dragons, phoenixes, flowers and trees, and were embossed on the top."[29] The two daises referred to here must be the same as those we have come across previously, one for the

---

[28] It is most fortunate that Ennin gave such a detailed description of the procedure followed in the popular lecture, for the account here serves to supplement the outline given in the Pelliot manuscript.

[29] *Tu-yang tsa-pien* 3.13a, *Hsüeh-tsin t'ao-yüan* ed. This episode is also recorded in the *CTS* 19A.18a, but the time is placed in the fifth month, and not in winter. The passage reads: "The Emperor went to the An-kuo Monastery and presented a high dais made of agaru wood to the monks lecturing on the sutra."

master who lectured on the sutra, and one for the disciple who explained the sutra in the vernacular for the edification of the multitude.

What do the Tun-huang manuscripts have to offer concerning this problem of procedure? On the reverse side of Pelliot 3849, there is a step-by-step account of the proceedings in a popular lecture. The order is as follows:

1. Chanting of the psalms
2. Reciting the names of the bodhisattva a couple of times
3. A speech to calm the audience
4. Reading[30] the *Wen-shih-ching*[31]
5. Reading and explaining the title of the sutra to be discussed
6. Invocation to the Buddha
7. Announcement that the lecture on the sutra is to commence
8. Another invocation to the Buddha
9. Explanation of the title, word by word
10. Lecture on the contents of the sutra
11. Recital of the ten *pāramitās*
12. Recital of psalms praising the Buddha
13. Utterance of the earnest wish
14. Another invocation to the Buddha
15. Repetition of the earnest wish
16. Dispersal

Also on the back of the same manuscript but in another place, there is another account of the procedure:

1. Chanting of the psalms
2. Invocation to Avalokiteśvara

[30] In the original document there is an expression *su-chiu*, the meaning of which is not clear. Chou I-liang, *op.cit.*, 377, has suggested that this *su-chiu* should be emended to *su-ch'ang*, reading in a clear voice without tune, and I have followed this emendation.

[31] *Wen-shih-ching*, said to be translated by An Shih-kao (see *T* 14.802c-803c). This sutra extols the benefits of taking baths. The *CSTCC* 2,*T* 55.8a ascribes the translation of the sutra to Dharmaraksha.

3. Reading the text to calm the audience
4. Request to recite the text of the sutra, *Vimalakīrti*
5. Explanation of the title of the sutra
6. Psalms of praise
7. Invocation to the Buddha
8. Division of the text into two or three parts
9. Invocation to the Buddha
10. Explanation of the title of the sutra word by word
11. Lecture on the sutra
12. Chanting some psalms praising the Buddha
13. Utterance of earnest wish by donors
14. Repetition of the earnest wish
15. Dispersal

These two versions in Pelliot 3849 are not as detailed as the exposition by Ennin, but a comparison reveals close resemblances in procedural details. The only new element introduced by Pelliot 3849 is the *ya-tso-wen*, the meaning of which is not entirely clear. Scholars like Hsiang Ta and Sun K'ai-ti have interpreted the term as a reference to some kind of literature whose objective was to calm and settle the audience or to hold its attention and prepare it for the lecture on the sutra.[32] It is also possible, though not likely, that the term may refer to a summary of the hidden meaning of the sutra.

What was the nature of the texts used in these popular lectures? Ennin reported that the monks lectured on such Mahāyāna sutras as the *Lotus, Hua-yen, Diamond Cutter,* and the *Nirvāṇasūtra.* Now these are advanced Mahāyāna scriptures, preaching ideas that are extremely abstruse and difficult to be understood by the uneducated multitudes. Obviously such texts would not be suitable as vehicles for propagating the religion to the masses unless they are modified to some extent. Such modifications were in fact made by the

[32] Hsiang, *Ch'ang-an yü Hsi-yü wen-ming*, 305; Sun, *Ts'ang-chou-chi* 1.53. Examples of such *ya-tso-wen* have been found in Tun-huang, and in Stein 2440 may be found three samples, published in *Taishō* 85. In Pelliot 4524 and 4615, one finds this *ya-tso-wen* before the *Chiang-mo-pien.*

monks, and the modified versions of the sutras preached in these popular lectures were designated *pien-wen*.

There has been considerable discussion concerning the meaning of the expression *pien-wen*. Cheng Chen-to[33] interprets the character *pien* to mean change, changing the style of the Buddhist sutras to become texts used in the popular lectures. As for the term *pien-hsiang*, he interprets this to mean changing the episodes in the sutras into pictures. Chou Shao-liang and Chou I-liang[34] have a different interpretation. They think what happened was that monks took hold of some marvelous events or episodes (*shen-pien*) in the sutras, elaborated and embellished them, and then used them for spreading the message of the Buddha. If the monks used pictures to illustrate the marvelous events, the pictures were called *pien-hsiang*, but if they used literature to describe the episodes, then the literature was called *pien-wen*, or texts of marvelous events. All agree that the *pien-wen* was composed primarily to serve as texts for the popular lectures.

In style, the *pien-wen* consists of a mixture of prose and poetry. The nucleus of the *pien-wen* is, as we said, an episode taken from a Buddhist sutra, and greatly expanded by fanciful embellishments for the purpose of catching and holding the interest of the audience. The audience which the monks sought to reach through these popular lectures consisted often of the multitudes of common people who congregated on the grounds of the Buddhist monasteries during festival days. On such an audience a straightforward lecture on a sutra would not make the faintest impression, but if the lectures were interspersed with all kinds of stories, parables, anecdotes, marvelous events, etc., then the attention of the masses could be captured, so that they would be in a mood to listen to the message of the Buddha.

Of the Buddhist *pien-wen*, probably the two most popular are the *Mu-lien pien-wen* and the *Wei-mo-chieh pien-wen*. A number of the former have been found in Tun-huang. In

---

[33] *Chung-kuo su-wen-hsüeh-shih* (Peking 1957), 1.190.
[34] Chou Shao-liang, *Tun-huang pien-wen-hui-lu* (Shanghai 1954), p. x. Chou I-liang, *op.cit.*, 381-383.

Paris alone, for instance, the story may be found in Pelliot 2193, 2319, 3107, 3485, and 4988. The chapter on Ethical Life, above, gives a detailed account of the contents of this *pien-wen*. As an indication of the expansion process, the request of the Buddha to Maitreya asking the latter to visit the sick layman is presented in only 14 characters in the *Vimalakīrti*, but in the *pien-wen*, the episode is expanded into 633 characters in prose and sixty-five lines of poetry, with each line consisting of 7 characters. The request to Mañjuśrī is also expanded from 14 to 570 characters in prose and seventy-two lines of poetry.

The *pien-wen* is not exclusively concerned with Buddhist subjects. Judging from the titles of some of them, they also dealt with Chinese historical subjects. Among the Pelliot manuscripts, for instance, there are such titles as *Shun-tzu chih-hsiao pien-wen* (*A Pien-wen on the extreme piety of Shun-tzu*[35] [Pelliot 2721]); *Han-chiang Wang Ling pien* (*A Pien-wen on the Han general Wang Ling*[36] [Pelliot 3627]); *Chao-chün-pien* (*A Pien-wen on Chao-chün*[37] [Pelliot 2553]).

[35] Shun-tzu was a legendary emperor renowned for his piety.

[36] Wang Ling, d. 184 B.C. During the struggle between Liu Pang and Hsiang Chi at the founding of the Han dynasty, Wang raised an army of several thousand men. Hsiang seized Wang's mother in the hope of securing the aid of her son, but the old woman ended Hsiang's hope by killing herself. For his help, Wang was rewarded with high offices by the Han emperors, but he later incurred the wrath of Empress Lü Hou when he opposed her over the line of succession to the throne. See *Ch'ien-Han-shu* 40.18a-21a.

[37] Chao-chün, whose name was Wang Ch'iang, 1st century B.C. According to the popular story, Emperor Yüan of the Han dynasty had such a large harem that he could not see all his concubines, so he commanded a court painter to paint the portraits of his ladies. The concubines bribed the painter to beautify their portraits, but not Chao-chün, who was the most beautiful of all the ladies. This led the painter to paint a very uncomplimentary picture of her. Some time later, it was necessary to present a bride to a Hsiung-nu general, and Emperor Yüan, after looking over the portraits, selected Chao-chün. When he finally saw her in person and realized that she was the most beautiful of all his concubines, he sought to renege on his promise, but the Hsiung-nu general refused to let him. So Chao-chün went north to become the queen of the Hsiung-nu. See *Ch'ien-Han-shu* 94B.7b.

In such instances, it is thought that the Buddhist monks who composed these *pien-wen* decided to include some Chinese historical episodes with which the audience was familiar for the purpose of holding their interest. Thus the non-Buddhist themes were added.

Discussion of these popular lectures will not be complete without some further remarks concerning Wen-hsü (variant Wen-shu). It will be recalled that Ennin noted during his sojourn in Ch'ang-an that this monk was the foremost among the popular lecturers in the capital. As early as the Yüan-ho era (806-820, reign of Hsien-tsung) Wen-hsü was active as a popular lecturer in Ch'ang-an.[38] Next we are told that during the Ch'ang-ch'ing era (821-824) there was a popular lecturer Wen-hsü who was most proficient in chanting the sutras, and that he possessed a soft and pleasant voice which moved people.[39] When Emperor Ching-tsung during the sixth month of the second year of Pao-li (826) paid a visit to the Hsing-fu Monastery, this same monk Wen-hsü was delivering a popular lecture there.[40] During the reign of Wen-tsung (827-840) Wen-hsü enjoyed the prestige of a great virtuous monk who was permitted to enter the imperial precincts, but was banished because of some offense against the emperor.[41] The period of banishment was apparently over by the Hui-ch'ang period, for during the first year of Hui-ch'ang (841), he was back in Ch'ang-an, where he was mentioned by Ennin as the lecturer on the *Lotus Sutra* in the Hui-ch'ang Monastery. The career of this remarkable monk therefore spanned the reigns of five emperors—Hsien-tsung, Mu-tsung, Ching-tsung, Wen-tsung, and Wu-tsung—from 806 to 846. By all accounts he must be considered an outstanding individual. Ennin, for instance, introduced him as a monk of great virtue, debater of the Three Teachings, and wearer of the purple

[38] Tuan, *Yu-yang tsa-tsu hsü-chi* 5.11a.

[39] Tuan An-chieh, *Yüeh-fu tsa-lu, Wen-hsü t'iao, TSCC* ed., vol. 1659, p. 38.

[40] *T'ung-chien* 243 (Peking 1957), 4.7850.

[41] *Lu-shih tsa-shuo,* quoted in *TPKC* 204, *Wen-tsung t'iao* (Peking 1959), 3.1546.

robe.[42] One would therefore expect to find his name mentioned in the biographies of monks, but strange to say, nowhere is he mentioned. A hint as to the reason for this non-inclusion may be found in an entry in Chao Lin, *Yin-hua lu*:[43] "There was a certain Wen-shu who gathered multitudes in order to speak to them. He acted as if he were speaking on the sutras and treatises, but [in reality] what he discussed was none other than base, vulgar, and filthy subjects. . . . Ignorant men and fascinated women delight in hearing him speak, and his audiences choke up the monasteries. They regard him with respect and consider him the [ideal] monk. . . . However, those followers of the Buddha who know the truth and are even slightly skilled in the literature all ridicule him."[44]

This passage by Chao Lin is very revealing, for it provides a good insight into the nature of the audiences that listened to the popular lectures. These were not the educated laymen and the learned monks, but the unlettered and rustic masses. It indicates also that the subject matter of the lectures, though undoubtedly Buddhist in nature, was diluted and embellished, and then related in the earthy and robust vernacular so attractive to the common people that they swarmed into the monasteries to listen to them. Chao Lin, a *chin-shih* and a bureaucratic official, reflected what must have been the rather widespread antagonism among the literati toward these popular lectures, and this attitude was probably shared by the learned monks in the saṅgha. It was this antagonistic attitude toward Wen-hsü that undoubtedly prevented his inclusion in the collections of biographies of monks.

[42] *Ennin* 3.84.

[43] Ch. 4, *chüeh-pu*, TSCC ed., vol. 2831, p. 25.

[44] The name is written Wen-shu here, as it is in Tuan, *Yu-yang tsa-tsu*. In the other sources, however, it is written Wen-hsü. This difference has led Naba to surmise that there were two different individuals involved. See his article, "Chū Tō jidai zokkōsō Bunsho hōshi shakugi," *Tōyōshi kenkyū*, 4.6 (1939), 461-484. However, he appears alone in this conjecture, for all the other scholars think that the two names refer to one and the same person.

Festivals

Besides offering instructions on the teachings of the Buddha through lectures, debates, and dramatic performances, the Buddhist monks also performed another vital function in Chinese society, namely, the organization of the religious festivals that occupy such an important role in the daily lives of the common people. Such festivals were an expression of the religious fervor of the Chinese, and the intensity of this expression was a good indication of the degree of acceptance by the Chinese of Buddhism in China. Contemporary accounts describe what amounted to a mass religious hysteria on such occasions as the welcome of the Buddha's tooth into the capital of Ch'ang-an. Such festivals therefore provided the opportunity for the Chinese to participate personally in the activities of the religion and to identify themselves with the founder and the leading heroes of their faith. No longer was Buddhism just a religion for the select members of the monastic community; it was now a great surging movement drawing clergy and the laity together into a common effort. In celebrating the festivals collectively, all classes of Chinese society—the high and the low, the rich and the poor, the imperial family, the aristocracy, the monastic community, and ordinary people—were drawn together by the unity and the solidarity of a common faith. Such a feeling of communion may be traced to a great extent to the Mahāyāna emphasis on compassion and salvation for all sentient creatures. The Confucian rites in the Confucian temples and in the imperial court were altogether too formal, too remote, and too difficult for the ordinary Chinese to understand. Taoist practices were considered too coarse and vulgar to be acceptable to the court aristocracy and the literati. Only Buddhism fulfilled the religious yearnings of all. Finally, these festivals throughout the year provided the Chinese with an escape from their daily humdrum routine. By participating in these festivals, they could forget their toils and their worries, they could go out and enjoy themselves with their fellow men, they could shout and make whatever noises they wanted, they could sing, beat drums, dance, play musical instruments, and even mutilate themselves if they so desired. In short, these festivals possessed high therapeutic values for the religious emotions of the Chinese.

During the T'ang dynasty, there was one feature of the celebration of these festivals that distinguished it from that of other dynasties, namely the state or dynasty-oriented nature of some of the festivals. In these instances, the purpose of the festivals was mainly directed toward the support of the dynasty and the ruling family and had little or nothing to do with Buddhist religion *per se*. We now turn our attention to two of these festivals, the celebration of the imperial birthdays and the memorial celebrations in honor of deceased emperors.

The celebration of the imperial birthdays was designated by a number of terms, *ch'ien-ch'iu-chieh* (festival of the thousssand autumns), *t'ien-ch'ang-chieh* (festival of imperial longevity), or just *tan-sheng-chieh* (imperial birthday). According to the *Chiu-T'ang-shu*, in the seventeenth year of K'ai-yüan (729), on the fifth day of the eighth month (this day being the imperial birthday), the emperor Hsüan-tsung entertained his officials at a banquet in the Hua-e Pavilion. The officials presented a memorial, asking that every year this date (the fifth day of the eighth month) be set aside for the celebration of the imperial birthday, to be accompanied by banquet and music and a three-day holiday.[45] The very next year (730), it was decreed by the emperor that the day in question be celebrated as the imperial birthday in all the Buddhist and Taoist monasteries in the empire.[46] After this, it became the general practice for the Buddhist monasteries to celebrate this festival of the imperial birthday. The usual method of celebration was for the Buddhist monastery to hold a vegetarian feast. For instance, during the reign of Te-tsung (780-804), the ten main monasteries on Wu-t'ai-shan

[45] *CTS* 8.16a.   [46] *FTTC* 40, T 49.374c.

would prepare vegetarian feasts annually to feed 10,000 monks.[47] Sometimes, however, the celebrations were the occasion for Buddhist and Taoist monks to be invited into the palace chapel, where they would debate the merits of their respective religions. Ennin in an entry for the third month of 844, wrote: "It is a national custom that annually on the occasion of the imperial birthday, virtuous monks who were court priests and debaters and Taoist priests were invited into the palace to hold a vegetarian feast, and burn incense. The monks were invited to discuss the sutras, and the Buddhists and the Taoists debated with each other."[48]

Equally important was the celebration of the anniversary memorial service for deceased emperors, usually called *kuo-chi-jih*.[49] Concerning these memorial services, there is a long passage in the *T'ang-liu-tien*:

> During the national memorial anniversaries, two Taoist and two Buddhist monasteries in each of the two capitals should be designated to dispense the vegetarian feasts. Taoist priests and priestesses and Buddhist monks and nuns should all assemble at the places where the feasts are to be held. Civil and military officials in the capital of the

[47] *Kuang-ch'ing-liang-chuan* 2, *T* 51.1116a.

[48] *Ennin* 4.95-96. For other sources concerning these celebrations, see *SSL*, *T* 54.248b, during the reign of Tai-tsung, 763-779; *ibid.*, during the reign of Hsüan-tsung, 847; *SKSC* 6, *T* 50.744c-745a, during the reign of I-tsung, 860-873; *FTTC* 42, *T* 49.389c, during the reign of Chao-tsung, 889-904.

[49] Ōtani Kōshō in his study *Tōdai no bukkyō girei* (Tokyo 1937), 1.35, writes that such memorial services were already celebrated as early as 628, and based this on an entry in the *THY* 49.5b. However, a closer reading of the pertinent passage in the *THY* indicates that it is at fault. The passage reads: "Second year of Chen-kuan, fifth month, nineteenth day, decree. The Chang-ching Monastery was established during the previous reign. From now on, whenever it is the anniversary of the death of the previous emperor, one should always prepare a vegetarian feast and burn incense there. Let this be the constant practice." There is a glaring discrepancy here, for as we have indicated previously, the Chang-ching Monastery was not yet in existence in 628. Obviously, the date, second year of Chen-kuan, is in error.

fifth rank and above, and pure lofty officials of the seventh rank and above, should all assemble to offer incense and then withdraw. In the case of the outlying departments, each should also designate one Taoist and one Buddhist monastery to dispense the vegetarian feast. There are eighty-one departments in which the department and prefectural officials are to offer incense and dispense the vegetarian feast. . . . Those Taoist priests and priestesses and those Buddhist monks and nuns who cultivate the *Tao* and dispense the vegetarian feasts should all be given incense, oil, and charcoal. If officialdom is sponsoring the vegetarian feast, then it should donate to each of the two religions, Taoism and Buddhism, thirty-five portions of materials, to be used for the maintenance of the two religions, and for copying the scriptures. To each Taoist priest and priestess and each Buddhist monk and nun twelve cash should be given. . . . In the case of memorial anniversaries of distant emperors, although there is no cancellation of work, still one should perform only the most urgent of military business.[50]

Such memorial services were usually held in the national monasteries, especially the K'ai-yüan-ssu which Hsüan-tsung had established in 738 throughout the empire.[51] Ennin, while in Yang-chou, witnessed on the eighth day of the twelfth month, 838, a memorial service in honor of Emperor Ching-tsung who was assassinated on this day in 826, and recorded it in great detail.[52]

He reported that on this day, a national memorial day, fifty strings of cash were donated to the K'ai-yüan-ssu by the throne to prepare a vegetarian feast for 500 monks. As early as 8 A.M. monks representing the various monasteries in the Yang-chou area, together with civil and military officials of the region, gathered within the monastery to participate in the ceremonies. Minister of State Li Te-yü and the command-

---

[50] *TLT* 4.17a.
[51] For the establishment of the K'ai-yüan-ssu, see *THY* 50.20b.
[52] *Ennin* 1.14-15.

ing general led the procession to worship the Buddha. As part of the ceremonies, the participating monks held flowers and banners, burnt incense, and chanted psalms praising the Three Jewels. The chanting of the psalms in unison by the monks created the most wonderful music to the ears of the Japanese visiting monk. There was also some chanting to glorify the spirit of the departed emperor.

After the worship ceremonies, the civil and military officials with their retinue went to the great hall in the monastery to participate in the vegetarian feast, while the monks dined in the galleries. These monks sat row by row, and were served by managers sent by the different monasteries. After the feast was completed, the monks returned to their original monasteries.

During the Hui-ch'ang persecution of Buddhism in 845, Emperor Wu-tsung banned the celebration of these memorial services, but his successor Hsüan-tsung resumed the practice after he ascended the throne upon the death of Wu-tsung.[53] and the practice continued until the end of the dynasty.[54]

Some data on attendance at these memorial services exist. In 773, when a memorial service was held to honor T'ai-tsung, some 4,000 people were present at the Fu-ch'eng Monastery,[55] while 1,000 monks were present at the service held to honor Wen-tsung in the Chien-fu Monastery in Ch'ang-an on the fourth day of the first month, 841.[56]

The participation of the Buddhist monasteries in what were essentially dynastic functions serves to indicate the close relationship that had developed between the saṅgha and the imperial state. It might be said that by holding these celebrations in the Buddhist monasteries, the religion was fulfilling a very important role in the maintenance of the imperial cult and in protecting the imperial family and state against possible evil forces. Since these celebrations were usually held in those national monasteries established by the state, the monks living in them received the necessities of life from the im-

[53] FTTC 42, T 49.386b.   [54] THY 23.23b.
[55] TFYK 52.5a.   [56] Ennin 3.83.

perial treasury. In this sense, they were the elite of the monastic community, for they were under no obligation to seek sustenance from the ordinary laity. For instance, to cover the expenses of the memorial service held at the K'ai-yüan-ssu in Yang-chou in 838, the throne donated fifty strings of cash to arrange for a vegetarian feast for 500 monks.[57] The imperial treasury was likewise the main supporter of the huge complex of monasteries atop Wu-t'ai-shan. These monasteries were all dedicated to the bodhisattva Mañjuśrī, and they were constantly on the lookout for signs related to the appearance of Mañjuśrī on the sacred mountains. Such signs were considered to be auspicious for the reigning emperor and the imperial family, and were to be reported immediately to the ruling authorities. It is not surprising, therefore, to read in Ennin's diary that the imperial treasury would send commissioners annually to the mountains loaded with gifts for the monasteries.[58]

Turning now to those festivals that may be said to be Buddhistic in nature, the first one on the annual calendar is the Lantern Festival, celebrated during the middle of the first month of the year, usually for three days and nights, the fourteenth, fifteenth, and sixteenth.[59] It was the custom during T'ang times to have the lanterns lighted in the temples and in the streets of cities during the three nights of the festival, and to permit the populace to stay up through the night to revel in the festivities. This represented a concession on the part of the authorities. Ordinarily travel at night between wards in the cities was severely restricted, no one being permitted to be out on the streets except on some public business or critical illness. In the *T'ang-lü su-i*,[60] it is stipulated that "those

[57] *Ibid.*, 1.14.   [58] *Ibid.*, 3.70.

[59] See *ibid.*, 1.16-17 for the celebration in Yang-chou on the fifteenth day of the first month, 839. See also *THY* 49.8b-9a: "Decree of the eleventh month, 744. Every year in accordance with established precedence, the markets shall be open and lanterns lit on the evenings of the fourteenth, fifteenth, and sixteenth days of the first month. Let this be a permanent custom."

[60] *TLSI* 26.13a, *tsa-lü, shang, fan-yeh.*

261

who violate the curfew shall be bambooed twenty times." The commentary on this passage reads:

According to the regulations of the Palace Guards, when the drum at the Shun-t'ien Gate is struck at the third portion of the fifth watch,[61] people are permitted to move about. When the day clepsydra is exhausted, the drum at Shun-t'ien Gate is struck 400 times. After the [Shun-t'ien] Gate is closed, then the drum is again struck 600 times. All the gates in the wards are now closed, and the populace forbidden to travel. Violators are bambooed twenty times. Therefore, the commentaries stipulated that after the drum has been sounded to close the gates, and before the drum is sounded to open the gates, travelers on the streets are violators of the curfew. However, in cases of urgent business, traveling is permitted only in those cases concerning the public weal. In cases of sickness or calamities in private families, it is permissible to go out only if the individual first obtains a permit from the local ward or subprefectural officials. . . . [The curfew, however] restricts travel only from one ward to another; travel within one ward is not affected.

In the T'ang-liu-tien[62] we read that the duties of the guards in the city are "to question travelers on the city streets at night. If the traveler does not respond, the guard should sound his bow by snapping it. If the traveler still does not respond, then he should shoot the arrow beside him, and if there is still no response, the guard should now shoot him." During the three nights of the Lantern Festival, however, all such restrictions were lifted, and the inhabitants were permitted to roam around the city streets all through the evening.

[61] Each night was divided into five watches. The first watch was from 8 P.M.-10 P.M.; second, 10-12 midnight; third, 12-2 A.M.; fourth, 2-4 A.M.; fifth, 4-6 A.M. Each watch in turn was divided into five portions, with each portion consisting of about twenty-four minutes each. The third portion would therefore commence about 5:12 A.M.
[62] TLT 25.13b.

It was also customary for the monasteries to donate the oil necessary to keep the lanterns burning. For instance, in Pelliot 2049, the following entry is noted in the expense account of the monastery: "oil, three *sheng,* for the use of lanterns on the night of the fifteenth day of the first moon." In Pelliot 3034, the entry indicated that two and a half *sheng* of oil was provided for the lanterns.

Next on the calendar is the celebration of the birthday of the Buddha. In China, two dates were celebrated, the eighth day of the second month, and the eighth day of the fourth month,[63] whereas in India it was the eighth day of the fourth month. Fa-hsien, a Chinese monk, while in Magadha witnessed such a celebration and left behind a vivid detailed description of the event. He wrote that on the particular day, a procession of images was held, with the images of the Buddhas and bodhisattvas paraded through the streets of the city on carriages elaborately decorated with painted figures of deities, accompanied by silken streamers and canopies. The carriages themselves were about five stories high, with the superstructure held together by bamboo. In the procession were also singers and musicians who scattered flowers and incense. Monks and the laity within the kingdom were invited to participate in the procession, and the celebration lasted all through the night, with lamps burning and music resounding.[64]

While in Khotan, he witnessed a similar celebration and again gave a detailed description of the event. Streets in the city were swept clean beginning with the first day of the fourth month. Over the city gate a large, elaborately decorated tent was pitched, which served as a temporary residence for the king and his retinue of ladies. In the procession, the vehicle carrying the image of the Buddha was so large that it resembled a monastery. Within the carriage was displayed the seven precious substances,[65] accompanied by silken

[63] *SSL, T* 54.235b-236a.   [64] *Fa-hsien-chuan, T* 51.862b.
[65] Saptaratna, gold, silver, lapis lazuli, rock crystal, ruby, diamond, agate. See *Sacred Books of the East* 11.249.

streamers and canopies. When the vehicle bearing the image neared the gate, the king took off his crown and changed his dress, and then walking on his bare feet went forth to greet the image, carrying flowers and incense. In the presence of the image, he paid homage to its feet, and then scattered flowers and incense. When the image entered the gate, the ladies in the gallery showed their adoration by scattering all kinds of flowers. The celebration lasted from the first to the fourteenth day of the month, and on each day, a different carriage from a different monastery carried the image into the city.[66]

These two accounts indicate that an essential part of the festival was the parade of the Buddha images. Such was also the case in China. As early as the Northern Wei dynasty, we are told that "on the eighth day of the fourth month, the Buddha images are put on carriages and paraded through the broad thoroughfares. The emperor personally ascended the tower above the gate to gaze at the procession, and scattered flowers as a sign of respect."[67] In the *Lo-yang ch'ieh-lan-chi* is a most vivid description of this procession of images in Lo-yang during the era 520-524. On the seventh day of the fourth month, all the images in Lo-yang were assembled in the Ching-ming Monastery. Then on the following day, the images were paraded through the streets in the direction of the imperial palace. When the procession arrived there, the emperor personally appeared above the gate to welcome it and to scatter flowers. The procession itself was a gala affair. Some of the participants carried flowers made of gold that sparkled in the sunlight. Others carried ornamented parasols and brilliantly colored banners and pennants. Along the course of the procession, so much incense was burnt by the devoted populace that the incense fumes blanketed the streets like mist. All the while, the skies resounded and the earth trembled with the music and the chants given forth by the exuberant throngs, who decided that the occasion was to be one of joyous abandon and spirited play. With troops of monks and elders milling about, and with the ground covered

[66] *Fa-hsien-chuan, T* 51.857b.   [67] *Wei-shu* 114.10a.

by the flowers dropped by the people, a magnificent confusion was the predominant order of the day.[68]

As part of the birthday celebration, there was also the ceremony of the bathing of the Buddha image. This ceremony was based on the legend that when Śākyamuni was born, devas in heaven poured down streams of scented water to bathe the child.[69] This practice of bathing the image must have started at some early period, for in the biography of Fo-t'u-teng[70] there is already mention of a certain monk going to the monastery to bathe the Buddha image. Scattered notices of the ceremony during the North-South dynasties may also be found.[71] During the T'ang dynasty, however, there is a notice that placed the ceremony of bathing the image on the eighth day of the second month.[72] The ceremony was in vogue as late as the Sung dynasty, for we read in the *Tung-ching meng-hua-lu*:[73] "On the eighth day of the fourth month,

[68] *Lo-yang ch'ieh-lan-chi* 3, T 51.1010b.

[69] See *P'u-yao-ching* 2, T 3.494ab; *Jātaka* 1.52-53: "Yathā pana aññe sattā mātukucchito nikkhamantā paṭikūlena asucinā makkhitā nikkhamanti na evam bodhisatta. Bodhisatto . . . mātukucchisambhavena kenaci asucinā amakkhito suddho visado . . . . mātukucchito nikkhami. Evaṁ sante pi Bodhisattassa ca Bodhisatta-mātuyā ca sakkāratthaṁ ākāsato dve udakadhārā nikkhamitvā Bodhisattassa ca mātu c'assa sarīre utuṁ gāhāpesuṁ." "When other people issue forth from the mother's womb, they are smeared with disagreeable impurities, but not the bodhisatta. The bodhisatta, ... not smeared by any impurity originating from the mother's womb, issued forth from his mother's womb pure and spotless. . . . Nevertheless, for the purpose of honoring the bodhisatta and his mother, two streams of water came from the skies to wash away the discharge on the bodies of the bodhisatta and his mother."

[70] *KSC* 9, T 50.384b.

[71] *Sung-shu* 47.9a. Biography of Liu Ching-hsüan: "On the eighth day of the fourth month, Ching-hsüan saw the multitudes bathing the image of the Buddha." See also *FTTC* 36, T 49.346a: "On the eighth day of the fourth month, sixth year of Ta-ming (462), the emperor bathed the image of the Buddha and arranged for a vegetarian feast for the monks in the inner palace."

[72] *HKSC* 22, T 50.616a. Biography of Hsüan-yüan, who died in the tenth year of Chen-kuan (636) at age 75.

[73] *Tung-ching meng-hua-lu* 8.1a, Hsüeh-tsin t'ao-yüan ed.

every one of the ten great Ch'an monasteries [of the eastern capital, Lo-yang] held assemblies to bathe the Buddha image and to arrange for vegetarian feasts."[74] What is indeed curious is the silence on the part of Ennin concerning this ceremony. Nowhere in his diary did he mention it on the eighth day of the second month or the eighth day of the fourth month. Does this silence mean that the ceremony was not carried out during his sojourn in China, or that it was carried out but that he did not have occasion to witness it?

As part of the birthday festival there was also another ceremony, that of welcoming and reverencing the relics of the Buddha. Such relics, consisting of bones or teeth of the Buddha, were regarded by the faithful as visual symbols of the Buddha and were therefore highly venerated. Ennin reported that there were four teeth of the master in Ch'ang-an, one from India, one from Tibet, one from Khotan, and one from heaven. These were kept in the Ta-chuang-yen Monastery, Ch'ung-sheng Monastery, Chien-fu Monastery, and Hsing-fu Monastery. For the year 841, he reported that on the eighth day of the second month, the teeth were placed on display in Ch'ang-an. Evidently the display was not always related to the birthday of the Buddha. For the celebration in Ch'ang-an, Ennin wrote that the various monasteries arranged and offered all kinds of medicines, foods, fruits, flowers, and incense to the Buddha's tooth. The tooth itself was the object of adoration of all the famous monks in the city. As for the common inhabitants, they rushed to make donations to the relic. One man donated a hundred *shih* of rice and twenty *shih* of millet, another donated copious quantities of biscuits, while a third donated enough cash to provide the

[74] See also *SSL, T* 54.236a: "At present it is the practice in the Eastern Capital to bathe the Buddha image on the eighth day of the twelfth month, as it is said that this is the birthday of the Buddha." See also *Shih-shih yao-lan, T* 54.288c, "Nowadays the people in the Chiang-che area bathe the Buddha image on the eighth day of the fourth month." It is curious that the former source places the birthday of the Buddha on the eighth day of the twelfth month. See also Teng Chih-ch'eng, *Tung-ching meng-hua-lu chu* (Hongkong 1961), 209-210.

meals for the monks in the various monasteries in the city. In addition, they tossed coins like rain toward the hall where the tooth was kept.[75]

Probably the best known of these relics is the finger bone kept in the Fa-men Monastery in Feng-hsiang just outside of Ch'ang-an. According to the *Fa-yüan-chu-lin*[76] the monastery was one of the 80,000 built by Emperor Ashoka. It was said to have been destroyed at the downfall of the Chou dynasty, and was not rediscovered and restored until the fourth year of Hsien-ch'ing (659). When the stupa was opened, it was said, the relic was discovered. After that, it was periodically taken from the monastery, presented as offering to the imperial palace, and then returned to the monastery. It was the occasions of these presentations to the palace in 790, 819, and 873 that were the inspiration for the most frenzied outbursts of religious emotions by the Chinese.[77]

[75] *Ennin* 3.84. [76] *FYCL* 38, *T* 53.586 abc.

[77] *CTS* 13.4b, entry for the sixth year of Chen-yüan (790): "The Ashoka Monastery in Ch'i-chou has a finger bone of the Buddha measuring more than an inch. It was first taken into the imperial precincts to receive offerings, then on the eighth day it was returned to the original monastery." *CTS* 15.16a, *Hsien-tsung pen-chi*: "Yüan-ho fourteenth year, first month (819). [The Emperor] welcomed the Buddha relic from the Fa-men-ssu in Feng-hsiang into the capital, where it remained in the imperial palace for three days before it was presented to the different monasteries. Princes, dukes, members of the aristocracy, and commoners rushed to and fro to make offerings, as if afraid that they would be late. Han Yü, vice-president of the Board of Punishment, presented a memorial in which he severely protested the evil effects of the deed." *CTS* 19.21a, *I-tsung pen-chi*: "On the third day of the third month (873), it was decreed that monks from the two halves of the capital go to Fa-men-ssu in Feng-hsiang to welcome the relic of the Buddha. It rained this day, turning the ground into a sea of yellow mud everywhere. On the eighth day of the fourth month, the relic reached the capital. From the K'ai-yüan Gate to the An-fu Gate, decorated arches lined the streets, while the voices invoking the Buddha shook the earth. The emperor ascended the An-fu Gate to welcome and venerate the relic. He welcomed the relic into the royal chapel for three days. After that it was displayed in the various monasteries within the capital. Never since antiquity has there been such an assemblage of men and women or such a rich display of rituals."

267

Concerning these displays of the relic, there are some detailed descriptions of the emotional reaction of the faithful Buddhists in 819 and 873. Here is an account of the 819 display: "Princes, dukes, aristocracy, and commoners looked with respect at the relic and rushed to make their donations, as if fearing they would be late. Among the common people, there were those who abandoned their occupations and exhausted their fortunes, or who burnt their heads and scorched their arms, saying that they were making offerings to the relics. Some mischievous lads from shops, who willingly endured the pain of burning and branding, cauterized their flesh under the pretext that they were making offerings to the Buddha. . . . Many farmers abandoned their spring activities and poured into the capital."[78]

It was such excessive exuberance leading to mutilation of the body that led Han Yü to present his strongly worded memorial against Buddhism in 819. For after all, a good Chinese should follow the admonitions of the *Hsiao-ching* and return his body intact to his ancestors. Han Yü was so aghast by the unfilial conduct of the people that he felt constrained to denounce Buddhism as the religion that brought about such a situation. In his memorial, he wrote:

The Buddha was originally a barbarian who did not understand the language of China and whose costume also differed from ours. His mouth did not utter the standard sayings nor did he wear the standard dress of our former kings. He did not know the relationship between prince and subject, nor did he understand the feelings between father and son. If he were alive today and were sent to our capital from his country as an envoy, Your Majesty would have received him ceremoniously with one audience and one banquet, presented him with one set of clothing, and then would have sent him under guard to the border so that he would not deceive the people. But now that he is

[78] *THY* 47.13b. See also *CTS* 160.3a, where we are told that the faithful burnt their heads and roasted their fingers.

dead for such a long time, how is it fitting that his decayed and rotten bones and his evil and unclean remains be permitted to enter the forbidden precincts? Confucius said, "Respect the spirits but keep them at a distance." The feudal lords of ancient times, whenever they went on visits of condolences, usually commanded exorcists to go before them with brooms and peach-tree branches to uproot and destroy all unlucky influences before proceeding. Now, without any reason, you have taken this unclean object and examined it without being preceded by any exorcist and without any broom or peach-tree branches being employed. Your ministers do not point out the error, your censors do not indicate the omission. I am truly ashamed of them. I beg that Your Majesty cast this bone into water or fire, so that the roots would be eternally cut off, thereby dispelling all the doubts of the empire and preventing future generations from being deluded. By so doing, you will cause people in the empire to know that the actions of a great sage surpass those of ordinary man by a million times. Is this not something admirable, is this not an occasion for rejoicing?

If the Buddha has the supernatural power to bring about misfortunes, may the calamities befall on my person. Let heaven descend to witness this, I do not repent nor regret.[79]

An even more vivid description may be found concerning the festival of 873, written by a contemporary witness:

On the eighth day of the fourth moon of 873, the bone of the Buddha was welcomed into Ch'ang-an. Starting from the An-fu Building at the K'ai-yüan Gate, all along the way on both sides, cries of invocation to the Buddha shook the earth. Men and women watched the procession of the relic respectfully, while monks and nuns followed in its wake. The emperor went to the An-fu Temple, and as he personally paid his respects, tears dropped down to moisten his

[79] *CTS* 160.4a.

breast. He thereupon summoned the monks of both sides of the city to offer gifts of varying quantities to it. Moreover, to those venerable old men who had participated in welcoming the bone during the Yüan-ho era (806-820) he bestowed silver bowls, brocades, and colored silks. The prominent families of Ch'ang-an all vied with one another in ornamenting their riding carriages for this occasion. Streets in every direction were filled with people supporting the old and assisting the young. Those who came to see the spectacle all fasted beforehand in order that they might receive the blessings of the Buddha. At the time, a soldier cut off his left arm in front of the Buddha's relic, and while holding it with his hand, he reverenced the relic each time he took a step, his blood sprinkling the ground all the while. As for those who walked on their elbows and knees, biting off their fingers or cutting off their hair, their numbers could not be counted. There was also a monk who covered his head with artemisia, a practice known as disciplining the head. When the pile of artemisia was ignited, the pain caused the monk to shake his head and to cry out, but young men in the market place held him tight so that he could not move. When the pain became unbearable, he cried out and fell prostrate on the ground. With his head scorched and his deportment disorderly, he was the object of laughter of all the spectators.

The emperor welcomed the bone into the palace chapel, where he built a comfortable couch with curtains made of golden flowers, a mat made of dragon scales, and a mattress made of phoenix feathers; he burnt incense of the most precious quality, and offered cream made of the essence of milk, all materials offered by Kalinga in 868. Immediately after welcoming the bone, the emperor decreed that in the capital and vicinity people were to pile up earth along the roadside to form incense posts to a height of ten to twenty feet. Up to about nine feet they were all decorated with gold and jade. Within the capital, there were approximately 10,000 of these posts. Legend has it that when these posts shook, rays from the Buddha and auspicious clouds lighted up the roadside, and this was regarded repeatedly as a supernatural sign by the happy people. Within the city the rich families one after another sponsored preaching assemblies, and along the streets they tied together silks to form pavilions and halls, poured mercury to form pools, set up gold and jade as trees, and competed against each other to assemble the monks or to establish Buddha images. They blew the conch shell and struck the cymbals, they lighted lamps and candles without interruption. They also ordered several barefooted children with jade girdles and golden headgear to sing praises and to play as they wished. Likewise they tied brocades and embroideries to form small carts to convey singers and dancers. In this fashion, they filled the imperial capital with their fun and gaiety, with the inhabitants of Yen-shou Lane putting on the most gorgeous show.[80]

Next on the calendar is the Buddhist All-Souls' Feast, celebrated on the fifteenth day of the seventh month, commonly referred to as the Ullambana Feast. In the chapter dealing with the ethical role, we dealt at length with this festival, which was described by Ennin as "a most flourishing festival."[81] In that discussion we indicated that one of the chief reasons why the festival was so popular and widespread was that it was identified in the Chinese mind with the important Confucian virtue of filial piety. Another reason for its popularity was that the Buddhist monasteries during T'ang times took advantage of the occasion to display their rare and valuable treasures; in some instances, rich laymen in the vicinity of the monasteries also placed their treasures on exhibition. Such a display of seldom-seen treasures was, of course, a powerful magnet drawing the multitudes to the Buddhist monasteries. Very often there was open competition among

[80] Su E, *Tu-yang tsa-pien, chüan-hsia*, translated in K. Ch'en, *Buddhism in China*, 280-282.
[81] Reischauer, *Ennin's Diary*, 344.

the various monasteries in Ch'ang-an to see which one could put up the most attractive display.

During such festival days, when throngs of spectators gathered at the monastery grounds, there would often be dramatic performances by the monks to entertain the people. The themes of such performances were undoubtedly based on episodes in the Buddhist scriptures, especially those connected with the life of the Buddha during his previous rebirths or during his last rebirth just prior to attainment of nirvana. There were very likely also puppet shows just for pure entertainment. Then there were those performances of magic feats by Buddhist monks who were proficient in such arts. Buddhist philosophy considers all the dharmas as illusory and devoid of reality. The world is māyā, an illusion. From such a philosophy, the idea of illusion was popularized, and this fostered and abetted the development of the magic art. The magician created situations and objects which appear to be real to the audiences but which are in reality magical creations that are false and illusory. Many of the Buddhist monks in China were skillful practitioners of thaumaturgy, and a whole section in the *Kao-seng-chuan*[82] is given over to the biographies of such experts. Undoubtedly such monks were valuable assets in spreading the message of Buddhism to the masses. Such monks were said to have the ability to travel over long distances within a short time, to cure sickness by means of charms and spells, to walk over water, to predict the future, and to produce rain. In this connection one recalls the words ascribed to the Buddha in the *Divyāvadāna*, "A magical feat quickly wins over the minds of worldlings."[83]

In a work entitled *Sou-shen-chi* by Kan Pao of the Chin dynasty, four categories of magical feats are ascribed to the Buddhist magicians in China. These were:

1. Cutting the tongue in twain and connecting it again. We

[82] *KSC* 9-10, *T* 50.383b-395b.
[83] E. B. Cowell and R. A. Neil, *Divyāvadāna* (Cambridge 1888), p. 192, line 8; p. 313 line 15: "ācu prithagjanasya riddhir āvarjanakarī"; also p. 133, line 9: "ācu prithagjanāvarjanakarī riddhir."

are told that the magician first shows his tongue to the audience, then cuts it in two. Blood splatters on the floor. The magician puts the cut-off section in a vessel and shows it to the audience. He also shows the remaining portion of the tongue in the mouth. Then he puts the sliced-off piece back into his mouth and after a moment or two shows the whole tongue to the audience again. A variation of this trick is to pierce the tongue with a coarse needle, then pull out the needle, leaving behind no trace of blood on the tongue.

2. Cutting a ribbon and joining the two pieces together. Two people are asked to hold both ends of a long narrow piece of silk. The magician cuts it right in the middle. After a while, he blends the two pieces together, and they become one piece again.

3. Swallowing and spitting fire.

4. Causing objects to be immune to fire. In this feat, the magician throws paper or string into the fire before the eyes of the spectators. After the fire has burnt its course, the magician would then extract from the ashes the objects he had thrown into the fire.[84]

One of the favorite tricks of the Buddhist magician was the creation of a lotus flower. The lotus, as is well known, is the favorite symbol of the Buddhists; the Buddha is often seated in the lotus position on top of a lotus, and the lotus is also often found at the base of the Buddha image. Among the best-known practitioners of lotus magic was Fo-t'u-teng, whose method was to put water in an empty bowl, mutter some secret formula, and within moments, the lotus plant would appear first, then the flower.[85] Later magicians made some changes in this method by creating the lotus out of a bowl of fire or a cup of boiling water.

The famous monk Kumārajīva was known for his ability to swallow needles. According to his biography,[86] he often exhibited this skill before multitudes of spectators. Chinese ma-

---

[84] *Sou-shen-chi,* ch. 2, *TSCC* ed., vol. 2692, p. 13.

[85] See his biography, *T* 50.383c; *Chin-shu* 95.12a.

[86] *Chin-shu* 95.22a.

gicians later took over this feat and refined it, for we read that not only were needles swallowed, but also thread, and after some moments, the magician would pull out the needles and thread together, with the needles all threaded.[87]

Probably the most revealing account of such magic feats is furnished by Yang Hsüan-chih in his *Lo-yang ch'ieh-lan-chi.* Yang was an eyewitness of the splendors and glories of the Buddhist monasteries in Lo-yang during the heyday of Buddhism there, and his work, completed in 547, is a valuable historical source for the study of contemporary conditions in that city. In describing a temple fair at Ching-lo-ssu, he wrote: "Musicians were assembled to demonstrate their art within the temple, while rare birds and strange beasts danced within the courtyard. Acrobatic stunts, deceiving magical acts, and strange skillful feats such as had never previously been seen by people were assembled and performed before the crowds. Some magicians skinned a donkey in a moment, others dug a well and drew water. Some made dates and melons grow on the spot and become edible instantly. Such sights were indeed amazing and bewildering to the spectators."[88]

The magic feats and black arts performed by the Buddhist monks are also referred to in the following entry:

I have heard that there are many Buddhist monks and their followers who are immersed in the current practices of the people. Some pretend to be spirits who recklessly transmit tales of the weird and supernatural. Some falsely call themselves healing wizards, seeking gains through their heretical practices. Some burn and pierce their bodies and skins to startle and frighten ignorant multitudes. Or they may make their way to the offices of government officials to bribe them. All such practices are damaging to the sacred religion. Our imperial desire is to protect and sustain the religion, and there must never be any relaxation or leniency

[87] Wu Tzu-mu, *Meng-liang-lu* 20.12b.
[88] *T* 51.1003b, translated in *China Quarterly* (April-June 1965), 30.

in this. From now on, we must command all officials to abide by the six codes.[89]

Such references in this passage to the monks pretending to be spirits, piercing their bodies and skins, or claiming to be healing wizards, are all allusions to the magical feats performed by the Buddhist monks. The presence of such magicians is also indicated in the edict issued on the ninth day of the tenth month, 842, which specified that monks who practiced alchemy, sorcery, and the black arts should be laicized.[90]

Recitation of magic tales must have also figured prominently in the temple fairs. Probably one of the most famous of such tales is the one entitled "The Goose Cage and the Student." According to this tale, a certain Hsü Yen was carrying a cage filled with geese. While passing over a mountainous range, he met a student who said that his feet were tired of walking and asked whether or not he could be carried in the cage with the geese. Hsü Yen consented, and put him in the cage with the geese. Both student and geese had no trouble keeping themselves comfortable in the crowded cage. Soon afterward, the student came out of the cage, and from his mouth he spat out wine, wine cups and some food, which he shared with Hsü Yen. Then he spat out a girl, the girl in turn spat out a boy, the boy in turn spat out another girl. In the end everyone returned to the mouth of the spitter, and the wine and wine cups to the mouth of the student.[91]

The source of this interesting tale must be the *Chiu tsa-pi-yü-ching*, translated by K'ang Seng-hui in the third century

[89] *FTLT* 11, *T* 49.569b; Gernet, *Économique*, 242-244. This entry is recorded under the eleventh year of Wu-te. However, the era Wu-te did not last eleven years. The first year of Wu-te is 618, so that the eleventh would be 628. The year 628 was already the second year of Chen-kuan. It seems that the Buddhist chronicler was in error here. The six codes are the six rules observed by a prince in governing people, to grant life and to execute, to reward and to punish, to grant and to deprive. See Morohashi, *Dai Kanwa jiten* 2.76d.

[90] *Ennin* 3.90; Gernet, *op.cit.*, 243.

[91] Lu Hsün, *Chung-kuo hsiao-shuo shih-lun* (Hongkong 1958), 32-34.

A.D. In this sutra, we find the story of the religious student who by magic spat out a jar that contained within it a girl. While the student rested, the girl practiced some magic of her own. She spat out a flask, within which was a boy. After sleeping with the boy, the girl swallowed the jar and the boy at the same time. The religious student now awoke, put the girl back into the jar, and swallowed it.[92]

Vegetarian Feasts

Still another vehicle for the propagation of the religion was the *chai* or vegetarian feast. Such feasts may be carried out any time during the year, and the occasions for holding them were surprisingly variegated. In the Buddhist calendar, certain regular periods known as the fasting days were also set aside. For instance, there were the three long months (the first fifteen days of the first, fifth, and ninth months), and the six fasting days (eighth, fourteenth, fifteenth, twenty-third, twenty-ninth, and thirtieth). On these days, the monks were not supposed to eat after the noon meal. During the Sui and T'ang eras, it was also decreed that during these fasting periods, there would be no execution of criminals, or killing of living animals. Such decrees were issued in 583 and 619,[93] reaffirmed in 692, and remained in force until 844, when they were discontinued by Emperor Wu. We are not so much concerned with these fasting days which apply primarily to the monastic community. What we are concerned with are those vegetarian feasts which affect not only the clergy but also the laity.

The occasions for such vegetarian feasts may be the birthday of the Buddha or that of the reigning emperor, it may be the date of nirvana, it may be the memorial days of deceased emperors or of deceased patriarchs of the different Buddhist

[92] *T* 4,514a.

[93] *HTS* 1.5b: "It is decreed that henceforth, during the first, fifth, and ninth months, there shall be no execution of criminals and killing of animals."

schools. These are the more commonplace occasions. Sometimes, the occasion may be the completion of construction or repair of a Buddhist image or a pagoda or a monastery. There is an interesting anecdote about a vegetarian feast which celebrated the end of the remodeling of the An-kuo Monastery. During the celebration of the feast, the emperor Hsi-tsung (reign 874-888) struck the temple bell ten times and donated 10,000 strings of cash. He then invited the various officials present to strike the bell also, and added that when they did so, they were to contribute 1,000 strings of cash for each stroke. After the feast was over, a certain Mr. Wang, who had probably drunk a little too much wine, meandered over to the bell and struck it a hundred times. He was forced to hand over to the monastery 100,000 strings of cash.[94] During the eighth day of the twelfth month, 732, a huge vegetarian feast was held at the Shih-pi Monastery to celebrate the completion of an image of Maitreya.[95]

Sometimes the vegetarian feast was arranged as the expression of gratitude for some good fortune, boon, or benefit received. For instance, we read of the case of a certain official, Ts'en Wen-pen, president of the Grand Imperial Secretariat, and a native of Chiang-ling, who since his youth had been a Buddhist devotee and who constantly recited the *p'u-men* section of the *Lotus Sutra*. One day the boat he was riding in sank in the river, and of all the people on board the boat, only he was saved. As he was in the water, he remembered someone telling him that if he were in danger, he should invoke the name of the Buddha. He did this, and was carried to the river banks by the current. To express his gratitude he arranged for a vegetarian feast in his own residence, to which he invited monks and laymen.[96] Sometimes a feast was intended to express gratitude for rain produced by a monk. For instance, Pu-k'ung (Amoghavajra) was once asked by the emperor to relieve the drought that had plagued the capital

[94] *TPKC* 499.4095-4096 (Peking 1959 ed.).
[95] *Chin-shih ts'ui-pien* ch. 84, *Shih-pi-ssu t'ieh Mi-le-hsiang.*
[96] *Ming-pao-chi, chung, T* 51.795a.

during spring and summer. Amoghavajra set up the altar, performed the necessary rituals, and on the next day, adequate rain fell. The emperor rewarded him with the title "master of the purple robe," and presented him with 100 bolts of assorted materials. He also arranged for a thousand-monk vegetarian feast as an expression of gratitude.[97] There are also instances of vegetarian feasts being arranged because of hospitality received. Ennin, for instance, sponsored several such feasts as partial payment for food and lodging he received in the monasteries.[98] Or a feast could be in the nature of a welcome or farewell party. While in Teng-chou in Shantung and on Wu-t'ai-shan, Ennin was sent off by the Chinese monks with a vegetarian feast.[99] Mention has already been made of vegetarian feasts staged during the various Buddhist festivals. Then there are the vegetarian feasts arranged for the benefit of departed souls. Such feasts were called *lei-ch'i, chai-ch'i,* or *ch'i-ch'i.* In the *Fo-tsu t'ung-chi,* we read: "Nowadays, people arrange for a vegetarian feast every seventh day after the death of a person to pray for the benefit of the deceased. This is known as the *chai-ch'i.*"[100] Finally there are those vegetarian feasts staged by the monasteries for the benefit of the religious associations connected with them. These will be discussed in greater detail later on.

Whether the sponsors of vegetarian feasts be members of the imperial family or private individuals, it can be said that they were motivated by one underlying concern, the accumulation of merits by their acts. When members of the imperial family sponsored the vegetarian feasts during the imperial birthdays or memorial services, they hoped by their deeds to accrue enough merits to ensure adequate protection of their persons and fortunes by the spiritual forces of Buddhism. The private individual, besides expressing his gratitude for certain boons or benefactions, also hoped that he would acquire enough merits to ensure a better rebirth in his future lives.

[97] *SKSC* 1, *T* 50.712b.   [98] *Ennin* 1.8, 1.12.
[99] Reischauer, *Ennin's Travels,* 178-179.
[100] *FTTC* 33, *T* 49.320c. See also *Shih-shih yao-lan, T* 54.305b.

Such vegetarian feasts were usually held in the Buddhist monasteries. For those connected with the imperial birthdays or memorial services, the scene was the national monasteries established by the state. During the T'ang dynasty, these were the Ta-yün-ssu, Lung-hsing-ssu, and K'ai-yüan-ssu. However, there are instances when the feasts were held in private residences, such as Ts'en Wen-pen's. It is also recorded that the minister Li Lin-fu on his birthdays would invite monks to his private residence for the vegetarian feast.[101] Sometimes, if the number of people present was extremely large, the feast would not be confined to one monastery, but would be spread out over a number of monasteries. This happened during the Chen-yüan era (785-804) when feasts sponsored by Emperor Te-tsung on imperial birthdays attracted over 10,000 people and had to be held spread out over the ten monasteries on Wu-t'ai-shan.[102] There were even instances when the feasts were held within the imperial precincts, as seen in the following passage: "During the twelfth year of Hsien-t'ung (871) Emperor I-tsung staged a feast for 10,000 monks within the imperial palace, and he personally ascended the platform to utter praises to the Buddha."[103]

Such vegetarian feasts were generally mixed gatherings of monks and laymen mingling on the basis of equality. Ennin has some pertinent comments on this point. In his entry for the second day of the seventh month, 840, while he was on Wu-t'ai-shan, he wrote that in the vegetarian feasts on the mountain, monks, the laity, men and women were all served equally with no regard as to whether they were high or low, great or small.[104] He reported an interesting legend to account for this feature. Once a pregnant woman came and sat down for the feast. The patron gave her one portion, but the woman demanded another for her unborn child. The patron refused, saying that the child was not there to eat it. The woman replied that if the child was not given its share, she

---

[101] *Yu-yang tsa-tsu, hsü* 5.11b.
[102] *Kuang-ch'ing liang-chuan, T* 51.1116a.
[103] *FTTC* 42, *T* 49.389a.   [104] *Ennin* 3.72.

would not eat, whereupon she left the dining hall, transformed herself into Mañjuśrī, and flew away into the sky. The assembly of people present were dumbfounded by this miracle; they then raised their voices in repentance, beseeching Mañjuśrī to return, but he never even looked back. The assembly then made a vow that henceforth all were to be served equally. Ennin then concluded: "Now when vegetarian feasts are held in the dining hall, there is a row of men, a row of women, some of whom may perhaps be carrying babies, who also receive their shares, a row of boys, a row of novices, a row of senior monks, and a row of nuns, all of whom receive their offerings of food while seated on their benches. The patron donates equal shares to all, and if anyone asks for more, he is not reprimanded but is given whatever he asks for."[105]

The number of people present at such feasts varied from a few to tens of thousands. The expression *wan-seng-chai* occurs very often in the literature. Fa-tsang, for instance, arranged a feast for 10,000 monks,[106] while Tai-tsung in 773 staged a 10,000-monk feast in Tz'u-en Monastery.[107] Liang Wu-ti once arranged in 529 a feast attended by 50,000 monks and laymen.[108] Emperor Kao-tsung in 656 ordered by imperial edict a feast for 5,000 monks in the Tz'u-en Monastery,[109] while Emperor I-tsung sponsored a feast for 10,000 people in the royal palace in 871.[110] Emperor Chen-tsung in 1011 staged a feast for 30,000 in the P'u-hsien Monastery on Mt. Omei in Szechuan.[111] Such huge feasts were the exceptions, however; usually the attendance would be 500, 1,000, or 5,000.[112]

After the meals there occurs what is known as the *dakshina* ceremony, which consists of offering a gift to the monks present. The gift may consist of a bolt of cloth or silk, or a certain amount of cash. The latter was the prevailing

[105] *Ibid.*, 3.73.
[106] *HKSC* 19, *T* 50.581b.
[107] *TFYK* 52.5a.
[108] *FTTC* 37, *T* 49.350b.
[109] *FTTC* 39, *T* 49.367a.
[110] *Ibid.*, 42, *T* 49.389a.
[111] *Ibid.*, 44, *T* 49.404b.
[112] *Ennin* 1.14, 1.12, 2.61-62, 3.83.

practice, with each monk receiving around thirty cash. During the ceremonies attending the feast, there was the recital of an essay, detailing the name and contribution of the donor. The monk composing this essay would be rewarded with a much bigger present, around 400 cash. The monks could use this cash in any way they wished. Some spent it on their personal needs, others used it to free animals, buy food for criminals, aid the needy, or to repair and decorate the temples. Such expenditure of the *dakshina* cash for social services became fairly common during the T'ang period.

Buddhist Societies

As Buddhism claimed more and more converts among the Chinese, religious associations, consisting of faithful and devoted laymen as members under the leadership of monks, began to emerge, with faith in the Buddha as the uniting bond. Such societies were organized by the laity for a variety of purposes: constructing monasteries and statues of the Buddha, copying and reciting the sacred scriptures, arranging for vegetarian feasts, printing images of the Buddha, or performing some pious deeds for the accumulation of merits. Such societies varied in size, ranging from small groups consisting of about twenty members to large groups claiming more than 1,000 members. One society organized by a monk Nan-ts'ao in Hang-chou was said to have a membership of over 100,000.

Such societies are known to have existed during the period of the North-South dynasties, and became very widespread under the Northern Wei. In the early stages, they were called *i, i-i,* or *i-hui.* Members were called *i-jen,* while the leader of the group would be called *i-chu, i-chang,* or *i-wei-na.* Each group usually had as spiritual preceptor a monk who was given the title *i-shih.*[113]

For such groups of faithful laymen, the instrument to deepen and strengthen their faith was a sutra forged during the

[113] The terms *i-i* and *i-hui* appear in Pelliot 3128, while *i-jen* appears in Pelliot 5529.

Northern Wei period by a Buddhist monk named T'an-ching and entitled *T'i-wei Po-li-ching (Sutra on Trapuśa and Bhallika)*. It evoked widespread interest because it put forth in simple language a detailed course of religious discipline that a layman could practice. Concerning T'an-ching, we read that because the texts translated previously had been destroyed by fire, and because people were being misled concerning the dharma owing to the absence of texts, he produced the *T'i-wei Po-li-ching* in two chapters for the purpose of enlightening the public. However, his language was said to be false and reckless. During the K'ai-huang era (581-600) of the Sui dynasty, it was said that people took to studying the forged sutra in droves, members of the religious associations carried their robes and bowls and staged their monthly vegetarian feasts.[114]

During the Northern Wei period, the societies were mainly concerned with statue-building. At Yün-kang and Lung-men, numerous inscriptions accompanied the carving of the statues, which provide invaluable information concerning the identification of the figures carved and the individual patron or group responsible for the carving. In many of these inscriptions, the terms *i-jen*, *i-chu*, and *i-i* appear. One inscription, found in Yün-kang and dated 483, noted that a society consisting of fifty-four faithful devotees constructed statues for the benefit of the state, and ended with an earnest wish that the members of the society from then on would have their faith deepened and their conduct purified. The names of three monks, P'u-ming, T'an-hsiu, and Fa-tsung, were listed as *i-shih* or spiritual preceptors.[115]

Many more references to these societies were found in Lung-men. One, dated 502, reveals that a group of more than 200 members, headed by two local officials named Sun Ch'iusheng and Liu Ch'i-tsu, created a stone statue of the Buddha,

[114] Biography of T'an-yao in *HKSC* 1, *T* 50.428a. See also *CSTCC* 3, *T* 55.39a, where it is indicated that the text was forged during the period 454-464 by T'an-ching.

[115] Tsukamoto, *Shina bukkyōshi kenkyū, Hokugi-hen*, 497-498.

and they hoped that by this act the state would flourish forever, that the Three Jewels would be universally manifested, that their parents and children would ascend to the heavens, and that all living beings in the five states of existences would share in the fruits of this earnest wish.[116]

Another inscription of the same year introduced a certain Kao Shu as the *i-chu*, heading a group of thirty-two members in creating a stone image of the Buddha. The term *i-chu* was used here to designate the individual who contributed the most toward the expenses of constructing the image. Sometimes the term *hsiang-chu* was used.[117] Two inscriptions, also in Lung-men and dated 519 and 520, record the activities of a monk, Hui-kan, who was the spiritual leader of two societies. One was led by the *i-chu* Sun Nien-t'ang and the other by the *i-chu* Chao A-huan. The latter group consisted of thirty-three members and constructed a statue of Maitreya, the Future Buddha. Of Chao and his society, it is said that they "knew that their bodily forms were like floating clouds, and their lives like the frosty dew. So they banded together and exhausted their family fortunes to construct a statue of Maitreya."[118]

It is apparent that during the Northern Wei dynasty the various religious associations were concerned mainly with statue-building. Such construction activities required rather large societies with ample resources, hence the existence of groups with membership running into the hundreds and even into the thousands.

Other than the lithic records, there are also some literary accounts attesting to the existence of these early religious societies. In the *Hsü Kao-seng-chuan* we read of a certain monk named Pao-ch'iung (d. 634) in Szechuan, of whom it was said that "whenever he formed a society it must consist of thirty members who meet to recite the *Pañcaviṁśati-sāhasrikā prajñāpāramitā*, or the *Perfection of virtue in 25,000 verses*, with each member reciting a chapter. Each month, a vegetarian feast would be organized, at which time the members

[116] *Ibid.*, 479.   [117] *Ibid.*, 489.   [118] *Ibid.*, 483.

283

would recite in turn. Such societies as these numbered more than a thousand."[119]

Beginning with approximately the seventh century, however, the term *i* or *i-hui* began to disappear and a different term appeared to refer to these societies. Now they were called *she* or *she-i*. Since ancient times in China, villagers from one locality had organized such *she* for the purpose of offering sacrifices and burning incense to the deities of the soil during the spring and autumn. The new designation used for the Buddhist associations was very likely borrowed from this ancient term. However, though the terminology had changed, the nature of the Buddhist *she* remained the same as the earlier *i* or *i-hui*, namely, its purpose was to accumulate merits primarily through the performance of pious deeds. This is indicated in the following passage concerning a *mi-she* or rice association, organized by a monk Chih-ts'ung (550-628). It is recorded that "Ts'ung thought that his monastery in the mountain forest was too remote and distant and difficult to reach to be supplied with grains. So he organized 300 faithful devotees in Yang-chou to form a Rice Association, with each member contributing one *shih*, and the contribution to be sent once a year to the monastery. In this fashion, the rations of the monastic community were adequately supplied."[120] There is also one Shen-hao who in 759 organized a *Hsi-fang fa-she* (A Society seeking rebirth in the western paradise), the members of which recited regularly the *Lotus Sutra*.[121]

Then there is an interesting notice concerning two societies dedicated to the bodhisattva Samantabhadra which relates that several hundred families in T'ung-chou, Shensi, during the early years of the K'ai-yüan era (713-741) organized two societies, called the East and West Samantabhadra Societies. A woman servant in the Eastern Society once gave birth to a boy on the day of the vegetarian feast and named him P'u-hsien, after the patron saint of the society. When the boy

[119] *HKSC* 28, *T* 50.688a.   [120] *HKSC* 20, *T* 50.595b.
[121] *SKSC* 15, *T* 50.803a.

reached eighteen, he was given a menial job within the society. On the day of the vegetarian feast, the youth suddenly pushed aside the statue of the bodhisattva Samantabhadra and took its place instead. This act naturally angered the members of the society, who reviled and struck him, whereupon the youth P'u-hsien cried out, "You see the real P'u-hsien and do not reverence him; instead you reverence this clay figure, what is the use?" Having said this, he changed his body into a golden color, mounted on a six-tusked elephant, and flew away into the sky, all the while emitting a great light. The society members now realized that the youth was the real bodhisattva P'u-hsien in disguise, and felt ashamed of themselves for not having recognized him.

As for the Western Society, we are told that at one vegetarian feast, a pregnant woman suddenly appeared and said that she was going to give birth to her child in the hall of the bodhisattva. Efforts to dissuade her proved to be futile, and the birth impurities that soiled the altar led to intense resentment among the people. Suddenly the woman disappeared, and the child became P'u-hsien the bodhisattva himself, shining brilliantly, and causing all the impurities to become fragrant flowers. He then mounted an elephant and disappeared into the sky, to the intense embarrassment of the people who were not able to recognize the bodhisattva when they saw him in person.[122]

It doesn't matter that the tales recounted in the above versions have the flavor of the marvelous that the common people delight in; what is important is the indication that there were two societies dedicated to the same bodhisattva in the same locality. This provides some evidence of the prevalence of such societies among the common people. It is probable that some sort of rivalry existed between the two societies, and that the fables connected with each was created to show that each society had a more marvelous story to tell about the bodhisattva than the other. Such rivalry reminds one of that which existed among the various societies in Hang-chou dur-

[122] For this account, see *TPKC* 115.800 (Peking 1959).

ing the Sung dynasty as recorded by Wu Tzu-mu in his *Meng-liang-lu* 19.9ab, where we read that on certain occasions known as the *keng-shen hui*, the women of the city attended the meetings bedecked in elegant costumes, precious gems, and rare treasures, so that the occasions were called by the populace "Meetings to Compete in Gems."

While the earlier *i* or *i-hui* during the Northern Wei dynasty was mainly concerned with statue-building, the *she* or *she-i* during the T'ang period appears to have undergone a shift in emphasis. The T'ang societies were more interested in arranging for vegetarian feasts, copying and reciting sutras, helping in the popular lectures, or invoking the name of the Buddha. Such activities usually did not require large numbers; hence, the societies during the T'ang were often smaller in number than their predecessors of the Northern Wei. Very often such societies were attached to the monasteries. In other words, they were organized and sponsored by the monasteries to assist in the various programs which the monasteries carried out to spread the religion among the populace. Membership was made up mainly of devoted laymen who lived in the vicinity of the monasteries. More often than not, each monastery would sponsor a number of such societies and during the numerous festivals, members of all the societies connected with the monasteries would turn out to participate in the celebration and to assist in whatever way necessary. Such occasions were therefore in the nature of grand reunions, where the participants enjoyed themselves in eating, drinking, and making merry. Sometimes the food and wine were supplied by the monasteries as a reward for the help furnished by the members of the society, but there were also occasions when the members themselves had to furnish their own food and drink.

The best source for the study of these societies during the T'ang period are the rare and valuable manuscripts taken from Tun-huang. Sir Aurel Stein brought out some 9,000 manuscripts in 1907, and these are now kept in the British Museum, while Paul Pelliot brought out some 5,000 items, of which over 2,500 are in Chinese, now stored in the Bibliothéque Nationale. Among the manuscripts in Paris, there are a considerable number which contain data bearing on these societies sponsored by the Buddhist monasteries. Most of the manuscripts are in the nature of notices announcing a meeting at a certain place and time, but there are also others giving some information about the society's aims and activities. There are also a number of manuscripts noting the existence of societies having nothing to do with Buddhism and the monasteries; such societies were organized sometimes for social fellowship, sometimes for mutual assistance in time of sorrow, sometimes for self-improvement. Let us consider some of this latter type before proceeding to a discussion of those connected with Buddhism.

In Pelliot 3266, we read: "The candidate Tung Yen-ching since birth has been entirely useless. So far he has led a life of idleness, and does not belong to any society. Now he has become acquainted with your honorable society, and he now wishes to apply for admittance as a member, so that he can dispel ill-luck and pursue good fortune."[123]

This document is not dated, but Pelliot 3989, which contains data of a similar nature, is dated 894. It tells of a society in Tun-huang consisting of thirteen members, none of whom was a monk, which met for social improvement and cultivation of personal character. Members were called upon to render mutual assistance in instances of personal misfortunes, to observe order at meetings, and to punish members who became drunk and caused disorders.

Of a similar nature is Pelliot 3730, which reads: "All those who belong to the society should first pursue good fortune and dispel ill-luck. If there should be tragedy among the families in the society, then the families should assist one another to the utmost." Pelliot 3707 also tells of a society composed of members of a K'ung family, which met after the death of the mother in the family, with each member contributing

[123] This Tung was not too well-educated, for in the document a number of characters are erroneously written.

wine and grains for the memorial party. Sometimes a meeting of a society would be called to celebrate the return of a member from a long journey, with members contributing the food and drink for the party. Notices of such meetings may be seen in Pelliot 3441 and Stein 1475.

Finally, there is the very interesting document in the Stein collection (Stein 527) which describes a society of fifteen women devoted to the promotion of friendship among women. The document, dated 959, opens with the statement that our parents give birth to this body but friends increase its value; in times of danger we support each other, in times of misfortunes we rescue each other. In dealing with friends, our words are to be trustworthy. The older members are to act as older sisters, the young ones as younger sisters, with the younger ones paying deference to the older ones. The regulations are established with the mountains and rivers as witnesses. On the feast days of the society, each member is required to contribute some oil, wine, and flour for the occasion. During the meetings, proper discipline must be maintained, and if anyone creates a disturbance, or disregards precedence, or is guilty of disobedience before a superior, then that individual will be forced to contribute enough wine and food to feed the entire group. Once having joined the group, a member would be bambooed three times if she wished to leave the club, and she would be forced to give a feast for the others.[124]

Let us now turn to those documents describing societies connected with the monasteries. As indicated previously, many of the documents contain notices calling for meetings of the society, as illustrated in the following examples. In Pelliot 3372, a circular sent by an official of the society reads:

> On the day set aside for the accumulation of blessings, each member shall bring one *tou* of grain, two cakes, one arrow

[124] It is difficult to see how the last treatment could be carried out. Obviously a member, knowing what the penalty was, would not announce before the group her wish to withdraw her membership.

288

made of the feathers of the eagle, and one bow made of *hua-pei* [?]. It is requested that all the members reading this circular will gather at the entrance of the Tuan-yen Monastery at the hour of *mou* [6 A.M.] on the fourth day of the coming month for a vegetarian feast.[125] The last two persons to arrive will be seized and fined one beaker of wine. Those who are absent will be fined half a flask of wine. This notice is to be circulated rapidly among the members, and no one is permitted to hinder its distribution. If there is any delay, the guilty party shall be punished in accordance with established practices. After the notice has been circulated, then it should be returned to the present office, which will use it as a basis for punishing offenders. Office of the secretary, twenty-second day of the twelfth month, year *jen-shen*.[126]

At the end of the notice, the names of the members appear, twenty-five in all. However, the name of one member appears twice, so that in reality there were only twenty-four members. What is of interest to us here is the list of officials in the society, *she-kuan, she-chang,* and *she-lao,* which could be translated respectively as society official, society leader, and society elder. Besides the above, there was the secretary, thus making four officials in the association. Similar notices may be found in Pelliot 2975, 3037, 3145, 3286, 3319, 3391, 3503, and 3666. The only difference would be in the place of meeting. The last manuscript carried the date "first year of Wen-te," which would be 888. In some of these manuscripts, for instance Pelliot 2975, we find the term *ch'un-tso chü-hsi.* According to Ku Yen-wu,[127] the reading *chü-hsi* refers to a

---

[125] The original reads *chin-yüeh,* the present month, but this must have been a scribal error and should be emended to *lai-yüeh,* the coming month. The reason for this emendation is to be found in the date given at the end of the document, twenty-second day of the twelfth month. Obviously the meeting could not be held on the fourth day of the present month.

[126] The year *jen-shen* could be either 852 or 912.

[127] *Jih-chih-lu,* ch. 17.

feast. The above term points therefore to a feast held during the spring.

Pelliot 3382 indicates that the meeting was to be held on the fourth day of the first month of the year. Pelliot 3037 also specifies the fourth day, and although it has no indication of the month, it probably would be safe to assume that the first month was involved. The time is significant here, for during the T'ang period the spring series of public popular lectures given by the monasteries usually commenced around the fourth day of the first month. Such popular lectures were also staged, as previously noted, during the fifth and ninth months, and in connection with these lectures, vegetarian feasts, designated in the manuscripts as *hsia-tso* and *ch'iu-tso chü-hsi*, were likewise prepared in the monasteries for the benefit of the society members who assisted in the proceedings.

In one of the Buddhist texts, there is an interesting explanation as to why these months, the first, fifth, and ninth, were chosen for the occasion of the feasts and the lectures accompanying them. Śakra, Lord of Heaven, illuminated the four great continents of the four directions with his great precious mirror to look into the good and evil conduct of man. During the first, fifth, and ninth months, the mirror shone on Jambudvīpa, and hence during these three months, all killings are avoided and meritorious deeds are cultivated.[128] In Pelliot 4536, reference is made to these three feasts: "Every year during the three long [months of fasting], meetings for the production of prosperity are arranged. The pavilions and residences are sprayed and cleansed, the chapels are decorated, famous incense is burnt, and rare delicacies are displayed."

How were such vegetarian feasts supplied with the food necessary to feed those present? Some indication is given in the circular announcing the feasts. For instance, Pelliot 3391

[128] *Shih-men cheng-t'ung* 4, *Hsü Tsang-ching* IIB/3/5.405a. See also *Pai-chang ch'ing-kuei* 1, *T* 48.1114c, where we are told that Vaiśravaṇa makes an annual inspection of the four great continents, and during the first, fifth, and ninth months, he is in Jambudvīpa.

reads: "For the spring and autumn feasts, each member is to contribute one catty of oil and one catty of flour, plus wheat and other grains." Pelliot 3037 reads: "On the day for the creation of merits, each member is to bring a couple of cakes and a *tou* of millet," while Pelliot 3145 reads: "for the spring feast, members are to proceed to the home of Ts'ao Pao-nu, with each one bringing one *tou* of millet, one catty of flour, and half a *sheng* of oil, to be presented at the home of the host." Similar information may be found in Pelliot 3286, 3319, and 3391, where the amount contributed by each member was usually one *tou* of wheat, one *tou* of millet, and half a *sheng* of oil.

However, it is likely that such contributions by society members were not sufficient to provide for all the food required during the vegetarian feast. In such instances, the monastery felt obliged to contribute something toward the requirements of the feast. Data for such monastery contributions may be found in the financial reports presented by the monastery accountant to the monastery community at the end of each year. Many such reports are included in the Tun-huang manuscripts. They are usually written on the reverse side of the document. Such reports give detailed information about the income and expenses of the monastery, and to these reports we now turn. Pelliot 2032, report of the Ching-t'u Monastery in Tun-huang: "Millet five *tou*, wine, for the consumption of monks during the autumnal feast. Flour one *shih* six *tou* five *sheng* for the consumption of monks during the autumnal feast." Pelliot 2049, dated 924, report of Ching-t'u Monastery: "Millet seven *tou*, wine, for consumption of monks during spring feast. Oil three *sheng*, for consumption of monks during spring feast." Pelliot 2032, report of Ching-t'u Monastery: "Flour three *tou* five *sheng*, oil half *sheng*, made available to Ch'ien-yüan Monastery for feast after the popular lecture."[129]

On other festival days, the monasteries also supplied society members with food and drink, ostensibly for help con-

[129] This Ch'ien-yüan Monastery, according to Pelliot 2250, had about twenty-five monks in residence.

tributed by them during the festival. For example, Pelliot 2032 has the following entry: "Flour, one *shih* one *tou*; oil, four and a half *sheng*; millet, one *shih* eight *tou* five *sheng*; wine, for consumption during vegetarian feast by society members and monks on the eighth day of the second month."

The eighth day of the second month is one of the grand Buddhist festivals celebrating the birthday of the Buddha,[130] and clearly this entry referred to the items furnished by the Ching-t'u Monastery for the vegetarian feast given to monks and laymen. Soon after that, however, another entry appears: "Flour, six *tou* five *sheng*; oil, one and a half *sheng*; millet, two *shih* one *tou*; wine, for consumption by members of a new society drawing up regulations for that new society." From this we learn that after the feast of the eighth day, another feast was held the following day to entertain the members of a new society. Pelliot 2049, also a report of the Ching-t'u Monastery, has the following item: "Millet two *shih* one *tou*, wine, for the vegetarian feast on the eighth day of the second month, consumed by those society members and those monks who carried the images of the Buddha during the procession of the images." Again Pelliot 2049: "Oil, four *sheng* one *ch'ao*, for use in preparing *fu-yü* [fermented bean-curd] in vegetarian feast during the eighth day of the second month, consumed by society members and monks." Pelliot 3234: "Oil one *sheng* and a half, for preparation of food consumed by the society members who gathered and paraded images of the Buddha."

These various entries extracted from the financial reports of the monasteries do not tell us very much about the nature of the societies connected with the monasteries, but at least they furnish some hints about the relations between the two. On the whole, it is evident that the T'ang societies, according to the manuscripts, still follow the traditions of the earlier societies, and were engaged in much the same activities as their predecessors. They were likewise composed of laymen under the leadership of the clergy. A very close relationship

[130] *SSL, T* 54.235b-236a.

existed between the societies and the monasteries. Very often, a number of such societies, varying from one to ten or fifteen, were organized by a monastery, each one under the leadership of one or more spiritual preceptors who were monks in the monastery. Membership in each would vary from twenty-five to forty members. Such societies would gather for grand reunions during the various festivals. At such reunions, the members of the societies were given the opportunity to participate in the religious programs of the monastery: they helped in various capacities such as raising funds, assisting in the popular lectures to spread the teachings of the master, staging vegetarian feasts, or copying or reciting the sutras. By such activities they shared in the development of the monastery, and they basked in the glory of having done something concrete and constructive for the religion. They realized that as individuals their efforts might count for very little, but working as a group and with other groups they knew that their contributions might be quite substantial, and the amount of merits accumulated could be considerable. The cohesion of the societies was assured by their participation in the numerous vegetarian feasts. By being members of these societies, the individual gained status and personal benefit, but it must also be pointed out that he took over new duties which were permanent. For instance, he had to attend the meetings of the society; failure to do so resulted in his having to pay a fine. Moreover, whenever he attended a meeting, he had to be on time or incur a penalty. He was also obliged to contribute something toward the vegetarian feasts which were sponsored by the monasteries.

Besides the Tun-huang manuscripts, is there any further data furnished by contemporary literature? Po Chü-i, the famous T'ang poet, gives an illuminating account of the Society for the Recitation of the Avataṁsakasūtra, which the cleric Nan-ts'ao organized in Hang-chou. When Po was governor of Su-chou in 825, he became a member of the society, and was asked by the founder Nan-ts'ao to compose a record of the society, which Po did. According to Po, each member of the society, which was said to have a membership of over 100,000, would recite one chapter of the *Avataṁsaka*, and the whole society would meet quarterly for a vegetarian feast.[131]

CHARITABLE ACTIVITIES

One would suppose that Buddhism with its advocacy of mendicancy, its acceptance of the doctrine of karma, and its practice of withdrawal from society, would not have very much to do with the sick, the needy, and the unfortunate in the world, since the condition of these people is considered a result of their past karma and therefore little could be done to assist them. However, such a view of Buddhism fails to take into account the Mahāyāna thrust toward compassion and altruism, based on the fundamental idea that all sentient beings have the Buddha-nature within them. The Mahāyāna draws from this the conclusion of the equality of all mankind and the unity of all things. These are the main ideas emphasized by the Hua-yen school in China, for instance, with its teachings of interpenetration and mutual identification. Interpenetration, the Hua-yen teaches, means that the absolute (Buddha) and phenomena (all sentient beings) are interfused with each other. Mutual identification, according to the Hua-yen, means that since all phenomena are manifestation of the absolute, it follows that each individual is related to every other individual, thus establishing the equality and unity of all.

In Mahāyāna Buddhism the spirit of compassion is manifested concretely by the first of the ten *pāramitās* or perfections, *dana* or charity, the giving of gifts. The greatest of charity is the giving of life to another. In actual practice, this meant providing the means to keep the flame of life burning in the needy, or the medicine to heal and to restore to life

---

[131] *CCC* 59.7a; *FTTC* 42, *T* 49.384c. It is unlikely that the society had such a large membership, for it would have been difficult to stage a vegetarian feast for so many people at one time and at one place. Probably ten thousand would be a more reasonable figure.

those who are sick. These people to whom aid is given constitute what the Mahāyāna calls the field of merit or the field of compassion, for charity on their behalf gives rise to great merits. In a sense, the concept of the field of merits is changed somewhat here. In early Buddhism, the Buddha and the saṅgha were considered the ideal fields of merits, for a devotee in offering gifts to the Buddha and the saṅgha was storing up merits for the future, just as a farmer in planting seeds in his fields during spring was making provision for an ample harvest in the fall. In some schools, the saṅgha was considered to be a greater field of merit than the Buddha. In Mahāyāna Buddhism, the situation is reversed. Instead of the laity offering gifts to the monastery and monks, it is the monks and the monastery who are offering the gifts, and the people are the recipients; the people are now the field of merit or compassion.

Such a change of attitude is illustrated in the following passage taken from a forged sutra, *Hsiang-fa chüeh-i-ching:*

> In various sutras I have stressed the perfection of charity, for I wish that my disciples, both monks and laymen, would cultivate the compassionate heart, and give to the poor, the needy, the orphaned, and the aged, even to a famished dog. However, my disciples did not understand my idea, and only offered gifts to the *ching-t'ien* [field of respect] and not to the *pei-t'ien* [field of compassion]. When I speak of the field of respect, I refer to the Three Jewels, the Buddha, the dharma, and the saṅgha. When I speak of the field of compassion, I refer to the poor and the needy, the orphaned, the aged, and even the ant. Of these two categories, the field of compassion is the superior one.[132]

[132] *T* 85.1336ab. This sutra, printed in *T* 85.1335c-1338c, contains a prediction by the Buddha concerning the decline of the law during the period of the counterfeit dharma (*hsiang-fa*). During the decline, monks and nuns would ridicule the dharma, would not repair the sutras, statues, or buildings, would disregard the teachings of the masters and regard their own opinions as true. They would be interested only in wealth, they would practice business, fortune telling,

In another sutra, entitled *Fo-shuo chu-te fu-t'ien-ching* [translated by Fa-li and Fa-chü, of the Western Chin period], we are told that there are seven types of activities that constitute the field of merits. These are:

1. Construction of stupas, monastic halls, and pavilions
2. Establishment of fruit gardens, bathing tanks, and trees
3. Dispensing medicine for sick
4. Construction of sturdy boats to ferry people
5. Construction of bridges
6. Digging of wells along well traveled roads
7. Construction of toilet facilities for the convenience of the public[133]

The point to be noted here is that with the exception of the first, all the rest are aimed at the welfare and convenience of the public. Consequently we may conclude that this concept of the field of merit or field of compassion was responsible for what may be termed in modern parlance the Buddhist social welfare program.[134]

---

magic, and the like. They would regard saṅgha property as their own, and spend all their time eating delicious foods. As a result the laity would be contemptuous of the Tree Jewels. During such a decline, it is necessary to practice charity and compassion, to regard all beings as our brothers and sisters, and to look upon donor, receiver, and gift as empty and nonexistent. The sutra is mentioned by Chih-i, *Miao-fa lien-hua-ching hsüan-i*, ch. 10b, *T* 33.809c; Chi-tsang, Fa-hua hsüan-lun, ch. 8, *T* 34.424c; ch. 10, *T* 34.450a; *FYCL* 81, *T* 53.884c. The sutra is listed as spurious in *Chung-ching mu-lu* 2, *T* 55.126b; *KYL* 18, *T* 55.675b; *Yen-tsung-lu* 4, *T* 55.172c. Because it was considered a forgery, it was not included in the Sung, Yüan, Ming, and Korean editions of the Tripitaka. The judgment now is that it was forged during the North-South dynasties to combat the ills of the era. See Mochizuki, *Bukkyō daijiten* 4.3112b-3113b.

[133] *T* 16.777b.

[134] Passages concerning the field of merit may also be found in the *Tsa-a-han* 36, *T* 2.261c-262b; *Ch'ang-a-han* 2, *T* 1.13b. Discussions of such programs may be found in Ch'üan Han-sheng, "Chung-ku fo-chiao ssu-yüan-ti tz'u-shan shih-yeh," *Shih-huo* 1.4.(1935).1-7; Michihata, *Tōdai bukkyōshi no kenkyū*, 388-440; and in the latest and most complete book on the subject by the same author, *Chūgoku bukkyō to shakai fukushi jigyō* (Kyoto 1967), 248 + 6 pp.

As part of their social welfare program, the Buddhist monasteries established a number of institutions. Foremost among these is the field of compassion. Whereas formerly in India this was an abstract concept, now in China the concept took on concrete dimensions in the form of actual fields of compassion connected with the monasteries, with the income derived from these fields being used for altruistic purposes.

There are only a few scattered notices concerning these fields of compassion in the secular literature. Apparently the term came into usage during the reign of Empress Wu Tse-t'ien, if we rely on a memorial by Sung Ching presented during the fifth year of K'ai-yüan (717), which reads as follows: "Fifth year of K'ai-yüan, memorial by Sung Ching. As for the field of compassion and hospital, from the Ch'ang-an period (701-704) down to the present, officials have been established to govern them."[135] The memorial goes on to say that in the beginning, the business of the field of compassion was under the jurisdiction of the state. "In having compassion toward the orphaned and the poor, in aiding the aged and healing the sick, so that they would all be safely sheltered, officials of the state shall oversee each activity." Apparently improper practices arose in connection with the state-sponsored fields of compassion, and Sung Ching recommended in his memorial that the institution be entrusted to the Buddhist monastery. This suggestion was received favorably, and thereafter, the fields of compassion became part of the Buddhist establishment.[136]

While Sung Ching's memorial would indicate that the support for the fields of compassion was still furnished by the state, it is also reasonable to assume that in some cases the expenses for altruistic activities were born by the monasteries themselves.

The question of the fields of compassion arose again during the persecution of Buddhism in 845. During that persecution, monks were laicized and monastery lands were appropriated by the state. Realizing that this jeopardized the program of

[135] *THY* 49.9a. [136] *Ibid.*, 49.9b.

social welfare sponsored by the monasteries through the fields of compassion, Li Te-yü, the minister of state, memorialized the throne as follows:

Now since all the monks and nuns in the various circuits have been laicized, there is no one left to oversee the operation of the fields of compassion, and I am afraid that this would leave the sick and the poor with no place to go to, thereby causing more misery and suffering. Your minister has considered the matter. He proposes that the fields of compassion, which originally arose within Buddhism, be converted into institutions to heal the sick. In the two capitals and in the various departments, from among the venerable senior citizens, let one person be chosen who is well known for his upright conduct, who is cautious and trustworthy and praised by his fellow men, and command him to manage the matter. He proposes also that in the two capitals, ten *ch'ing* of monastery land be given; in the large departments and market towns, seven *ch'ing*; while in the other departments, let the intendants estimate the number of poor and sick and grant five *ch'ing* of land to provide food for the needy.[137]

The emperor agreed with the suggestion advanced by Li, and in the eleventh month of 845 issued this decree:

As for the fields of compassion and the hospitals, these have no one to manage them since the monks returned to lay life. I am afraid that the infirm and the sick would have no one to look after them. Let the two capitals estimate and make available monastery land that could be used for relief purposes, with the department or prefecture granting seven to ten *ch'ing* of land to be used as the field of compassion. Each field would be administered by a venerable old man chosen for the purpose. The harvest from the land would be used to supply the food needed.[138]

[137] *Ibid.*, 49.9ab.
[138] *CTS* 18A.15b; *THY* 49.10a.

In Buddhist literature, there are also scattered notices concerning these fields of compassion. In the *Tō Daiwajō tōseiden* by Genkai, a Japanese monk, we learn that when the monk Chien-chen was in Yang-chou, he arranged a *moksha* assembly for the field of compassion to rescue the poor and the sick.[189] Here and there in the *Hsü Kao-seng-chuan* there are also some references.[140] Working in conjunction with the fields of compassion were the hospitals established in the monasteries to assist the sick and the ailing.[141] Such hospitals gave free services to those who needed them. The Buddha often referred to himself as the great physician who cured the ills of the world. Of course, he was speaking in the spiritual sense, but later monks took the passage literally and became healers of the flesh. It is not surprising therefore, to find among the Buddhist monks in China a number who were proficient in medicine. An Shih-kao (second century), Fo-t'u-teng (fourth century), and Buddhayásas (fifth century) were acknowledged masters in the art of healing. During the T'ang dynasty, there were two well-known Indian physicians who attended the T'ang emperors. Although it is not known definitely whether or not they were Buddhist monks, the likelihood is that they were. One was named Na-lo-erh-p'o-sa, who arrived in China in 648 and was commissioned by T'ai-tsung to make some longevity pills. The other was Lu-chia-i-to, physician to Kao-tsung, who also consulted him about longevity pills.[142]

In the Chinese records, the fields of compassion and the hospitals were often mentioned together, *pei-t'ien yang-ping-*

[189] *T* 51.992b.

[140] *HKSC* 29, *T* 50.698b, biography of Hui-chen; *HKSC* 29, *T* 50.697a, biography of Te-mei; *HKSC* 15, *T* 50.541b, biography of Fa-ch'ang; *HKSC* 25, *T* 50.664a, biography of Fa-yün.

[141] See Chao I, *Kai-yü ts'ung-k'ao* 27.577, Commercial Press ed. (Shanghai 1957): "During T'ang times, hospitals were under the management of monasteries and monks."

[142] See article on "Byo" in Hōbōgirin 3.225-265; Pierre Huard and Ming Wong, *La Medécine Chinoise au cours des Siècles* (Paris 1959), 27-32.

fang. Not only did the hospitals take care of the sick, but also the beggars. For instance, we learn from one source that "in the tenth month of the twenty-second year of K'ai-yüan [734] beggars were prohibited in the capital, and it was ordered that hospitals should gather them together and take care of them."[143] A similar notice is found in another source, "Beggars are forbidden in the capital; they are to be put in hospitals and fed there."[144]

There are some instances of individual monks establishing a hospital. For instance, Narendrayaśas is said to have established separate facilities to take care of male and female sick patients in a beautiful valley near some springs in the western hills of Chi-chün (present-day Chi-hsien in Ho-nan).[145]

Through these fields of compassion and the hospitals, the Buddhist monks were able to render significant service in caring for the aged, the infirm, and the poor, in healing those who were afflicted with sickness, and in dispensing medicine to all who needed it. In times of calamity such as a famine, they often engaged in relief work to alleviate conditions. We read of one Fa-chin, a native of Liang-chou, who during a great famine urged the state to open its granaries to succor the hungry, and when the granaries were exhausted, he offered his own flesh to the hungry. The latter however refused to accept the offer.[146] Probably the most common method practiced by the Buddhist monastery to feed the hungry multitude was the convening of assemblies which were in effect huge vegetarian feasts open to all equally. During the reign of Emperor Wu of the Liang dynasty, such assemblies were frequent and gigantic affairs, and throughout the T'ang period, they continued to be held and to draw huge throngs.[147]

The various altruistic activities carried out by the Buddhist monks and monasteries mentioned above were directed primarily toward those who were less fortunate in life, the poor,

[143] *THY* 49.9b; *CTW* 704.3b-4a.
[144] *T'ung-chien*, ch. 214, *T'ang-chi* 30, Peking ed., 3.6809.
[145] *HKSC* 2, *T* 50.432c.   [146] *KSC* 12, *T* 50.404b.
[147] *SKSC* 1, *T* 50.713b for a feast staged by Amoghavajra.

the aged, the sick, and the hungry. Some of the other welfare projects, directed more toward the benefit and good of the general public, were road- and bridge-building activities, clearing and deepening of river channels, digging wells, providing bath houses, planting trees, maintaining inns for pilgrims going to famous mountains or shrines. To honor such public-spirited monks, special sections in the biographical collections were devoted to them, designated as *hsing-fu-p'ien* (Section on monks who increase merits). The section in the *Hsü Kao-seng-chuan* (c. 29) mentioned seventeen such monks, while *Sung Kao-seng-chuan* (c. 27 and c. 28) mentioned fifty-six in all. Frequently the notices concerning the public welfare works are too short and meager to be meaningful. One exception is a notice concerning a monk Ming-yüan written by the poet Po Chü-i. We are told by Po that the region between Huai-shui and Ssu-shui was frequently flooded during heavy rains. Ming-yüan, with the cooperation of the local prefect, planted 10,000 trees in the area; when the trees matured, the floods were controlled.[148]

In the notice concerning the Ching-lo Monastery in the *Lo-yang ch'ieh-lan-chi* (c. 1), we learn that monks planted trees, then dug a well nearby. Water from the well was drawn up and stored in a trough, and near it were iron cups for travelers who rested under the trees. The well was called an *i-ching*, or public well.[149]

As for bathhouses we read of a certain monk Shou-ju who in 722 wanted to build a bathhouse in Fukien. However, the site he had in mind was too high, for the spring that would supply the water was below it. One night, another spring began gushing water above the site. Shou-ju considered this to be a sign that the Buddha was giving his approval to the site as a bathhouse, which he then built to accommodate monks and the laity.[150] Another passage described the bathhouse built by monk Chih-hui in Lo-yang. After it was completed,

[148] *Po Hsiang-shan-chi*, ch. 60, *Kuo-hsüeh chi-pen ts'ung-shu* ed., 9.55.
[149] *T* 51.1003b.   [150] *SKSC* 26, *T* 50.875b.

the inhabitants of Lo-yang, monks and laymen, high and low, rich and poor, flocked to the bathhouse. It was open the first five days of every month, and when it was in business, customers came ceaselessly. All in all, it was estimated that there were between two and three thousand customers who patronized the bathhouse annually during the seventy or so days it was open.[151]

The last example of public service carried out by the monks and monasteries are the *p'u-t'ung-yüan* or common cloisters established for the benefit of pilgrims who traveled to Wu-t'ai-shan to visit the sacred shrines there. Wu-t'ai-shan, located in the northeastern corner of the present province of Shansi, was during T'ang times an important monastic center dedicated to the cult of Mañjuśrī, the bodhisattva of wisdom. Because of the numerous miracles said to have taken place there and attributed to Mañjuśrī, and also because of the beautiful scenery everywhere in the mountains, Wu-t'ai-shan was a favorite goal for pious pilgrims. However, the mountainous area was sparsely settled, and pilgrims making the difficult and arduous journey from the plains of north China to the top of the mountains where the sacred shrines were located would have experienced considerable difficulty and hardship in finding lodgings along the way. For the benefit and well-being of weary lay pilgrims and traveling monks, the Buddhist saṅgha established what were called common cloisters all along the main routes to the top of the mountains. They were so called because they were open to all without discrimination: any traveler on the road could avail himself of the facilities of these common cloisters.[152]

To go back to the question raised at the beginning of this chapter, what were the methods used by the Buddhists in popularizing their religion among the Chinese? We have examined the techniques and methods devised by the Bud-

[151] *SKSC* 28, *T* 50.884a.

[152] In the chapter on economic activities, there is already an extended discussion of these common cloisters, based mainly on the diary of Ennin, and so there is no need to repeat here what has already been written there.

dhists to extend their teachings to the general public, the different individuals engaged in this process of education and their roles, the types of literature created by the Buddhists to convey the message of the Buddha and the numerous festivals sponsored by the Buddhist saṅgha throughout the year. As we have seen, such festivals attracted huge throngs, and they served as one of the most effective means to draw the masses of Chinese to the religion because they combined pleasure with the serious business of propagating the tenets and practices of Buddhism, and they provided the people with an easy way of expressing their religious fervor. Then there were the vegetarian feasts staged for many reasons by the monasteries, monks, and pious laymen. These feats, as we have also seen, provided opportunities for social fraternizing between the clergy and the laity on a basis of equality, thus encouraging a spirit of friendship, cooperation, and camaraderie between the two. Such friendship and cooperation were nurtured and encouraged by the religious societies sponsored by the monasteries for various purposes. The societies created cordial relations between the monasteries and the communities in which they were located, and the members of the societies were made to feel that they were contributing substantially toward the progress of the religion. Finally, we must mention the charitable activities which the monasteries sponsored. In the light of such a variegated program, it comes as no surprise that so many Chinese during the T'ang dynasty, when the religion was at its highest point of development in China, were attracted to the religion and participated faithfully and fervently in the different activities of the monasteries. Buddhism had now become thoroughly acclimated to the Chinese scene, it had become an integral part of the Chinese cultural pattern.

BIBLIOGRAPHY

I. PRIMARY SOURCES

Book of the Discipline, tr. by I. B. Horner, London, vol. 1, 1938; vol. 2, 1940; vol. 4, 1951.

Ch'an-yüan ch'ing-kuei, in *Hsü Tsang-ching* II/16/5.

Ch'ang-a-han-ching, tr. by Buddhayaśas, *T* 1, no. 1.

Chao Tzu-ku erh-shih-ssu hsiao shu-hua ho-pi, by Chao Meng-chien, Peking, 1933.

Chen-yüan hsü-k'ai-yüan-lu, by Yüan-chao, *T* 55, no. 2156.

Chen-yüan hsin-ting shih-chiao mu-lu, *T* 55, no. 2157.

Chi ku-chin fo-tao lun-heng, by Tao-hsüan, *T* 52, no. 2104.

Chi sha-men pu-ying pai-su teng-shih, by Yen-tsung, *T* 52, no. 2108.

Ch'ien Han-shu (Po-na ed.).

Chih-kuan fu-hsing ch'uan-hung-chüeh, by Chan-jan, *T* 46, no. 1912.

Chin-kuang-ming-ching wen-chü, by Chih-i, *T* 39, no. 1785.

Chin-shih ts'ui-pien, by Wang Ch'ang.

Chin-shu (Po-na ed.).

Ching-lü i-hsiang, by Pao-ch'ang, *T* 53, no. 2121.

Chiu tsa-pi-yü-ching, tr. by K'ang Seng-hui, *T* 4, no. 206.

Chiu T'ang-sshu (Po-na ed.).

Chu-ching yao-chi, *T* 54, no. 2123.

Ch'u San-tsang chi-chi, by Seng-yu, *T* 55, no. 2145.

Ch'üan Tang-wen.

Chung-a-han-ching, tr. by Sanghadeva, *T* 1, no. 26.

Chung-ching mu-lu, by Fa-ching, *T* 55, no. 2146.

Dialogues of the Buddha, tr. by T. W. Rhys Davids, London, vol. 1, 1899.

Dīghanikāya.

Divyāvadāna, ed. E. B. Cowell and R. A. Neil, Cambridge, 1888.

Eihei shingi, by Dōgen, *T* 82, no. 2584.

Ennin's Diary, tr. by E. O. Reischauer, New York, 1955.

Fa-hsien-chuan, *T* 51, no. 2085.

Fa-hua hsüan-lun, by Chi-tsang, *T* 34, no. 1720.

Fa-yüan chu-lin, by Tao-shih, *T* 53, 2122.

Fan-wang-ching, tr. by Kumārajīva, *T* 24, no. 1484.

Fo-i chiao-ching, tr. by Kumārajīva, *T* 3, no. 389.

Fo sheng T'ao-li-t'ien wei-mu shuo-fa-ching, tr. by Dharma-raksha, *T* 17, no. 815.

Fo-shuo chu-te fu-t'ien-ching, tr. by Fa-li and Fa-chü, *T* 16, no. 683.

Fo-tsu li-tai t'ung-tsai, by Nien-ch'ang, *T* 49, no. 2036.

Fo-tsu t'ung-chi, by Chih-p'an, *T* 49, no. 2035.

Fu-chiao-pien, by Ch'i-sung, *T* 52, no. 2115.

Fu-mu-en nan-pao-ching, tr. by An Shih-kao, *T* 16, no. 684.

Gradual Sayings, tr. by E. M. Hare, London, 1935.

Hou Han-shu (Po-na ed.).

Hsiang-fa chüeh-i-ching, *T* 85, no. 2870.

Hsiao-tzu-chuan, by Liu Hsiang, *Shih-chung ku-i-shu* ed.

Hsin T'ang-shu (Po-na ed.).

Hsü Kao-seng-chuan, by Tao-hsüan, *T* 50, no. 2060.

Hsü Ch'ing-liang-chuan, by Chang Shang-ying, *T* 51, no. 2100.

Huan-chu ch'ing-kuei, in *Hsü Tsang-ching* II/16/5.

Hung-ming-chi, by Seng-yu, *T* 52, no. 2102.

Jen-wang-ching, tr. by Kumārajīva, *T* 8, no. 245; tr. by Amoghavajra, *T* 8, no. 246.

Jen-wang-ching su, by Chih-i, in *Hsü Tsang-ching* I/40/4.

Jih-chih-lu, by Ku Yen-wu.

K'ai-yüan shih-chiao-lu, by Chih-sheng, *T* 55, no. 2154.

Kai-yü ts'ung-k'ao, by Chao I, Shanghai, 1957.

Kao-seng-chuan, by Hui-chiao, *T* 50, no. 2059.

Ken-pen shuo-i-ch'ieh yu-pu p'i-nai-ya, *T* 24, no. 1448.

Kuan-ting-ching, tr. by Śrīmitra, *T* 21, no. 1331.

Kuang-ch'ing-liang-chuan, by Yen-i, *T* 51, no. 2099.

Kuang-hung-ming-chi, by Tao-hsüan, *T* 52, no. 2103.

Lai-nan-lu, by Li Ao, *SPTK* ed.

Liang-ching hsin-chi, by Wei Shu, in *Yüeh-ya-t'ang ts'ung-shu*.

Liu Meng-te wen-chi, by Liu Yü-hsi, *SPTK* ed.

Liu-tu chi-ching, tr. by K'ang Seng-hui, *T* 3, no. 152.

Lo-yang ch'ieh-lan-chi, by Yang Hsüan-chih, *T* 51, no. 2092.

Lu Hsüan-kung-chi, by Lu Chih, *SPPY* ed.

The Mahāvaṁsa, tr. by W. Geiger, London, 1912.

The Mahāvastu, tr by J. J. Jones, London, 3 vol., 1940-1956.

Les Mémoires historiques, tr. by E. Chavannes, Paris, vol. 1, 1895.

Meng Hao-jan-chi, by Meng Hao-jan, *SPTK* ed.

Meng-liang-lu, by Wu Tzu-mu.

Miao-fa lien-hua-ching, tr. by Kumārajīva, *T* 9, no. 292.

Miao-fa lien-hua-ching hsüan-i, by Chih-i, *T* 33, no. 1716.

Middle Length Sayings, tr. by I. B. Horner, London, vol. 1, 1954.

Ming-pao-chi, by T'ang Lin, *T* 51, no. 2082.

The Minor Readings, tr. by Ñanamoli, London, 1960.

Mo-ho-seng-ch'i-lü, *T* 22, no. 1425.

Nittō-guhō junrei gyōki, by Ennin, in *Dainihon bukkyō zensho*, vol. 113.

Pai-chang ch'ing-kuei, *T* 48, no. 2025.

Pai-chang ta-shih ch'an-shih yü-lu, in *Ku-tsun-su yü-lu, Hsü Tsang-ching* II/23/2.

Pao-p'u-tzu, by Ko Hung.

Pelliot 2032, 2040, 2049, 2193, 2285, 2319, 2418, 2507, 2553, 2686, 2721, 2932, 2975, 3004, 3037, 3051, 3107, 3124, 3145, 3153, 3234, 3266, 3286, 3319, 3361, 3372, 3391, 3441, 3453, 3472, 3485, 3503, 3627, 3666, 3707, 3730, 3849, 3919, 3959, 3989, 4525, 4536, 4615, 4988.

Pien-cheng-lun, by Fa-lin, *T* 52, no. 2109.

P'o-hsieh-lun, by Fa-lin, *T* 52, no. 2109.

Po Hsiang-shan-chi, by Po Chü-i, *Kuo-hsüeh chi-pen ts'ung shu* ed.

Po-shih Ch'ang-ch'ing-chi, by Po Chü-i, *SPTK* ed.

Pu-k'ung piao-chih-chi, *T* 52, no. 2120.

P'u-sa Shan-tzu-ching, *T* 3, no. 174.

P'u-yao-ching, tr. by Dharmaraksha, *T* 3, no. 186.

The Questions of King Milinda, tr. by T. W. Rhys Davids, New York, 2 vols., 1963.

Seng-shih-lüeh, by Tsan-ning, *T* 54, no. 2126.

Shan-tzu-ching, tr. by Sheng-chien, *T* 3, no. 175.

Shang-shu ku-shih, by Li Ch'o, *TSCC* ed.

Shih-chi (Po-na ed.).

Shih-men cheng-t'ung, by Tsung-chien, in *Hsü Tsang-ching* IIB/3/5.

Shih-shih yao-lan, by Tao-ch'eng, *T* 54, no. 2127.

Shih-shih chi-ku-lüeh, by Chüeh-an, *T* 49, no. 2037.

Shih-sung-lü, *T* 23, no. 1435.

Stein PI, S527, 1475, 2051, 2084, 2440, 2614, 3704, 3728, 4445.

Sou-shen-chi, by Kan Pao, *TSCC* ed.

Ssu-fen-lü hsing-shih-ch'ao tzu-ch'ih-chi, by Yüan-chao, *T* 40, no. 1805.

Sung Kao-seng-chuan, by Tsan-ning, *T* 50, no. 2061.

Sung-shu (Po-na ed.).

Ta fang-kuang fo hua-yen-ching, tr. by Śikshānanda, *T* 10, no. 279.

Ta-jih-ching su, by I-hsing, *T* 39, no. 1796.

Ta-pan nieh-p'an-ching, tr. by Dharmakshema, *T* 12, no. 374.

Ta-T'ang Hsi-yü-chi, by Hsüan-tsang, *T* 51, no. 2087.

Ta-tz'u-en-ssu san-tsang fa-shih-chuan, by Hui-li and Yen-tsung, *T* 50, no. 2053.

Ta-yün-ching, tr. by Dharmakshema, *T* 12, no. 387.

T'ai-p'ing kuang-chi.

T'ang-hui-yao.

T'ang-liu-tien.

T'ang-lü-su-i.

T'ang Wang Yu-ch'eng-chi, by Wang Wei, *SPTK* ed.

Traité des Functionaires et Traité de l'Armée, tr. by Robert des Rotours, Leiden, 1947, 2 vol.

Ts'e-fu yüan-kuei.

Tu-yang tsa-pien, by Su E, *Hsüeh-tsin t'ao-yüan* ed.

Tu-yang tsa-tsu, by Tuan Ch'eng-shih, *Hsüeh-tsin t'ao-yüan* ed.

Tung-ching meng-hua-lu, by Meng Yüan-lao, *Hsüeh-tsin t'ao-yüan* ed.

Tzu-chih t'ung-chien, Peking, 1957.

Wei-mo-chieh so-shuo-ching, tr. by Kumārajīva, *T* 14, no. 475.

Wei Shu, Treatise on Buddhism and Taoism, tr. by L. Hurvitz, Kyoto, 1956.

Wen-cheng-kung-chi, by Fan Chung-yen, *SPTK* ed.

Wen-shih-ching, tr. by An Shih-kao, *T* 16, no. 701.

Wu-fen-lü, T 22, no. 1421.

Yen-shih chia-hsün, by Yen Chih-t'ui, *SPPY* ed.

Yen-tsung-lü, T 55, no. 2147.

Yin-hua-lu, by Chao Lin, *TSCC* ed.

Yü-lan-p'en-ching, tr. by Dharmaraksha, *T* 16, no. 685.

Yü-lan-p'en-ching su, by Tsung-mi, *T* 39, no. 1792.

Yü-lan-p'en-ching su, by Yü Jung, *Hsü Tsang-ching* I/87/4.

Yü-tao-lun, by Sun Ch'o, *T* 52, no. 2102.

Yüeh-fu tsa-lu, by Tuan An-shih, *TSCC* ed.

II. Secondary Sources

Brown, W. Norman, "The Basis for the Hindu Act of Truth," *Review of Religion* (November 1940), 36-45.

Burlingame, E. W., "The Act of Truth," *JRAS* (July 1917), 429-467.

Ch'en, Kenneth, *Buddhism in China,* Princeton, 1964.

———, "Anti-Buddhist Propaganda during the Nan-Ch'ao," *HJAS* 15 (1952), 166-192.

———, "The Sale of Monk Certificates during the Sung Dynasty," *Harvard Theological Review* 49.4 (1956), 307-327.

———, "Economic Background of the Hui-ch'ang Persecution," *HJAS* 19 (1956), 67-105.

Ch'en Yin-k'o, *Yüan Po shih-chien cheng-kao,* Shanghai, 1958.

Ch'en Yüan, *Tun-huang chieh-yü lu,* Peking, 1931.

Cheng Chen-to, *Chung-kuo su-wen-hsüeh shih,* Peking, 1957.

Chou I-liang, *Wei Chin Nan-Pei-Ch'ao lun-chi,* Peking, 1963.

Chou Shao-liang, *Tun-huang pien-wen hui-lu,* Shanghai, 1954.

Duyvendak, J.J.L., "The Buddhist Festival of the All-Souls in China and Japan," *Acta Orientalia* 5.1 (1926), 39-48.

Eitel, J., *Handbook of Chinese Buddhism*, Hongkong, 1888.

Feifel, E., "Biography of Po Chü-i," *Monumenta Serica* 17 (1958), 255-311.

Fuchs, W., Huei-ch'ao Pilgerreise durch Nordwest-Indien und Zentral-Asien um 726," *Sitzungsberichte der Preussischen Akademie der Wissenschaften*, Phil-hist. kl. 30 (1938), 456-457.

Fukui Fumimasa, "Zokkō no imi ni tsuite," *Philosophia* 53 (1968), 51-64.

———, "Tōdai zokkō gishiki no seiritsu wo meguru shomondai," *Taishō daigaku kenkyū kiyō* 54 (1968), 307-330.

Gernet, J., *Les Aspects Économiques du Bouddhisme dans la Société Chinoise du Vᵉ au Xᵉ Siècle*, Saigon, 1956.

Goodrich, L. C., "The Revolving Book Case in China," *HJAS* 7.2 (1942), 130-161.

Grousset, R., *In the Footsteps of the Buddha*, London, 1932.

Hanabusa Hideki, *Haku-shi monjū no hihan teki kenkyū*, Kyoto, 1960.

Hayakawa Junzaburō, *Ryō no shūge*, Tokyo, 1912-13.

Hirano Kenshō, "Haku Kyoi no bungaku to bukkyō," *Ōtani-daigaku kenkyū nempō*, Kyoto, 1964, 119-187.

Hiraoka Takeo, "Haku Rakuten no shi to Rinanshi-jiin wo chūshin toshite," *Tsukamoto Hakushi shojū kinen bukkyō-shigaku ronshū*, Kyoto, 1961, 596-614.

Hsiang Ta, "T'ang-tai su-chiang-k'ao," *Yen-ching hsüeh-pao* 16 (1934), 119-132.

———, "T'ang-tai su-chiang-k'ao," *Wen-shih tsa-chih* 3.9/10 (1944), 40-60.

———, "T'ang-tai su-chiang-k'ao," *Kuo-hsüeh chi-k'an* 6.4 (1950), 1-42.

———, *T'ang-tai Ch'ang-an yü Hsi-yü wen-ming*, Peking, 1957.

Hurvitz, L., "Render unto Caesar," *Sino-Indian Studies* 5.3-4 (1957), 96-114.

Huard, Pierre and Wong, Ming, *La Médecine Chinoise au cours des Siècles*, Paris, 1959.

Iwamoto Yutaka, *Mokuren densetsu to urabon*, Kyoto, 1968.

Julien, St., *Méthode pour déchiffrer et transcrire les noms Sanscrits*, Paris, 1861.

Kanaoka Shōkō, "Tōgodai hembun no igi," *Proceedings of the Okurayama Oriental Research Institute* I (1954), 129-140.

Kato Shigeshi, *Shina keizaishi kōshō*, Kyoto, 1952.

Kuroita Katsumi, *Kokushi taikei*, vol. 23, Tokyo, 1943.

Lu Hsün, *Chung-kuo hsiao-shuo shih-lun*, Hongkong, 1958.

Michihata Ryōshū, *Tōdai bukkyōshi no kenkyū*, Kyoto, 1957.

———, *Chūgoku bukkyō to shakai fukushi jigyō*, Kyoto, 1967.

———, *Chūgoku bukkyōshi no kenkyū*, Kyoto, 1970.

———, "Chugoku bukkyō to dorei no mondai," *Tsukamoto Hakushi*, 764-783.

———, *Bukkyō to Jukyō rinri*, Kyoto, 1968.

Miura Hiroyuki, *Hōseishi no kenkyū*, Tokyo, 1919.

Mori Keirai, "Tō no kindenhō ni okeru sōni no kyūden ni tsuite," *Rekishigaku kenkyū* 4.1 (1935), 53-59.

Moroto Tatsuo, "Tōsho ni okeru bukkyō kyōdan no tōsu," *Bunka* 16.6 (1952), 66ff.

Naba Toshisada, "Chūban Tōjidai ni okeru giransō ni kansuru ichi kompon shiryō no kenkyū," *Ryūkoku-daigaku bukkyō-shigaku ronsō*, Tokyo, 1939, 129-140.

———, "Chūban Tōjidai ni okeru Tonkō chihō bukkyō jiin no tengai keiei ni tsuite," *Tōa keizai ronsō* I (1941), 549-577, 847-874; 2 (1942), 535-556.

———, Ryō-ko-kō, *Shina bukkyō shigaku* 2.1 (1938), 1-40; 2.2.27-68; 2.4.30-82.

———, Zokkō to hembun, *Bukkyō shigaku* 1.2 (1950), 60-72; 1.3.73-91; 1.4.39-65.

———, Chūtō jidai zokkōsō Bunsho hōshi shakugi, *Tōyōshi kenkyū* 4.6 (1939), 461-484.

Nanjō, B., *Catalogue of the Chinese Translation of the Buddhist Tripitaka*, Oxford, 1883.

Niida Noboru, *T'ang-ling shih-i*, Tokyo, 1964.

Niida Noboru, *Tō Sō hōritsu bunsho no kenkyū*, Tokyo, 1937

Ogasawara Senshū, "Tō no haibutsuronsha Fu Eki ni tsuite," *Shina bukkyō shigaku* 1.3 (1937), 83-93.

Ōtani Kōshō, *Tōdai no bukkyō girei*, Tokyo, 1937.

Pelliot, Paul, "Meou-tseu ou les doutes levées," *T'oung-pao* 19 (1920), 255-433.

Reischauer, E. O., *Ennin's Travels in T'ang China*, New York, 1955.

Sarkisyanz, E., *Buddhist Backgrounds of the Burmese Revolution*, The Hague, 1965.

Seiiki Bunka Kenkyūkai, *Tonkō Toroban shakai keizai shiryō*, fasc. 1, Kyoto, 1959.

Sun K'ai-ti, "T'ang-tai su-chiang chih k'e-fan yü t'i-ts'ai," *Kuo-hsüeh chi-k'an* 6.2 (1936), 1-52.

――――, "T'ang-tai su-chiang kuei-fan yü ch'i pen chih t'i-ts'ai," *Ts'ang-chou-chi*, vol. 1, Peking, 1965.

Suzuki, D. T., *Studies in the Lankāvatāra*, London, 1957.

Takigawa Masajirō, "Ryō no shūge ni mieru Tō no hōritsu sho," *Tōyō gakuhō* 18 (1929), 35-41.

T'ang Yung-t'ung, *Han Wei Liang-Chin Nan-Pei-Ch'ao fo-chiao-shih*, Shanghai, 1938.

Teng Chih-ch'eng, *Tung-ching meng-hua-lu chu*, Hongkong, 1961.

Tsukamoto, Zenryū, "Kokubunji to Zui Tō no bukkyō seisaku narabi ni kanji," *Nisshi bukkyō kōshōshi no kenkyū*, Tokyo, 1944, 1-47.

――――, *Shina bukkyōshi kenkyū, Hokugi-hen*, Kyoto, 1942.

――――, "Shingyō no sangaikyōdan to mujinzō ni tsuite," *Shūkyō kenkyū* 3.4 (1926), 571-586.

――――, "Sō no zaiseinan to bukkyō," *Kuwabara Hakushi kanreki kinen Tōyōshi ronsō*, Tokyo, 1934, 549-594.

――――, "Tōchūki irai no Chōan kudokushi," *Tōhō gakuhō* (Kyoto) 4 (1933), 368-406.

Twitchett, D. W., "The Monasteries and China's Economy in Medieval Times," *BSOAS* 19.3 (1957), 526-549.

――――, "Monastic Estates in T'ang China," *Asia Major*, N.S., 5 (1956), 123-146.

Chu-ching yao-chi 諸經要集

Chu Fo-nien 竺佛念

chü-jen 舉人

Chu Li 朱禮

Ch'u-san-tsang chi-chi
出三藏記集

Ch'uan-fa-t'ang-pei 傳法堂碑

Ch'üan Han-sheng 全漢昇

Ch'üan Hou-wei wen 全後魏文

Ch'üan T'ang-wen 全唐文

chuang-hu 莊戶

chuang-k'e 莊客

Chūban Tōjidai ni okeru giransō ni kansuru
ichi kompon shiryō no kenkyū
中晚唐時代に於ける偽濫僧
に關する一根本史料の研究

Chūban Tōjidai ni okeru Tonkō chihō bukkyō
jiin no tengai keiei ni tsuite
中晚唐時代に於ける燉煌地方
佛教寺院の碾磑經營に就いて

chüeh 覺

Chüeh-an 覺岸

chüeh-pu 角部

Chūgoku bukkyō to dorei no mondai
中國佛敎と奴隸の問題

Chūgoku bukkyō to shakai fukushi jigyō
中國佛敎と社會福祉事業

Chūgoku bukkyō to sosen sūhai
中國佛敎と祖先崇拜

Chūgoku bukkyōshi no kenkyū
中國佛敎史の研究

Chūgoku rinri to Tōdai bukkyō
中國倫理と唐代佛敎

Chūgoku shakai no okeru bukkyō rinri no
keitai 中國社會に於る佛敎
倫理の形態

Chūgoku shomin seikatsu to bukkyō rinri
中國庶民生活と佛敎倫理

ch'un-tso chü-hsi 春坐局席

Chung-a-han-ching 中阿含經

Chung-ching mu-lu 眾經目錄

Chung-chou 忠州

Ch'ung-fu-ssu 崇福寺

Ch'ung-hsüan-shu 崇玄署

Chung-ku fo-chiao ssu-yüan-ti tz'u-shan
shih-yeh 中古佛敎寺院的
慈善事業

Chung-kuo she-hui ching-chi-shih chi-k'an
中國社會經濟史集刊

Chung-kuo su-wen-hsüeh shih
中國俗文學史

chung-sheng 眾生

Chung-tsung 中崇

Chung-yung 中庸

Chū Tō jidai zokkōsō Bunsho hōshi
shakugi 中唐時代俗講僧
文溆法師釋疑

Dainihon bukkyō zensho
大日本佛敎全書

Eihei shingi 永平清規

en-tu 恩度

Ennin 圓仁

Erh-shih-ssu-hsiao ya-tso-wen
二十四孝押座文

317

Fa-an 法安

Fa-ch'ang 法常

Fa-chü 法炬

Fa-hua 法華

Fa-hua hsüan-lun 法華玄論

Fa-kuo 法果

Fa-li 法立

Fa-lin 法琳

Fa-men-ssu 法門寺

Fa-ning 法凝

Fa-pao 法寶

Fa-tsang 法藏

Fa-tsung 法宗

Fa-wei 法戚

Fa-yüan chu-lin 法苑珠林

Fa-yün 法運

Fan Chung-yen 范仲淹

fan-nao 煩惱

Fan T'ai 范泰

Fan-wang-ching 梵網經

Fang Hsüan 房玄

Feng (surname) 馮

Feng-kuo-ssu 奉國寺

Feng Ssu-hsü 馮思勗

Fo-i chiao-ching 佛遺教經

Fo sheng T'ao-li-t'ien wei-mu shuo-
fa-ching 佛昇忉利天為母
說法經

Fo-shuo chu-te fu-t'ien-ching
佛說諸德福田經

Fo-shuo hsiao-tzu-ching
佛說孝子經

Fo-shuo shan-sheng-tzu-ching
佛說善生子經

Fo-tsu li-tai t'ung-tsai
佛祖歷代通載

Fo-tsu t'ung-chi 佛祖統紀

Fu-ch'eng-ssu 服成寺

Fu-chiao-pien 輔教編

Fu I 傅奕

Fu-jen hsüeh-chih 輔仁學誌

Fukui Fumimasa 福井文雅

Fu-kuo ta-chiang-chün
輔國大將軍

Fu-mu en-chung-ching 父母恩重經

Fu-mu en-chung-ching chiang-ching-wen
父母恩重經講經文

Fu-mu en-chung su-wen
父母恩重俗文

Fu-mu-en nan-pao-ching
父母恩難報經

fu-yü 餺飳

Genkai 元開

Hai-an 海岸

Hai-ch'ing 海清

Haku Kyoi no bungaku to bukkyō
白居易の文學と佛教

Haku Rakuten no shi to Rinanshi-jiin wo
chūshin to shite 白樂天の詩と
臨安志一寺院を中心として

Haku Shi monjū no hihan teki kenkyū
白氏文集の批判的研究

Han (kingdom) 韓

318

Han-chiang Wang Ling pien

漢將王陵變

Han-T'ang shih-chien hou-chi

漢唐事箋後集

Han Wei Liang-chin Nan-pei-ch'ao fo-chiao-

shih 漢魏兩晉南北朝

佛教史

Han Yü 韓愈

Hanabusa Hideki 花房英樹

Hayakawa Junzaburō 早川純三郎

Heng-chi 恒寂

Hirano Kenshō 平野顯照

Hiraoka Takeo 平岡武夫

ho 河

Ho Ch'ung 何充

Ho-lien-po-po 赫連勃勃

Ho-lin yü-lu 鶴林玉露

Hōseishi no kenkyū 法制史の研究

Ho Yüan-te 何願德

Hou-Han-shu 後漢書（百衲本）

Hou Pa 侯霸

Hsi-fang fa-she 西方法社

Hsia 夏

Hsia-kuei 下邳

hsia-tso 夏座

hsiang-chu 像主

Hsiang-fa chüeh-i-ching

像法決疑經

Hsiang Ta 向達

hsiao-hsiang 小祥

Hsiao-tzu-chuan 孝子傳

Hsien-ch'un-chih 咸淳志

Hsin-cheng 新鄭

Hsin T'ang-shu

新唐書（百衲本）

Hsin T'i-fou 辛替否

hsing-fu-p'ien 興福篇

Hsing-fu-ssu 興福寺

Hsing-kuo-shang-jen

興果上人

Hsing-shan-ssu 興善寺

Hsiu Hsiang-shan-ssu-chi

修香山寺記

Hsü Ch'ing-liang-chuan 續清涼傳

Hsü Hsün 許詢

Hsü Kao-seng-chuan 續高僧傳

Hsü Liu-t'ung 徐留通

Hsü Sung 徐松

Hsü-ta-na 須大孥

Hsü Tsang-ching 續藏經

Hsü Yu 許由

Hsüan-tsang 玄奘

Hsüan-tsung 玄宗

Hsüan-ying 玄應

Hsüan-yüan 玄琬

Hsüeh Huai-i 薛懷義

Hsüeh-tsin t'ao-yüan 學津討原

Hsün Chi 荀濟

Hu Yüan-li 胡元禮

hua-pei 畫被

Hua-yang 華陽

Hua-yen-ching 華嚴經

Huai-hai 懷海

Huai-jang 懷讓

huai-se 壞色

Huan Ch'ien 桓謙

Huan-chu ch'ing-kuei

幻住清規

Huan Hsüan 桓玄

hui 慧

Hui-ch'ang-ssu 會昌寺

Hui-ch'ao 慧超

Hui-chen 慧震

Hui-chou 慧冑

Hui-jih-ssu 慧日寺

Hui-kan 惠感

Hui-li 慧立

Hui-lin-ssu 慧林寺

Hui-neng 慧能

Hui-shen 惠深

Hui-yüan 慧遠

Hung-fu 弘福

Hung-lu-ssu 鴻臚寺

Hung-ming-chi 弘明集

hung-yüan 弘願

i 邑

i-chang 邑長

i-ch'ien 依前

i-chu 邑主

i-hui 邑會

i-i 邑義

i-jen 邑人

I-ch'ieh-ching yin-i

一切經音義

i-ching 義井

i-shih 邑師

I-shih-chuan 逸士傳

i-tzu 邑子

Iwamoto Yutaka 岩本裕

i-wei-na 邑維那

Jen-wang-ching 仁王經

Jen-wang-ching su 仁王經疏

Jen-wang pan-jo-ching

仁王般若經

Jih-chih-lu 日知錄

Jui-ying pen-ch'i-ching

瑞應本起經

Kai-yü ts'ung-k'ao 陔餘叢考

K'ai-yüan shih-chiao-lu

開元釋教錄

Kan Pao 干寶

Kanaoka Shōkō 金岡照光

K'ang Seng-hui 康僧會

kang-wei 綱維

Kao Hsing 高行

K'ao-ku hsüeh-pao 考古學報

Kao-seng-chuan 高僧傳

Kao Shu 高樹

Kato Shigeshi 加藤繁

Ken-pen shuo-i-ch'ieh yu-pu

p'i-nai-ya 根本說一切有

部毗奈耶

Keng-shen hui

庚申會

Ko Hung 葛洪

Kokubunji to Zui Tō no bukkyō seisaku

narabi ni kanji 国分寺と隋唐

の佛教政策並に官寺

320

CHINESE & JAPANESE WORDS

Kokushi taikei 國史大系

Koremune Naomoto 惟宗直本

kou-fen-t'ien 口分田

Kou-tang ching-ch'eng chu-ssu-kuan
hsiu-kung-te-shih 勾當京城諸
寺觀修功德使

Ku-chu 孤竹

Ku hsiao-tzu-chuan 古孝子傳

Ku-shan 孤山

Ku-tsun-su yü-lu 古尊宿語錄

Ku Yen-wu 顧炎武

Kuan 觀

Kuan-ting-ching 灌頂經

Kuan wu-liang-shou-ching
觀無量壽經

Kuang-ch'ing-liang-chuan
廣清涼傳

Kuang-hung-ming-chi 廣弘明集

Kuang-ying 光影

Kuei-ts'e-chuan 龜策傳

k'ung-men 空門

kung-te-fen-ssu 功德墳寺

kung-te-shih 功德使

kung-te-yüan 功德院

Kuo-ch'ing 國清

Kuo Chü 郭巨

Kuo-hsüeh chi-k'an 國學季刊

Kuo Tsu-shen 郭祖深

Kuo Tzu-i 郭子儀

Kuroita Katsumi 黑板勝美

Kuwabara Hakushi kanreki kinen Tōyōshi
ronsō 桑原博士還曆紀念
東洋史論叢

Lai-nan-lu 來南錄

lan 嵐

Lan-t'ien 藍田

Lang 郎

Lao-lai-tzu 老萊子

lei-ch'i 累七

Li 麗

Li Ao 李翱

Li Chi-fu 李吉甫

Li Ch'iao 李嶠

Li Chien 李建

Li Ch'o 李綽

li ch'u yü-lan-p'en
力出盂蘭盆

Li Ho-ho 李和和

Li Hsün 李訓

Li Lin-fu 李林甫

Li-pu 禮部

Li Shih-chi 李師稷

Li Shih-min 李世民

Li Te-yü 李德裕

Li Teng 李登

Li Yüan-tsung 李元琮

Liang 梁

Liang-ching hsin-chi
兩京新記

liang-hu 梁戶

liang k'e 梁課

Liang-kuo-kung 梁國公

321

liang-tzu 浪子

Liao Yung-hsien 廖用賢

Ling-chü-ssu 靈居寺

Ling-hu Fa-hsing 令狐法性

Ling-yin-ssu 靈隱寺

liu (penalty) 流

Liu Ch'i-tsu 劉起祖

Liu Ching-hsüan 劉敬宣

Liu Ch'ung-hsün 劉崇訓

Liu Fen 劉汾

Liu Hsiang 劉向

liu-ken 六根

Liu Meng-te wen-chi
劉夢得文集

Liu Tsung-yüan 柳宗元

Liu-tu chi-ching 六度集經

Liu Yü-hsi 劉禹錫

Lo Chen-yü 羅振玉

Lo-pu 羅卜

Lo Ta-ching 羅大經

Lu 魯

Lu Chih 陸贄

Lu Hsüan-kung-chi 陸宣公集

Lu Hsüan-kung tsou-i
陸宣公奏議

Lu-shih tsa-shuo 盧氏雜說

lüan-lüan 戀戀

Lung-chou 隴州

Lung-hsing-ssu 龍興寺

Ma Ch'i-lin 馬其隣

Ma Ling-chih (chuang)
馬令痓 (莊)

Ma Ting-nu 馬定奴

Ma-tsu Tao-i 馬祖道一

Makita Tairyō 牧田諦亮

mao-tao fan-fu 毛道凡夫

Matsubara Saburō 松原三郎

men-tso-lo 門左羅

men-tso-nang 門左囊

Meng Hao-jan-chi 孟浩然集

Meng-liang-lu 夢梁錄

Meng Yüan-lao 孟元老

ming 明

Miao-fa lien-hua-ching hsüan-i
妙法蓮華經玄義

Michihata Ryōshū 道端良秀

Ming-chi 明稧

Ming-ch'üan 明佺

Ming-chun 明準

Ming-pao-chi 冥報記

Ming-sha shih-shih i-shu
鳴沙石室佚書

Ming-yüan 明遠

Miura Hiroyuki 三浦周行

Miyamoto Shōson 宮本正尊

Mizuno Seiichi 水野清一

Mo-ho-seng-ch'i-lü
摩訶僧祇律

Mokuren densetsu to urabon
目連傳説と盂蘭盆

Mori Keirai 森慶來

Moroto Tatsuo 諸戸立雄

Mou-tzu li-huo-lun 牟子理惑論

Mu-lien yüan-ch'i 目連緣起

Mu-lien pien-wen 目連變文

Naba Toshisada 那波利貞

Nagahiro Toshio 長廣敏雄

Nai 素

Nan-ch'an-ssu 南禪寺

Nan-t'ao 南桃

Nan-ts'ao 南操

nei-tao-ch'ang 內道場

Nieh Cheng 聶政

Nieh-p'an-ching 涅槃經

nien-hao 年號

nien-wei 碾磑

Niida Noboru 仁井田陞

Nisshi bukkyō kōshōshi no kenkyū
日支佛教交渉史の研究

Nittō guhō junrei gyōki
入唐求法巡禮行記

Niu Seng-ju 牛僧孺

Ogasawara Senshū 小笠原宣秀

Ōmura Seigai 大村西崖

Ōtani-daigaku kenkyū nempō
大谷大學研究年報

Ōtani Kōshō 大谷光照

pa-chien-chieh 八漸偈

Pao-ch'iung 寶瓊

pa-k'u 八苦

Pai-chang ch'ing-kuei
百丈清規

Pai-chang ta-shih ch'an-shih yü-lu
百丈大師禪師語錄

pai-hsing-seng 百姓僧

pai-t'u 白徒

p'an-pa-ts'ui 判拔萃

Pao-liang 寶亮

Pao-p'u-tzu 抱朴子

Pao-shou-ssu 保壽寺

P'ei Chi 裴坦

Pei-Chou hui-fo chu-mou-che
    Wei Yüan-sung 北周毀佛
    主謀者衛元嵩

P'ei Hsüan-chih 裴玄智

pei-t'ien yang-ping-fang
悲田養病坊

Pen-hsing chi-ching
本行集經

p'en-tso-na 盆佐那

Pien-cheng-lun 辯正論

pien-hsiang 變相

Pien Ssu-chih 卞嗣之

pien-wen 變文

p'in-tao 貧道

Po Chi 伯姬

Po Chi-keng 白季庚

Po Chü-i 白居易

Po Hsiang-shan chi 白香山集

P'o-hsieh-lun 破邪論

Po Lo-t'ien 白樂天

Po-shih ch'ang-ch'ing-chi
白氏長慶集

Po I 伯夷

P'u-chi 普濟

p'u-ch'ing 普請

pu-erh-fa-men 不二法門

P'u-hsien 普賢

Pu-k'ung piao-chih-chi

不空表制集

p'u-men 普門

P'u-ming 普明

P'u-sa shan-chieh-ching

菩薩善戒經

P'u-sa Shan-tzu-ching

菩薩睒子經

P'u-sa ti-ch'ih-ching

菩薩地持經

P'u-t'i-ssu 菩提寺

p'u-t'ung-yüan 普通院

P'u-yao-ching 普曜經

Rekishigaku kenkyū

歷史學研究

Ryō-ko-kō 梁戶考

Ryō-no-shūge 令集解

Ryō-no shūge ni mieru Tō no hōritsu

sho 令集解に見える

唐の法律書

Ryūkoku-daigaku bukkyō-shigaku ronsō

龍谷大學佛教史學論叢

san-kang 三綱

Sangaikyō no kenkyū

三階教の研究

Seiiki Bunka Kenkyūkai

西域文化研究會

seng-chi 僧籍

Seng-lang 僧朗

Seng-shih-lüeh 僧史略

seng-ts'ao 僧曹

Sha-men-t'ung 沙門統

Sha-men pu-ching wang-che-lun

沙門不敬王者論

Shan-chien 善見

Shan-tao 善導

Shan-tzu 睒子

Shang-shu ku-shih 尚書故實

Shang-yu-lu 尚友錄

Shao-lin-ssu 少林寺

she 捨

she-chang 社長

she-i 社邑

she-kuan 社官

she-lao 社老

She-li-fo wen-ching 舍利佛問經

Shen-chao 神照

Shen-chao Ch'an-shih t'ung-su

神照禪師同宿

Shen-chi 神寂

Shen-hao 神皓

Shen Hsüan-ming 沈玄明

Shen-lung 神龍

shen-pien 神變

Shen-tsou 神奏

Sheng-chien 聖堅

Sheng-shan-ssu 聖善寺

sheng-ssu-lun 生死輪

Shih-chia-lo yüeh liu-fang li-ching

尸迦羅越六方禮經

Shih-chung ku-i-shu

十種古逸書

Shih Hu 石虎

CHINESE & JAPANESE WORDS

Shih-huo-chih 食貨志

Shih-lao-chih 釋老志

Shih-men cheng-t'ung

釋門正統

Shih-pi-ssu t'ieh Mi-le-hsiang

石壁寺鉄彌勒像

shih-shen ju fou-yün

(a) 視身如浮雲
(b) 是身如浮雲

shih-shen ju p'ao pu-te chiu-li

是身如泡不得久立

shih-shen ju tien nien-nien pu-chu

是身如電念念不住

Shih-shih chi-ku-lüeh

釋氏稽古略

Shih-shih yao-lan 釋氏要覽

Shih-sung-lü 十誦律

Shina bukkyōshi kenkyū Hokugi-hen

支那佛教史研究比魏篇

Shina bukkyō shigaku

支那佛教史學

Shina keizaishi kōshō

支那經濟史考證

Shingyō no sangai-kyōdan to mujinzō ni

tsuite 信行の三階教團
と無盡藏に就いて

Shou-ju 守如

Shou-yang 首陽

Shu Ch'i 叔齊

shu-ch'ien-wan-ch'ing 數千萬頃

Shuang 霜

Shun-tzu chih-hsiao pien-wen

舜子至孝變文

So (abbot) 索

Sōni-ryō 僧尼令

Sō no zaiseinan to bukkyō

宋の財政難と佛教

Sou-shen-chi 搜神記

ssu 死

Ssu-fen-lü 四分律

Ssu-fen-lü hsing-shih-ch'ao tzu-ch'ih-chi

四分律行事鈔資持記

Ssu-piao 嗣標

Ssu-pu pei-yao 四部備要

Ssu-pu ts'ung-k'an 四部叢刊

su-ch'ang 素唱

su-chiang-seng 俗講僧

su-chiu 素舊

Su E 蘇鶚

Sun Ch'iu-sheng 孫秋生

Sun Ch'o 孫綽

Sun K'ai-ti 孫楷第

Sun Nien-t'ang 孫念堂

Sun Sheng 孫盛

Sung Ching 宋璟

Sung Kao-seng-chuan 宋高僧傳

Sung-shan 嵩山

Ta-Chou k'an-ting chung-ching mu-lu

大周刊定衆經目錄

Ta-chuang-yen-ssu 大莊嚴寺

Ta-fang-kuang fo hua-yen-ching

大方廣佛華嚴經

Ta-fo ting-shou-leng-yen-ching

大佛頂首楞嚴經

325

CHINESE & JAPANESE WORDS

ta-hsiang 大祥

Ta-hsiang-ssu 大像寺

Ta-hsing-shan-ssu 大興善寺

Ta-ming 大明

Ta-Mu-kan-lien ming-chien chiu-mu pien-
  wen ping-t'u 大目乾連冥間
  救母變文並圖

Ta-pan nieh-p'an-ching
  大般涅槃經

Ta-pi-ch'iu san-ch'ien wei-i
  大比丘三千威儀

Ta-sheng-tz'u-ssu 大聖慈寺

Ta-T'ang Hsi-yü-chi
  大唐西域記

Ta-T'ang nei-tien-lu
  大唐内典錄

Ta-tz'u-en-ssu san-tsang fa-shih-chuan
  大慈恩寺三藏法師傳

Ta-yün-ching 大雲經

Ta-yün-ssu 大雲寺

T'ai-p'ing-ching 太平經

T'ai-p'ing kuang-chi 太平廣記

T'ai-po 泰伯

Takigawa Masajirō 瀧川政次郎

t'an (Julien No. 1730) 談

t'an (Julien No. 1718) 曇

T'an-ch'ien 曇遷

T'an-ching 曇靖

T'an-hsiu 曇修

tan-sheng-chieh 誕聖節

T'an-yao 曇曜

T'ang-hui-yao 唐會要

T'ang Liang-ching ch'eng-fang-k'ao
  唐西京城坊考

T'ang-ling shih-i 唐令拾遺

T'ang-liu-tien 唐六典

T'ang-lü su-i 唐律疏議

T'ang-tai Ch'ang-an yü Hsi-yü wen-ming
  唐代長安與西域文明

T'ang-tai shui-pu-shih
  唐代水部式

T'ang-tai su-chiang-k'ao
  唐代俗講考

T'ang-tai su-chiang chih k'e-fan yü t'i-
  ts'ai 唐代俗講之科範
  與體裁

T'ang-tai su-chiang kuei-fan yü ch'i
  pen chih t'i-ts'ai 唐代俗講
  軌範與其本之體裁

T'ang Wang Yu-ch'eng chi
  唐王右丞集

T'ang Yung-t'ung 湯用彤

Tao-ch'eng 道成

Tao-hsüan 道宣

Tao-hui 道慧

Tao-jen-t'ung 道人統

T'ao-kuang 韜光

Tao-piao 道標

Tao-seng-ke 道僧格

Tao-shih 道世

Tao-shun 道䜒

Tao-tsung 道崇

Tao-ying 道英

Teng Chih-ch'eng 鄧之誠

ti-chu-seng 地主僧

t'i-hsü 体虛

Ti-tsang p'u-sa pen-yüan-ching
地藏菩薩本願經

T'i-wei Po-li-ching
提謂波利經

t'ien-ch'ang-chieh 天長節

tien-chia 佃家

tien-hu 佃戶

tien-k'e 佃客

tien-min 佃民

tien-p'ao-shen 電泡身

ting 定

Ting Lan 丁蘭

Tō Daiwajō tōseiden
唐大和上東征傳

Tō no haibutsu ronsha Fu Eki ni tsuite
唐の排佛論者傳奕に就いて

Tō no kindenhō ni okeru sōni no kyūden ni
tsuite 唐の均田法に於ける
僧尼の給田に就いて

Tō-Sō hōritsu bunsho no kenkyū
唐宋法律文書の研究

Tōa keizai ronsō
東亞經濟論叢

Tōdai bukkyōshi no kenkyū
唐代佛教史の研究

Tōchūki irai no Chōan kudokushi
唐中期以來の長安功德使

Tōdai no bukkyō girei
唐代の佛教儀禮

Tōdai zokkō gishiki no seiritsu wo
meguru shomondai 唐代俗講儀式
の成立をめぐる諸問題

Tōgodai hembun no igi
唐五代變文の意義

Tonkō Toroban shakai keizai shiryō
敦煌吐魯番社會經濟史料

Tonkōbon Daii-kyō no kenkyū
敦煌本提謂經の研究

Tō sho ni okeru bukkyō kyōdan no
tōsei 唐初に於ける佛教
教團の統制

Tou Wen-ch'ang 竇文場

Tōyō Gakuhō 東洋學報

tsa-ling 雜令

tsa-lü, shang, fan-yeh
雜律上犯夜

Tsan-ning 贊寧

Ts'ang-chou-chi 滄州集

tsao-fo-p'en 造佛盆

Ts'ao Pao-nu 曹保奴

tsao yü-lan-p'en 造盂蘭盆

Ts'e-fu yüan-kuei 冊府元龜

Ts'en Wen-pen 岑文本

Tseng Ts'ao-t'ang Tsung-mi shang-jen
贈草堂宗密上人

tso-chu men-sheng t'iao
座主門生條

Tso-shen-ts'e hu-chün chung-wei
左神策護軍中尉

Tso-wei-wei ta-chiang-chün
左威衛大將軍

Ts'ui An-tu 崔安都

Ts'ui Ch'ün 崔群

Tsukamoto Hakushi shōju kinen bukkyō
shigaku ronshū 塚本博士
頌寿記念佛教史學論集

Tsukamoto Zenryū 塚本善隆

Tsung-chien 宗鑑

Tsung-mi 宗密

Tsung-shih 宗實

Ts'ung-shu chi-ch'eng 叢書集成

t'u (penalty) 徒

tu-chiang 都講

Tu Hung-chien 杜鴻漸

Tu T'ang-tai su-chiang-k'ao
讀唐代俗講考

Tu Tsung-ching 杜宗敬

tu-wei-na 都維那

Tu-yang tsa-pien
杜陽雜編

Tuan An-chieh 段安節

Tuan Ch'eng-shih 段成式

Tun-huang chieh-yü-lu
敦煌叙籙錄

Tun-huang i-shu tsung-mu-lu so-yin
敦煌遺書總目錄索引

Tun-huang pien-wen 敦煌變文

Tun-huang pien-wen hui-lu
敦煌變文彙錄

t'ung 通

Tung-ching meng-hua-lu chu
東京夢華錄注

Tung Chung-shu 董仲舒

tung-hsiang-tso-t'iao
東向坐條

t'ung-hsing 童行

T'ung-hua 通化

Tung Yen 董黯

Tzu-chih t'ung-chien 資治通鑑

Tz'u-pu 祠部

Tzu-sheng-ssu 資聖寺

Wan-nien 萬年

wan-seng-chai 萬僧齋

Wan-shou ssu 萬寿寺

Wang Chi 王寄

Wang-chi-ssu 周極寺

Wang Ch'iang 王女晉

Wang Chien 王儉

Wang Chih 王志

Wang Chih-hsing 王智興

Wang Chin 王縉

Wang Fang-i 王方翼

Wang Hsiang 王祥

Wang Mi 王謐

Wang Ming-kuang 王明廣

Wang Wei 王維

Wei Chin Nan-Pei-ch'ao lun-chi
魏晋南北朝論集

wei-hu 磑戶

wei-ju 磑入

Wei-k'uan 惟寬

wei, kung 為共

wei-lan-seng 偽濫僧

Wei-mo-chieh 維摩詰

wei-na 維那

wei-po-shih 磑博士

Wei-shih 唯識

Wei Shou 魏收

Wei-shu 魏書

Wei Shu 韋述

Wei Yüan-sung 衛元嵩

Wen-ch'ang 文暢

Wen-cheng-kung-chi 文正公集

Wen-chü 文舉

Wen-hsü 文淑

Wen-shih-ching 溫室經

Wen-shih tsa-chih 文史雜誌

Wen-shu 文淑

wu-chin-ts'ai 無盡財

wu-chin-tsang 無盡藏

Wu Ch'ing-shun 吳慶順

Wu-fen-lü 五分律

wu-hsin 五辛

wu-lan-p'o-na 烏藍婆拏

Wu-lin-shan 武林山

Wu Meng 吳徸

Wu Tzu-mu 吳自牧

Wu-ying-tien chü-chen-pan 武英殿聚珍版

Wu Yüan-heng 武元衡

Ya-tso-wen 押座文

Yabuki Keiki 矢吹慶輝

Yang Chia-lo 楊家駱

yang-nü 養女

Yang Ssu-fu 楊嗣復

Yang Su 楊素

Yang Yen 楊炎

Yao Ch'ung 姚崇

Yen Chih-t'ui 顏之推

Yen-ching hsüeh-pao 燕京學報

Yen-shih chia-hsün, kuei-hsin-p'ien 顏氏家訓歸心篇

Yen-tsung-lu 彥悰錄

Yen-tzu 剡子

Yin-hua-lu 因話錄

Ying 盈

Yü Ch'ao-en 魚朝恩

Yü Chia-hsi 余嘉錫

Yü-chia shih-ti-lun 瑜伽師地論

Yü Fa-k'ai 于法開

yu-hsing-seng 遊行僧

yu-hua-seng 遊化僧

Yü Jang 豫讓

Yü-jung 遇榮

Yü-lan-p'en-ching 盂蘭盆經

Yü-lan-p'en-ching su 盂蘭盆經疏

329

Yü-lan-p'en-ching su hsiao-heng-
　　ch'ao 盂蘭盆經疏
　　孝衡鈔
Yu-p'o-sai-ching
　　優婆塞經
Yü Ping 庾冰
Yü-tao-lun 喻道論
Yu-yang tsa-tsu hsü-chi
　　酉陽雜俎續集
Yüan-chao 元照
Yüan Chen 元稹
Yüan Chen 袁震
Yüan-chien 圓鑒
Yüan-chien 元簡
Yüan-ching 圓鏡
Yüan-jen-lun 原人論
Yüan K'o-chih 元恪之
Yüan Po shih-chien cheng-kao
　　元白詩箋證稿
Yüan Tsai 元載
Yüeh-ya-t'ang ts'ung-shu
　　粵雅堂叢書
Yüeh-fu tsa-lu 樂府雜錄
Yün-hua-ssu 雲化寺
Yün-kao 雲皋
Yung-ch'üan 永護
yung-yeh-t'ien 永業田
Zokkō no imi ni tsuite
　　俗講ノ意味に就いて
Zokkō to hembun
　　俗講と變文

INDEX

Act of Truth, 21-22
Ai, Emperor, 130
Ajātasattu, King, dialogue with Buddha, 65-66
Āḷavī Monastery, 146
All-Souls' Feast, 83, 120, 271-72
Amitābha, 6, 8; Western Paradise of, 204-5, 224-25, 233, 234, 238, 284
Amitāyus, 241
Amoghavajra, 7, 86, 108-9, 277-78; governmental activities, 118-19
An-hsi, 111, 112*n*
An-kuo Monastery, 131, 249, 277
An Lu-shan rebellion, 90, 128
An Shih-kao, 19, 299
ancestral worship, 50-55; filial piety and, 30, 31, 50-51; memorial services, 51-55, 109-10, 112
Anguttaranikāya, 66*n*
Anhui, 91
Ashoka, Emperor, 267
Aṣṭasāhasrikā, 242
Avalokiteśvara, 6-8, 224
Avataṁsakasūtra, 9, 11, 159-60, 238, 293-94; see also *Hua-yen-ching*
Avīci hell, 26-27, 98

bathhouses, 301-2
Bhāishajyaguru, 197
Bimbisāra, 65
Bodhiruci, 195*n*
bodhisattvas: Ch'an view of, 11; representations of, 6-8, 10

Buddha, 29-31, 220, 221*n*; Ajātasattu's dialogue with, 65-66; Amitābha, *see* Amitābha; birthday of, 83, 263-67, 276, 292; bones of, 266-71; Ch'an view of, 11-12; on commercial transactions, 158-59; on farm labor by monks, 146-47; filial piety of, 29-31, 34-35, 42-43, 50; images of, penalty for stealing or destruction, 100; images of, used in ceremonies, 263-66; on magic, 272; Maitreya (Laughing Buddha), 7-8; *see also* Maitreya; Mu-lien and, 24-25, 27, 28*n*, 30; relics of, 266-71; sutras preached by, 9-10; teeth of, 256, 266; on women as rulers, 111
Buddhayaśas, 19, 299
Buddhism: ancestral worship, 52-55; in art, 12*n*; charitable activities, 294-303; Chinese adaptation (Sinicization), 5-12, 59-60, 67-68, 114, 124; church and state, 105-24; eight characters, essence of discipline, 187-90; eight miseries, 224*n*; festivals, 256-76, 303; filial piety and, 15-50; five cardinal precepts (sīlas), 55-59; five pollutions, 224*n*; five precepts for monks, 70; four evil destinies, 224*n*; Han Yü's memorial against, 268-69; in India, 65-67; killing of living

INDEX

Kuo Tzu-i, biography of, 153
Kuo-yüan Common Cloister, 171, 173

land: equal-field system, 130*n*, 132; measurement, 126-27; of monasteries, *see* monastery lands; mortgages, 130; rental, 144-45; sale, regulation of, 129-30; taxes, 138-42, 144-45
Laṅkāvatāra, 195*n*, 238
Lantern Festival, 261-63
Lao-lai-tzu: story of, 35
Lao-tzu, 47, 78, 132-33
laws: on monks, regulation of behavior, 95-105; penalties for violation of, 96, 99-104
lectures on Buddhism, 240-55, 290
Li (clan), 78, 132-33, 179
li (proper conduct): concept of, 67-68, 70, 71
Li Ao, 174
Li Chi-fu, prime minister, 138, 179
Li Ch'iao: on laymen in monasteries, 138
Li Hsün, premier, 93
Li Lin-fu, 279
Li-pu (Ministry of Rites), 117, 121
Li Shih-min, 92*n*
Li Teng: donation to monastery, 128, 160
Li Te-yü, 179, 259; memorial on charities, 298
Li Yüan-tsung, 119
Liang-ching hsin-chi, 161-63
Liang dynasty, 159
Liang-ling Common Cloister, 171, 172
Liang-pen, 108
Liang Wu-ti, Emperor, 10-11, 280
Ling, Empress Dowager, 83
Ling-chü Monastery, 131

Ling-nan, 174
Ling-t'u Monastery, 165, 166*n*
Ling-yin Monastery, 205
literature, 179-239
Liu Ch'i-tsu, 282
Liu Ch'ung-hsün, 119
Liu Fen: merit cloister established, 140-41
Liu-shih Common Cloister, 171
Liu Sung dynasty: controversy on monks, 77*n*, 78
Liu Tsung-yüan, 193
Liu-tu chi-ching, 23
Liu Yü-hsi, 236; poems, 180, 210*n*
Lo-pu, story of, 26-27
Lo Ta-ching, 145
Lo-yang, 90, 106, 113, 121, 128, 160, 187, 194, 207, 208, 213, 215, 220-22, 225, 231, 232, 234, 264, 274, 301-2
Lo-yang ch'ieh-lan-chi, 264-65, 274
loans: from Inexhaustible Treasury, 161; interest rates, 161, 167-70; of money, 169-71; of seeds, 165-66, 168; of silk, 166-67
Lotus Sutra, 6, 7, 10, 11, 20*n*, 88, 241, 246, 251, 254, 277, 284
Lu-chia-i-to, 299
Lu Chih, on land regulations, 130-31, 144, 145
Lu-shan Monastery, 72, 201-6, 220, 233
Lung-ch'uan Common Cloister, 172
Lung-hsing Monastery, 112, 126, 131, 143, 167, 210, 279
Lung-men, 6, 8, 219, 231, 282-83

Ma-tsu Tao-i, Ch'an master, 199
Magadha, 263
magic, 272-76; misuse of, forbidden, 101-2

337

INDEX

Ullambana Feast, *see* All-Souls' Feast

Vajrabodhi, 7
vegetarian feasts, 120, 257-61, 276-81, 300, 303; of societies, 282, 286, 288-94
Vimalakīrti (Wei Mo-chieh), 80, 182, 223-24, 238
Vimalakīrti (Vimalakīrtisūtra), 80, 159-60, 194, 203*n*, 206, 212*n*, 223-24, 238, 241, 242, 251, 253
Vinayas (Rules of discipline), 95, 97, 99, 100, 146-47, 151, 158, 159

Waley, Arthur, 184, 230-31
Wan-shou Monastery, 136
Wang-chi Monastery, 175
Wang Ch'iang (Chao-chün), 253*n*
Wang Chien, 77*n*
Wang Chih, 175
Wang Chih-hsing, 91
Wang Chin, 118
Wang Hsiang: story of, 14-15, 35
Wang Ling, 253*n*
Wang Mi: in controversy on monks, 74-75
Wang Ming-kuang, 46
Wang Wei, 182-83; poems, 179-81, 183
water: Buddhist rules on use of, 146-47; for irrigation and mills, regulation of 152-53
water-powered mills, *see* mills
Wei-k'uan, Ch'an master, 199, 232
Wei Mo-chieh (Vimalakīrti), 80, 182, 223-24, 238
Wei-mo-chieh pien-wen, 252-53
wei-na, 83, 84, 115-16
Wei Shou (506-572), 58-59
Wei Shu (T'ang dynasty), on Inexhaustible Treasury, 161-63

Wei-shu, 58-59, 135
Wei Yüan-sung, 46, 136
Wen, Emperor, 110, 116; land donated to monastery, 126
Wen-ch'ang, 193
Wen-chü, 131
Wen-shih-ching, 250
Wen-shu (Wen-hsü), lecturer, 245, 246, 254-55
Wen-te, Empress, 89
Wen-teng-hsien, 247
Wen-tsung, 52, 260
Western Paradise of Amitābha, 204-5, 224-25, 233, 234, 238, 284
White Tara, 7
Wisdom Sutras, 10
women: as heads of state, 111; society of, 288
work, Ch'an attitude toward, 148-51
Wu, Emperor (Liang dynasty), 143, 159, 300
Wu, Emperor (T'ang dynasty), *see* Wu-tsung
wu-chin-tsang, see Inexhaustible Treasury
Wu Ch'ing-shun, slave, 143-44
Wu-fen-lü, 99
Wu-lin Mountain, 205-06
Wu Meng: story of, 15
Wu-t'ai, Mt. (Wu-t'ai-shan): monasteries, 110, 139, 257-58, 261; monastery hostels, 171-72, 302; vegetarian feasts, 120, 257-58, 278-80
Wu Tse-t'ien, Empress, 87, 106, 110-13, 163, 164, 219*n*, 297; decree favoring Buddhism, 117; Hsüeh Huai-i associated with, 111, 113
Wu-tsung (Wu), Emperor, 230, 231, 254, 276; persecution of Buddhists, 121, 136, 260